Integrated Pitchfork Analysis

Basic to Intermediate Level

For other titles in the Wiley Trading Series
please see www.wiley.com/finance

INTEGRATED PITCHFORK ANALYSIS

Basic to Intermediate Level

Dr. Mircea Dologa

A John Wiley and Sons, Ltd., Publication

Other Wiley Editorial Offices

John Wiley & Sons Inc., 111 River Street, Hoboken, NJ 07030, USA

Jossey-Bass, 989 Market Street, San Francisco, CA 94103-1741, USA

Wiley-VCH Verlag GmbH, Boschstr. 12, D-69469 Weinheim, Germany

John Wiley & Sons Australia Ltd, 42 McDougall Street, Milton, Queensland 4064, Australia

John Wiley & Sons (Asia) Pte Ltd, 2 Clementi Loop #02-01, Jin Xing Distripark, Singapore 129809

John Wiley & Sons Canada Ltd, 6045 Freemont Blvd. Mississauga, Ontario, L5R 4J3 Canada

Wiley also publishes its books in a variety of electronic formats. Some content that appears in print may not be
available in electronic books.

Library of Congress Cataloging-in-Publication Data

A catalogue record for this book is available from the Library of Congress

British Library Cataloguing in Publication Data

A catalogue record for this book is available from the British Library

ISBN 978-0-470-69434-3(H/B)

Typeset in 10/12pt Times by Aptara Inc., New Delhi, India
Printed and bound in Great Britain by CPI Antony Rowe, Chippenham, Wiltshire

Contents

Dedication   x
About the Author   xi
Acknowledgements   xii

    Introduction   1

    Prelude   7

1   The Birth of Pivots and the Pitchfork   17
    1.1   Defining the Market Context and its Limits   18
    1.2   Pivots: Definition, Characteristics and Function   19
    1.3   Constructing the Pitchfork   22
    1.4   Creating Pivots: Case Studies   23
    1.5   Key Learning Points   27

2   Choice of Pivot   31
    2.1   Optimal Pivots   31
    2.2   Kinematic Study of the Pivot   32
    2.3   Kinematics of the Pitchfork Embedding the Global Market   33
    2.4   Pivot Choices: Case Studies   33
    2.5   Penultimate Pivots of an Ending Correction: Case Studies 54
    2.6   Key Learning Points   55

3   The Magnet-Like Power of Median Lines   59
    3.1   Magnet-like Effect and Symmetry Axis Power   60
    3.2   Triple Action Potential   60
    3.3   Zooming and Piercing   60
    3.4   Testing and Retesting   60
    3.5   Failures   61
    3.6   Median Line-related Market Strength or Weakness: Double
          Six Parameter Rules   62
    3.7   Other Functions of the Median Line   63

3.8   Using the Median Line: Case Studies   64
3.9   Key Learning Points   72

4   The Mini-Median Line   75
4.1   Definition, Characteristics and Function   75
4.2   Border Mini-Median Line   76
4.3   Inside Mini-Median Line: Horizontal Orientation   78
4.4   Inside Median Line: Oblique Orientation   84
4.5   Reverse Mini-Median line   85
4.6   Mini-Median Line with steep downsloping ML   86
4.7   Mini-Median Line with a twin pivot ML   87
4.8   Key Learning Points   95

5   Warning Lines   97
5.1   Definition, Characteristics and Function   97
5.2   Warning Lines: Case Studies   98
5.3   Key Learning Points   101

6   Trigger Lines   103
6.1   Signal Line Function   103
6.2   The Hagopian Rule and Line   104
6.3   The Trigger Line as a Border Line   105
6.4   Variability of the Trigger Lines Quantifies the Trade Risk 105
6.5   Trigger Lines: Case Studies   112
6.6   Key Learning Points   119

7   Sliding Parallel Lines   121
7.1   Definition   121
7.2   Price Behaviour and Sliding Parallel Lines   121
7.3   Parallelism Criteria of Sliding Parallel Lines   122
7.4   Money Management   122
7.5   Sliding Parallel Lines: Case Studies   123
7.6   Key Learning Points   132

8   Unorthodox Trend Lines   133
8.1   Definition   133
8.2   The Degree of the Slope   134
8.3   Fan Lines   134
8.4   Specific Trend Lines   134
8.5   Degree of Strength   135
8.6   Redrawing a Trend Line   135
8.7   Confirming a Trend Line   135
8.8   Confirming a Breakout   135
8.9   Breakout Efficiency of a Trend Line   136
8.10 Money Management and Trend Lines   136
8.11 Unorthodox Trend Lines: Case Studies   137
8.12 Key Learning Points   145

9 Multiple Pitchfork Trading   147
   9.1   Definition   147
   9.2   Creating Multiple Pitchforks   148
   9.3   Kinematics of Multiple Pitchforks as Integrated Patterns   149
   9.4   Multiple Pitchfork Integration: Case Studies   150
   9.5   Key Learning Points   159

10 Schiff Pitchforks and Affiliates   161
   10.1   Definition   161
   10.2   Constructing the Schiff Pitchfork   162
   10.3   The Efficiency of the Schiff Pitchfork: 1   163
   10.4   Efficiency of Schiff Pitchfork: 2   165
   10.5   The T-Pitchfork   172
   10.6   The 'Hybrid' Pitchfork   176
   10.7   The Reverse Pitchfork: Building the Future   179
   10.8   Key Learning Points   184

11 Action and Reaction Lines   185
   11.1   Definition and Historical Foundation   185
   11.2   Comprehension and Build-up   186
   11.3   Characteristics and Function   186
   11.4   Foundation and Development   187
   11.5   Constructing Traditional Action and Reaction Lines   188
   11.6   Constructing Gap A&R Lines: Image Mirroring Technique   192
   11.7   A&R Lines and the Price Translation Across the Market Slots 194
   11.8   Constructing Double A&R Lines: Criss-cross Pattern Technique 197
   11.9   Constructing Double A&R Lines: Symmetrical Pattern Technique 204
   11.10 Pre-close Breaking-Up/Down Trend Lines   207
   11.11 The Straight Pivot Alignment Pitchfork   214
   11.12 Key Learning Points   215

12 The Gap Median Line   217
   12.1   Definition   217
   12.2   Building the Pitchfork with a Gap Median Line   218
   12.3   Multiple Gap Median Lines and Other Chart Patterns   236
   12.4   Key Learning Points   240

13 Breakaway and Runaway Gaps   243
   13.1   Definition   243
   13.2   The Gap Context and the Systematized Visualization Tool   244
   13.3   Gap Mechanisms: Foundation and Development   246
   13.4   Array of Tradable Gaps   249
   13.5   Trading the Island Reversal   256
   13.6   Gap Trading: Gap Median Line versus A&R Lines   257
   13.7   Key Learning Points   259

14 Fibonacci Price Lines   261
    14.1   Definition and Brief Historical Basis   261
    14.2   Price Fibonacci Tools   262
    14.3   Fibonacci Price Ratio (Horizontal) Lines: Case Studies   266
    14.4   Dynamics of Integration: Pitchfork and Fibonacci Price Ratio
           (Horizontal) Lines   269
    14.5   Dynamics of Integration: Pitchfork and Fibonacci Price Ratio
           (Oblique) Lines   276
    14.6   Key Learning Points   283

15 Confluences   285
    15.1   Definition and Function   285
    15.2   Double Line Intersection Confluences: Case Studies   286
    15.3   Multi-level Line Intersection Confluences: Case Studies   289
    15.4   Multi-zone Confluences with Multi-level Line Intersections:
           Case Studies   291
    15.5   Confluence vs Cluster   292
    15.6   Key Learning Points   298

16 Mirror Bars   301
    16.1   Definition and Function   301
    16.2   Mirror Bars: Case Studies   302
    16.3   Mirror Bars and their Pitchfork Applicability: Case Studies   308
    16.4   Key Learning Points   313

17 Energy-Building Rectangles   315
    17.1   Definition and Function   315
    17.2   Micro and Macro Aspects of Energy-building Rectangles:
           Case Studies   317
    17.3   Measuring Techniques and Energy-building Rectangles:
           Case Studies   324
    17.4   Mapping the Context and Local Market: Case Studies   327
    17.5   Key Learning Points   328

18 The Pitchforks' Journey Through Multiple Time Frames   329
    18.1   Definition and Function   329
    18.2   Multiple Time Frames and Fractal Geometry   330
    18.3   Multiple Time Frames and Photographs from Space: An Analogy   330
    18.4   Global Behaviour   333
    18.5   Monthly Time Frame   336
    18.6   Weekly Time Frame   337
    18.7   Daily Time Frame   337
    18.8   Operational Time Frame: the 60-minute Time Frame   338
    18.9   Multiple Time Frames and Pitchforks: Practical Aspects   339
    18.10 Key Learning Points   353

19 Case Studies and Money Management   355

    19.1 Zoom and Retest Technique: After a German Dax Energy
           Building Rectangle   355

    19.2 Zoom-and-Test Technique: ES Energy-Building Rectangle
           and Trigger Line   362

    19.3 Zoom-and-Test (Entry) and Retest (Add-on) Technique   374

    19.4 Zoom-and-Test Technique: German Dax Median Line   382

    19.5 Breakout of the Narrow Range: German Dax Median Line   387

Appendices   395

    Appendix I: Historical Basis: Using the Concept of the Pitchfork
        as a Tool   395

    Appendix II: The 80:20 Percent Rule   401

    Appendix III: Bibliography and References   402

    Appendix IV: Contents of Volumes II and III (in preparation)   403

    Epilogue   404

Glossary   407

Index   433

Dedication

This book is dedicated to

Richard W. Schabacker, a giant of Technical Analysis, who devoted his entire life to pioneering research of the financial markets. His books, published in 1930 and 1932, still reflect the quintessence of modern charting analysis – price movements with their patterns and volume – and are so relevant today it seems that both works have just been written. This giant has not only paved the way for the 21st century trader but also provided an astonishing wealth of charting information which modern market technicians would do well to use!

Apprentice traders today, who are so eager to gather and assimilate trading information.

Cassandra and Kim-Tracy, my beloved daughters, probably the youngest apprentice traders around; they are 14 and 18 years old.

About the Author

Dr Mircea Dologa began his investment and trading career in the pharmaceutical and real estate industries in 1987. Once he passed the Series 7 and Series 3 exams, he realized the scarcity of the true 'know how' tools in financial literature and seminars. As a Commodity Trading Advisor (CTA), he founded a new teaching concept, mainly based on practical aspects of trading, for both newcomers and experienced traders. He is an international contributor to trading magazines in the USA (*Technical Analysis of Stocks & Commodities*, *Futures*); the United Kingdom (*The Technical Analyst*); Germany (*Traders* - English- and German-language editions); Australia (*Your Trading Edge*) and Asia (*The Trader's Journal*).

After reading hundreds of trading books and attending numerous seminars, the same question kept popping up: Where is the meat? Most of the time. . . it wasn't there!

The author's main thought during the two years of planning, conceiving and writing this book was how to revealing the practical aspects of trading. The key topic, continuously present in his mind, is described below.

This *Integrated Pitchfork Analysis* workbook is a way of bringing risk control to the trader using this technique. Risk control is the only factor that counts when building consistency – the same principle applies in any entrepreneurial activity. Risk dominance will be always present because of the trader's professional life. He knows that, of all businesses, trading is the only one that imposes planned losses. Risk management is the only element which will enable him 'to be or not to be' a consistent trader. The main idea throughout the book is: 'How to build consistency', and for that you have to religiously respect the saying: 'You make money, if you don't lose money'. The author sincerely hopes that he has accomplished this hard task of teaching and implementing trading consistency, but will let you, the trader, be the sole judge!

Dr Mircea Dologa attended New York University and Cooper Union School of Engineering and Science in New York and graduated from the latter with a B.S. in Theoretical Physics. He obtained his Doctorate in Medicine from the School of Medicine in Paris. After graduation and internship at the Mount Sinai Hospital in New York City and Xavier Bichat Hospital in Paris, he worked in the medical field of gastroenterology, and also took MBA courses in finance and business management at the University of South Carolina in Columbia and the French School of Business and Finance (HEC Paris France). After holding the position of Medical Director and later General Manager in a French pharmaceutical company, in 1992 he decided to focus exclusively on his investments and since then he has devoted his activity to financial markets. He lives with his wife and two daughters in Paris, France.

Email: mircdologa@yahoo.com
Founder of www.pitchforktrader.com

Acknowledgements

I can never thank enough my wife, Felicia. Without her continuous support, patience and dedication I could have started writing, but certainly never have finished. As with trading, writing demands tremendous peace of mind. . . and she was always there. . . year after year!

Thanks too, to the Wiley Finance Publishing team, which has detected in *Integrated Pitchfork Analysis* an original trading topic worth publishing. The Chichester team has done a tremendous job to help me with the manuscript: Caitlin Cornish, the very efficient Finance Publisher; Aimée Dibbens, Caitlin's assistant, was worth her weight in gold in promptly answering any questions I might have; Lori Boulton and Louise Holden, the marketing team, have been indispensable in their advice about the book's launching; and Rachael Wilkie, the English expert who has initiated me into the science of editing, showing me elegant rephrasing indispensable to the wellbeing of our readers.

The assistance of Pamela van Giessen – the US Editorial Director – was for me very valuable when it came to harmonizing communication across the ocean.

Last but not least, I would like to thank Johannes Petrus Joubert, my student who has become an efficient trader in South Africa. Besides other human and trading qualities, his talent in proofreading has really made the publication of this book possible.

As all authors already know, the making of a book takes almost as long as writing it. . . no detail is to be forgotten!

Would I do it again? Yes, I would!

Introduction

Human nature tends to see what it expects to see . . . (Anon)

Common sense compels us to acquire a consistent technique that gives us the confidence to learn how to trade. This will not come without 'sweat and tears' but, as the Eastern sage says: 'What first brings pleasure, in the end gives only pain, but what at first causes pain, ends up in great pleasure.'

Trading should not be too difficult if you build on a solid foundation . . . just watch the basics!

Integrated Pitchfork Analysis is a coursebook focusing on the branch of Technical Analysis which uses the Andrews' pitchfork trading technique. The process begins with the underlying theory (basic and intermediate knowledge) and then, step by step, the practical aspects about the low-risk high-probability trade from its inception until its termination are covered. The emphasis is on the trade's management and money management. No prior knowledge of trading is required.

The course is divided into two parts. Volume I focuses on developing the basic knowledge of the pitchfork's morphology (study and description of a defined structure: definition, form, inflexion, derivation, and compounding) and its dynamic principles. It is indispensable to have this knowledge before using the more advanced concepts. Volumes II and III (in preparation) will focus on developing the multiple integrative methods that will greatly improve the chances of the trader being consistently successful.

Any professional trader will freely admit that it is vital to master just one main technique at a time. Once the learning process is accomplished, he can then apply his own rules and perceptions to help him become a trading force. Because each trader behaves slightly differently, he will use different methods to make decisions about entering a trade, exiting, stop losses, trail stops or projecting profit targets.

PUSH THE LIMITS OF YOUR LEARNING CURVE

The trading learning curve is like that of any other discipline. A neurosurgeon, an engineer or a teacher are continuously faced with new problems which are similar but not exactly identical to those previously encountered. In order to acquire consistently positive results, these professionals must repeatedly analyze problems from their past which will help them with those of the present. Would you allow your child to have surgery performed by an intern, or would you rather it was performed by the chief surgeon? No physician would dare to operate alone after just a couple of weeks, months or even five years of learning the surgical techniques!

We cannot emphasize enough that chart interpretation and the wisdom of technical market behaviour cannot be learned overnight. This being said, we shouldn't be surprised that many of the 'wannabe' traders lose money and disappear after a couple of months. The richer the storehouse of experience, the more efficient the problem analysis will be. As a consequence, the consistency will improve and the trading results will ameliorate. However, most novice traders jump the gun and start trading after only a couple of months, if not weeks. Their thinking probably goes along the lines of, 'Even a stopped clock is right . . . twice a day!'

OMISSION AND INACTION

I couldn't proceed further with this process of imparting trading knowledge without mentioning the work of Jonathan Baron (http://www.sas.upenn.edu/~baron/), a 61-year-old psychology professor at the University of Pennsylvania. He has dedicated many years of his life to the study of judgement and decision-making, which he has described in wonderful detail in his latest book, *Thinking and Deciding*.

Knowing at least a bit about the omission phenomenon, coupled with inaction and decision-making processes, will greatly enhance our trading performance (see Chapter 19). Now, please don't get me wrong! My book is not about psychology even if, as a physician, I consider it is as important as food and shelter in the development of modern civilisation. This book is about short-term trading or, more specifically, about the pragmatic aspects of integrated pitchfork trading which will assist the novice trader in achieving a consistent performance.

NEVER AGAIN THE SNAKE OIL . . .

If the trader does not take the right approach to learning, not only could it cost him his shirt but he could be eliminated before he has had a chance to start making any money. After reading this book, common sense will dictate that you practise all the rules in order to get the most out of the charts.

- If you are a beginner, go to the web references listed below (we illustrate Dow Jones Cash Index and German Dax Cash Index URLs), and you'll find free delayed access for most of the securities:
  - http://www.futuresource.com/charts/charts.jsp?s=DJY
  - http://www.futuresource.com/charts/charts.jsp?s=DAXY
  - http://www.prorealtime.com
- We recommend the Advanced GET Charting, which is one of the most efficient, ergonomic and prolific charting tools available to the trader. We have been using it for years. You can take a 30-day free trial and see if the tool fits with your everyday practice: http://www.esignal.com
- Draw as many pitchforks as you can, especially in the pre-open. Become familiar with the intricacies of the pitchforks, rectangles, failures, and so on.

- Follow the charts during the day, simulating scenarios. Let the market come to you. Assess your post-market work and see if your judgements were good and, if not, why they failed.
- Discern whether there is some kind of correctable error in your judgement, a mistake in understanding the learning curve topics, or a sudden unexpected market condition.

More often than not, the novice traders do not focus on risk and money management as an essential part of their trading practice. This is due to greed and also to a poor understanding of the learning curve. As a first trading approach, their goal is to be right more than 50% of the time. However, trading is a business which is different to any other type of business. It is the only one where losing money is part of the way of life. The trader must understand the vital importance of the difference between losing tiny bits on average and consistently winning. Once you have learned how to lose these tiny bits, then and only then will you really start making money!

WHY A BOOK ON INTEGRATED PITCHFORK ANALYSIS?

As mentioned above, common sense encourages us to acquire a consistent technique that will give us confidence. Once you have decided to enter the highly competitive field of trading, you will quickly realize that this immense field can never be totally mastered. But one question arises: 'Do we really need to know all these topics?' The answer is, of course, 'No!'

The essence of becoming a consistently-successful trader is to understand the overall context of the market, and specialize in one of the techniques that works for various markets in any kind of tendency: trending or non-trending. In your quest for the 'Holy Grail' technique, you should be aware that by learning and cruising along with the 'smart money' people, you will acquire an inexhaustible edge.

As we have previously stated (at www.pitchforktrader.com):

> ...You should realize that in 2005 a large portion of the Chicago Mercantile Exchange (CME) floor traders and Chicago Board of Trade (CBOT) floor traders specialized in practising the pitchfork technique. They rely on it as part of their trading arsenal, in an off-floor environment. Our colleague, Timothy Morge, from www.medianline.com, conducted these professional and high quality exchange-sponsored seminars. We have for him, the deepest admiration and gratitude. We consider him, not only a master trader, but also a great teacher that has massively contributed to the development of the hyper-specialized field of pitchfork analysis, originated more than three quarters of a century ago and then continued by the late Dr. Alan H. Andrews, since the early 1960s.
>
> So...sit down and think for a moment...if these people having the opulence of the smart money, who are using the best trading techniques that money can buy, are learning the pitchfork technique, what does it mean? Do they know something that the novices or the non-consistent traders ignore? The answer is a big 'Yes'.
>
> They are convinced that the pitchfork technique should belong to their trading arsenal, because they have seen it at work...and it works. It is one of the best ways to consistency...so they adopted it. While the crowd is still far behind...

As we all know, the market price evolves in a *time−price* virtual space. In order to be consistent, both parameters should be taken into consideration. More often than not, traders do not apply time—price related techniques, using only price-related ones. It is also true to say that there are not many techniques around capable of using the time—price intricacy.

The potential technique should be tested, valued and reliable for both the trending market and for the sideways market.

The last, and probably the most important, parameters in choosing the most symbiotic and consistent technique are its sensitiveness and its feature applicability towards an ergonomic and profitable employment of risk control and money management.

Vocabulary Warning: We would like to warn the novice trader about some aspects of employing the right trading words. Most of the charting programs, which plot the ratios, are not limited to Fibonacci ratio applications only. When the Fibonacci ratio icon is clicked, the program calculates and plots whatever the value of ratio is entered, without any concern abut who invented it. Therefore we will follow the same procedure and use only the words Fibs or Fibonacci (ratios), whatever the name of the inventor. For accuracy's sake, the possible choices are listed below:

- Fibonacci ratios: 0.146, 0.236, 0.382, 0.500, 0.618, 0.786, 0.886, 1.000, 1.618, 2.618, 4.25 and 6.85.
- Dow ratios: 0.333 and 0.666; also their halves.
- Gann ratios: 0.25, 0.50, 0.75 and 1.00; also their halves and eighths.

EPISTEMOLOGY . . . ALWAYS HAS THE LAST WORD!

Even if you are lucky and have discovered the most consistent and symbiotic technique, there remains the problem of assimilating and practising it.

Epistemology is the science of learning, building knowledge from the basement, and understanding its limits and its validity. We will try to make full use of it throughout the entire book.

The method of building knowledge blocks (modules) is used in all the books in such a way that the information is assimilated very easily, and then it is put together for immediate memory retention and applicability. The methodology used to explain the concepts is simplified in such a way that the novice can quickly understand it without any prior knowledge.

The intermediate level trader might want to skip the beginning chapters (see Contents), advancing directly to the more complex topics.

CONCLUSION

After several years of hard work, I have decided to share our research with trading colleagues, at a very reasonable price compared with other trading techniques available on the market. My educational background and professional ethics do not allow me to publish unreliable or inconsistent information. I know the affection that an author has for his or her work, but in my case I have tried to do my best, as objectively as possible, in the name of advancing the science of technical analysis.

I firmly believe that Integrated Pitchfork Analysis is one of the most reliable and consistent techniques. It harmoniously respects and is guided by the four principles listed below:

- The edge of learning and practicing along with the 'smart money' techniques.
- Learning to navigate in the time—price virtual space of the contextual market, enclosing the local market flow.

- The diversified efficiency in the various trending and sideways markets.
- And finally, the ergonomic and profitable trading efficiency in synergy with risk control.

Dr Mircea Dologa, MD, CTA
November, 2008
Paris, France
mircdologa@yahoo.com
Founder of www.pitchforktrader.com

Please read below the current disclaimer that the Federal Trade Commission (FTC) has proposed must be prominently displayed by anyone offering an investment course to the public.

Disclaimer

The purpose of this material is to provide you with a very powerful trading technique, named 'Integrated Pitchfork Analysis', a valuable tool in the financial markets. The text, the chart examples, or any part of this material are not to be taken as 'investment advice'. They are purely and strictly for educational purposes. Ultimately, you are responsible for all of your investment decisions. The data used in this material is believed to be from reliable sources but cannot be guaranteed.

There is no guarantee that this tool will continue to work in the future. 'Past performance is not indicative of future results'. You should understand that there is considerable risk of loss in the stock, futures or options markets. Neither the author, nor anyone else involved in the production of this material, will be liable for any loss, damage or liability directly or indirectly caused by the usage of this material.

Prelude

HOMEWORK FOR THE READER: SPOTTING AND MANAGING A TRADE

0.1 Homework Instructions

In order to evaluate the reader's knowledge in comparison with that of the book's presentation we will assign in this section some homework for the reader, using the first three charts (Figs 0.1, 0.2 and 0.3). Your learning task is to study them carefully and try to find the best low-risk high-probability trading opportunity.

Figure 0.1 Homework chart: market under observation (Courtesy of www.pitchforktrader.com)

Figure 0.2   Homework chart: market under observation (cont.) (Courtesy of www.pitchforktrader.com)

Figure 0.3   Entire trade chart, including unmarked entry and exit (Courtesy of www.pitchforktrader.com)

Do it in writing and take your time to study this example. Use only your trading experience as a guide. If you encounter difficulties, it means that this book is for you and that you will improve your knowledge after you have read and assimilated the information in this book.

Very few people are at ease in front of a naked chart. So do not blame yourself for any-thing . . . just study it. It takes what it takes!

After the three assignment charts, we will present in detail which trade will represent the best low-risk high-probability opportunity. Please do not be tempted to jump the gun and go straight to the chart solution. It will not be in your interest!

We wish you good luck!

Do not go to the next page, unless you have finished the homework!

0.2 Homework Solutions

Figures 0.4–0.10 offer a concise presentation of the homework and reveal the logical mechanisms of spotting and managing a low-risk high-probability trade. The synopsis table and the new lessons from the trade's execution, located at the end of this chapter, complete the assignment.

Figure 0.4 will help you implement your valuable chart markings:

– down-sloping trend line;
– labelling of the most current move (ABC swing);
– applying Fibonacci tools to monitor the activity of the local market.

All these start to take away the emptiness and incomprehension of the naked chart and begin the development of a competitive edge.

Figure 0.4 Implementing chart markings (Courtesy of www.pitchforktrader.com)

Figure 0.5   Local market movement (Courtesy of www.pitchforktrader.com)

Figure 0.6   A retest starts the trade (Courtesy of www.pitchforktrader.com)

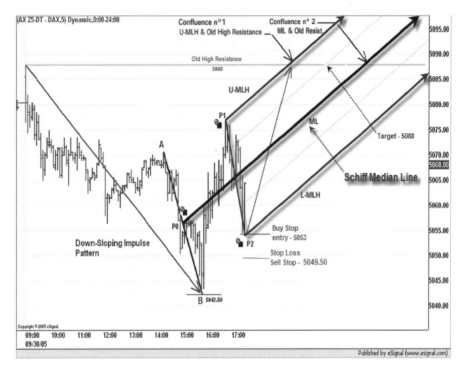

Figure 0.7 Replacing the A&R Lines with a Schiff median line (Courtesy of www.pitchforktrader.com)

Figure 0.8 Schiff median line trade (Courtesy of www.pitchforktrader.com)

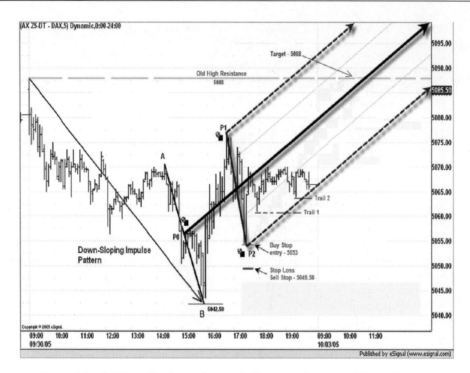

Figure 0.9   Schiff median line trade (cont.) (Courtesy of www.pitchforktrader.com)

Figure 0.10   Reaching the logical profit objective (Courtesy of www.pitchforktrader.com)

The corrective moves of the local market (Fig. 0.5) should encourage you to do the following:

- Construct the Action and ReAction Lines. This approach is dictated by the attainment of the 61.8% Fibonacci ratio retracement level and the absence of an efficient traditional pitchfork set-up (anchor and P1−P2 swing).
- Consider the eventuality of a test-and-retest trade applied to the Center Line.
- Implement the three-pawn technique: prearranged entry, initial stop loss an target.
- Decide on the most optimal money management strategy: R/R ratio, degree of the trade's probability, number of trading units and number of contracts per unit.

A retest of the Center Line starts the trade (Fig. 0.6), once the entry order has been executed.

Next (Fig. 0.7), replace the A&R Line with a more efficient contextual structure, the Schiff median line. Thus we can visualize and manage the trade better at this stage of its development and at this market price level.

Be ready to follow the rules: discipline and patience. The automatic control mode (refer to the Three Pawn Technique) of the trade will bring you to either the target or to the planned stop loss (Fig. 0.8). The dice have already been thrown . . .! You cannot lose more than the already-planned and psychologically-accepted amount.

Follow closely the hard-earned money through the trailing process, break-even set-up (right after the market advanced one ATR move), trails nos1 and 2, both snugged under the last low of the swing (Fig. 0.9).

The logical profit objective has been attained and the trade terminated (Fig. 0.10). None of the four trailing stops were used. Proceed to the conclusion of the trade, including the trader's journal (refer to Table 0.1: Trade Synopsis Table below).

Table 0.1   Trade synopsis table

Trade Synopsis Table
Test and Retest of the *Center Line* Technique

1	**Spotting the Trade**	**Test-and-Retest of the Center Line**
2	**Finding the Optimal Set-up**	**5-min time frame chart**
3	**Time Frame Alignment**	**Upper Time Frame aligned upwards**
4	**Three Pawn Technique** *(long trade)*	**Entry -** *buy stop* **- 5053** **Stop Loss -** *sell stop* **- 5049.50** **Logical Profit Objective -** *sell stop* **- 5088** **Money Management:** Risk - 3.5 pts Reward - 35 pts R/R ratio - 10
5	**Profit & Loss Statement**	Trading units - 3 Break-even - 5053 Trailing stops - 4 Exit - targeted out 5088 P/L - 105 pts/contract (3x35) - 2625 euros ($3333) Time spent in trade - from day's afternoon until the next day's morning
6	**Trader's Journal**	**New lessons out of this trade:** Energy building rectangles Trailing relay locations Secret revelation of the Market Direction

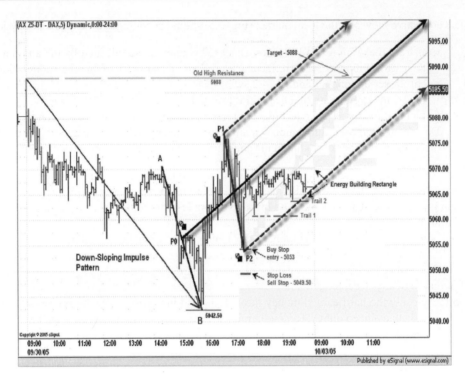

Figure 0.11   Formation of a narrow consolidation (Courtesy of www.pitchforktrader.com)

Figure 0.12   Optimal location of a trading stop (Courtesy of www.pitchforktrader.com)

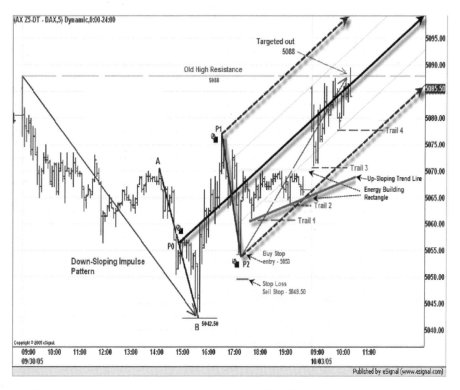

Figure 0.13   Revealing the future direction of the market flow (Courtesy of www.pitchforktrader.com)

0.3   Trader's Journal: New Lessons out of This Trade

As always, don't neglect the importance of writing down your thoughts for later use!

Detect any energy-building rectangles that could be the foundation of a future trend. Observe carefully in Fig. 0.11 the formation over several hours of a narrow consolidation. The lower boundary is often used as the trailing stop's most trusted location. Whatever the case will be, be prepared for a next day exploding momentum.

The outburst of restored energy within the rectangle projects the market price to several times its initial height (Fig. 0.12). The trusted location of the trailing stop is once more confirmed: the upper/lower boundaries of the energy-building rectangle, right under the low of the up-swings.

The up-sloping trend line located between trail nos 1 and 2 (Fig. 0.13) is worth a thousand words. It will reveal the future direction of the encapsulated market flow energy and offer the trader a hidden competitive edge.

1
The Birth of Pivots and the Pitchfork

The darkness of the unknown has always intrigued me. Whilst doing part of my residency in a New York City hospital, I was forever marvelling as our Emergency Medicine professor performed what seemed to be an almost magical examination on a comatose patient. He would spend only a few minutes observing the physical signs and quickly make his diagnosis. Then we eagerly waited for the results of the laboratory tests, which confirmed or negated the diagnosis. Most of the time, the professor's diagnosis was correct. Only years later have I come to understand the mechanism of his intuitive approach.

Whatever you decide to do in life, when starting from scratch you should always be aware of the 'knowledge building blocks' which will help you on your way, and trading is no different. Once you have mastered them, then and only then can you pursue more complex topics with competency. The approach given in this book guarantees a thorough understanding of the subject of pitchfork trading, and one that will shorten your learning curve, especially if you consistently practise the practical aspects. If you do so, you will be well on your way to applying intuition as part of your approach. Although it took him years of training and learning, my Emergency Medicine professor finally arrived at his goal: the planned intuition level. He could 'smell' a comatose junkie just by looking at him, or detect a potential suicide while inspecting the patient's nails, hair or clothes.

It might seem strange to associate Emergency Medicine and trading, but they both have the same strong impact on the psyche of the uninitiated person. When a person decides to take up trading, he or she will always be surprised by the emptiness of the chart, and will have the same feelings as the medical student on his first day in the Emergency Room. The emptiness, or 'nakedness', of the chart clearly illustrates the part of trading that new traders find the most perplexing (Fig. 1.1). With his eyes locked on to the vertical and horizontal axes, to the new trader the market appears to be completely motionless. At first, he is rather lost and, even if he has some idea of what trading is all about, does not know where to start.

This book will help the trader get over his initial bewilderment, and the charts are mapped in such a way that the left-to-right market movement on the time-wise horizontally oriented axis is clearly delineated.

Figure 1.1 Emptiness of the chart (Courtesy of www.pitchforktrader.com)

1.1   DEFINING THE MARKET CONTEXT AND ITS LIMITS

In order to trade, we must first become familiar with the market's flow. Second, we need to think about trading decisions. One of the best methods of understanding the market context (its layout), is to mark out its cardinal orientation:

- Where is the price coming from?
- Where does it seem to be going?
- Is the market trending or non-trending?
- What is the market's exact location within the whole context?
- How high/low is the morning, afternoon or day's apogee (highest high)?
- What is the slope like, or how did the price reach the current location?
- Was there continuous movement, or did the price jump directly towards the high/low of the chart?
- How did the day finish – at an extreme point of the chart, or was there a last gasp in pre-close with the market closing with a huge counter price bar?

As you have probably noticed, the above list only relates to the *price-related* market features. For the moment we have refrained from talking about any time-related chart factors. Why? In real trading, many traders don't use the time parameters. However, potentially this could upgrade the trading results. It is like shooting a revolver instead of firing a high-calibre machine gun from a US Navy warship. Time−price relation is dealt with in detail in Volume II (in preparation).

Let us go back to our empty chart and look at timing (Fig. 1.1). Even if the emptiness seems bewildering and mostly meaningless, closely observe the market flow and try to understand the following:

- What time length corresponds to each bar? This will allow us to calculate the time frame.
- What is the time period of the chart (duration of the chart from left to right)?
- What is the interval between two lows or two highs?
- How quickly/slowly does the price reach its morning, afternoon or day's extreme positions?
- How long does it take for the price to end its up-sloping/down-sloping tendency?
- What kind of rhythm does the price perform (cadenced, random, rapid, slow)?

The time–price relation is intricate, but it can explain much more clearly the market's movements and its random or sequential flow. In order to progress we must understand what will happen when we use a real-time chart where the price is rolling on the low time frame chart, like a small but very active mercury bubble. Ideally, we should embed the market flow energy into a hypothetical meandering river. Its winding movement will be optimal only if it takes the path of least resistance. This topic is treated in more detail in Volumes II and III (in preparation).

1.2 PIVOTS: DEFINITION, CHARACTERISTICS AND FUNCTION

The simplest concept can become the most powerful and most efficient tool.

In order to understand the meaning of the price movements, we create a map of the market with the help of landmarks, called *pivots*, which constitute the basics of pitchfork construction.

A pivot is defined as: *a critical point having a major or central role, function or effect . . . a shaft or pin on which something turns* (Merriam-Webster's Collegiate Dictionary 10th edition, 2002).

Therefore the dual role of the pivot is to both perform an important function and be a platform on which something else can turn. We could not agree more about these dual functions. Not only are they useful for trading but, in a way, they also become synergetic with each other. Whatever their degree of importance, pivots are easily-detected landmarks. They can be used to trace out both the immediate past and the current market positions, thus projecting the market price into the time–price space.

In Fig. 1.1 we can see that the price curve is not straight but resembles a sine curve. The market flow has been disturbed by small, middle-sized or very visible troughs (up-trend) or peaks (down-trend). Every time the price reaches a turning point, whether as a tiny stumbling move or a complete reversal, a pivot is formed. Its characteristics depend on the market's strength or weakness, slope and direction; in other words, how long the market maintains a particular price movement. By their shape and depth and/or height, the following four types of pivot can be identified:

- primary pivots (P), chiefly used to detect the high/low of a trend;
- major pivots (J), frequently seen immediately before the trend is completed;
- intermediate pivots (I), a kind of bridge between J and M pivots;

- minor pivots (M), called pullback pivots. They are often present at the beginning and end of the pullbacks.

The trader can mark pivots on the chart, but this requires some experience in evaluating the degree of importance of each type of pivot or by utilising ergonomic charting software (see, for example, *The Tools, the Power, the Knowledge* – Tom Joseph's Advanced GET User's Guide from eSignal, 1989–2003). Choosing the most optimal three-pivot set-up is not easy, especially during your apprenticeship. You should discipline yourself by keeping in mind that the whole market context (*think globally*) should be considered as an integral part of the local action of the market (*act locally*).

Figures 1.2–1.5 give examples of how and where to mark the pivots. The primary pivots (P) on Fig. 1.2 mark the most vigorous price movements while the local market is performing a counter-trend movement. As we can see from Fig. 1.3, the major pivots (J) often accompany the primary pivots (P). The former have less impact on the market tendency than the latter. Figure 1.4 indicates the position of intermediate pivots (I). The degree of impact on the market bias is less compared with that of the major pivots (J).

The minor pivots (M) perfectly integrate with the other types of pivot (Fig. 1.5 on p. 22). These pivots are the least important in terms of their impact on the market tendency. However, they ought not to be neglected because they have their role for entries and exits, especially when the trader goes to a lower time frame (optimal pivot visibility).

Figure 1.2   Primary pivots (P) (Courtesy of www.pitchforktrader.com)

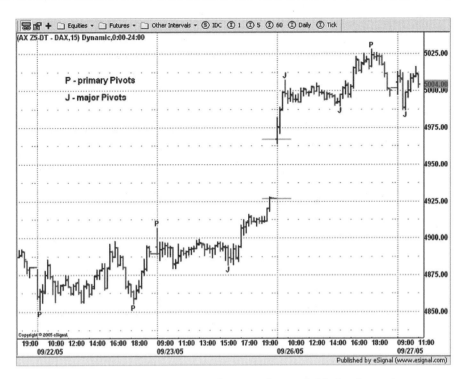

Figure 1.3   Major pivots (J) (Courtesy of www.pitchforktrader.com)

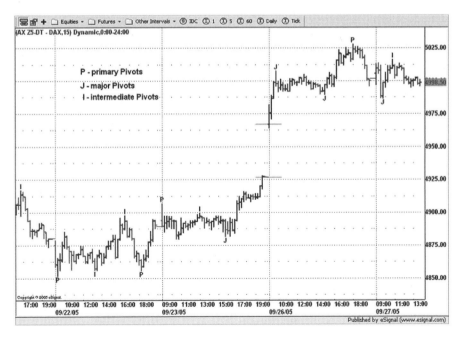

Figure 1.4   Intermediate pivots (I) position – lesser degree market impact compared with that of the major pivots (J). (Courtesy of www.pitchforktrader.com)

Figure 1.5   Minor pivots (M) (Courtesy of www.pitchforktrader.com)

1.3   CONSTRUCTING THE PITCHFORK

Whilst on the subject of embedding the energy flow of the market, there probably isn't a better way to guide this tremendous power than the pitchfork invented by Dr Alan Hall Andrews. Inspired by a course taught by Roger W. Babson, another entrepreneur from the first half of the 20th century, Andrews explained the mechanism of the median line (ML) closely guarded by two parallel trend lines (see Appendix 1: Historical Basis). These median lines are present on almost all charting software under the name of *Andrews pitchfork*.

It is not our intention to treat in detail the work of Babson or Andrews; the former was working over 75 years ago, and the latter in the early 1960s. Rather, we focus on how their pioneer work has evolved into the technical market concepts integral to everyday trading. Although Fundamental Analysis flourished during their time, both of them struggled and succeeded in creating the foundation of modern Technical Analysis. Even though much time has gone by (rather quickly for some of us), their work is as valid today as ever.

The geometrical structure of the pitchfork closely resembles a channel made out of three equidistant parallel trend lines, where the median is anchored farther away from the channel's main body. The cardinal orientation is usually slanted; otherwise it would have been called a rectangle. Most of the time the pitchfork is optimally drawn by suitable software and the trader only has to choose the best landmarks, which could be a single pivot or a mixture of the pivots already described: primary, major, intermediate and minor.

If you had to retain just one concept from these three volumes (over 1000 pages and more than 1200 charts), it would be the following:

> *The choice of pivots underpins the efficiency of pitchfork trading, which in turn is expressed by how well the market is described.*

I call this principle 'the Holy Grail of the pitchfork'. Please keep it in mind while you read on.

The physical construction of the pitchfork is easily understood and carried out, even manually. Each pitchfork needs three physical or virtual pivots and the construction sequence is usually as follows: High–Low–High or Low–High–Low except in the case of specific pitchforks using virtual pivots or midpoint pivots of a virtual (or not) swing (for instance, the 'suspended' anchor pitchfork, the T-pitchfork, the straight alignment pitchfork described further). The initial pivot, usually marked P0, firmly fixes the structure into the market, and is therefore named the *anchor*. The other two pivots are usually marked P1 and P2. After selecting the optimal three-pivot set, draw a *trend line* (median line or ML) joining the anchor (P0) to the middle of the swing formed by the P1–P2 duo. Once the current market builds a pivot, you should look for a possible location for the next one.

Very briefly, we mention here the *warning lines* (WL) which run parallel to the extreme upper and lower parallel lines (U-MLH and L-MLH), which in turn are parallel to the ML. The WL is parallel to the MLH at same distance as that of the MLH to the ML. The space between the ML and each MLH, or between the WL and any neighbouring MLH, may be divided following a Fibonacci ratio measure, thus creating the *Fibonacci trend lines*. You will find more information on these topics in Chapters 5 and 14.

Now for a brief word about whether or not to mix the four types of pivot (primary, major, intermediate and minor). We would say it does not really matter how you choose these pivots as long as you keep in mind the 'Holy Grail of the pitchfork'. There is more on pivot choice criteria in Chapter 2.

1.4 CREATING PIVOTS: CASE STUDIES

German Dax Futures Index Charts

Constructing a pitchfork is carried out with only one denominator in the trader's mind: an ideal market description (Fig. 1.6). As you can see, whatever its type, each pivot is marked in the same fashion; its relationship with the others ideally embeds the market flow and converts a seemingly random market into a railroad-like structure, less random than it first seems.

The choice of all the primary (P) pivots seems to be workable for the first part of the chart (Fig. 1.7). On 26 September 2005, the strength of the market creates a very large market interruption (*gap*), which translates the market flow from inside the body of the pitchfork farther upwards, to over 100% of the pitchfork's height.

Drawing lines parallel to the U-MLH reveals once again the position of the optimal primary (P) pivot (Fig. 1.8). The market rides perfectly on these trend lines. The gap opens right on the upper warning line, above the upper 150% Fibonacci line and U-MLH. Even a 100% upward market translation cannot disturb the optimal market description ('the pitchfork's Holy Grail').

In spite of their different degrees of importance, the primary (P) and the major (J) pivots perform nearly the same role of stopping the upward market move, right above the upper 350% Fibonacci line (Fig. 1.9).

Two of the best qualities of the pitchfork are its flexibility and versatility. Figure 1.10 demonstrates that, by slightly changing the location of the anchor and the P1−P2 swing alignment (from P−P to P−J), the market is described even better.

Changing the anchor location and the P1−P2 swing alignment enables the creation of a dual set of interdependent pitchforks (PF). The most recent PF better embeds the market with the help of the older PF (Fig. 1.11).

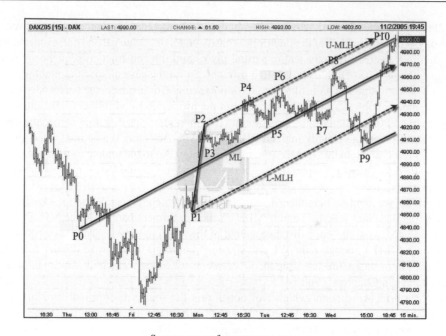

Source: www.futuresource.com
Figure 1.6   Pitchfork construction (Courtesy of www.pitchforktrader.com)

Figure 1.7   Choice of primary pivot (P) (Courtesy of www.pitchforktrader.com)

Figure 1.8 Optimum primary pivot choices (Courtesy of www.pitchforktrader.com)

Figure 1.9 P and J pivots stopping the upward market move (Courtesy of www.pitchforktrader.com)

Figure 1.10   Flexibility and versatility of the pitchfork (Courtesy of www.pitchforktrader.com)

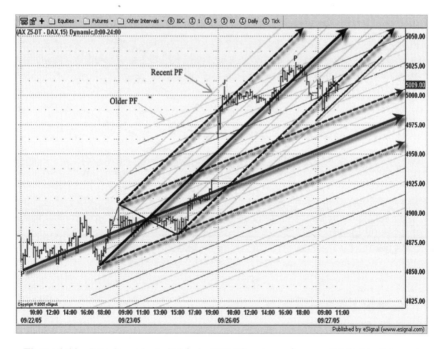

Figure 1.11   Interdependent pitchforks (PF) (Courtesy of www.pitchforktrader.com)

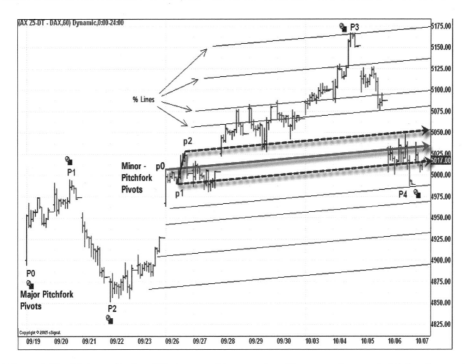

Figure 1.12   Major and minor PF pivots working together (Courtesy of www.pitchforktrader.com)

The major and minor pitchfork concept is treated in detail in Chapter 9. For our present purpose, the chart in Fig. 1.12 shows how the two different sets of pivot, the minor PF (p0, p1 and p2) and the major PF (P0, P1, P2, P3, and P4), are working together. Pivots P3 and P4 halt the market cold, upwards and downwards respectively, and are well embedded within the outer limits of the p0-p1-p2 pitchfork.

Figure 1.13 shows the two different sets of pivots creating two pitchforks. The larger PF encloses the market price movements (the market context); the smaller PF, which is the more recent, is right on top of the immediately developing market. It is interesting to note that they share a common pivot (p0 = P2). We will see later that this feature is very common when the trader tries to embed the ongoing correction of a just-finished positive trend. This is done right after the confirmation of the bottom.

Look at the two sets of pivots in Fig. 1.14. One set describes the contextual pitchfork (P0, P1 and P2) and the second (p0, p1 and p2 − not drawn here) belongs to the pitchfork which is closer to the market's ongoing downward movement. For clarity and learning purposes we have drawn only the corresponding MLs.

The pattern in Fig. 1.15 (on p. 29) completes the contextual pitchfork of Fig. 1.14 where only the first set of pivots, the median line with its accompanying lines and the P1−P2 swing are drawn.

1.5   KEY LEARNING POINTS

- The most simple concept can become the most powerful and efficient tool.
- Pivots can be easily used to trace out both the immediate past and the current market positions, thus projecting the market price into the time−price space of the immediate future.

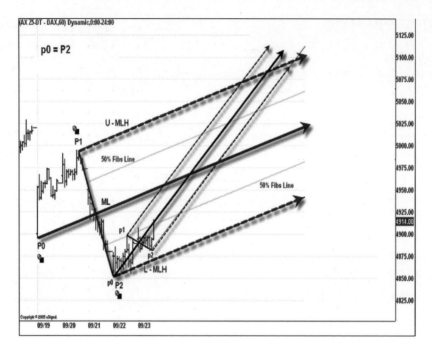

Figure 1.13   Creation of two PFs (Courtesy of www.pitchforktrader.com)

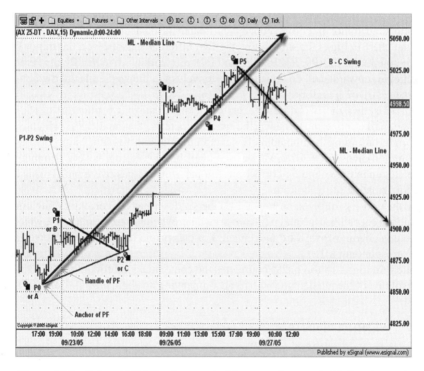

Figure 1.14   Stripped PF: MLs drawn only (Courtesy of www.pitchforktrader.com)

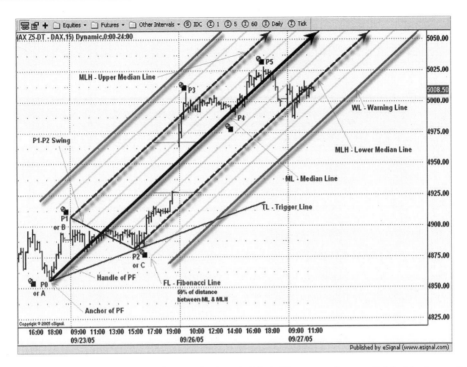

Figure 1.15   Complete set-up of an up-sloping pitchfork (Courtesy of www.pitchforktrader.com)

- The whole market context (think globally) should be considered in conjunction with the local action of the market (act locally).
- The choice of pivots underpins the efficiency of pitchfork trading, which in turn is expressed by how well the market is described. We call this principle 'the Holy Grail of the pitchfork'.
- The quality of a pivot should be always observed:
  - a bigger swing with a big reversal bar (*shooting star*) gives the best pivot;
  - the cleanness of the bars within a swing;
  - the pivot range indicates market volatility at that moment.
- The pitchfork construction procedure is fully realised when there is only one denominator in the trader's mind: an ideal market description. Whatever the type of pivot used, their compatibility ideally embeds the tortuous market flow, converting a seemingly random market into a railroad-like structure, less random than it first appears.

2
Choice of Pivot

We cannot stress too strongly the 'Holy Grail' of the pitchfork discussed in the previous chapter:

> *The choice of pivots underpins the efficiency of pitchfork trading, which in turn is expressed by how well the market is described.*

As long as this is kept in mind at all times, trading results will be optimal. All this emphasizes the power of the choice of pivot.

It goes without saying that, when using the pitchfork technique, capital accumulation will not be possible if the right pivots are not chosen. The pitchfork embodies both the true market price kinetics and the interactions of the millions of participating traders, and takes into account the price as well as the time variable. We cannot emphasize fully enough how important it is to make the time−price space part of everyday trading decisions. It is far more efficient than taking just one variable. The choice of pivot contributes hugely when assessing how these dual temporal−spatial variables interact.

The pivots are located either within a *swing* (distance between the two nearest pivots) or at its extremities. The swing is located within a *trend* (distance between two market reversals). Several swings may constitute a trend toward a given direction. Classically, the market is said to be *up-trending* when the price climbs to higher highs and higher lows, and *down-trending* when the price drops to lower highs and lower lows. A non-trending market is called a *sideways* or *trading range*.

2.1 OPTIMAL PIVOTS

There is one obvious question: How does the trader choose the optimal pivots? We will try to answer this question by evaluating the pivots' characteristics.

- Consider them as Cartesian coordinates sitting on the top/bottom of a pullback (in up-trends) and on the top/bottom of a peak (in down-trends). The pullback and the peak movements are *resting areas*, indispensable as trends develop. Other resting locations would be considered as less common within the trend: the high/low/midpoint of a gap or on the curvature inflexion of two intersected/joint moving averages (see Fig. 11.19).
- The size of the pullback/peak swing containing the pivots has four degrees of importance (see Fig. 2.2): the bigger they are, the greater the impact of the pivots on the market bias.

Their measurement is carried out in two ways:
- as a percentage compared with its current swing; or
- as a percentage of its height (in points, dollars or currency) compared to the value of the absolute security ((high-low)/low and vice versa in a down-trend).
- Consider the type of pivot: primary, major, intermediate and minor.
- The number of consecutive pivots located on the same trend, usually numbered from 0 to 5, and less frequently from 0 to 7 or even from 0 to 9. In the case of a prolonged tendency, the number of pivot markings may reach 11. The reversal price potential is omnipresent when the price reaches the 3rd, 5th, 7th, 9th or 11th pivot.
- Location within its current swing.
- Location within its trending swing.
- Location compared with the prior trending swing.

As we already know a pitchfork is composed of three pivots (see Fig. 2.3):

- the anchor, represented by P0;
- the pitchfork's P1–P2 swing;
- the median point, located at the intersection of the 50% portion of the P1–P2 swing with the median line. It constitutes one of the supports when drawing in the pitchfork.

2.2 KINEMATIC STUDY OF THE PIVOT

From the point of view of the pitchfork's kinematics (the branch of dynamics that deals with the aspects of motion apart from mass and force), we have two variables:

- The anchor's (P0) location is defined by:
  - The P0's Cartesian position (time, price), which is most often situated on a pivot (a turning point of variable importance), usually giving birth to a *traditional pitchfork*, as illustrated in Fig. 2.3.
  - The P0's non-pivotal location, situated on the midpoint of the swing opposite the pitchfork's own P1–P2 swing. This is described in detail in Chapter 10 and is called the *Schiff pitchfork* (Fig. 10.2).
  - The P0's non-pivotal Cartesian position, located on the midpoint of a virtual swing opposite to the pitchfork's real P1–P2 swing. To our knowledge, this is the first time that this type of pitchfork has been described and we have taken the liberty of calling it the *T-pitchfork* (see Fig. 10.18). This topic is treated in more detail in Chapter 10.
  - The P0's non-pivotal location, situated on a 'suspended' market point, born through the Action/Reaction (AR) Line development which is described in detail in Chapter 11. In this case, the functional role of the pitchfork is of rather a 'hybrid' nature, because the A/R Lines already perform the market embedding. The P0 pivot's location gives rise to the name of this type of chart formation: the *hybrid* or *suspended pitchfork*. Another version of this pattern is the *retrograde pitchfork* (see Fig. 2.33).
- The P1–P2 swing (see Fig. 2.3), which in turn depends on the location of its constituent P1 and P2 pivots. Their exact position will:
  - directly engender the swing orientation in time–price space;
  - indirectly impose the pitchfork's alignment within the same space.

2.3 KINEMATICS OF THE PITCHFORK EMBEDDING THE GLOBAL MARKET

Once the characteristics of the pitchfork's pivots are in place, we can then discuss the kinematical part of the pitchfork as a whole, and its role in embedding the market flow. At this point, we must once again discuss the 'naked' chart. When observing the naked chart of any market, in any time frame, two aspects should be thoroughly considered:

- The overall picture, describing the layout of the trending, non-trending or mixed directional aspects of the global time—price virtual space of the market.
- The exact location of the current market price (the most recent move) within:
  - its own swing;
  - the swing of its most recent trend;
  - its last global swing or previous trend.

Optimal results are given by the combined study of multiple time frames (at least three, including the operational one).

2.4 PIVOT CHOICES: CASE STUDIES

S&P 500 e-minis & DJIA Cash Index Charts

Figure 2.1 shows a naked S&P 500 e-mini chart which will be studied in detail over Figs. 2.2—2.7. Close observation of the apparent emptiness of the chart reveals the following:

- Globally, the market is downtrending (left side of the chart). It is currently situated in the middle of a correction (right side of the chart).

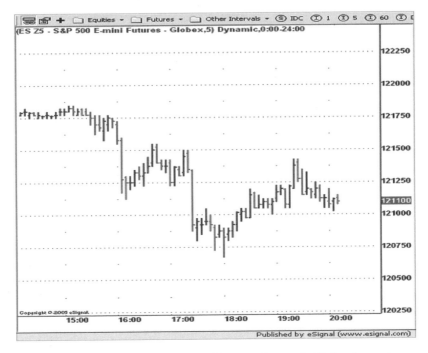

Figure 2.1   S&P 500 e-mini chart (Courtesy of www.pitchforktrader.com)

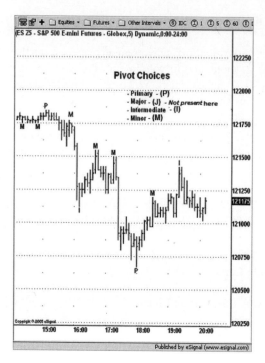

Figure 2.2 Pivot choices: three of the four possible types of pivot are present
(Courtesy of www.pitchforktrader.com)

- Locally, the price retraces the most recent swing (18:00 hrs to 19:30 hrs), trying to rebound in order to finish the correction of the entire down-swing (left side of chart up to 18:00 hrs).
- The terminal bars of this 5-min ES chart are located around 20:00 Central European Time (CET), corresponding to the 14:00 US ET.

In Fig. 2.2, out of the four possible types of pivot, only three are present: primary, intermediate and minor. The major type (J) is not present here. The two primary (P) pivots, at the start and end of the trend, are illustrated in the left half of the chart. This is completely in line with the definition of this type of pivot, which usually shows the trend's extremities. The minor (M) pivots are the most numerous. The correction shown on the right half of the chart is topped by an intermediate (I) pivot, which fails to reach the double minor (M) levels on the down-sloping trend (left half of the chart).

The labelling of the listed pivots is performed by the eSignal Advanced Charts from www.esignal.com. The charting software I use is provided by eSignal.

Figure 2.3 provides the same information as Figs. 2.1 and 2.2, but the trend is in a terminating phase. The construction of the down-sloping pitchfork uses a minor (M) pivot for the anchor (P0), an intermediate (I) pivot for P1, and another minor (M) pivot for P2. The pitchfork stresses the steep slope of the trend. As the market reaches the bottom, illustrated by the P3 primary pivot, a possible correction phase is starting which might be brought to term. If this reversal is valid, the P3 pivot will be the lowest low of this down-sloping pitchfork. Another set of pivots

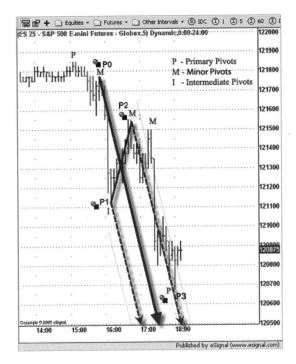

Figure 2.3   S&P 500 e-mini chart (Courtesy of www.pitchforktrader.com)

should be prepared to be marked in the opposite direction. In the case of a false reversal, the current pitchfork P4, P5−P11 pivot markings should continue.

In Fig. 2.4, the P2 of the pitchfork is moved lower to impersonate the second minor (M) pivot. Why is this done? The answer is to obtain a better market description. (Remember the pitchfork's 'Holy Grail': *The choice of pivots underpins the efficiency of pitchfork trading, which in turn is expressed by how well the market is described.*)

With the P4 pivot already marked, we are still within the pitchfork's main territory at its upper border and at this point the down-sloping market flow is continuing. It is ensured by the close of the last P4 bar, which is a reversal bar (close lower than the open, situated in the lowest quarter of the bar).

Figure 2.5 shows an upward trend going beyond the inner body of the down-sloping pitchfork. It is reasonable to replace the P4 marking (see Fig. 2.4), and create a counter-trend pitchfork (p0, p1, p2 and p3). The local market is retracing pretty well on its preceding P2−P3 swing (1215−1207 zone), and even on the entire P0−P3 down-sloping swing (1218−1207 zone).

The market zooms through the p1 resistance (1210.50) and a double retest ensues. A low-risk, high-probability trade is being set up (long entry at 1211 level, with a tiny stop at 1209, one and a half ES points under the p1 resistance). The profit target will be the upper median line of the up-sloping pitchfork. All of this is achieved through the three prearranged orders: entry, stop loss and then the logical profit objective. These orders compose the *three pawn technique* (see Chapter 19).

In Fig. 2.6 (on p. 37), we can see that the market is climbing as expected, right through the upper median line of the up-sloping pitchfork, after intense local activity at the 1210.50 level, which this time is forming a strong support (old resistance). The p0-p1-p2 pitchfork masters the

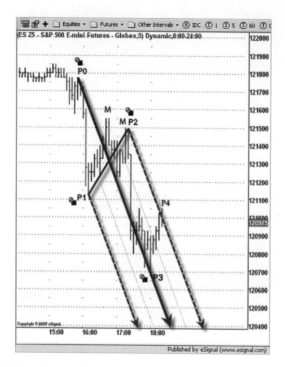

Figure 2.4   S&P 500 e-mini chart (cont.) (Courtesy of www.pitchforktrader.com)

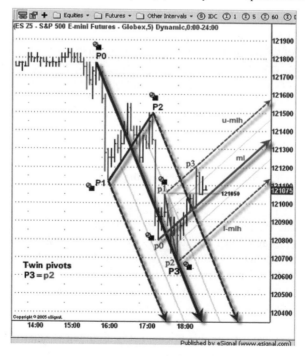

Figure 2.5   S&P 500 e-mini chart (cont.) (Courtesy of www.pitchforktrader.com)

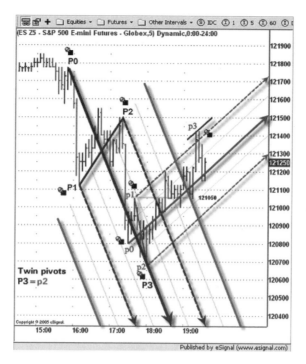

Figure 2.6   S&P 500 e-mini chart (cont.) (Courtesy of www.pitchforktrader.com)

embedding of the local market flow almost within its inner limits. The market closes above the upper median line (at the p3 pivot level) of the up-sloping pitchfork and then drops like a stone toward its up-sloping median line. By now the price, even if it is still beyond the inner limits of the initial pitchfork (P0, P1, P2 and P3), is ready to drop, reaching its initial low levels once again.

The mirror bars illustrated in Fig. 2.7 form the p3 pivot, and constitute very strong resistance as they send the price in the opposite direction, straight down to the lower median line of the up-sloping pitchfork. It seems that the 1210.50, p1 old resistance level has now become a very strong support, already responsible for multiple retests and piercings (see Figs. 2.6 and 2.7). Thus the p4 pivot has been created – and it seems to hold.

Figure 2.8 illustrates an empty chart in a 5-minute time frame. It is important to study as many of these charts as possible in order to hone your observational and interpretational skills, so you can immediately put the global situation into the local context and understand the effervescence of the most current movement (local action). Several time frames are studied in Figs. 2.8–2.11.

After the movements on the Wednesday morning, the Dow jumps 100% of its morning range, hitting the very strong 11045 resistance in the afternoon. The following morning, the price starts a two-day down-sloping trend, dropping like a stone until midday Friday. An inceptive correction or maybe even a reversal (it's too early to know yet) timidly tries to take over by the end-of-day market.

To summarize, the naked chart in Fig. 2.8 (on p. 39) shows, from left to right:

- a sideways movement in the morning;
- a two-day, down-sloping trend;
- and, finally, a probable ensuing correction or reversal.

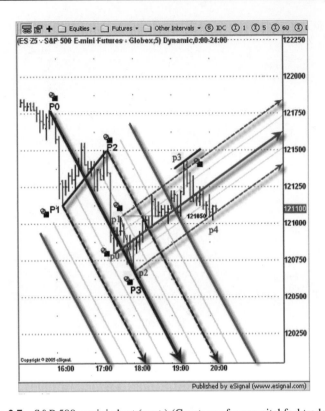

Figure 2.7 S&P 500 e-mini chart (cont.) (Courtesy of www.pitchforktrader.com)

All this is taking place over a 3-day time period of a 5-minute chart.

The naked chart presented in Fig. 2.8 gives a pretty good idea of the ongoing price movements for the duration of the charted three days (Wednesday, Thursday and Friday). Now all the three movements already mentioned − sideways, trend and eventual correction or reversal − must be enclosed within one or two pitchforks (Fig. 2.9 on p. 40). For that we have chosen two sets of pivots (P0, P1 to P 5 and p0 to p3).

As you can see, the first pitchfork (major) choice, has three possible anchors.

The second choice, the minor pitchfork, will function under the influence of the major pitchfork. Its role is to describe, as best it can, the ensuing correction or reversal. As a result of the three choices of anchor (P0, P00 and P000), there are three possible major pitchfork drawings. Which one will be the most optimal? The one that best describes the market! How are we going to know which one this is? Simply by trying out all three!

One plausible option is to have the anchor in P00 (Fig. 2.10 on p. 40). By drawing its corresponding pitchfork we encapsulate a market movement running through the lower part of the major pitchfork parallel to the channel formed by the ML and the internal upper 25% Fibonacci Line. The latter halts the market exactly at the minor pitchfork's p3 pivot.

The second pitchfork choice, having a 'suspended' pivot P0, is born out of an Action/Reaction Line set-up (Fig. 2.11 on p. 41). Detailed information on this process is provided in Chapter 11. This time the market has changed its cruising channel and runs on the upper side of the major pitchfork. The breakout of U-MLH improves the visibility of the incoming correction/reversal.

Figure 2.8   An empty chart with a 5-minute time frame (Courtesy of www.pitchforktrader.com)

Note: The P000 pivot pitchfork choice (Fig. 2.9) was abandoned because it did not optimally fit the market. Our preference goes to the P0 'suspended' pivot pitchfork, which best describes the market.

Figure 2.12 (on p. 41) is an empty 15-minute chart covering a 9-day time period. For the global context, the chart covers (from left to right) a trend inception phase (Tuesday morning), followed by a 7-day time period trend. The ensuing down-sloping correction starts with a huge reversal down-sloping bar on Thursday morning, which has lasted, so far, for two days.

Figure 2.13 (on p. 42) shows two sets of pivots (p0 to p9 and P00 to P02). They faithfully follow the corresponding context of the naked chart and the local market. The trend contains ten pivots numbered 0 to 9. The projected pitchfork drawn by utilizing pivots P00, P01 and P02 encloses the local market flow and illustrates the most recent phase of the market.

Figure 2.14 (on p. 42) is a 15-minute chart illustrating the influence of the upper 30-minute time frame (TF) upon the lower one (15-min TF). Even if the market flow of the trend is assiduously guided by the median line (ML) of the upper TF, our chosen pivots (p0 to p9) perform a magnificent job in describing the market. This ML magnetizes and holds the market's up-side potential (p1, p3, p5 and p9) and serves as a symmetry axis through the swing p7—p8. The p4 pivot holds

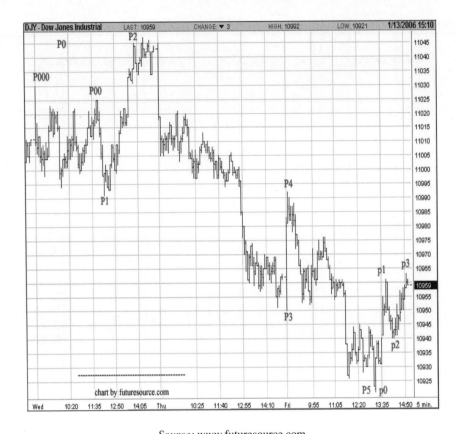

Source: www.futuresource.com

Figure 2.9   Choices of the most optimal pivot: three sets (Courtesy of www.pitchforktrader.com)

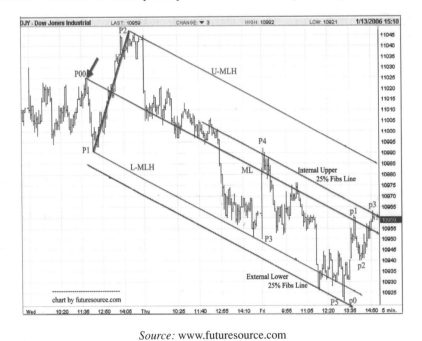

Source: www.futuresource.com

Figure 2.10   Choice of pitchfork with anchor in P00 (Courtesy of www.pitchforktrader.com)

Source: www.futuresource.com

Figure 2.11   Pitchfork arising from an Action/Reaction line set-up (Courtesy of www.pitchforktrader.com)

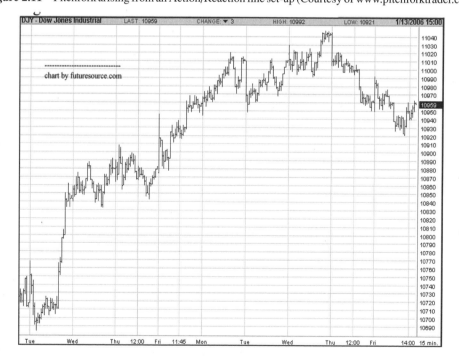

Source: www.futuresource.com

Figure 2.12   Naked chart covering a 9-day time period (Courtesy of www.pitchforktrader.com)

Source: www.futuresource.com

Figure 2.13   Illustration of contextual and local market flows (Courtesy of www.pitchforktrader.com)

Source: www.futuresource.com

Figure 2.14   Influence of the upper time frame on the lower time frame
(Courtesy of www.pitchforktrader.com)

Source: www.futuresource.com

Figure 2.15   Using the T-pitchfork to understand market flow (Courtesy of www.pitchforktrader.com)

the downside momentum of the market. Out of ten pivots only three (p2, p6 and p8) are not directly implicated. It is rare that the market's description uses every pivot; if this does happen, then the potential of the trader's results is greatly enhanced.

Figure 2.15 underlines the fact that the market is still trending upward. The use of P0 to form what is called a 'T-pitchfork' is clear (this technique is treated in more detail in Chapter 10). We can see that this type of pitchfork enhances the role of the upper time frame pitchfork in the process of optimally describing the market. In this way, the market flow can be better pinpointed on this 15-min lower time frame chart.

The 30-min chart in Fig. 2.16 covers almost one month of trading days. The mid-point of this chart illustrates the final part of the down-trend (until Tuesday morning's low). Then, a strong up-sloping trend ensues. An abrupt huge reversal bar on Thursday afternoon starts the corresponding up-sloping corrective movement, ending on the right side of the chart.

In order to better observe the market flow, a 30-min chart (Fig. 2.17) is marked with three types of pivot. From left to right:

(i)   p0-p1-p2 to p11 in order to project the up-sloping tendency of the whole market;
(ii) P1-P0-P2 to enclose the same up-sloping trend, but with a more optimal median line;
(iii) p00-p01-p02-p03 which projects the most recent ongoing correction.

If we consider the first set of pivots (p0 to p11) displayed on the 30-min chart shown in Fig. 2.18, we notice that the price climbs all the way up to the external upper 50% Fibonacci Line as discussed in Fig. 2.17. We are far from the main body of the pitchfork, situated in the territory limited by U-MLH and L-MLH.

Source: www.futuresource.com

Figure 2.16 One month of trading days on a 30-min chart (Courtesy of www.pitchforktrader.com)

Source: www.futuresource.com

Figure 2.17 Three types of pivot on a 30-min chart (Courtesy of www.pitchforktrader.com)

Source: www.futuresource.com
Figure 2.18   Detecting the market flow out of the body of the main pitchfork
(Courtesy of www.pitchforktrader.com)

Of all the choices described in Fig. 2.17, the pitchfork shown in Fig. 2.19 is the most optimal
in describing the market flow. We made an exception when we named this pitchfork's anchor
pivot P1 instead P0, because we wanted to preserve the classic pivot P0-P1-P2 labelling sequence
of market development. The best argument in favour of this choice is the slope alignment of the
median line, which the market roughly follows about 66% of the duration of the trend (multiple
tests, retests, piercings and zooms). The more a median line is tested from below, the greater its
resistance role.

Together with the 15-min chart, the 60-min chart illustrated in Fig. 2.20 is the time frame used
most often in intra-day trading. The time period covers almost two months of trading days. The
left half of the chart, with more than a month's correction, is terminated on Tuesday morning.
The ensuing up-trend lasts $7\frac{1}{2}$ days. Its ongoing sharp corresponding up-sloping correction
terminates on the right side of the chart.

As we advance our study to a higher time frame (Fig. 2.21 on p. 47), the market is more
concise. Fewer pivots are needed to cover the market flow. In this chart, a single pivot set is used.

The pitchfork illustrated in Fig. 2.22 (on p. 47) optimally describes the market, using the low
of a prior swing as an anchor (P0) and a P1−P2 swing that ends the down-sloping trend (see the
first two-thirds of the chart, left to right). Thus, the up-sloping trend is very visible. The median
line is used as a symmetry axis (from Tuesday afternoon through to Friday) and acts as a very
strong support (see the last Friday to the right of the chart).

Figure 2.23 (on p. 48) is a daily chart illustrating $11\frac{1}{2}$ months of market flow activity. It starts
as an up-sloping trend in the middle of April 2005. Then the market flows with deep swings until

Figure 2.19   Optimal pivot choice (Courtesy of www.pitchforktrader.com)

Figure 2.20   A 60-min chart commonly used in day trading (Courtesy of www.pitchforktrader.com)

Figure 2.21   Using a single pivot set to cover the market flow (Courtesy of www.pitchforktrader.com)

Figure 2.22   Pitchfork with an anchor at the low of the prior swing (Courtesy of www.pitchforktrader.com)

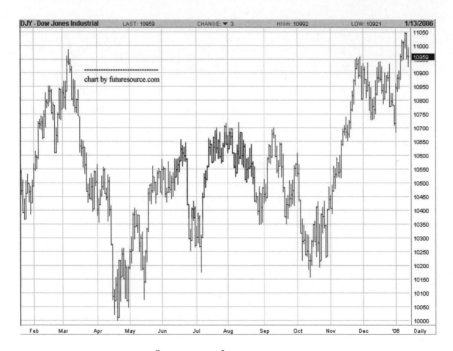

Source: www.futuresource.com
Figure 2.23   Eleven-and-a-half months of market flow activity (Courtesy of www.pitchforktrader.com)

the beginning of August 2005. After a short-lived downward zigzag correction (mid-August to mid-October 2005) the price improves with a steep upward slope, exceeding the old high of March 2005.

The set of pivots illustrated in Fig. 2.24 is classic, as the trend is well advanced in its development. At the beginning of the trend we have the choice of using the low of the penultimate swing as an anchor (p0 in this case). As the trend develops, using P0 is more optimal than p0 and the market flow will be better described.

The set of pivots P0 to P5 in Fig. 2.25 gives a faithful market description.

The weekly chart shown in Fig. 2.26 covers $4\frac{1}{2}$ years of market activity. We can see that since the low of October 2002 the market is in a steady up-sloping trend. The first part of the trend, ending in February 2004, has a steep gradient with a slope above 45°. After that, the slope diminishes by at least half. It then makes a new annual high, but still cannot get beyond the high of summer 2001.

The role of the pivots (see Fig. 2.27) is very important in selecting which is the most suitable to optimally describe the incoming trend (P0 to P7). Out of several possibilities, the only way to decide is by drawing all of them (more on this technique at the end of the chapter).

The market naturally chooses its most optimal *gliding bed*, cruising along the path of least resistance (Fig. 2.28). The P0 to P7 pivot set has built an optimal pitchfork: the U-MLH serving as a strong resistance, the ML and L-MLH both tested several times. They also serve as a symmetry axis. Finally, the market is halted by the warning line (WL) (see Chapter 5 for information on WLs).

Source: www.futuresource.com

Figure 2.24   Classic set of pivots (Courtesy of www.pitchforktrader.com)

Source: www.futuresource.com

Figure 2.25   Pivots describing a faithful market description (Courtesy of www.pitchforktrader.com)

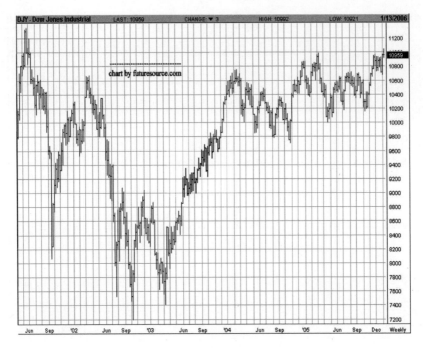

Source: www.futuresource.com

Figure 2.26 Chart illustrating 4.5 years of market activity (Courtesy of www.pitchforktrader.com)

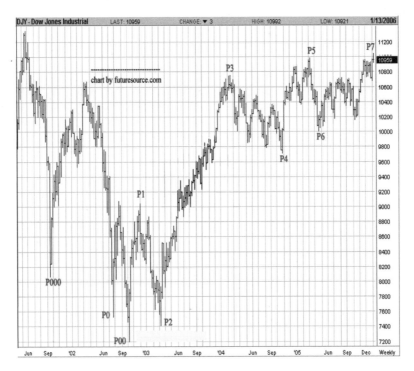

Source: www.futuresource.com

Figure 2.27 Marking all possible pivots in order to select the most suitable
(Courtesy of www.pitchforktrader.com)

Source: www.futuresource.com
Figure 2.28   Optimal pitchfork (Courtesy of www.pitchforktrader.com)

The monthly chart shown in Fig. 2.29 illustrates very long-range market activity, clearly identifying 20 years of market flow. After a mildly sloping trend ending in February 1995, the market achieves a high rate of momentum (March 1995 breakout), raising the slope of the chart to more than 45°. It finally culminates in January 2000, after which the market is in a corrective pattern. The only pivot available to embed the trend of the market flow is that illustrated in Fig. 2.30. It is a classic use of pivots for a trending market.

The pitchfork in Fig. 2.31 (on p. 53) faithfully describes the up-sloping market. The most recent market activity is very well embedded between the median line and the internal lower 50% Fibonacci line.

The study of the pitchfork in Fig. 2.32 (on p. 53) is carried out in parallel with that of Fig. 2.33 (on p. 54). There are two choices of pivot for establishing the efficient anchor of the most optimal pitchfork. In the first scenario (Fig. 2.32) we chose the P00 pivot as anchor, the high of the last down-swing (P00-P1) preceding the down-sloping trend. The advantage of this version is that it can be drawn into the trend's development; right after the P2 is formed.

The pitchfork shown in Fig. 2.33 is a '*retrograde*' variation of the traditional pitchfork. Its median line is drawn through the middle of the P1−P2 swing and the P5 pivot, with the purpose of projecting the market price of the ongoing reversal movement (p0-p1-p2). Comparing the pitchforks of Figs. 2.32 and 2.33, the latter optimally describes the market flow and shows the p0 to p3 correction more efficiently. Its disadvantage is that it can be drawn only after the P5 pivot has already formed, but right on time for trading the up-sloping correction, with the assistance of the p0 to p3 pitchfork.

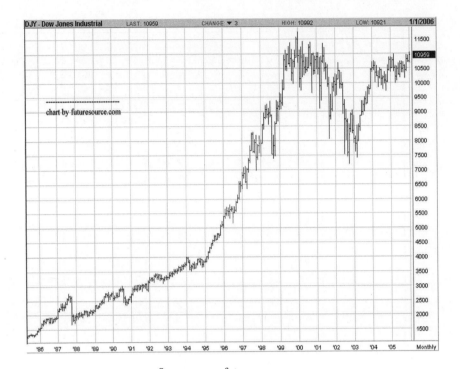

Source: www.futuresource.com

Figure 2.29 Long-range monthly activity (Courtesy of www.pitchforktrader.com)

Source: www.futuresource.com

Figure 2.30 Classic pivots in a trending market (Courtesy of www.pitchforktrader.com)

Source: www.futuresource.com

Figure 2.31 Pitchforks describing the up-sloping market (Courtesy of www.pitchforktrader.com)

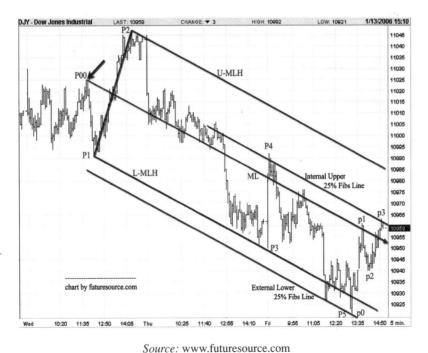

Source: www.futuresource.com

Figure 2.32 Down-sloping pitchfork and 25% Fibonacci ratio lines
(Courtesy of www.pitchforktrader.com)

Source: www.futuresource.com
Figure 2.33   Retrograde pitchfork (Courtesy of www.pitchforktrader.com)

2.5   PENULTIMATE PIVOTS OF AN ENDING CORRECTION: CASE STUDIES

DJIA Cash Index, FTSE 100 Cash Index Charts

The role of the pivots preceding the correction's lowest low is more forceful because they are near the inception trend zone. The antepenultimate low (P000), the penultimate low (P0) and the lowest low (P00) of the correction are just a few of the possible pivotal choices.

There are several choices for the most optimal pivot for the construction of a pitchfork, which will embed the market flow of the ensuing up-sloping trend after the preceding correction is confirmed. This is possible only after the first swing of the ongoing up-sloping trend has developed, so it can be used for constituting the P1−P2 of the pitchfork. Once the P1−P2 swing is defined, we have to verify which of the possible pivots situated in front of this swing can best be used as an anchor as we draw in the up-sloping pitchfork of the current trend.

First, we must carefully observe the zone preceding the end of the correction in order to locate the possible pivotal choices and analyze the corrective swings to find an adequate pivot. A study using five pivot choices is presented below. Where there is no suitable pivot, there are still three possibilities:

- use the Action/Reaction Line set-up (see Chapter 11) to get a hybrid pitchfork;
- use the Action/Reaction Line set up to get a retrograde pitchfork;
- search for a T-pitchfork (more details in Chapter 10).

The pitchfork in Fig. 2.34 uses the antepenultimate pivot (P000). The market is well described, with the ML and the L-MLH being tested several times. The pitchfork in Fig. 2.35 (on p. 56) uses the penultimate pivot (P0). The market is well described, running along the channel formed by the inner parallel trend line (TL) and the L-MLH; they have both been tested several times.

Figure 2.34   Antepenultimate pivot choice (no. 1) of the anchor location
(Courtesy of www.pitchforktrader.com)

The version that we call a T-pitchfork is very well illustrated in the DJIA Cash Index weekly chart (Fig. 2.36). The 'suspended' anchor (P−AB) is at the middle of the virtual AB swing. The market flow monopolizes the upper part of the pitchfork, going beyond the U-ML, but is well-contained in channels formed by the ML, U-MLH and WL (more details on this in Chapters 5 and 10).

Pivot choice 4 (Fig. 2.37 on p. 57) forms a typical Schiff pitchfork, which will be treated in detail in Chapter 10. For now, we can say that this particular pivotal choice translates the market upward in the channel formed by the U-MLH and external upper 250% Fibonacci lines, well above the pitchfork's main body.

Figure 2.38 (on p. 57) shows the P00 pivot (the lowest low) as an anchor, provoking a very steep slope on the constructed pitchfork. This is less practical because the price will quickly get out of the main body. The use of multiple WLs is imposed.

Conclusion: The optimal pivot for an ideal anchor location to describe the flow of the market is either 1 or 2.

2.6   KEY LEARNING POINTS

- Evaluate the pivots' characteristics: the size of the swing (%), which gives the pivots their degree of importance; type; number of consecutives pivots (numbering); and their locations on the three different swings.

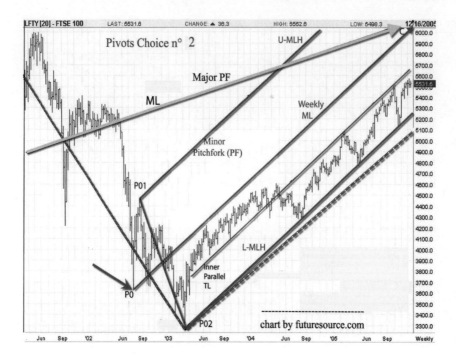

Source: www.futuresource.com
Figure 2.35 Penultimate pivot choice (no. 2) of the anchor location
(Courtesy of www.pitchforktrader.com)

Source: www.futuresource.com
Figure 2.36 T-pitchfork: a virtual pivot choice (no. 3) of the anchor location
(Courtesy of www.pitchforktrader.com)

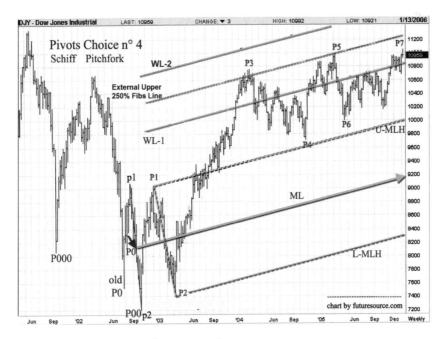

Source: www.futuresource.com

Figure 2.37 Schiff pitchfork: a preceding swing midpoint anchor choice (no. 4)
(Courtesy of www.pitchforktrader.com)

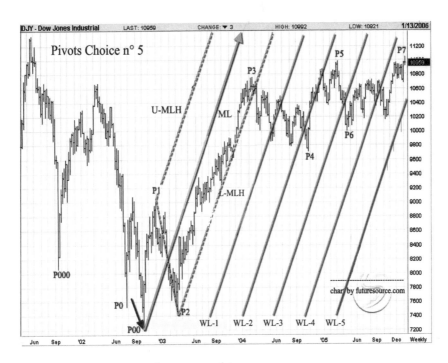

Source: www.futuresource.com

Figure 2.38 Lowest low pivot choice (no. 5) of the anchor location
(Courtesy of www.pitchforktrader.com)

- Kinematics of the anchor's location and its consequences: traditional pitchfork, Schiff pitchfork, T-pitchfork, the hybrid or 'suspended' pitchfork, and the 'retrograde' pitchfork.
- Kinematics of P1–P2 swing.
- Penultimate pivots of an ending correction.
- The quality of a pivot should be always observed:
  - a bigger swing with a big reversal bar (called a 'shooting star') gives the best pivot;
  - the cleanness of the bars within a swing;
  - the pivot range, which indicates market volatility at that moment.
- Two very important points to remember:
  - the global context and the local market effervescence, as treated in the case studies;
  - the variability of the pitchfork's alignment just before the start of a new trend.

3
The Magnet-Like Power of Median Lines

The median line (ML) is the line that joins the anchor (P0) with the middle of the P1−P2 swing. The forerunner of this line first appears in the work of Roger W. Babson (1875−1967) in the first decades of the twentieth century. Babson successfully used his charts to forecast the October 1929 stock market crash, well ahead of the event. Its precise name was the Normal Line; on a Babson chart its presence delimited the market flow in two territories:

- above the line, where prosperity reigned,
- below the line, where depression surged.

The late Dr Alan Hall Andrews, being passionate about Technical Analysis, attended Babson's Action and Reaction Newtonian Principle seminar. In the early 1960s, Andrews organized the essence of this concept into a 60-page course, naming it the 'Action-Reaction Course' as a tribute to Roger Babson. His work − described as the Median Line Method − showed drawn median lines on the charts and, as they resembled a pitchfork, these became known in most of the charting programs as the Andrews pitchforks.

The essence of a pitchfork resides in its median (ML) and accompanying lines: U-MLH, L-MLH, WL, TL, etc. The lines parallel to the ML, through the P1 and P2 pivots, form the upper median line (U-MLH) and the lower median line (L-MLH). (The letter H in this annotation is inherited from our 20th century teachers, indicating the parallelism of the two vertical lines of the letter H and those of MLHs.)

The median line is a virtual link between the trader and the market enhancing the understanding of the pitchfork's role. Without the ML the pitchfork would be just another channel. It could even be said that the pitchfork is the 'most noble of the channels'.

The median line is the main component of a pitchfork's framework, not only linking the anchor to the midpoint of the P1−P2 swing but also constituting a foundation guideline for drawing its subordinates: the upper and lower median lines, warning lines, Fibonacci lines and sliding parallel lines (more about these can be found in Chapters 5, 7 and 14). The constructed median line will also project into the price−time virtual space, the immediate past and the current market flow, as it is formed by the specific choices of anchor (P0) and the corresponding P1−P2 swing.

The seven main functions of the median line are synthesized below.

3.1 MAGNET-LIKE EFFECT AND SYMMETRY AXIS POWER

Dr Alan Andrews suggests that the median line's main role is to attract the market price. He taught his students that the price has a very high probability to return to the median line. Thus, the median line becomes the *minimum price objective*. It is one of the best components of the pitchfork and the most powerful in optimally describing the market flow. In order to confirm the optimal description of the market flow, we look for:

- multiple tests; as experienced traders would say: 'The final indicator is a tried and tested trend line'.
- symbiosis between the market price and the median lines responsible for:
  - restored energy through the energy-building rectangles; and
  - energy consumption in the process of building huge bars and swings.

The median line can be an excellent symmetry axis for the price which:

a)   mirrors the most dominant trend (usually a major pitchfork); or
b)   runs parallel to the minor trend's axis (a minor pitchfork).

The median line may play a support role (in down-trending), or a resistance role (in up-trending). An old support can rapidly become a new resistance and vice versa.

3.2 TRIPLE ACTION POTENTIAL

When the price approaches the median line, it creates one of three movements:

 (i)   a reversal (a top pivot is made);
 (ii)   a violent piercing, resembling a zoom through (see Section 3.3), well exceeding the ML; or
 (iii)   a narrow range, which will prepare for the next price outburst.

3.3 ZOOMING AND PIERCING

A zoom through the median line is the signature of a highly-charged movement and can be used to consider a potential low-risk high-probability trade (see Chapter 19). As soon as a level is broken, either the market will move on to the next level or the ML needs to be retested.

Piercing a median line is a complex phenomenon; its relative importance is situated between zooming and testing (retesting). No trade should be set up if only this element is present.

3.4 TESTING AND RETESTING

Testing the median line is a very important element of setting up a low-risk high-probability trade. First, let us clearly define this process. A trader tests a resistance or a support if he expects that the price will shortly come to a standstill or even start to reverse from the current trend. Testing gives the key of where the market will be heading in the immediate future.

Testing implies a pinpoint touch of the price on the support/resistance (S/R) level. No piercing or slight zooming is allowed — the price must rest exactly on the testing line. The degree of importance of the halt is greatly enhanced by studying the type of close the touching bar achieves:

- Is it in its lower quarter (a possible reversal for the current up-trend)?
- Is it in its first upper quarter (a possible reversal for the current down-trend)?

The space between the tested median line and the close of the touching bar should be measured in order to quantify the potential strength of the price trend to reverse or not. Once again, the larger the space, the stronger the trend's inclination to reverse.

Retesting is the rich parent of testing. Easy to understand, it happens when multiple tests occur. The number of tests determines the strength of the S/R trend line. The more numerous the tests, the stronger the S/R trend line becomes. Thus, if you have a support trend line that has been tested four times, and a resistance trend line that has been tested only two times, the market will selectively choose to break the resistance (only two touches), since it is not as strong as the support (four touches).

Generally speaking, the market will always take the path of least resistance. But beware, never trust an untested median line, except when at least one of the following strong levels is present (see Section 3.6). While on this topic, one thing is worth mentioning. Most traders consider that all the support/resistance (S/R) trend lines are created equal from the point of view of the halting strength. This is not true. There are S/R lines that count at least twice when evaluating the degree of their halting power. Among them are the following:

- the old high/low levels;
- the levels pertaining to gaps: the recent gap's high/low level and even the 50% gap's Fibonacci ratio level;
- the all-time high/low of a security (example: high/low of a futures contract or stock);
- the Fibonacci ratios 0.38, 0.50 and 0.618;
- round numbers, or those in exact tenths, fiftieths, hundreds or thousands;
- a vigorous trend line, especially the ML of a higher time frame;
- a multi-pivot trend line, also called an *unorthodox line* (see Chapter 8);
- a chart formation pattern: its symmetry axis, neckline or an apex line of a triangle.

When one of these strong lines is tested several times by the market price, there is a high probability it will increase the strength of its halting power.

With the S/R concept now seen in a different light, we emphasize that zooming, testing and retesting of these S/R trend lines is vital when setting up our low-risk high-probability trades.

3.5 FAILURES

The behaviour of the price as it approaches the median line tells much about the strength of the momentum and its final destination. If the market price can't reach the median line and turns back, it forms a *failure*, a sort of cut-off momentum move. In this case, we say that the price failed to reach the median line (refer to Fig. 6.1, which shows a double up-sloping failure).

The failure signals a reversal. Once the price reverses, it will take the direction of the opposing lower/higher median line. *The counter move will be more powerful than the initial approaching ML movement.* Please remember this — it will give you a real competitive edge.

The distance (space) between the ML and the newly-created failure pivot can and should be measured in order to quantify the degree of momentum weakness. Most traders are unaware of this feature.

3.6 MEDIAN LINE-RELATED MARKET STRENGTH OR WEAKNESS: DOUBLE SIX PARAMETER RULES

The median line can be used to evaluate the degree of the strength or the weakness (double six parameters) of the ongoing market. These features are extremely important for trading decisions, and can really change the outcome of the trading results.

3.6.1 Six Parameter Rules: Characteristics of ML-Related Up-Sloping Momentum

1.   No potential resistance ahead (the path of least resistance).
2.   A certain type of penetration of the ML or U-MLH with huge bars; prices close in their upper bars' level (above 50%), as high as possible from these lines. We can conclude: the higher the close, the stronger the upward momentum of the trend.
3.   The gap over the ML is a sign of strength. Its magnet-like power will draw the price backwards, and try to fill the gap. The absence or scarcity of strong resistance levels situated ahead of the market, facilitates the upward conquering of this path of least resistance.
4.   No testing of any MLs or L-MLHs belonging to any other pitchfork structure.
5.   We have the effect (strong upward momentum) but not the cause even if the source of this strong momentum is obvious: a stationary trading range forming an energy cluster lying on the L-MLH or farther up on the ML.
6.   The ML of the market context and the ML of the upper time frame are both upwardly-oriented, in sync with the direction of the trade.

3.6.2 Six Parameter Rules: Characteristics of ML-Related Down-Sloping Momentum

1.   No potential support below (the path of least resistance).
2.   A certain type of penetration of the ML or L-MLH with huge bars; prices close in their lower bars' level (under 50%), as low as possible from the mentioned lines. The lower the close location, the stronger the down-sloping momentum will be.
3.   A gap underneath the ML is a sign of weakness. There is a strong probability that its magnet-like power will draw the price backwards to try to fill the gap. The absence or scarcity of strong support levels situated beneath this down-sloping market facilitates the price sinking through the path of least resistance.
4.   No testing in view of any MLs or U-MLHs belonging to any other pitchfork structure.
5.   We have the effect (high-velocity downward momentum) but not yet the responsible chart formation. The probable cause is the resident trading range energy cluster lying on the U-MLH or farther down on the ML.
6.   The ML of the market context and the ML of the upper time frame are both oriented downwards, in sync with the direction of the trade.

3.7   OTHER FUNCTIONS OF THE MEDIAN LINE

Further characteristics of the median line are given below.

3.7.1   The A/R Line is the Parent of the Median Line

The ML can be perfectly assimilated with the Center Line (CL) of the Action/Reaction Line, as they are specialized instances of this set up. This explains the 'hybrid' pitchfork, which is nothing more than the result of an A/R Line set up (more details in Chapter 11).

3.7.2   The Median Line's Different Versions

An ML can also be named after its exact location in regard to another pitchfork or a gap: the mini-median line (see Chapter 4), gap median line (see Chapter 12) and the inside median line (see Chapter 4).

   The major ML encloses other minor median lines in the same way that the 60-min time frame ML dominates the market flow of the 15-min chart ML.

   The mini-median lines are usually constructed to pinpoint the direction of a small correction of 1 to 5 bars, called a pullback (in up-trends) or a small rally or peak (in down-trends). They are good indicators of an eventual reversal (this topic is treated in detail in Chapter 4).

3.7.3   Median Line of a Single Bar Pitchfork

A very little-known ML is a single bar pitchfork. The four components of a bar (open, close, high and low) are selected to get the three optimal pivots necessary to construct this minuscule pitchfork. However, the natural question is: what use can a trader get from such a tiny pitchfork? The answer is not obvious — the only possible use at this small fractal scale level of the trend is in money management or in setting up or verifying the stop loss strategy.

3.7.4   Borderline Concept of a Median Line

The borderline concept is perfectly illustrated by an ML as it is being pierced:

- if the market drops and there is a tiny pierce just under the ML but it closes back above the ML, a possible reversal is imminent.
- if the market is rising and there is a tiny pierce just above the ML but it closes back beneath the ML, a possible reversal is imminent.

3.7.5   Wide Median Line Context

Wide median lines should be treated like a wide channel. First divide it by 50% and see how well this describes the market. Where an optimal result is not obtained, apply a different Fibonacci ratio until the right proportion of the width's division is obtained.

3.7.6   The Newest Median Line – a Step Ahead of the Market

Prices always head towards the newest ML. The trader should be always ready to draw a new ML when a probable correction is suggested.

3.7.7   Multiple Median Lines

Multiple MLs having the same slope mean a strong trend, which probably will not last long and will probably terminate with a trading range.

3.8   USING THE MEDIAN LINE: CASE STUDIES

3.8.1   German Dax Futures Index Charts

Figure 3.1 illustrates the attraction that the ML has for the market price. After the ML has been tested three times (observe where the price touches the ML, just before the up-sloping failure), the price drops and closes right on the L-MLH.

Figure 3.1   German Dax chart illustrating the attraction of the market price toward the median line (Courtesy of www.pitchforktrader.com)

Figure 3.2 German Dax chart illustrating the attraction of the market price toward the median line (cont.) (Courtesy of www.pitchforktrader.com)

In spite of this upward trend, the following morning's opening cannot exceed the high of the day before, and it closes as it opened, making a typical 'uncertainty' bar (open and close at the same level). This bar signals the market's indecision for an up or a down bias, and illustrates its inability to reach the ML; as a result, an up-sloping failure is formed.

Figure 3.2 shows the continuation of the morning's down-sloping movements. The P03 pivot failure does a great job, rapidly turning the market downwards with a textbook reversal bar. The down-sloping move illustrates the magnet-like attraction of the ML for the down-sloping

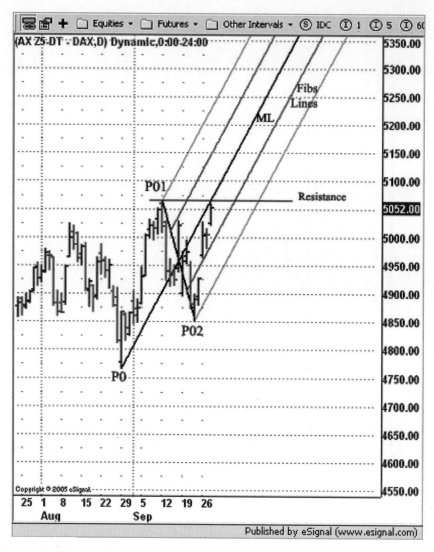

Figure 3.3 Morning period of a real-time daily chart (Courtesy of www.pitchforktrader.com)

pitchfork. The market takes the path of least resistance through the channel formed by the median line and the upper median line of the down-sloping pitchfork.

The magnet-like attraction of the ML is obvious on the daily chart shown in Fig. 3.3. The price tests the ML twice, reaching the level of the horizontal resistance at the P01 level. The two preceding gaps and the two small pullbacks (minor pivots), tell much about the high upward potential of the ongoing market; for the trader, a conservative approach would be to adopt 'a wait and see' attitude. The market is more likely to continue the up-sloping trend than to reverse, especially as the close of the last bar close is near its high. A glance at the volume indicator would tell more about how to project the next move. (Note: The snapshot of the chart in Fig. 3.3 was taken before the end-of-day.)

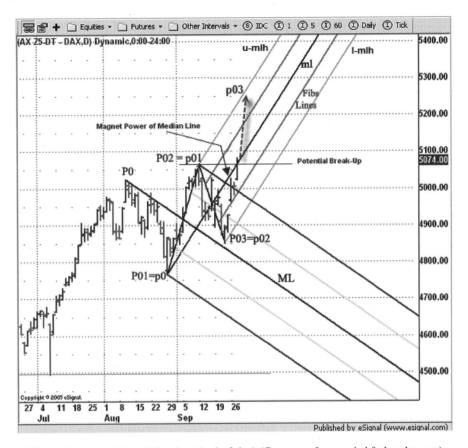

Figure 3.4 A real-time daily chart (end-of-day) (Courtesy of www.pitchforktrader.com)

The daily chart illustrated in Fig. 3.4 completes the previous chart (Fig. 3.3), being printed at the end-of-day. It can easily be seen that the price has broken the horizontal resistance of the P02 (p01) pivot level, and closes just above it. As mentioned above, the market has had high momentum, capable of breaking the strong resistance at the confluence of the p0-p01-p02 pitchfork ML and the P02 (p01) horizontal resistance.

Note: It would have been a great help if the following lines of the P0-P1-P2 down-sloping pitchfork had been drawn: the external upper Fibonacci lines and the warning line (WL-1). The minimum objective of the p02−p03 swing would be the measured distance of the p0−p01 swing.

The creation of the P5 pivot movement illustrated in Fig. 3.5 takes advantage of the morning's news announcement. The large market gap of 56 points lands the price right under the down-sloping ML − again demonstrating the magnet-like power of the median line. The gap is substantial, being even greater than the daily average trading range, which is currently around 50 Dax points. The path of least resistance is blocked here at the 5020 key level (a former big gap). Thus, the move of the down-sloping pitchfork's P5 pivot cannot totally profit from the inertia created by the huge momentum of the morning's news. A 10-point trading range is rapidly formed (20% of the trading range). This energy-building range is ideal for restoring

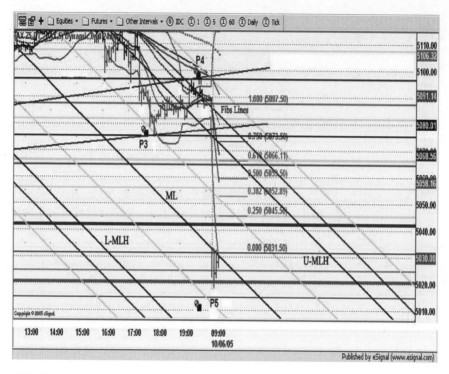

Figure 3.5 Down-sloping pitchfork illustrating the magnet-like power of the ML
(Courtesy of www.pitchforktrader.com)

the partially-exhausted energy of the market price. The location of the final P5 pivot and the presence of this trading range lead us to believe that the market will quickly reverse. Moreover, the nearness of the gap has the ability to vacuum-up the price, thus accelerating the *filling of the gap* phenomenon, through the 'rubber band' effect.

Figure 3.6 continues the story. In spite of the downward, heavily-guarded horizontal fence (5020 key level), the market drops almost twice the height of the preceding trading range. Another energy-building rectangle of the same height has formed.

Figure 3.7 shows how, finally, the market reverses and an up-sloping trend begins. The latter rectangle greatly restores the kinetic energy of the market flow. Very sharply, the market regains the lost ground by the height of almost three rectangles from the low of the huge gap.

The deciding level is at the low of the morning gap (5020 key level). Once the market closes above it, the path of least resistance appears more appealing to the trader, even if another smaller and older gap (5031.50 level) could temporarily endanger the wellbeing of the up-trending market development.

Our market closes above the down-sloping ML, ready for its final destination, the upper median line (U-MLH). We should be prepared to draw a new ML as soon as the present swing is terminated.

As we anticipated, the 5031.50 level (a small, older gap) causes a temporary obstacle in the development of the up-trend (Fig. 3.8). In order to be able to climb — and also to fill — the 56-point gap, the market needs to restore much more energy than it has already acquired. The more the price restores energy, the higher and the quicker the upward momentum will be.

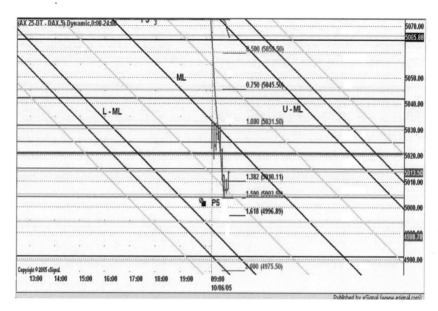

Figure 3.6   Energy-building rectangle just under the ML (Courtesy of www.pitchforktrader.com)

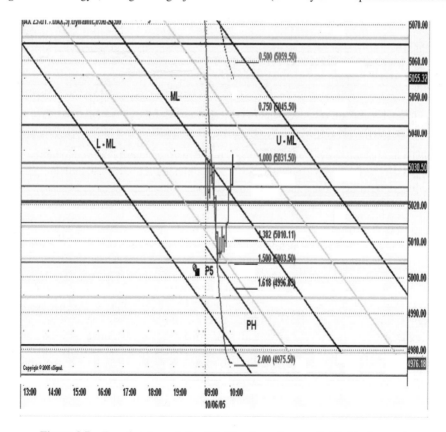

Figure 3.7   Zooming through the ML (Courtesy of www.pitchforktrader.com)

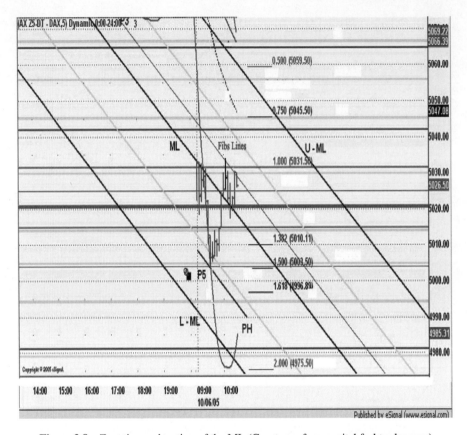

Figure 3.8   Zooming and testing of the ML (Courtesy of www.pitchforktrader.com)

It would be interesting to evaluate the quantity of the restored energy needed to fill the 56-point gap. How can this be done? By studying energy rectangles built in the past, and comparing their corresponding gap fillings. We should take into consideration:

- their height;
- their time length;
- how many gap points were filled, together with how many bars it took to build these energy rectangles in a specific time frame.

Of course, all this should be evaluated without any interference from external market factors such as news, the fundamentals (crude oil, gold and interest rates), currency markets, etc.

The median line shown in Fig. 3.9 forms a real symmetry axis. The up-trending market flow moves in a sinusoidal cycle around the ML, from below to above, several times. The channel formed by internal upper/lower Fibonacci lines guides the market's tremendous potential momentum upwards.

Figure 3.10 shows the same chart as in Fig. 3.1 which had an ML anchored at the chart's low (4850 level), illustrating the magnet-like attraction of its ML. By changing the location of the anchor (P0) to the high of the gap, Fig. 3.10 illustrates a different feature of the ML: the *symmetry axis*.

Figure 3.9 Forming a symmetry axis (Courtesy of www.pitchforktrader.com)

Figure 3.10 Illustrating the symmetry axis (Courtesy of www.pitchforktrader.com)

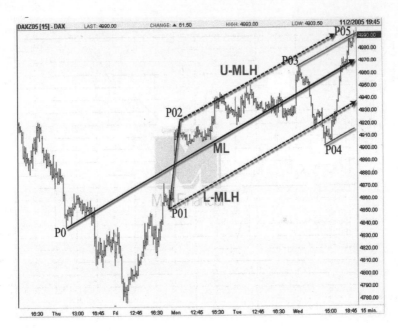

Figure 3.11   Market flow guided in the ML and U-MLH channel (Courtesy of www.pitchforktrader.com)

The beginning of the pitchfork illustrated in Fig. 3.11 shows first a market flow, perfectly guided in a channel formed by the ML and the U-MLH. The size of the channel is then doubled, and the flow glides along another railroad-like structure, bordered by the two parallels to the ML, through the P3 and P4 pivots.

Figure 3.12 shows that the testing of the ML in the pitchfork on this 5-min chart is almost continuous. The magnet-like power of the ML is stronger than ever.

3.9   KEY LEARNING POINTS

- The main component of a pitchfork, which optimally describes the market flow, is the median line (ML).
- Main characteristics:
  - magnet-like power;
  - minimum price objective;
  - excellent symmetry axis;
  - triple action potential: reversal, violent piercing and range;
  - zooming and piercing;
  - test and retest;
  - failures;
  - ML-related market strength/weakness (double six parameter rules);
  - other functions of ML (seven parameter rules).
- Construction: joins the anchor (P0) to the midpoint of the P1−P2 swing.

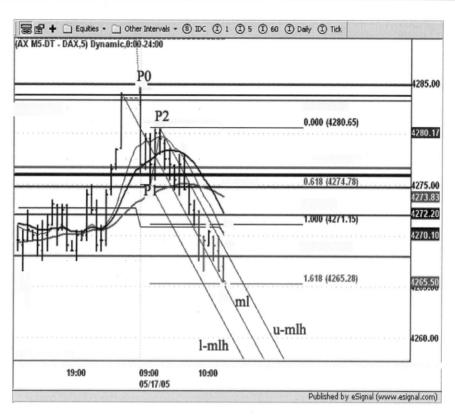

Figure 3.12   Testing the ML on a 5-min chart (Courtesy of www.pitchforktrader.com)

- The trader should routinely compare the position of the market flow with regard to the median line while selecting the optimal pitchfork. We prefer it when the market flow evolves above the median line rather than beneath it.
- The magnetic power of the ML is much greater than that of its parallels.

Ensure that you have understood and assimilated the two most important aspects of the ML:

- The principle of its magnetic power and the minimum price objective.
- The concept: '*The final indicator is a tried and tested trend line*'.

4
The Mini-Median Line

The mini-median line (mml) is one of the trend lines most frequently used to identify trend changes. Its ability to discern an earlier reversal, through the *pullback formation process*, does not need to be proved. Its anchor (P0) can act as the cornerstone of the incoming trend, guiding the market flow towards the termination of the detected trend. The sideways market sinusoidal movements are perfectly depicted when using this type of median line.

It is a kind of minor pitchfork, determined by the structure of the main major pitchfork and in itself highly dependable.

4.1 DEFINITION, CHARACTERISTICS AND FUNCTION

As mentioned above, this type of median line (ML) is of the highest value when looking at changing trends. When evaluating the previous trend development, which could be ready to reverse, it is important to choose the optimal pivots. The following points all need to be considered:

- the number of pullbacks;
- the length of the already-developed trend (bar count and momentum bars);[1]
- the number of any eventual gaps within the current trend;
- the type of pattern at the beginning of the trend's movement; knowing this greatly enhances our knowledge of its strength and our understanding of its behaviour.

The construction elements of the mml are identical to those of a traditional pitchfork. The smaller this pitchfork is, the more carefully we should proceed in our selection of the optimal pivots. One option is to switch to a lower time frame in order to obtain a better perspective of the operational time frame of the local price zone surrounding the pullback. A good idea is to use the alternate closes, instead of highs and lows, to choose the optimal pivots. Once again, let's apply the rule of the 'Holy Grail of the pitchfork' so valuable to the trader:

> *The choice of pivots underpins the efficiency of pitchfork trading, which in turn is expressed by how well the market is described.*

---

[1] Only the higher bars are counted in an up-trend and vice versa

This type of pitchfork is usually quite small, which allows a certain degree of freedom in its construction, taking into account the inside/outside major pitchfork locations:

- inside the main body (delimited by the U-MLH and L-MLH);
- right on the border of the pitchfork's main body. Some of these mmls use twin pivots, meaning that p0=P1 or p0=P2;
- outside the main body, in the *warning line territory* (see Chapter 5), where the slope of this type of pitchfork tells a great deal about its ability to describe the market:
  - the steeper the slope, the stronger the trend will be. However, it is very probable that the trend will not last;
  - in the case of a trading range, the zigzagging of the mmls of the multiple trend and counter-trend oriented pitchforks will give away the market's accumulation process.

4.2 BORDER MINI-MEDIAN LINE

Oblique Orientation: Price Projection Parallel to Market Direction

As can easily be seen on the hourly chart shown in Fig. 4.1, the choice of the three optimal pivots (p0, p1 and p2) for the mini-median line (minor pitchfork) was made as follows:

- on the close of the last bar of the day (09/27/05) for p0 pivot. This mml can also be called a *gap median line* (see Chapter 12);
- on the highest peak of the ongoing trend (p1);
- on the last low of the ongoing market (p2).

As we can see, when the price tested it, the magic of the magnet-like attraction of the mml worked right away, in the first single bar. We expect the length of the swing generated from the p2 pivot (p2–p3), to reach at least the measured swing p00 to p1.

Why did we choose this pivot? By looking at the preceding portion of this ongoing trend (the swing from levels 4855 to 5025), we first observe its steep slope. The next upswing (from p00 to p1) has a milder slope. Thus, we have chosen the optimal pivots that will produce an even milder slope, in preparation for the trend's end, once the market terminates the move equivalent to the p00 to p1 swing. The p3 pivot is now under construction (Fig. 4.1). Had we chosen p00 as an alternative to p0, the slope would have been much steeper. The same argument is valid for the new version of the p1 pivot, located at the high right behind the actual p1 pivot.

The mini trading range of only two bars preceding the p2 pivot gives the market the energy required to reach its immediate objective: the intersection of the external upper Fibonacci line and the upper mini-median line.

Let us say a word about the major pivot (P0-P1-P2). The current price is preparing to spill out of its traditional boundaries, situated between L-MLH and U-MLH. A very powerful sign of the trend's strength is the presence of the two gaps, revealing a *trend continuation* (more details in Chapter 13).

Figure 4.2 shows that, as we anticipated, the market simply jumps toward higher levels. We observe that the choice of pivots was optimal because the market is well described:

- Once the mml is twice zoomed, with two closes above, the price drops to l-mlh which starts to have the following functions:
  - as an attractor for numerous tests;
  - as a short height symmetry axis.

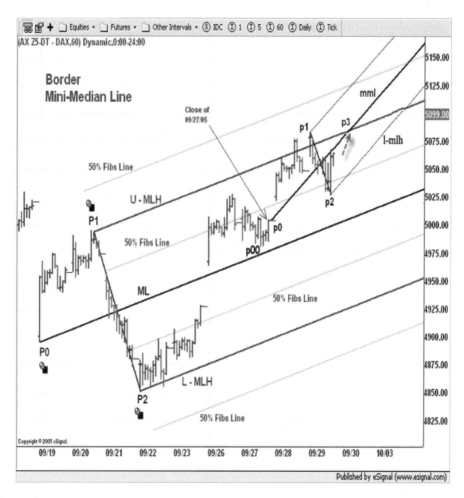

Figure 4.1   Choice of three optimal pivots on an hourly chart (Courtesy of www.pitchforktrader.com)

- The prices find a swift, almost frictionless, up-channel between the mml and l-mlh.
- The ML of the major pitchfork is able to temporarily halt the market rally (Fig. 4.2), after several persistent tests.

After up-zooming and testing (precisely on the U-MLH line), the market up-zoomed right through the external upper Fibonacci line of the major pitchfork (Fig. 4.3 on p. 79). The market is finally halted very close to the ML and a reversal ensues. Again, the pivot choice is optimally describing the market.

Figure 4.4 (on p. 80) shows, as we anticipated, that the ml has not only halted the price but also reversed the market. With the help of a middle-size down gap, the price lands right on the internal upper 50% Fibonacci line of the major pitchfork.

In Fig. 4.5 (on p. 80), we have purposely illustrated only the body of the minor pitchfork without the accompanying median lines. The market has dropped all the way down targeting the P2 (4850 level). The two descending gaps are indicative of the strong downward momentum.

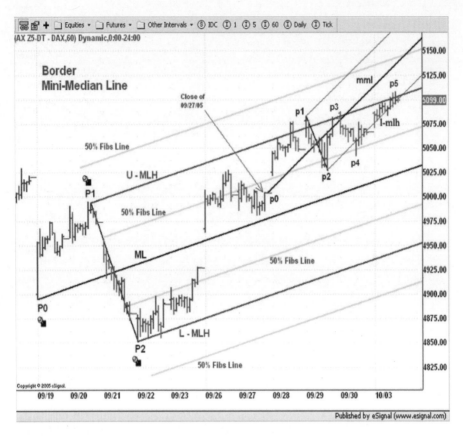

Figure 4.2   Choice of three optimal pivots on an hourly chart (cont.)
(Courtesy of www.pitchforktrader.com)

The influence of the major pitchfork on the market price is very obvious. The attraction of the Fibonacci lines is clear:

- first on the external upper Fibonacci line, serving also as a reversal zone;
- then on the internal upper 50% Fibonacci line;
- and finally on the internal lower 50% Fibonacci line.

Optimal trading results would have been obtained if we had drawn a down-sloping minor pitchfork with an anchor at the high of the market (actual p5 pivot). In this way the down-sloping market flow would have been optimally described.

4.3   INSIDE MINI-MEDIAN LINE: HORIZONTAL ORIENTATION

Price Projection Parallel to the Market Direction

In this section, we continue the study of the preceding market flow (Figs. 4.1−4.5) from the mini-median line point of view, but this time, horizontally oriented.

Figure 4.3   Choice of three optimal pivots on an hourly chart (cont.)
(Courtesy of www.pitchforktrader.com)

After the market reaches a high, it has one of the following three options:

- further trending;
- trading in a range, more or less tight;
- reversing.

Figure 4.6 (on p. 81) shows that the market could either continue its trend or move horizontally within a sideways rectangle. Whatever it decides to do, we expect our minor pitchfork to optimally describe the flow of the market.

What we know for sure is that, should the market continue trending, the price will be 'ladder climbing' on the minor pitchfork's accompanying trend lines. In other words, we expect multiple levels of warning lines (wl) and external upper Fibonacci lines. The terminal move announcing the reversal would be halted cold by a trend line parallel to the minor pitchfork or major pitchfork main lines. And this reversal will take place outside the pitchforks' main bodies.

On the other hand, if the market moves sideways, this kind of horizontal minor pitchfork will have an optimal symbiosis with the major pitchfork and the reversal will be detected earlier, right at its inception.

Figure 4.4 Choice of three optimal pivots on an hourly chart (cont.)
(Courtesy of www.pitchforktrader.com)

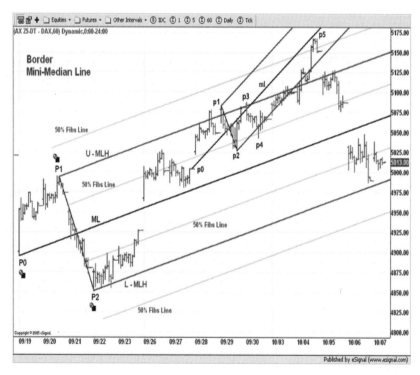

Figure 4.5 Choice of three optimal pivots on an hourly chart (cont.)
(Courtesy of www.pitchforktrader.com)

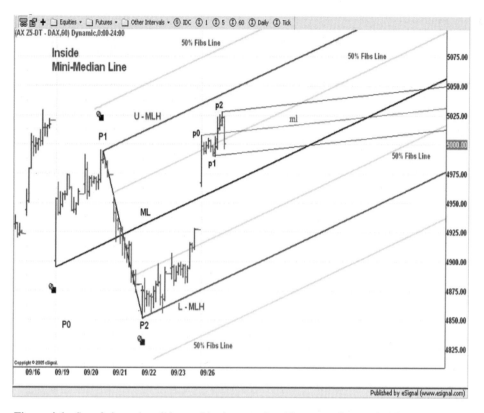

Figure 4.6   Set of pivots describing a ubiquitous market (Courtesy of www.pitchforktrader.com)

On the chart shown in Fig. 4.6, we have chosen as planned a set of pivots (p0, p1 and p2) capable of describing an immediate ubiquitous market: trending, non-trending or reversal market flow.

The next stage, as depicted in Fig. 4.7, shows the market first dropping slightly below the p1 level and then climbing vigorously with the help of a gap. The intersection of the external upper Fibonacci line of the minor pivot with U-MLH abruptly halts the up-sloping huge three bar movements. Again, as Fig. 4.8 shows, the external upper Fibonacci lines of the minor pivot have firmly halted the market, after multiple tests.

Figure 4.9 (on p. 83) shows the market dropping slightly, forming a nice big mirror bar set-up at the intersection of the upper mml and the internal upper 50% Fibonacci line of the major pivot. The last close is above the intersection of the internal upper 50% Fibs line of the major pitchfork and the upper mml of the minor pitchfork, thus confirming the very probable continuation of the up-sloping trend.

As Fig. 4.10 (on p. 83) shows, the market has continued to move upward; the last close (above the intersection) of the mirror set-up was correct. After an opening retest of the above intersection, the market implacably continues its up-sloping trend. Once again, the external upper Fibonacci line (level 3) of the minor pitchfork first double tests and then halts the market. In spite of all this resistance, the market can still go either way.

Figure 4.7 Set of pivots describing a ubiquitous market (cont.) (Courtesy of www.pitchforktrader.com)

Figure 4.8 Set of pivots describing a ubiquitous market (cont.) (Courtesy of www.pitchforktrader.com)

Figure 4.9 Set of pivots describing a ubiquitous market (cont.) (Courtesy of www.pitchforktrader.com)

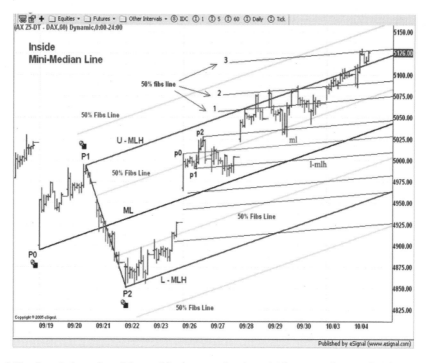

Figure 4.10 Set of pivots describing a ubiquitous market (cont.) (Courtesy of www.pitchforktrader.com)

Figure 4.11   Set of pivots describing a ubiquitous market (cont.) (Courtesy of www.pitchforktrader.com)

After testing the minor pitchfork's Fibonacci line three times (level 3) the market chooses to zoom up until it reaches the next external upper Fibonacci line (level 4) of the minor pitchfork. Figure 4.11 shows it testing the Fib line three times (right on the line), and finally deciding to reverse.

As Fig. 4.12 shows, the reversal was effective, and the strong down-momentum brought the price right under the U-MLH, testing it several times. The down-gap's strong momentum certainly helped.

After another round of testing the U-MLH, the market finally decides to fall all the way down to the L-MLH. Figure 4.13 (on p. 86) shows:

- the role of the double gaps in providing momentum (in both the up- and down-trend); and
- the symbiosis of the multiple Fibonacci levels of the minor pitchfork and the upper/lower median lines.

The choice of the 'ladder climbing' pitchfork was finally rewarding; it optimally described the market flow, not only during the up-trend but also during the down-trend.

4.4   INSIDE MEDIAN LINE: OBLIQUE ORIENTATION

Price Projection Parallel to the Market Direction

This new type of mini-median line belonging to the minor pitchfork is oriented upward towards the market direction (Fig. 4.14 on p. 87). The price approaches the L-MLH of the major pitchfork

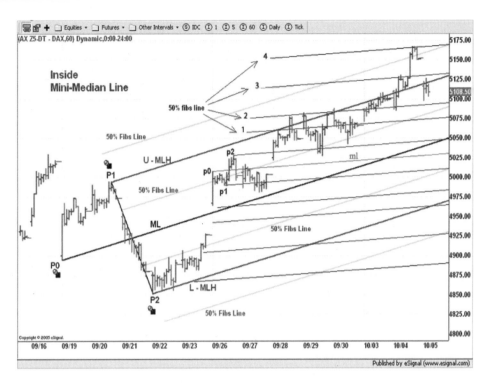

Figure 4.12   Set of pivots describing a ubiquitous market (cont.) (Courtesy of www.pitchforktrader.com)

but cannot test or pierce it. The market is preparing to make a reversal. The immediate objective will be the ML, with a possible rally to the U-MLH of the major pitchfork. This kind of minor pitchfork will attempt to optimally describe the local market flow, towards the designated upward direction.

4.5   REVERSE MINI-MEDIAN LINE

Price Projection Against the Market Direction

Figure 4.15 shows the reverse mml, constructed using an anchor (P0 at level 5001.50) at the midpoint of the biggest swing, which follows the previous trend's level 5025 reversal. The reverse mml will join this mid P0 pivot with the lowest low (P3) of the ongoing downtrend.

The reverse mml pitchfork shown in Fig. 4.16 optimally embeds the flow of the down-sloping market, through the channel created by its mml and u-mlh. The trend still has a strong downward momentum.

The reverse ML shown in Fig. 4.17 (on p. 89) has the anchor P0 at the intersection of the 50% Fibonacci level of the P1−P2 swing. First the P0 is selected, then the P3. The reverse ML naturally joins these two pivots. So far, the price optimally describes the market flow: a genuine channel formed by the ML and U-MLH. The P3 and P4 pivots are located right on these trending lines.

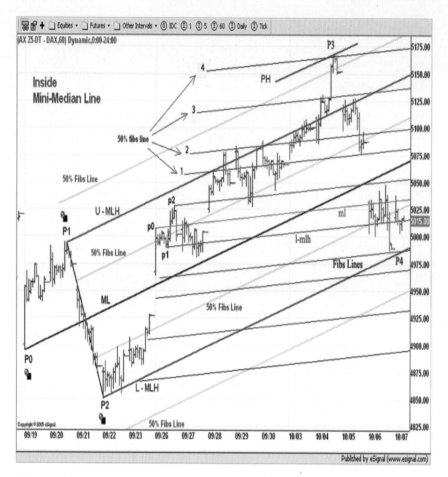

Figure 4.13 Set of pivots describing a ubiquitous market (cont.) (Courtesy of www.pitchforktrader.com)

As shown in Fig. 4.18 (on p. 89), the P4 pivot was a real turning point, reversing downwards the market flow through the newly-created U-MLH and ML channel. The minimum expected objective would be the P5 pivot level, probably located on the downward ML.

4.6 MINI-MEDIAN LINE WITH STEEP DOWNSLOPING ML

Price Projection Against the Market Direction

The trader might wonder: why use such a steep mini-median line? Well, when the market has tested the U-MLH of the major pitchfork so many times, we should start thinking about an eventual down move (Fig. 4.19 on p. 90). The first down-gap (above the p0 level) and the following retests of the U-MLH from below enhance the significance of the strong downward momentum.

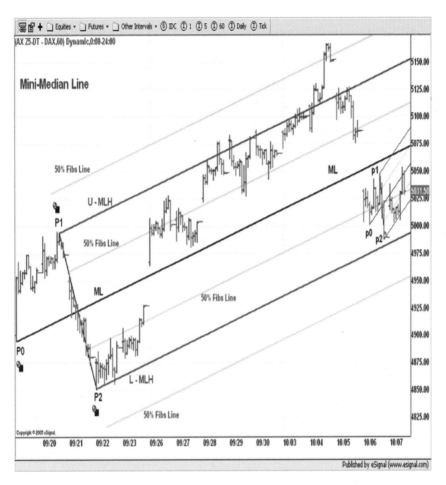

Figure 4.14 Set of pivots describing a ubiquitous market (cont.) (Courtesy of www.pitchforktrader.com)

Figure 4.20 (on p. 90) confirms that the pivots were well chosen, because the flow of the market drops steeply along the channel formed by the minor pivot's median and upper median lines. Even if the market seems to be in a sideways mode, the flow still obeys the minor pitchfork's lines; after the up gap, the price down-slopes steeply along the u-mlh (Fig. 4.21 on p. 91).

In spite of the sideways development, the minor pitchfork optimally describes the market flow: a halt caused by the outer Fib lines; a gliding channel formed by a warning line (wl); and the same external upper Fibonacci line (Fig. 4.22 on p. 91).

4.7   MINI-MEDIAN LINE WITH A TWIN PIVOT ML

Price Projection Parallel to the Market Direction

The twin pivots' median line is frequently used at market turning points (Fig. 4.23 on p. 92). They are called 'twins' because they both have the same price–time Cartesian coordinates, with

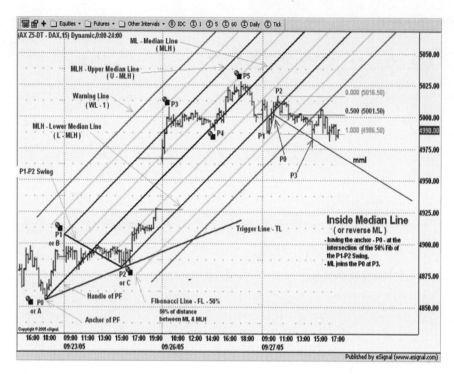

Figure 4.15 Isolated reverse mml (Courtesy of www.pitchforktrader.com)

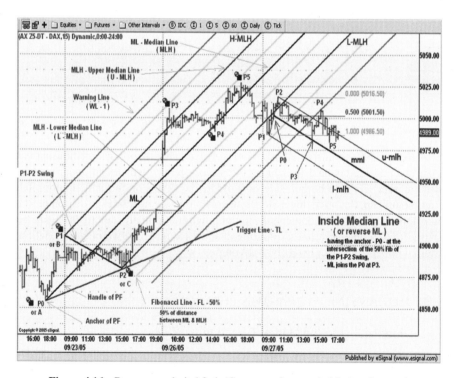

Figure 4.16 Reverse mml pitchfork (Courtesy of www.pitchforktrader.com)

Figure 4.17 Reverse ML (Courtesy of www.pitchforktrader.com)

Figure 4.18 Reverse ML (cont.) (Courtesy of www.pitchforktrader.com)

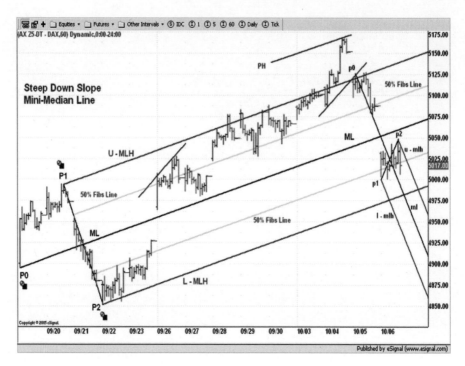

Figure 4.19 Predicting an eventual down move (Courtesy of www.pitchforktrader.com)

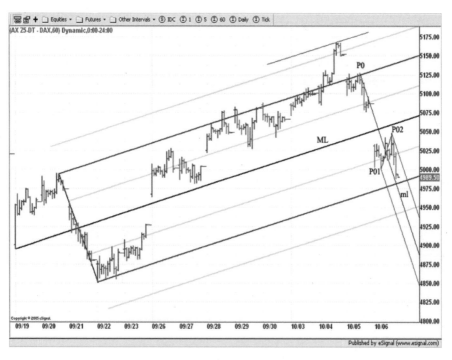

Figure 4.20 Market flow along the channel formed by the minor pitchfork's median and upper median line (Courtesy of www.pitchforktrader.com)

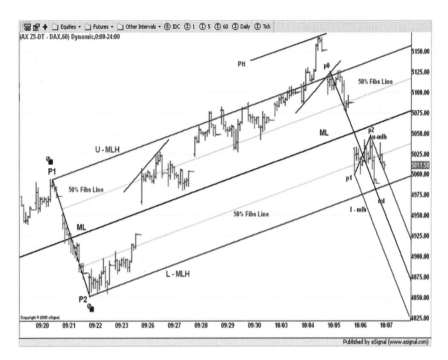

Figure 4.21 Market flow along the channel formed by the minor pitchfork's median and upper median line (cont.) (Courtesy of www.pitchforktrader.com)

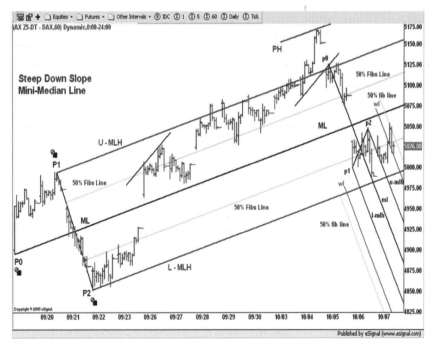

Figure 4.22 Market flow along the channel formed by the minor pitchfork's median and upper median line (cont.) (Courtesy of www.pitchforktrader.com)

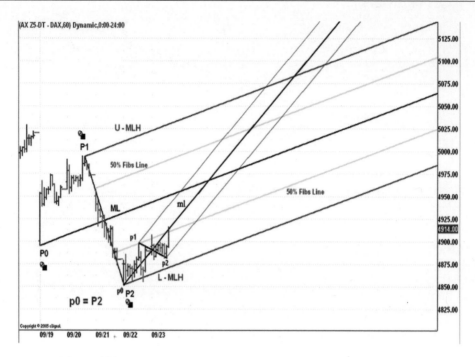

Figure 4.23   Market turning points (Courtesy of www.pitchforktrader.com)

the difference that one belongs to the major pitchfork (P2 pivot) and the second to the minor pitchfork (p0). Once again, the market flow glides through the ML channels, and the mml should optimally describe the local price market. The projected slope of the mini-median line looks as though it will reach a 45° angle or maybe there will be an even steeper trend-line orientation.

As the projected mini-median line anticipated, the price shoots up with an almost vertical slope (Fig. 4.24). The up-gap surely helps it to zoom through the ML. This strong momentum is expected to continue as a result of the presence of the up-gap. Afterwards, a huge bar is immediately followed by a small narrow pullback. The minimum expected objective is the upper median line (U-MLH) or maybe even higher.

As we expected, the price explodes until it reaches the external upper and outer 250% Fibonacci line of the minor pivot, forming the p3 pivot (Fig. 4.25). The marvellous magnet-like attraction of the mml has done the job once again, and the price sticks as if it is glued on, forming a mini energy-generating cluster. Once the intended up-sloping energy is restored, the market flow shoots up again through the ceiling, straight up to the intersection of the U-MLH and the upper warning line of the minor pitchfork. After a five small-bar time span when energy is being regained, the price shoots up again to the w1 level, forming the p5 pivot.

After a trading range of nearly two days, during which the p6, p7 and p8 pivots are formed, the market flow resumes its up-trend all the way to the p9 pivot, right under the mml of the minor pivot (Fig. 4.26 on p. 94). The formation of p9 signals a probable reversal zone. This is given away by the presence of the triple mirror bars (see Chapter 16), containing an inside bar followed by a reversal bar. The ensuing reversal move will probably reach its minimum expected objective at the intersection of the U-MLH and the line parallel to the lower warning line (w1).

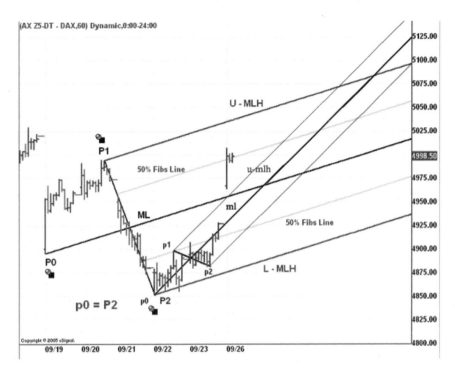

Figure 4.24   Market turning points (cont.) (Courtesy of www.pitchforktrader.com)

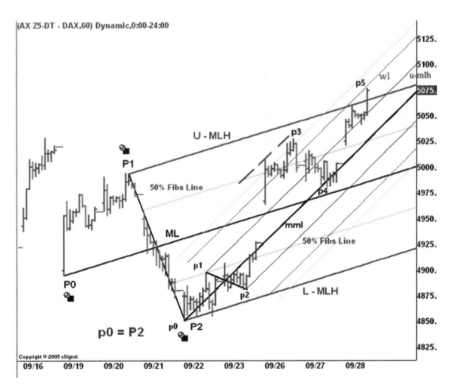

Figure 4.25   Market turning points (cont.) (Courtesy of www.pitchforktrader.com)

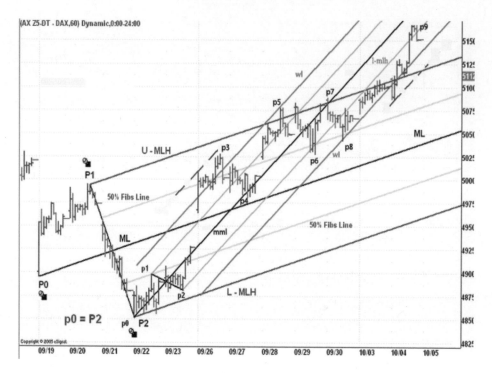

Figure 4.26 Market turning points (cont.) (Courtesy of www.pitchforktrader.com)

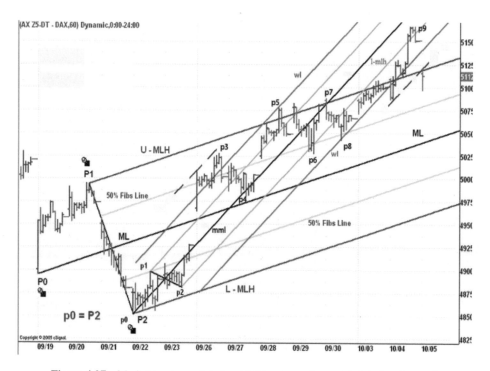

Figure 4.27 Market turning points (cont.) (Courtesy of www.pitchforktrader.com)

Mission accomplished! The price drops like a stone under the previously-mentioned intersection (Fig. 4.27). Now the market flow changes its course and it is time to prepare the drawing of the next minor pitchfork.

Without any doubt, the choice of the pivots p0 through p9 was more than optimal. For most of the time, the market flow remained near the main body of the minor pitchfork.

4.8 KEY LEARNING POINTS

- The mini-median line is an indispensable trading tool to be used whenever a reversal is in view.
- It is one of the few tools that allows the trader to determine the difference between a pullback and a reversal.
- Once the reversal is in view, choose the best type of mini-median line (border, inside, reverse, steep or twin).
- When the mini-median lines are tested, pierced and zoomed, they behave in the same way as any other median lines or non-pitchfork-related trend lines.

Ensure that you have assimilated two very important points:

- the principle of the minimum expected objective;
- when setting up the above principle, try to find an intersection between a trend line of the minor pitchfork and that of the major pitchfork.

5
Warning Lines

Once the flow of the market spills out over the main body of a pitchfork, situated between the L-MLH and U-MLH, the trader is alerted by the testing, piercing or zooming of the so-called *warning lines*.

5.1 DEFINITION, CHARACTERISTICS AND FUNCTION

Warning lines (WL) are defined as those trend lines which are parallel to the upper or lower median lines, at the same distance as that of the separating space between the ML and the MLH. Drawn at multiple distances from each other, but always equal, they are numbered from one to whatever level the flow of the market will attain. No warning line should be drawn as long as the price is within the main body area of the pitchfork, in order to avoid clouding the chart.

When the price starts to move outside the main body of the pitchfork, there should be at least one warning line ahead of the market flow. There may be up to four levels of warning line when the trend has a normal development of 13 to 21 bars. If the trend lengthens, going beyond the 2.618 Fibonacci ratio of the preceding move and corresponding to 34 or even 55 bars, then as many warning lines as the market requires may be used.

Always be ahead of the market by at least one level of warning line!

When the price reaches and moves beyond one warning line, the next warning line becomes the target. Thus a ladder-like price structure is obtained, very similar to that of the 'ladder' rectangles (described in Volume II — in preparation) on which the price may naturally climb. The levels of WL are frequently illustrated in extended trends. Should the market move sideways once it has exited the pitchfork's main body, then the warning lines will automatically construct a horizontal 'ladder' time structure. The passage from one warning line to another will be like measuring the cycle's time, rather than just the price.

Another characteristic of these warning lines is their intersection with the median line (ML) of other pitchforks or their associated lines. Thus it will create *confluences*, the landmarks of trade decisions (see Chapter 15).

The ultimate practical application of warning lines is the price translation across the market slots, an indispensable technique in trying to understand the market flow when searching for the low-risk high-probability trades (see Section 11.7).

Although the number of levels within the 'ladder' is not limited, there are two things to take into account:

1.   More levels imply a weakening of the WL's power, because the price is going beyond the main body of the pitchfork and escaping the influence of the ML.
2.   A persisting number of multiple levels is usually an indication that a probable reversal is in the making. There is then the choice of drawing a new pitchfork, preferably a mini-median line one, to achieve an optimal encasing of the market's flow.

These are not strict rules, because there are optimal trading intersections even at the seventh level of the WLs. The rest of the WLs' characteristics are the same as the other median lines (if necessary, refer back to Chapters 3 and 4).

5.2   WARNING LINES: CASE STUDIES

S&P500 e-mini and German Dax Futures Index Charts

As can be seen in Fig. 5.1, the upper warning line (WL-1) is parallel to the U-MLH, which in turn is parallel to the ML, through the P pivot. In its first half, the opening bar of the up-gap tests our WL-1. Just before the market closes, it serves as a wonderful symmetry axis.

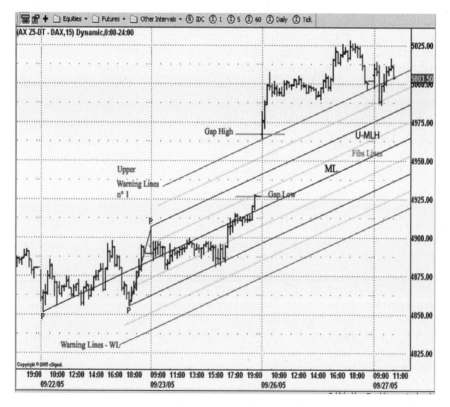

Figure 5.1   Warning line WL-1 (Courtesy of www.pitchforktrader.com)

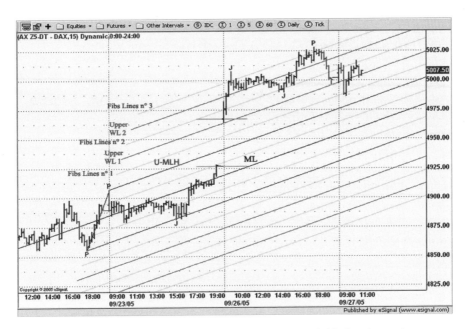

Figure 5.2   Warning line WL-2 (Courtesy of www.pitchforktrader.com)

As shown in Fig. 5.2, by adding the next warning line (WL-2) we can soon observe its efficient role as a symmetry axis between the two major (J) pivots and the primary (P) pivot.

The 5-min S&P 500 e-minis chart in Fig. 5.3 is a good example of the role that the warning line performs in exercising multiple functions at all levels:

- WL-01 (a test, a piercing and two retests)
- WL-02 (an intersection and an uncertainty bar)
- WL-03 (a trading range breakout)
- WL-04 (a zoom and a test)
- WL-05 (a zoom alone)
- WL-06 (a test and a zoom) and finally
- WL-07 (another test and zoom).

Warning line WL-1 shown in Fig. 5.4 is a good example of multiple tests; the presence of WL-2 here is only to participate in an eventual down-sloping move. Even so, we have noticed a higher low (second low) revealing a down-sloping failure. It seems as if the route to the path of least resistance is lying just in front of the market.

Figure 5.5 (on p. 101) contains almost a complete summary of the characteristics of warning lines:

- WL-1 is tested seven times by the market price in its down-sloping movement; we observe that, after a zoom and a test, the market jumps from the upper median line (U-MLH) straight to the warning line (WL-1) to form the double mirror bar.
- The passage from WL-1 to WL-2 is done in a single, three-bar movement; the halt of the market flow is very convincing, with the formation of mirror bars creating the P4 pivot. These double mirror bars are the prelude of a reversal, which occurs straight after.

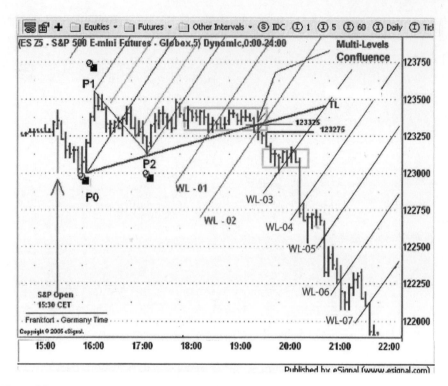

Figure 5.3   Warning lines in a 5-min S&P e-minis chart (Courtesy of www.pitchforktrader.com)

Figure 5.4   Example of multiple tests (Courtesy of www.pitchforktrader.com)

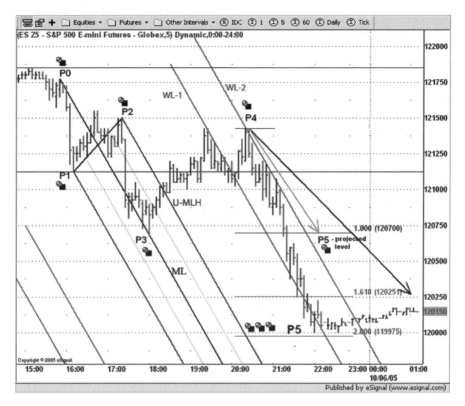

Figure 5.5 Summary of the characteristics of warning lines (Courtesy of www.pitchforktrader.com)

- After the P4 reversal, the WL-2 faithfully serves as a seven-times strong resistance; the market flow drops along the channel formed by WL-1 and WL-2. The multi-testing of WL-1 has switched to a multi-testing of WL-2; a trading range ensues, ready to restore the energy of the exhausted down-sloping market.
- Tiny bars at the trend's end, which witnessed the diminishing volatility of the market, form an energy-building rectangle. This situation is considered a prelude to the next strong move but the direction is not yet known. The presence of P5 emphasizes the possibility of a reversal, especially because the P4–P5 trend is of a medium size (20 bars, 1 bar off the 21 Fibonacci count).

5.3 KEY LEARNING POINTS

- The warning line is an indispensable indicator of the market flow when it goes outside the body of the main pitchfork, delimited by the U-MLH and L-MLH.
- Cultivate an automatic thinking process concerning the WL's usage and functions:
  - Think of employing the WL concept when the price spills over the pitchfork's main body.
  - Create the 'ladder'-like price or time structure.

- – Expect the market's reversal by evaluating the imminent end of the trend through the Fibonacci bars count, the number of pullbacks or the presence of any gaps.
- – Always create a mini-median line when the warning line is responsible for a reversal: piercing, multiple tests or failure (cut-off of the momentum).
- The testing, piercing and zooming of the warning lines behave in the same way as any other median line or non-pitchfork related trend lines.

Ensure that you have assimilated these two very important points:

- avoid clouding the chart but, on the other hand,
- don't be shy about going to seven levels of WL.

We have created an organized working context without falling into an *analysis paralysis syndrome*.

6
Trigger Lines

Although Alan Andrews did not christen this type of line, its use is of considerable importance. Whenever a failure (momentum cut-off) is imminent, the trigger line can be used to confirm the change of the trend.

It is easy enough to construct a trigger line (TL): its line joins the pivotal anchor (P0) with the P01 pivot (upper trigger line, or U-TL), or with the P02 pivot (lower trigger line, or L-TL) for an up-sloping pitchfork (Fig. 6.1).

6.1 SIGNAL LINE FUNCTION

The trigger line is mainly used as a signal line for routine confirmation and for a conservative trade entry; in a word, it's the legitimate mark of the trend's failure.

For an up-sloping failure:

- The market will fail on its way to reaching the ML of an up-sloping pitchfork (see Fig. 6.1). There is a short-trade entry opportunity when the lower TL (L-TL) is broken downward by the dropping market. This shows the double use of the trigger line (L-TL). In the first instance it has a support role, testing the P2 level when the market was up-sloping, and now it switches to a resistance role after the price makes a down-sloping breakout.

For a down-sloping failure:

- The market will fail on its way to reaching the ML of a down-sloping pitchfork (there is no diagram to illustrate this example). There is a long-trade entry opportunity when the upper TL (U-TL) is broken upward by the rising market. This shows the double use of the trigger line (U-TL). In the first instance, when the market was down-sloping it had a resistance role, and now it switches to a support role after the price makes an up-sloping breakout.

Note: Never forget the adage: 'An old resistance can always become a new support'.

The way these trigger lines behave when touched or penetrated is no different than that of the median or their associated lines, especially when it concerns testing, piercing or zooming.

Figure 6.1 Hagopian Rule (Courtesy of www.pitchforktrader.com)

6.2   THE HAGOPIAN RULE AND LINE

The *Hagopian rule* applies when an up-sloping market is approaching a significant trend line (slant, horizontal or curvilinear) but the market momentum is not strong enough to test it (for example, the ML of a up-sloping pitchfork).

The rule states that, after nearing the ML, the price will reverse vigorously in a big counter-move, dropping rapidly towards an opposite strong trend line (L-MLH and the L-TL in Fig. 6.1). Its reverse momentum is usually stronger than the initial momentum. In its strong counter-move, the price will meet the same trend line that it was drifting along before reversing. In our example, this is the lower trigger line (L-TL), which joins the anchor (P0) and the P2 of the up-sloping pitchfork (Fig. 6.1). It represents the *Hagopian line*, which has the merit of completing the set-up of the price failure rule.

Dr Alan H. Andrews clearly stated:

> *When prices reverse trend before reaching a line* (ML in our example) *at which probability indicates such a reversal could start, proper action may be taken in buying or selling, if prices cross the trend line* (L-TL in our example) *they were moving along before reversing.*

The Hagopian rule is clearly illustrated in Fig. 6.1, showing a 5-min German Dax Futures chart. After the two up-sloping failures in the 5073−5070 price zone (lower highs), the price drops suddenly in a huge counter-trend. It zooms through the Hagopian line (L-TL) and then twice retests the line before taking the path of least resistance, falling strongly downward. The numerous long down-sloping bars confirm it.

6.3 THE TRIGGER LINE AS A BORDER LINE

One thing must be emphasized here. This trigger line serves as a borderline for the whole market when it belongs to a contextual (major) pitchfork. Otherwise, the upper side of the market is found above the trigger line, and the lower side below it. Its function resembles that of the daily floor pivots, which are treated in Volume III (in preparation). The transition of the market flow from one side to another must inevitably pass through the strong support/resistance wall of the trigger line. The same thing happens if we draw a trigger line belonging to a higher time frame on the lower operational time frame.

If the trigger line belongs to a mini-median line (Fig. 6.2), the problem is different. Do not forget, here we are either on the higher/lower border or inside a major pitchfork. Whatever moves the market makes, within the limits of the mini-median line of the minor pitchfork the market flow will only describe the local market. Once the trigger lines of the mini-median line are left behind by the volatile market's huge bar moves (Fig. 6.2), only then will the major pitchfork's trigger lines have an impact on the trend's development.

6.4 VARIABILITY OF THE TRIGGER LINES QUANTIFIES THE TRADE RISK

At first sight, it seems far-fetched to talk about quantifying the risk of a trade in terms of the variability of trigger lines. However, a detailed analysis of several factors reveals the tenets behind this concept. It represents years of our research work in this field.

The 15-min chart in Fig. 6.3 (on p. 107) shows the median line and its associated lines describing the flow of the up-sloping market. The handle and the trigger line are clearly visible. Let us start by studying the parameters which make up this traditional pitchfork.

- The length of the handle affects its slope, for a given fixed P0 anchor (Fig. 6.4 on p. 107). In turn, it modifies the angle of the upper and lower trigger lines. (By 'handle' we mean the distance between the anchor (P0) and the midpoint of the P1−P2 swing.)
- The height and slope of the P1−P2 swing play an important role in creating the slope of the trigger lines. In this case the height and slope of the P1−P2 swing are tightly interdependent: a steep slope causes a taller height, and a smaller height is created by a slope of lesser degree (Fig. 6.5 on p. 108).

The variability of some of the parameters of the pitchfork (Fig. 6.5) will have a great impact on the trigger line:

- the handle and the P1−P2 swing characteristics as discussed above;
- the price location, especially when it is nearer to the upper/lower median lines;

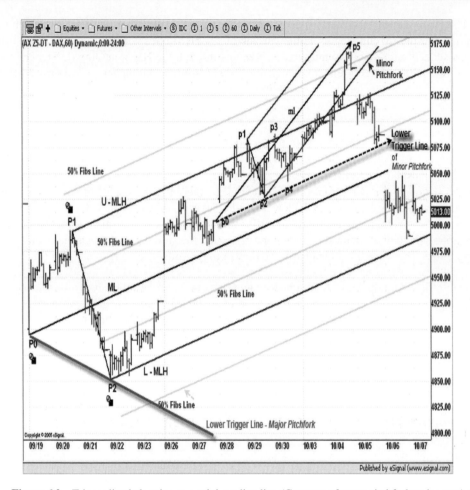

Figure 6.2   Trigger line belonging to a mini-median line (Courtesy of www.pitchforktrader.com)

- the proximity of the market flow to a failure zone, which could cause a strong counter-trend and convert the trigger line into a Hagopian line, following the Hagopian rule;
- and, finally, the slope of the trigger line, as a result of the above parameters.

Let us try to determine how (and if) the variability of these two parameters (the handle and the P1−P2 swing) could influence the risk of the trade. As an illustration, we take the framework of the up-sloping pitchfork as shown in Fig. 6.3. For simplicity's sake, the two parameters were not varied at the same time but carried out one after the other.

6.4.1   Variability of the Length of the Pitchfork's Handle

Note: The pitchfork illustrated in Fig. 6.3 is our structural framework.

On Fig. 6.4 we first look at the impact of the pitchfork's handle on the trigger line (TL); we have also drawn three versions of the latter. For comparative purposes, for each version we have

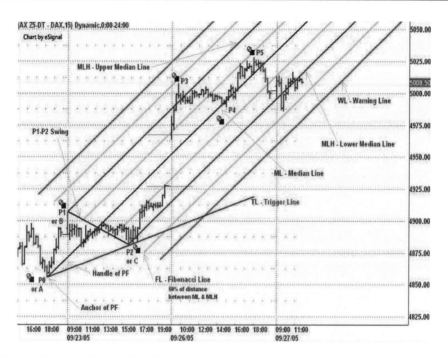

Figure 6.3   Complete pitchfork including a trigger line (Courtesy of www.pitchforktrader.com)

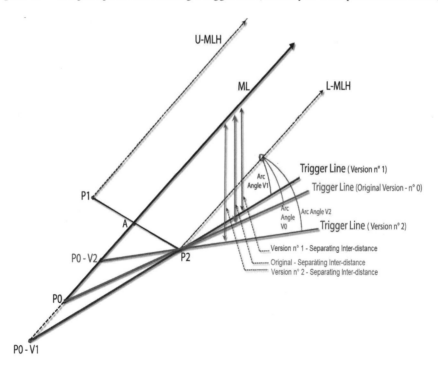

Figure 6.4   Variable pitchfork handle study: impact on the trigger lines

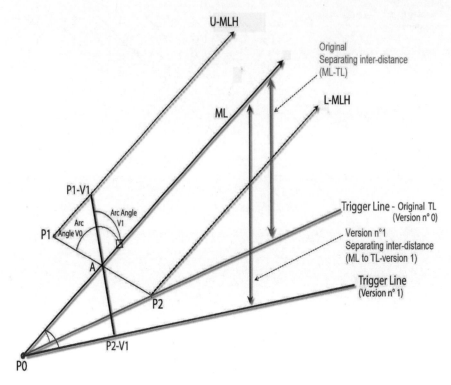

Figure 6.5   Role of the height/slope of the P1−P2 swing in creating the slope of the trigger line

measured the length of the handle and the angle formed by the lower median line and the trigger line:

- The original TL (no. 0), is identical with that in Fig. 6.3 and is described by:
    - a handle joining the P0 pivot to the midpoint A of the P1−P2 swing (its length is taken as our standard measure);
    - a trigger line joining the P0 and P2 pivots, forming the arc angle V0 (21°);
    - the angle of the P1−P2 swing line with the ML remaining still.
- TL version no. 1 shows:
    - a handle joining the P0−V1 pivot to the midpoint A of the P1−P2 swing. Its length increases, now representing 150% of the standard length;
    - the formation of a new trigger line joining the P0−V1 and P2 pivots, creating an arc with angle V1 (15°);
    - the angle of the P1−P2 swing line and the ML remaining unchanged.
- TL version no. 2 illustrates:
    - a handle joining the P0−V2 pivot to the midpoint A of the P1−P2 swing; its length decreases, representing now only 50% of the standard length;
    - the creation of a new trigger line joining the P0−V2 and P2 pivots, forming the arc angle V2 (32°);
    - the angle of the P1−P2 swing line and the ML remaining motionless.

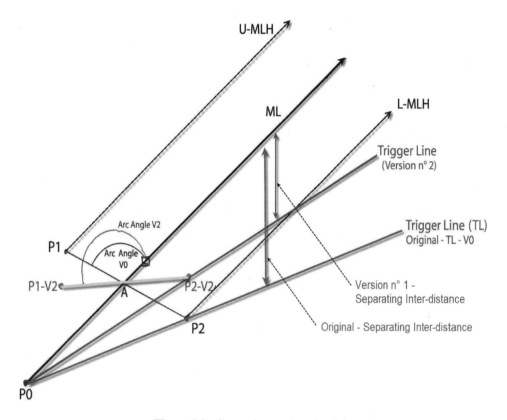

Figure 6.6 Comparing versions 1 and 2

The conclusion is that the length of the handle greatly influences the separating inter-distance between the L-MLH and the three versions of the trigger line. It is important to remind the reader that this study was done without considering any P1–P2 swing line rotations. The study's outcome can be summarized in three sentences:

- The shorter the handle, the deeper the trigger line will plunge, and the farther the separating inter-distance will be from the nearest L-MLH and, implicitly, from the ML to the trigger line.
- The bigger the size of the separating inter-distance, the more aggressive the entry will be; we assume that the trade's entry will be around the TL zone.
- The more aggressive the trade entry, the greater the risk and the smaller the reward/risk ratio will be.

The concluding triad is: the shorter handle – the greater risk – the smaller reward/risk ratio.

6.4.2 Variability of the Height and Angle of a Pitchfork's P1–P2 Swing

In order to avoid clouding the drawings and to enable a better grasp of the nuances of the swing angle rotation, we will first study only two drawings (Figs 6.5 and 6.6), each having an

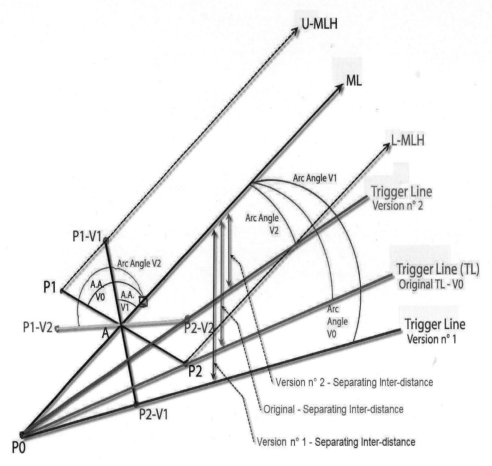

Figure 6.7 Risk and money management study using swing height and rotation, reward/risk ratio and separating inter-distance (from trigger line to MLs level)

angle rotation that will be compared to the original version. Afterwards, the observations will be summarized in Fig. 6.7. For our present purpose, in Figs 6.5 and 6.6 only the angle formed by the P1−P2 swing trend line and the median line (ML) has been measured, and not the angle between the median line and each trigger line.

We notice on Fig. 6.5 that:

- The original TL version (no. 0) is identical with that of Fig. 6.3, and is described by:
  - a P1−P2 swing line joining the P1 and P2 pivots, forming the arc angle V0 (116°);
  - a trigger line joining the P0 and P2 pivots;
  - the handle's length is not modified; the anchor remains still.
- TL version no. 1 illustrates:
  - a P1−V1 and P2−V1 swing line which joins these two pivots; it forms the arc angle V1 (62°). The clockwise rotation of the swing line decreases the angle between the original P1−P2 swing line's orientation and the median line;

- the creation of a new trigger line joining the P0 and P2—V1 pivots as a result of the swing line's clockwise rotation; this trigger line is below the original (version no. 0) with a bigger separating inter-distance from the lower median line;
- the handle's length is not modified; the anchor remains motionless.

Figure 6.6 compares the original version (TL 0) and a new version, TL 2. TL 2 reveals the following:

- a P1—V2 and P2—V2 swing line, which joins these two pivots, forms the arc angle V2 (141°) in the counter-clockwise rotation process of the swing line. Thus, the angle of the median line and the original P1—P2 swing line will be increased;
- the creation of a new trigger line joining the P0 and P2—V2 pivots as a result of the swing line's counter-clockwise rotation. This trigger line is below the level of the original TL 0 with a shorter separating inter-distance from the lower median line or ML respectively;
- the handle's length is not modified; the anchor remains the same.

As in the above study of the variable handle length, we conclude that the height/angle of the pitchfork's P1—P2 swing (Fig. 6.7) greatly influences the separating inter-distance from the median line (ML) to each of the three trigger line versions.

The argument seems to be clear: they have a dual character and affect angle and height variables. (We remind the reader that the latter part of the study was done with a fixed location of the anchor for all three trigger lines versions.)

To summarize the outcome of this study, from a trade's reward/risk point of view (see Fig. 6.7):

1. The triad: the bigger swing rotation – the taller swing – the smaller reward/risk ratio:
   - the bigger the clockwise swing, the taller the swing height, the deeper the trigger line will plunge and the further the separating inter-distance will be from the ML or L-MLH;
   - the bigger the size of the separating inter-distance, the more aggressive the entry, the greater the reward and risk (lengthier and riskier to reach targeting distance (entry to target)), will be;
   - the more aggressive the trade entry, the smaller the reward/risk ratio (average to big reward versus big risk), will become.
2. The triad: the smaller swing rotation – the smaller swing – the bigger reward/risk ratio:
   - the bigger the counter-clockwise rotation of the swing, the smaller the swing height, the higher the trigger line will rise and the shorter the separating inter-distance will progress towards the L-MLH or ML, respectively;
   - the smaller the size of the separating inter-distance, the less aggressive the entry, the lesser (to average) the reward (shorter and less riskier to reach targeting distance (entry to target)), will be;
   - the less aggressive (thus more conservative) the trade entry, the lesser the risk, and also the greater the reward/risk ratio (average reward versus smaller risk), will become.
3. The above risk and money management study is reworked in Fig. 6.8. The targeting distance replaces the separating inter-distance concept. All the other parameters remain the same! As homework, we invite the reader to study Fig. 6.7 in detail and draw the optimal conclusions.

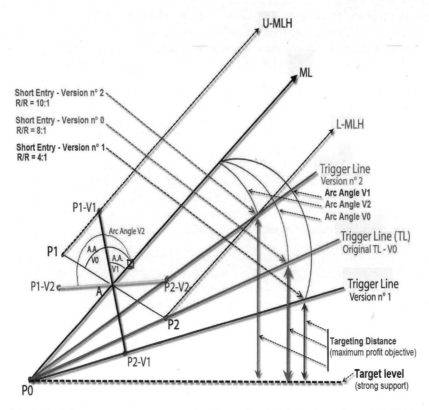

Figure 6.8 Risk and money management study using swing height and rotation, reward/risk ratio and targeting distance (entry to target level)

6.5   TRIGGER LINES: CASE STUDIES

S&P 500 e-mini and DJIA Cash Index Charts

As we see in Fig. 6.9, the classic trigger line joins the P0 and the P02 pivots of this up-sloping pitchfork. The trigger line starts to exercise its influence by attracting the market flow which is beginning to drift away. We also note with interest that the P0 pivot is located exactly on the low of the last bar where the up-trend started, situated at the extreme right of the energy-building rectangle.

As we expected, the market flow glides just above the TL, terminating its move with a small zoom (Fig. 6.10 on p. 114). The close of the last bar is beneath the TL. This increases the odds of a high-probability low-risk trade. The next action is a test or a retest of the TL. If this happens, we will enter the trade!

As we anticipated, we now have our test (Fig. 6.11 on p. 115). But – there is a slight problem! The testing bar is a doubly uncertain situation:

- first, the open is equal to the close, right in the bar's midpoint (uncertainty bar); and
- second, the bar is trapped between the trigger line (strong resistance) and the warning line no. 2 (a strong support). The next move will tell us which is stronger.

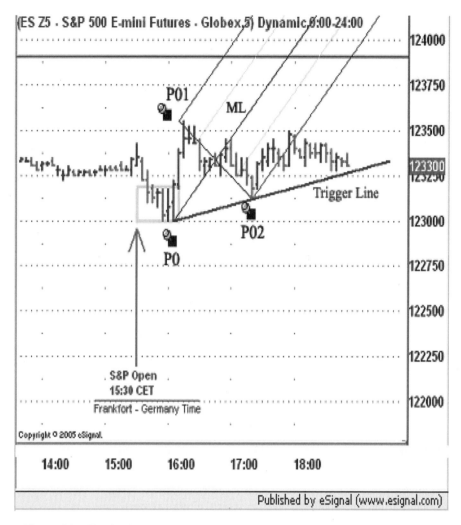

Figure 6.9   Classic trigger line on a 5-min chart (Courtesy of www.pitchforktrader.com)

The market seems hesitant and confused. The question is: What should we do in such a case? To answer this, let us be as logical as possible. There are two approaches:

1.   Take an aggressive attitude, leading to an immediate short entry at 1232.50 with a tiny stop loss of only three ticks at 1233.25 (only $150 per ES contract). With such a small risk the trade will easily have a risk/reward ratio well over 2.5. A more traditional (non-pitchfork) trader will adopt this approach.

2.   Take a conservative attitude and, with patience and self-control, wait for a confirming factor, such as a retest of the WL-2 after the price breaches it; only then execute a convenient short entry trade. The disadvantage of this choice is an increased risk and a diminished reward/risk ratio. This trade approach belongs to the arsenal of the pitchfork trader.

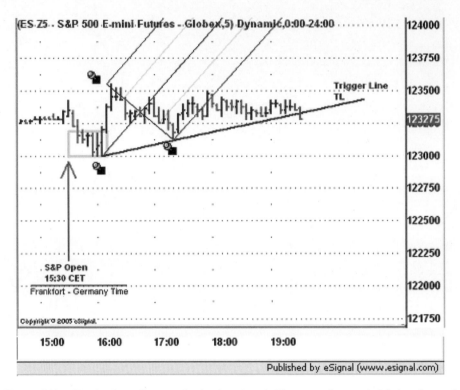

Figure 6.10   Classic trigger line on a 5-min chart (cont.) (Courtesy of www.pitchforktrader.com)

After considering the two trading decisions described above, it looks like the first choice is best suited in this case, because:

- there is a very profitable reward/risk ratio (superior to 2.5);
- the market already has a lower high; it seems as if the price has just come down from the prior 18 small bars trading range, in a sort of mini-range breakout;
- the Hagopian rule, which has converted the trigger line into a Hagopian line (a valiant resistance), has also faithfully confirmed the concept of completing the up-sloping failure. The immediate future projected market flow will be a consequence of this failure with a strong ensuing downwards counter-trend.

The Hagopian rule and the separating inter-distance concept were right (Fig. 6.12). After the test of the warning line (WL-2), the market flow was unlatched, propelled by a strong down-sloping momentum. This rather steep trigger line (Fig. 6.13) assumes most of the common features of the median lines:

- an attraction of the price (4985 and 5150 areas);
- a symmetry axis role (5025 and 5085 zones);
- an upper border channel of the up-trending market flow (5025 to 5165 gliding zone);
- an up-sloping failure (high at 5165).

The trigger line shown in Fig. 6.14 (on p. 117) has been converted into a Hagopian line as a result of the down-sloping market failure at level 4850 (twin P3 and p2 pivots). For the moment, the horizontal trend line, at the P02 and p1 twin level, temporarily obstructs the upward path of least

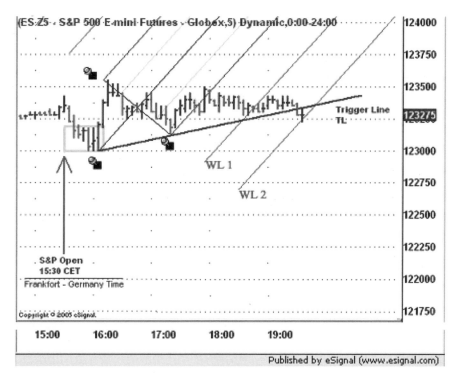

Figure 6.11   Classic trigger line on a 5-min chart (cont.) (Courtesy of www.pitchforktrader.com)

resistance. Once liberated from this obstacle, the flow of the market has every chance of breaking through the upper trigger line TL (Hagopian line). In spite of this, we should not neglect the possibility of an up-sloping failure at the P02 horizontal trend line level, or farther up in the zone demarcated by the intersection of the trigger line with the median line of the up-sloping pitchfork.

We show Fig. 6.15 (on p. 117) simply to illustrate the beauty of the test and retests of the trigger line.

Figure 6.16 (on p. 118) shows the multiple aspects of the trigger line characteristics:

- An up-sloping failure at 5070 level zone; the price tries to approach the lower median line (L-MLH) but does not have enough momentum.
- A test and multiple retests of the Hagopian line (TL) near the external lower 150% Fibonacci line.
- A big price drop is ensuing, all the way down to level 5043, ending with a huge reversal bar. Its energy helps the price to rally and retest the trigger line at the 5077 level. Then it returns to its initial downtrend direction, forming a big three-bar reversal structure. At the 5043 level we have drawn a main parallel to the trigger line, with its 50% Fibonacci line parallel to the TL, in order to better visualize the new up-sloping channel.

Figure 6.17 (on p. 118) continues from Fig. 6.16 with overlapping multiple Fibonacci and warning lines to try and identify the major multiple intersections. In spite of our good intentions, we can only reveal the symmetry axis role of the 50% Fibonacci line of the channel TL and main parallel TL and its multiple tests and retests.

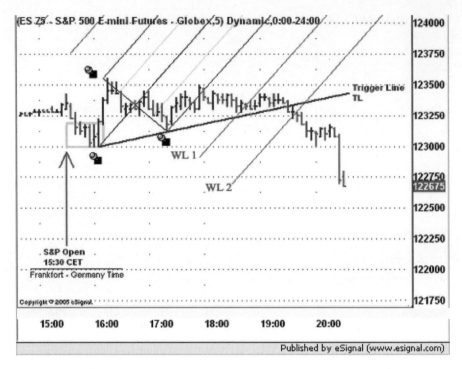

Figure 6.12   Classic trigger line on a 5-min chart (cont.) (Courtesy of www.pitchforktrader.com)

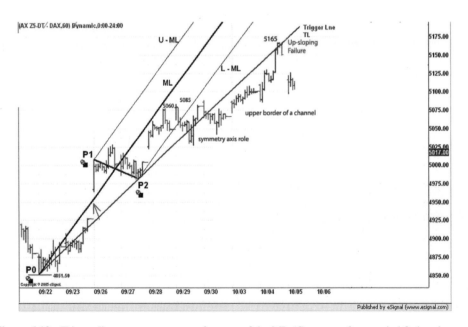

Figure 6.13   Trigger line assumes common features of the ML (Courtesy of www.pitchforktrader.com)

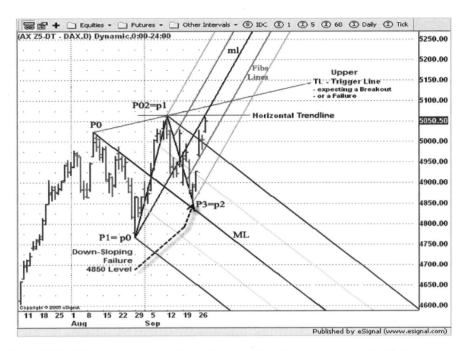

Figure 6.14   Trigger line converted into a Hagopian line (Courtesy of www.pitchforktrader.com)

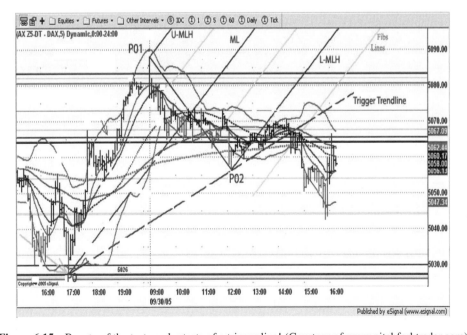

Figure 6.15   Beauty of the tests and retests of a trigger line! (Courtesy of www.pitchforktrader.com)

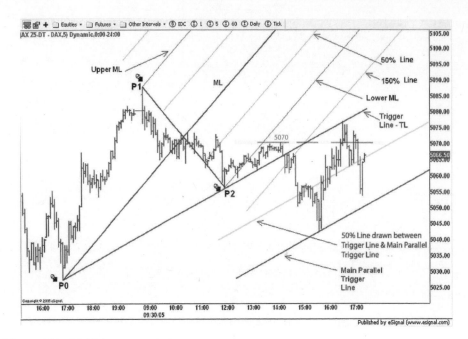

Figure 6.16   Multiple aspects of trigger line characteristics (Courtesy of www.pitchforktrader.com)

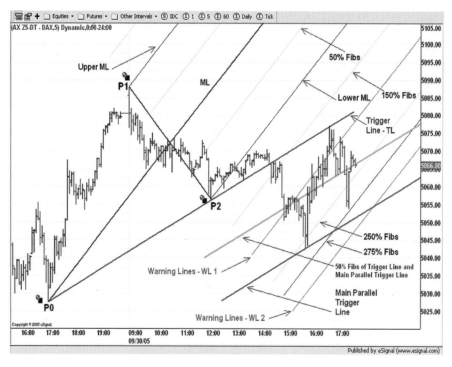

Figure 6.17   Multiple aspects of trigger line characteristics with multiple Fibonacci and warning lines (Courtesy of www.pitchforktrader.com)

6.6 KEY LEARNING POINTS

- The trigger line is an indispensable tool used for confirmation and entry decisions.
- A trend failure will convert a trigger line into a Hagopian line.
- Be aware of the intricacy of the trigger lines belonging to a major and a minor pitchfork on the operational time frame, and also those on other multiple time-frame pitchforks.
- The handle's size and the P1−P2 swing's angle rotation greatly influence the risk of the trade.
- When testing, piercing and zooming, the trigger lines behave in the same way as any other median or non-pitchfork related trend lines.

Ensure that you have assimilated and intensively practised the separating inter-distance and trend failure concepts, which are the guarantee of the low-risk high-probability trades.

7
Sliding Parallel Lines

Let us return for a moment to the subject of market failure. We saw in Chapter 6 how easily the Hagopian line can confirm and also complete the failure set up. However, this line is not the only one capable of confirming the failure.

Another tool able to confirm market failure is the *sliding parallel line* (PH), but this has a different degree of reliability. The main difference between these two confirming factors is in the timing of the failure phenomena. The sliding parallel line is created right at the extreme of the reversal bar (the inception site of the failure process), and the Hagopian line is created only when the counter-trend is well developed, when the trigger line is converted into a Hagopian line. (Some authors prefer the abbreviation SH instead of PH; we will use both of them.)

The uniqueness of these sliding parallel lines resides in the fact that their construction is not based on pivots, like all the other median lines, and we do not use pivots to draw them. It is not a fixed pivot-related line, but rather an unanchored trend line.

7.1 DEFINITION

As the name suggests, the sliding parallel line (PH/SH) is a line which passes through a high, a low or (even better) through multiple highs/lows. It is drawn parallel to another trend line, which can be an ML or its associated lines, a *multi-pivot trend line* (also called an *unorthodox trend line*, see Chapter 8) or a traditional trend line (see Fig. 7.3).

Market failures furnish significant highs (if an up-sloping failure) or lows (if a down-sloping failure) for the construction of the PH. Thus, the PH will slide along a channelled formation formed by median and associated lines. The best-known roles of the sliding parallel line are the guiding and blocking of the market flow functions. The trader can expect the price to reverse as it approaches the PH.

7.2 PRICE BEHAVIOUR AND SLIDING PARALLEL LINES

Using a sliding parallel line the market price can behave in several ways.

- It slides along the PH; this gives the line its name. If the price returns suddenly to inside the PH, a violent counter-trend can be expected. In this case the risk is minimal, and the reward/risk ratio is optimal, well above 3.

- It tests, pierces and zooms the sliding parallel line; in other words, the PH behaves in the same way as a median line.
- It creates multiple intersections with the MLs, which are themselves excellent turning points.
- And, as we have already mentioned, the trader can profit greatly when the market reverses, due to a blocking pattern. The PH provides valiant (ready-to-serve) resistance (in up-trends) and support (in down-trends), so do consider it very seriously.

7.3   PARALLELISM CRITERIA OF SLIDING PARALLEL LINES

Let us talk a moment about the different criteria of SH parallelism.

- Most of the time, the PH is parallel to the main trend, the ML of the major pitchfork. In this case, there is usually only a temporary reversal, and in an up-trend it certainly signifies a short-lived pullback. The market will finish the dip and retake its initial direction, possibly with a stronger momentum.
- However, the steeper the slope of the trend, the shorter and less temporary the reversal. In other words: short-lived and fewer bar pullbacks are the legitimate marks of strong trends. It is important to note that, in this context, a PH parallel to the major pitchfork ML does not create any intersections.
- When the PH is parallel to a mini-median line (mml) of a minor pitchfork the matter is completely different; the steeper the slope of the mml compared with that of the ML, the more intersections are produced, and thus more potential turning points are created (see Fig. 7.3).
- In the case of a horizontal pitchfork (a rectangle-like structure), the construction of a PH at a failure's high/low will tend to create a reversal rather than a pullback.
- As with the drifting away of the price from the main body of the pitchfork, we describe the possibilities of having inner or outer PHs.
- A PH can be an individual line alongside a trend line or be accompanied by other PHs, on the same side or opposite the symmetry axis which can be represented by MLs, U/L-MLHs, WLs, Fibonacci lines or trigger lines (TLs). The two PHs having a symmetry axis (see Fig. 7.4) constitute a drifting channel inside or outside the pitchfork's main body, which has the potential to guide the price farther away. Where these two SHs are valid only for a portion of the drifting away channel, we call them a *twin SH set-up* or a *mirror* inside or outside the SH.

7.4   MONEY MANAGEMENT

Another function, less well-known but nevertheless vital, is the use of the SHs as reliable and efficient initial or trailing stops. As we know, the implementation of a stop has its main role in allowing the trader to profitably execute his/her trade; it protects the trader from the noise and whipsaws of the market. The best stops are set behind a support (S) for a long trade or above a resistance (R) for a short entry, with two main conditions:

- The reliability of these R/S levels affects the degree of the trade's performance. These sliding parallel lines are some of the most efficient ready-to-serve (halting) levels (see Figs 7.1 and 7.2).

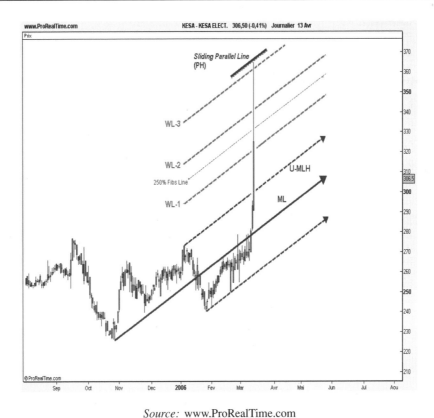

Source: www.ProRealTime.com

Figure 7.1 Watching and anticipating an impending failure (Courtesy of www.pitchforktrader.com)

- Be aware of the proximity of the market. Avoid the risk of an invasion by the tail of a whipsaw bar. The best distance between the market and the stop should be 1 to 2 ATR(21)s, which is the arithmetic average of the bars' true range for a defined period (last 21 bars, in this case) calculated on the operational time frame chart.

The occurrence of the sliding parallel line gives us a myriad of opportunities, especially when we are closely watching and anticipating an impending failure (Fig. 7.1).

The PH construction should be exercised immediately after the bar tail's invasive action on the warning line (WL-3), otherwise we risk remaining behind the markets (Fig. 7.2).

7.5   SLIDING PARALLEL LINES: CASE STUDIES

German Dax Futures Index Charts

Although classically the PH is placed just outside the U-MLH or L-MLH, Fig. 7.3 shows an inner PH, just outside the Fibonacci lines of the major and minor pitchforks. A closer look at the PH reveals that it can be superimposed by the warning line wl-2 of the minor pitchfork (not drawn here). The PH of the minor pitchfork in synergy with the intersection of the two pitchforks' Fibonacci lines is causing the up-sloping failure.

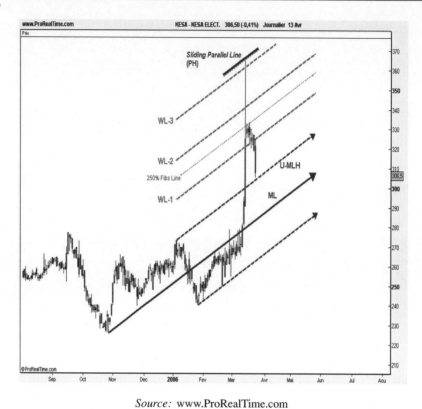

Source: www.ProRealTime.com
Figure 7.2   Occurrence of an up-sloping failure (Courtesy of www.pitchforktrader.com)

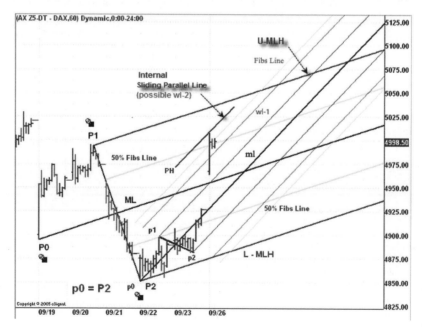

Figure 7.3   Inner PH just outside the Fibonacci lines of the major and minor pitchforks (Courtesy of www.pitchforktrader.com)

Source: www.futuresource.com

Figure 7.4 Inner and outer PHs locations compared with the pitchfork's main body territory (Courtesy of www.pitchforktrader.com)

Figure 7.4 shows the position of the inner and the outer PHs compared with the main body of the pitchfork, delimited by the U-MLH and the nearness of the L-MLH.

The daily chart shown in Fig. 7.5 depicts an inner PH, just up-zoomed by the first penetrating bar with its close right on it. The second bar (last on the chart) tests the PH, and creates a long trade with a very convenient stop loss and the corresponding reward/risk ratio.

The chart in Fig. 7.6 describes a classic location for a PH, just outside the upper median line of the down-sloping pitchfork, at the spike's high. The U-MLH is only pierced. Being outside the main body of the major pitchfork, it is called an *outer PH*.

By drawing the inner and outer PHs simultaneously (Fig. 7.7 on p. 127) we create a mini-channel employing the upper median line of the down-sloping pitchfork as a symmetry axis. The uncertainty bar, which equals the open and the close, right on the upper median line, is probably the first bar of a short duration pullback, caused by the strong up-momentum (steep slope).

Once the down-sloping mini-channel is set up (Fig. 7.8 on p. 127), we add a third PH right underneath, through the gap's high (*inner PH-1*). It adds to the mini-channel's trading potential, in the event there is a prolonged pullback in the immediate future, above the classic three bars. The presence of a gap between the two huge bars warns of an imminent continuation of the up-trend.

As we anticipated, the trend has shot straight up (Fig. 7.9 on p. 128), with a pullback of only one uncertainty bar; even that is a small one. We could very well say: the smaller and fewer the pullbacks, the stronger the trend will be!

As shown in Fig. 7.10 (on p. 129), a fifth PH (*outer PH-3*) has been projected which causes an intersection point with the ML of the up-sloping pitchfork. By observing the strong continuous up-trending price behaviour, another pullback can be expected at this intersection. The market

Figure 7.5 Double pitchforks criss-cross (Courtesy of www.pitchforktrader.com)

Figure 7.6 Classic location of a PH (Courtesy of www.pitchforktrader.com)

Figure 7.7 Creating a mini-channel with inner and outer PHs (Courtesy of www.pitchforktrader.com)

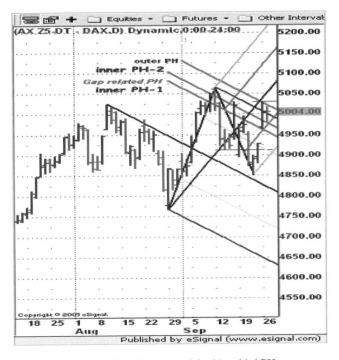

Figure 7.8 Adding to the mini-channel's trading potential with a third PH
(Courtesy of www.pitchforktrader.com)

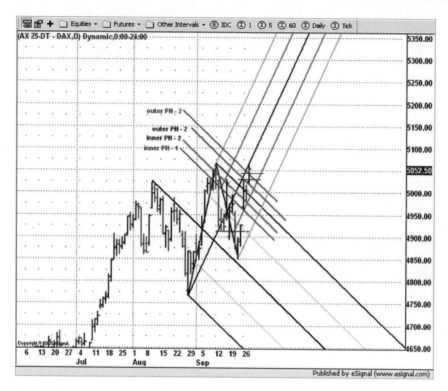

Figure 7.9   Adding to the mini-channel's trading potential with a third PH (cont.)
(Courtesy of www.pitchforktrader.com)

flow is not yet ready for a reversal, especially with the last big bar closed in its upper quarter and the length of the p2—p3 swing not yet at the 100% length of the p0—p1 swing.

The 5-min chart in Fig. 7.11 perfectly illustrates one of the most frequently met set-ups, the *mirror sliding parallel line*. The L-MLH serves as a symmetry axis and the last two bars are testing the outer PH. It looks like a reversal is about to happen.

Most traders don't think to look for what *isn't* happening on the chart. The concept of running out of steam gives the trader a competitive edge in revealing the up-sloping failures, especially in topping and bottoming markets (Fig. 7.12 on p. 130). The mirror PH set-up shown in Fig. 7.12 greatly enhances the trader's ability to recognise the up-sloping failure and its outcome.

Figure 7.13 (on p. 130) shows the same mirror sliding bars line set up with the same double testing of the outer PH as in Fig. 7.12, but this time on a 15-min chart. It looks as though this set up is travelling through time across multiple time frames. Once again, even on this time frame, the PH plays its ready-to-serve resistance role, being a border to an up/down-sloping channel.

Figure 7.14 (on p. 131) shows, as we anticipated, that the valiant (strong and vigilant landmark) outer PH has kept its promise of resistance and provoked the end of the four bar up-swing (P2 failure), allowing the down-trend to continue. Once the market flow reaches the trigger line of the up-sloping minor pivot, we can prepare for a short entry.

Figure 7.15 (on p. 131) looks clouded, covered with the mmls of the down-sloping pitchfork, the horizontal S/R trend lines and the PH's neighbouring oblique trend line. The purpose of this chart is to show you how a single PH can cause double up-sloping failures (levels 5049 and 5039.50), with ensuing double lower highs (levels 5023 and 5017). Then, the following morning,

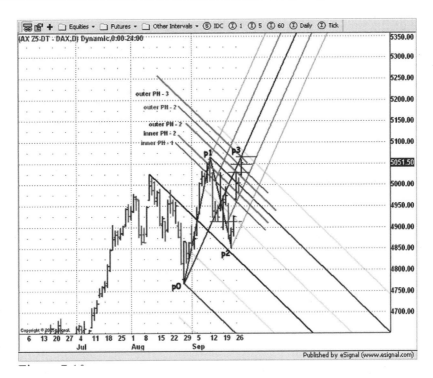

Figure 7.10 Making an intersection point with a fifth PH (Courtesy of www.pitchforktrader.com)

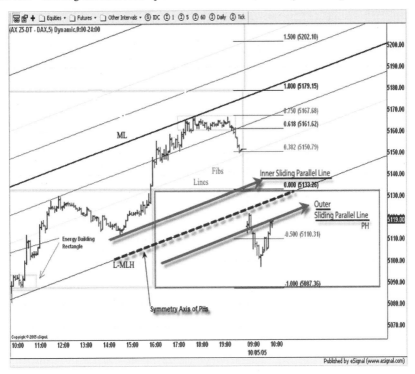

Figure 7.11 Mirror sliding parallel line (Courtesy of www.pitchforktrader.com)

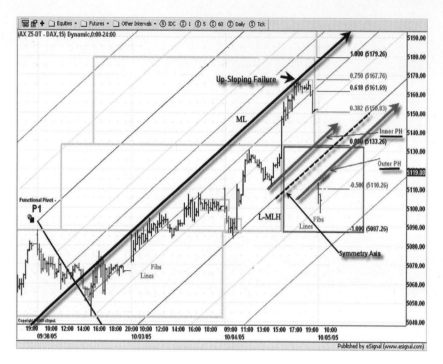

Figure 7.12 Topping and bottoming markets (Courtesy of www.pitchforktrader.com)

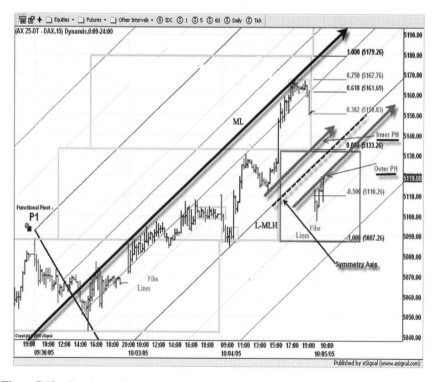

Figure 7.13 Topping and bottoming markets (cont.) (Courtesy of www.pitchforktrader.com)

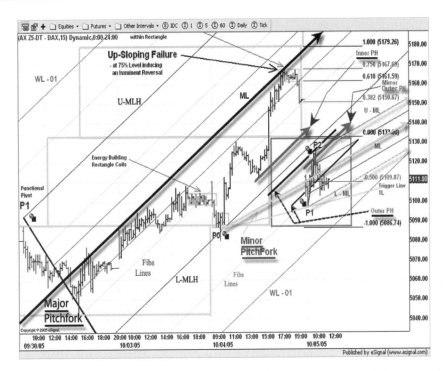

Figure 7.14 Topping and bottoming markets (cont.) (Courtesy of www.pitchforktrader.com)

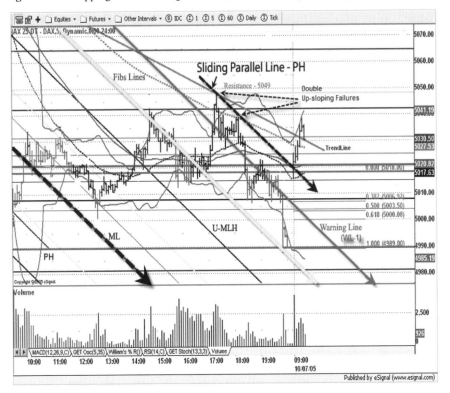

Figure 7.15 Single PH causing double up-sloping failures with ensuing double lower highs (Courtesy of www.pitchforktrader.com)

helped by an up-gap, the price zooms through the PH, validating once more the old adage: 'An old resistance becomes a new support.'

7.6   KEY LEARNING POINTS

- Make sure you understand the difference between the Hagopian line and the sliding parallel line.
- Keep in mind the best-known role of the SH: the creation of quick market reversals.
- Do not be parsimonious in using the SHs as initial and trailing efficient stops. Their use should become one of your reflex trading actions.
- When testing, piercing and zooming, SHs behave in the same way as any median or non-pitchfork related trend line, even though it is constructed without any ML pivots.

8
Unorthodox Trend Lines

As their name indicates, unorthodox trend lines illustrate the development of a trend, creating dynamic areas of support and resistance. They join two or more crossing points created from the interaction between the price and the trend lines. As a trading tool, they are very valuable because they illustrate a hidden facet of trading. A harmonious integration is revealed when used with other tools: pitchforks, chart patterns, angle lines, swings, breakouts and many others.

The main difference between traditional and unorthodox trend lines is expressed by the type of trajectory they travel. In this chapter, we look at their specific features and their integration with other chart formations.

8.1 DEFINITION

With regard to their trajectories there are two types of trend lines (TL):

- The orthodox (traditional) trend line joins at least two points: a series of higher highs (in an up-trend) or lower lows (in a down-trend). Its characteristic is that it does not traverse the market (the price bars).
- The unorthodox, or *multi-pivoted*, trend line is somewhat different. It links a series of higher highs or lower highs belonging to the same trend and/or other trends. It differs from the traditional trend line because it traverses the market, camouflaged between the numerous valleys and peaks. This is why many traders are not familiar with their existence.

Remember, we spoke about context. Whatever their type, the trend lines constitute one of the strongest elements in identifying the context of the whole market. We can also close in on the local (most recent) market, and look for the smaller swing trend lines (traditional and/or unorthodox) which might reveal a continuation of or, alternatively, a reversal of the market.

There are markets where traditional trend lines cannot be drawn. This occurs when the trend is not obvious, the market being in a non-trending state. In this case, the assistance of the unorthodox trend lines is valuable. They not only show us the past market flow movements, but also prepare us for immediate action.

One should never forget: *An old resistance line becomes a new support line.*

Other characteristics of both trend lines are fairly similar, and they have an equal role in the trader's arsenal of tools.

8.2   THE DEGREE OF THE SLOPE

The *degree of the slope* is one of the most important features when using an unorthodox trend line. It is known that a steep slope reveals either a sharp reversal or an imminent consolidation of the market, and a lesser degree slope informs about reversals rather than trading ranges. The degree of the slope tells the story of a trending or non-trending market. Generally, the steeper the slope of the trend, the stronger the momentum becomes, but the move tends to be of shorter duration. Concerning the projecting values of the trend lines, we may add that:

• the steeper the slope, the less valuable the projecting value; and
• the lesser the slope, the more important the out-bursting breakout.

The 45° trend line has a primordial role in the trending process, being the most important angle capable of giving the direction and strength of a trend. If this line is broken with huge bars, we can be sure that the market momentum is very strong. Alternatively, if the breakout or the price approach occurs with small trading range bars, we know that the current trend is starting to lose its power and that its termination could well be imminent. Whatever the type of breakout (swift or slow), it signals the beginning of a trend change, even if only a temporary one.

All the non-45° trend lines are excellent as support or resistance lines, or as target objectives. They are considered the equivalent of the 50% horizontal support/resistance level within a trading range. Most of the time the market price takes these values as the borderline between an up and a down bias. Once the price breakout is successful, breaching the trend line, the market flow travels fairly quickly through the path of least resistance. We can compare this relinquishing resistance action to a holed dam: when the pressure of the water finally causes the dam to burst, the water floods away until all the pent-up kinetic energy is used up.

8.3   FAN LINES

Multiple slope trend lines with the same original point (rather like an anchor) are called *fan lines*. Their usefulness is most apparent when the third fan line breakout signals the termination of the current trend and the start of a correction pattern (see Fig. 8.8).

8.4   SPECIFIC TREND LINES

Not all trend lines are linear. Where neither of the two (traditional or unorthodox) TLs is of any value, we can use a moving average (21 or 50-MA) to detect the slope and where the trend is in its development. In this case we are talking about a *curvilinear trend line*.

Many traders draw TLs only in an oblique inclination. A horizontal resistance or support is also a trend line, having a flat inclination.

8.5 DEGREE OF STRENGTH

The *degree of strength* depends on the number of trend touches (pivots or not) produced when the price reaches (and just touches) the trend line. If there are many touches, there is stronger legitimacy: the more touches mean a more significant event will occur when the price tries to break the line. Why? This is based on a Newtonian principle: *a body in motion tends to remain in motion through its inertia.* (If we go further and explain inertia we find that it is 'a property of matter by which it remains at rest or in uniform motion in the same straight line unless acted upon by some external force'.[1])

The strength of the legitimacy builds the authority of the trend line. Longer, more-tested trends give stronger signals than shorter trends. A trend line touched six times is harder to break than a trend line touched only three times. The length of the trend and the time frame in which it is drawn also describes its strength:

- The longer the trend, the stronger the trend line will become: the trend line of a 21-bars trend is much more resistant to being broken than that of a 13-bars trend.
- The higher the time frame, the more resistant its trend line: a trend line on a monthly chart is far stronger than a trend line on a daily chart.

Important hint: When projecting the trend line of an upper time frame on a lower (operational) time frame, notice how hard it is for the local market to break it.

8.6 REDRAWING A TREND LINE

It is crucial to redraw a trend line whenever there is a small penetration. We call this new line the *adjusted trend line*. It does not change our immediate strategy, but it will certainly take on more importance should the number of touches increase.

8.7 CONFIRMING A TREND LINE

A trend line is only confirmed after three touches, although it can be drawn after two touches.

8.8 CONFIRMING A BREAKOUT

It needs patience and the practical application of the 'wait and see' principle to confirm whether a trend line is breaking out. In spite of this, we still have some major clues.

1. The closing price: after piercing the line, the price might close two times in a row on the other side, in the direction of the reversal. Then it is very possible that the breakout will be confirmed.
2. The bar count method: the Fibonacci bars count and momentum bar count techniques are detailed in Volume II (in preparation).

[1] *Merriam-Webster's Collegiate Dictionary*, 10th edition, 2002

3.   Revealing the culmination of a trend, which will underpin the trend's termination and
      the breakout of the trend line. This is explained under the more advanced techniques
      described in Volume II (in preparation):
      – measured moves, especially for chart patterns – triangles, rectangles, head-and-
         shoulder and others;
      – circular points using Fibonacci circles and ellipses;
      – square root increments and percentage change;
      – the square of nine by Gann, in time and price;
      – and others.
4.   Confirm the breakout of the trend line when a certain arithmetic price limit percentage
      value is reached, away from the breaking point:
      – a penetration of 1% for intra-day; and
      – a penetration of 3% for swing trading.

8.9   BREAKOUT EFFICIENCY OF A TREND LINE

The breakout efficiency of a trend line depends on the degree of legitimacy, which in turn reveals
the degree of fragility or strength of the trend. A bigger volume is needed to break a stronger
trend line. Once the trend line is broken we have several possible situations.

- An *efficient first time breakout* is the exception, not the rule. If it does take place we could
  well say: 'the bigger the burst, the higher the thrust' (of the breakout).
- A *false breakout* is when, in the case of an up-trending move, the price returns to the
  newly-labelled support line (old resistance) within a few bars. Once it touches the support
  line it can either bounce away again or return to its departure point under the newly-created
  support.
- A *throwback* is when the returned price goes further through the breaking line, until it is
  quickly halted by a stronger support level.
- A *bull trap* is a version of the throwback described above, but in which the price drops
  beyond the 100% retracement of the previous swing.
- The behaviour of a chart after the *termination* of a strong trend is mostly made up of a
  consolidation area, especially if the trend line was very steep.
- The *duration* of a trend line should never be questioned. There are two specific aspects:
  – the duration of a trend during its three phases (inception, development and termina-
     tion), which will be valid until the weight of evidence confirms the reversal. Its trend
     line plays the S/R functions during the duration of the trend;
  – the duration of a trend line can last as long as the cash markets exist. As for the futures
     market, it will be there for the duration of the contract. It could reverse from a support
     function to resistance and vice versa.

8.10   MONEY MANAGEMENT AND TREND LINES

The initial stop loss and trail stop levels are frequently determined by utilizing trend lines; it
is an ergonomic and very efficient way of money management. Once the trend line breakout is
confirmed, the stops can be easily snugged on the opposite side of the trend line.

8.11   UNORTHODOX TREND LINES: CASE STUDIES

FTSE100, German Dax and S&P500 Index Charts

In Fig. 8.1, the trend line crosses the market through the high of the gap, and is touched (tested) four times by the price. The last touch strongly contributes to its legitimacy, halting the correction that started on the Friday of the previous week.

Figure 8.2 illustrates the dual aspects of a trend line: the orthodox and unorthodox. On this chart they form an expanding triangle.

The steep up-trend of the FTSE 100 15-min chart shown in Fig. 8.3 (on p. 139) is very handy for drawing the two types of trend line. It is important to choose the best future touching points that may increase the visibility of the market flow with a better participation in trading decisions. A good integrating tool is to mark most of the pivots in advance, so the opportunities can be better distinguished.

The pivot markings will assist the trader in understanding the past, the current and the immediate future market movements. When the unorthodox or traditional trend lines are drawn, the bedding of the market flow is emphasized and is much more visible. In this manner the inner and the outer limits of the whole market movement have been marked out.

Let us proceed and see how all these trend lines and pivots can contribute in such a way that the trader's results will be greatly enhanced. With time and practice this technique should be part of the daily trading routine.

The first clue we have in Fig. 8.4 (on p. 140) is about the context of the market flow. We observe an up-sloping trend which obviously marks the whole chart context. After drawing

Source: www.futuresource.com

Figure 8.1   TL touched four times by the price (Courtesy of www.pitchforktrader.com)

Source: www.futuresource.com
Figure 8.2   Dual aspects of a TL (Courtesy of www.pitchforktrader.com)

several hypothetical TLs, we have selected those which optimally describe the trend, the eventual incoming reversal (p5 level) or a trading range.

We can easily see that the timing of these two unorthodox trend lines is in arithmetical order (no. 1 and then no. 2). The first line, the link of P02 to p3 and p5, has been tested several times; its slope is almost 45°, meaning that it can specify the direction and the strength of the trend. The big price bars have bounced on it several times. It is an almost optimal symmetry axis role.

The second trend line (linking P04 to p4) is reinforced by its passage through the gap's low. As we can see, it also traverses the market with huge bars. The market flow goes up and down across these two lines, without deciding on an absolute gliding bed, although the main trend remains upward.

Figure 8.5 (on p. 141) differs from Fig. 8.4 only by the presence of the third unorthodox TL (no. 3). Its purpose is a complementary one: it marks a possible termination of the ongoing trend, and prepares the stage for a market failure (observe the last huge reversal bar); if this is the case, the next few bars will settle the matter.

The drawing of the major and minor pitchforks in Fig. 8.6 (on p. 141) organizes the rather random-looking market into a systematized, up-sloping market flow. This optimally described pattern will be concluded through the use of double channelling:

–   first, formed by the ML and its inner Fibonacci lines of the major pitchfork; and
–   second, concomitant running in the same direction, formed by the ml and u-mlh of the minor pitchfork.

Source: www.futuresource.com
Figure 8.3 Orthodox and unorthodox TLs on a FTSE 100 15-min chart
(Courtesy of www.pitchforktrader.com)

Figure 8.7 (on p. 142) is an almost perfect example of the complementarities between the traditional and unorthodox trend lines. We intentionally skipped the middle unorthodox trend line to better see this pair. They fulfil their obligations better than ever: multiple tests and a perfect triangular channel. The market could not have been better described! In spite of this, there is a missing link – a third line, which is an unorthodox trend line (Fig. 8.8 on p. 142). This latter line strengthens the relationship among all three, giving birth to a well-known pattern: the *triple fan lines* set up. This lowest trend line should be closely monitored in the direction of the ongoing trend. Looking at the last huge bar, we can see that it is closing exactly on the third line. We cannot be confident yet that the market trend will change – the next few bars will tell the difference.

The two trend lines shown in the chart in Fig. 8.9 (on p. 143) are both traditional at this stage of the market development. The down-sloping trend line is used as a diagnostic tool to detect an eventual upward-opening breakout. After testing the market from beneath, the price gaps up, retests the same line, and finally takes off with a really huge up-thrust. Its role is perfectly

Source: www.futuresource.com
Figure 8.4   Context of the market flow with two unorthodox TLs (Courtesy of www.pitchforktrader.com)

accomplished. So far, the up-sloping trend line plays only a passive role, although it has been tested several times. In the near future, we should expect this to act as a slant support trend line. We will study the same market further (Fig. 8.10 on p. 143) in order to see what the future holds.

As we expected, the passive role of the up-sloping trend line is converted into a very dynamic one (Fig. 8.10). After multiple tests and retests it plays first the support and then the resistance role several times. We can see how an innocent, orthodox up-sloping trend line has been converted into an unorthodox trend line, traversing the market without any pity!

The chart in Fig. 8.11 (on p. 144) uses the synergy between the two unorthodox lines (nos 1 and 2) and the up-sloping pitchfork. The intersection of the ML and the unorthodox trend line no. 1 gives birth to a strong confluence (level p04) which not only halts the market but also reverses it. The unorthodox line no. 2 was resistant enough to halt the corrective p01–p02 swing, enhancing the up-slope of the market flow through the restorative mechanism of the kinetic energy-building process.

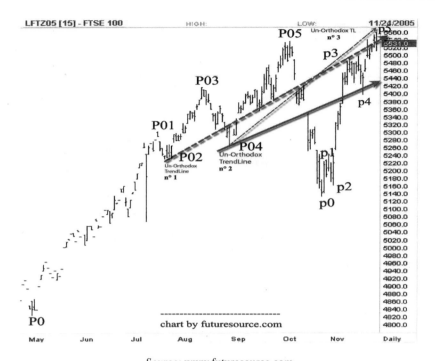

Source: www.futuresource.com

Figure 8.5 Context of the market flow with three unorthodox TLs (Courtesy of www.pitchforktrader.com)

Source: www.futuresource.com

Figure 8.6 Major pitchfork encapsulating the minor pitchfork (Courtesy of www.pitchforktrader.com)

Figure 8.7   Complementarities between traditional and unorthodox TLs
(Courtesy of www.pitchforktrader.com)

Figure 8.8   Triple fan lines (Courtesy of www.pitchforktrader.com)

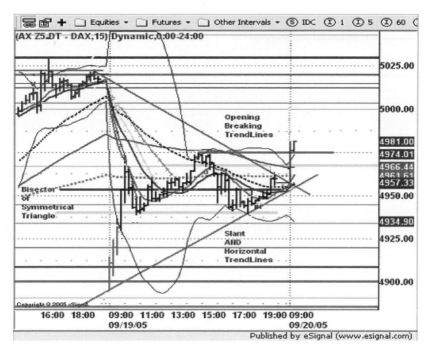

Figure 8.9   Opening breaking-out trend lines – before opening (Courtesy of www.pitchforktrader.com)

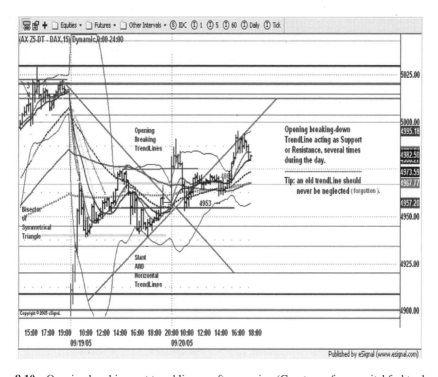

Figure 8.10   Opening breaking-out trend lines – after opening (Courtesy of www.pitchforktrader.com)

Figure 8.11 Using the synergy between the up-sloping pitchfork and unorthodox TLs
(Courtesy of www.pitchforktrader.com)

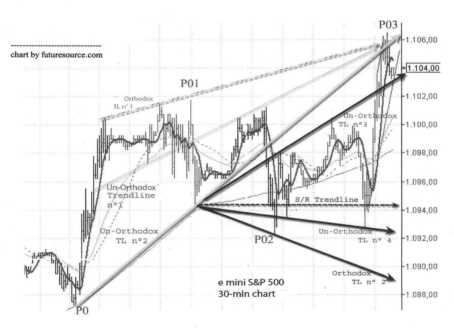

Figure 8.12 Systematized trend lines approach: a resourceful idea for trades
(Courtesy of www.pitchforktrader.com)

Figure 8.12 seems a little clouded. In spite of this, if we are organized and progressively draw the trend lines, taking into account the merits and the tasks of each one, we can obtain maximum information, thus enhancing our trading potential.

From this pattern we will only mention the merits of the following three trend lines: an orthodox trend line (no. 1) and two unorthodox trend lines (nos 1 and 2), which have given birth to a very strong confluence (level P03) whose role of halting and reversing the up-sloping market is obvious. I will let the reader discover the weaknesses or otherwise of the other drawn trend lines.

Conclusion: The use of orthodox and unorthodox trend lines dissipates the initial market chaos. The gradual disappearance of randomness is in direct proportion with the improvement in reading the charts.

8.12 KEY LEARNING POINTS

* Get used to a daily routine, and to detecting the hidden unorthodox trend lines combined with the fan line concept.
* Don't hesitate to look for specific trend lines: curvilinear and flat.
* Excel in the following topics: slope, strength and breakouts of a trend line.
* Don't neglect to confirm the efficiency of a trend line breakout.
* Even if it seems obvious, ensure that you understand and practise the difference between the trend and trend line terminations.

Ensure that you have assimilated and intensively practised the money management techniques, using the snugging concept behind the trend lines.

9
Multiple Pitchfork Trading

Multiple pitchfork trading appeals naturally to the trader, even if he or she is not totally familiar with it. Most traders practise this technique instinctively in their bid to achieve ever-greater profits. Very few have a predetermined multi-pitchfork strategy, and even fewer have a thorough understanding of the best ways to analyze a multiple pitchfork formation. It is difficult, if not impossible, for the novice trader to understand a chart with multiple pitchforks criss-crossing everywhere and numerous pairs of parallel lines, some overlapping others.

So the natural question is: How can any profit be made from using such a crowded pattern? Well, the answer may be obvious for the astute trader but is certainly not clear-cut for inexperienced traders.

The chart might seem unbearably messy, but this method is indispensable for understanding the market flow. It systematizes the apparent chaos of the market, turning it into an environment where it is much easier for the trader to make a decision. It is just a question of becoming familiar with it − or, should I say, becoming addicted!

9.1 DEFINITION

We would argue passionately that the multiple-pitchfork pattern greatly enhances the potential of trading results, with a qualified emphasis on consistency. Observing this pattern closely we realize that, most of the time:

- a bigger (major) pitchfork envelopes the smaller (minor) one(s);
- the smaller one(s) is/are distributed in meaningful location(s) connected to the major pitchfork: at its extremities, in the middle of its main area, or outside;
- if the multiple pitchforks are not overlapping, rather being arranged in a sequential chaining structure, we can easily see that the preceding pitchfork prepares the activity of the next one and that the bigger pitchfork guides the minor pitchfork.

When using multiple pitchfork strategy, your attitude must be adapted to both the type of the market and the specific situation that you are faced with.

- You must understand the market in a systematic manner. You will be trained well enough that, when looking at the naked chart (before the pitchforks are drawn), you will be able to distinguish between the context of the market flow and the local price turbulences which are ready to reverse or to explode. Once you have reached this level of skill, you are only one step from knowing how to draw pitchforks that optimally describe the market. You will be able to observe whether any chart pattern is developing that will enhance the potential of the pitchfork(s), thus leading to an eventual trade.

- As you know by now, the pivots and the resulting pitchforks play an indispensable role in finding the market flow bedding. Once these pivots are marked, search for any relationships among pitchforks, and traditional or unorthodox trend lines.
- Do not overcrowd the chart with multiple pitchforks if it is not really useful. As they say, 'The workplace must be always clean!'

9.2   CREATING MULTIPLE PITCHFORKS

It is not easy to plan, draw and manage a single pitchfork. So what will it be like doing the same with multiple pitchforks? Willpower and sheer effort are indispensable if you are to attain the essential skill of being consistent. To understand the mechanism of how a pitchfork functions, first you must learn how it is formed. The methodology of pitchfork trading is based on a few criteria of a structural and dynamic nature. The list below is not exhaustive.

9.2.1   Structure-related Criteria

- Double channelling (ML and U-MLH, and ML and L-MLH): the process of moving from one channel into the other signals a continuation or a reversal of the trend – only a single pitchfork (PF) is needed.
- The magnet-like role of the median line and its associated lines dominate everything else here – only a single PF is needed.
- The intersecting potential with single or multiple linear or curvilinear structures, such as: trend lines, chart pattern formations, Fibonacci ratios levels (arcs or lines), angle lines and others. The intersection of at least two lines gives birth to confluence zones, which are responsible for creating an energy cluster, the basement of kinetic energy building zones – only a single PF is needed.

There are several priorities to consider when building multiple pitchforks:

- First, the creation of the *confluence zones* (see more details in Chapter 15). This is by far the most important priority.
- Second, it greatly helps to understand the intricacies of the market flow context and the most recent market phase (local market).
- Third, the trader gets an invaluable edge when using the multiple pitchfork technique across the time frames. The projection of the ML of an upper frame pitchfork on the trading time frame greatly enhances the trade potential.
- Fourth, the beginning of a correction or an impulse pattern cannot be efficiently traded without the intricacy of at least two, if not three, drawn pitchforks, not to mention a fourth pitchfork belonging to an upper time frame. Refer back to Chapter 2 and the discussion about penultimate pivot pitchforks for a reminder about the importance of the multiple pitchfork set up.

9.2.2 Dynamics-related Criteria

Once we have defined the structure and it has become operational, let us go on to describe the functional aspect of the pitchfork's mechanism.

- Trading opportunities come around on specific occasions. Piercing, testing, retesting and zooming are part of trade management. Their continuous use will generate low-risk high-probability trades.
- Even though it has already been mentioned above, we would like to stress that the confluence zones have widespread usage with regard to price dynamics as they:
  - constitute excellent entry points;
  - represent great locations for snugging the initial and trailing stops;
  - greatly influence the pre-arranged (or not) exits;
  - plainly enhance the trader's self-control and confidence.

9.3 KINEMATICS OF MULTIPLE PITCHFORKS AS INTEGRATED PATTERNS

In his book *Crime and Punishment*, Fyodor Dostoyevsky wrote: '. . . the facts aren't everything. At least half the case is knowing what to do with the facts.' This statement is eminently applicable to pitchfork analysis once the anchor and the P1−P2 swing are defined.

Most of the time, optimal pitchfork trading should use two pitchforks, except in specific situations:

- a *major* pitchfork which will embed the global market;
- a more recent *minor* pitchfork, closer to the ongoing market and situated within the reach of the first pitchfork, either inside or outside its main body.

Careful now . . . I am not saying that pitchfork trading is not possible using a single pitchfork. I am just advising that using dual pitchforks is preferable because of their inherent advantages.

The major pitchfork guides the market price dance, from the start of an important movement until a consistent up/down translation move occurs, from the field of its main body. If this type of pitchfork forms a directional channel with the following P3, P4 and P5, then be ready for a reversal, with the price going outside the main body of the pitchfork. If this happens, prepare for a real reversal, and be quick to search for a new set of pivots, giving birth to a new potential pitchfork (see Fig. 9.8).

If, however, this move is a false reversal, then the next pivot (P6 in our case) will be created within the existing set of pivots (see Fig. 11.2). The same procedure is applied when P7, P9 or P11 occur (see Fig. 1.6).

Returning to the dual pitchfork technique, here are some of its advantages.

- Embedding: the market flow is better enclosed from a global and local (immediate current level) point of view.
- Continuity: the major pitchfork guides the price development of the trend along the 'railway track'; it could glide along smoothly, continuously, almost effortlessly. During this time, the minor pitchfork applied to any valuable 'resting areas', such as ongoing pullbacks or peaks, will reveal temporary disruptions. If these disruptions are strong enough, they could signal the presence of an imminent reversal.

- Reversal: the symbiosis of the two pitchforks will certainly help the trader detect a potential reversal.
- Multiple time frames: the major pitchfork can remain on an upper time frame and also be projected on the operational time frame (lower time frame) while the trade is being managed. Here, there is justifiable use of a third pitchfork. For further details see Chapters 18 and 19.

9.4 MULTIPLE PITCHFORK INTEGRATION: CASE STUDIES

German Dax Futures Index Charts

As can be seen in Fig. 9.1, the single drawn pitchfork ideally describes the up-sloping trend. So far, we could have traded the market flow without the help of a minor pitchfork. Once the P5 pivot level is attained, the need for a second pitchfork (a minor pitchfork having the p0 anchor in the P5 location) becomes imperative.

As anticipated, the new pitchfork becomes indispensable when a reversal needs to be described (Fig. 9.2). The median lines are always drawn first, in order to see how suitable they are for providing an optimal description of the incoming market flow.

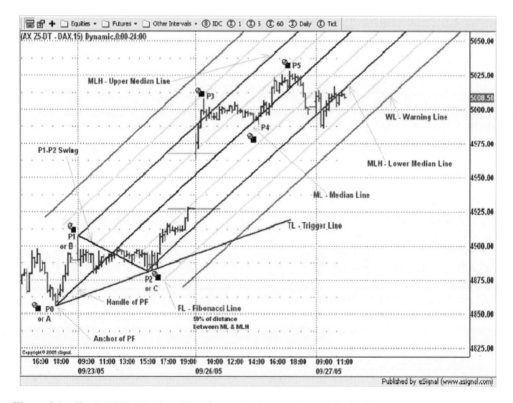

Figure 9.1 Single PF ideally describing the up-sloping trend on a 15-min chart
(Courtesy of www.pitchforktrader.com)

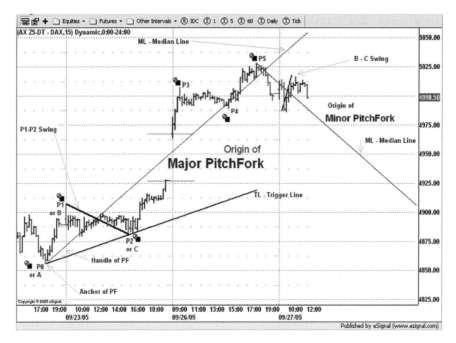

Figure 9.2   Using a new PF to describe a reversal (Courtesy of www.pitchforktrader.com)

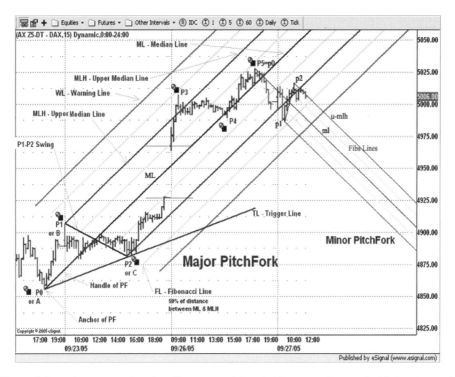

Figure 9.3   Using a new PF to describe a reversal (cont.) (Courtesy of www.pitchforktrader.com)

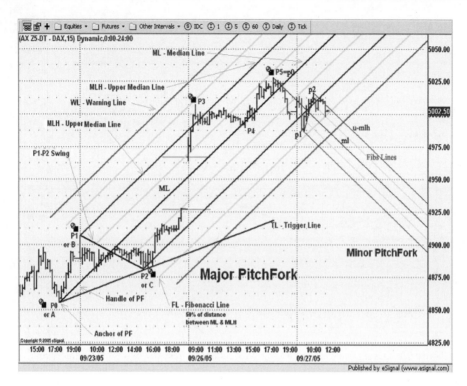

Figure 9.4   Using a new PF to describe a reversal (cont.) (Courtesy of www.pitchforktrader.com)

Figure 9.3 (on p. 151) shows how the minor pitchfork has readily adopted the most recent market flow, with the recent price testing its upper median line (u-mlh) several times. The internal Fibonacci 50% lines drawn on the chart will, together with the ml, possibly serve as components of future channels to help the price flow.

Figure 9.4 shows the same chart as Fig. 9.3, but 15 minutes later. The market makes a sudden halt at the confluence of the lower Fibonacci line of the major pitchfork and the upper Fibonacci line of the minor pitchfork.

Figure 9.5 is a continuation of Figs. 9.3 and 9.4. The minor pitchfork's upper channel, formed by the u-mlh and the ml, is ready for functioning. The upper Fibonacci 50% line seems to hold the down-sloping movement.

Continuing the sequence, Fig. 9.6 shows that the upper channel, delineated by the u-mlh and upper 50% Fibonacci lines of the minor pitchfork, serves as a bias indicator for immediate market decisions: an up-sloping tendency when the price moves above the channel and a down-sloping bias where the price looks like dropping. Whatever the direction, its warning lines (wls) will greatly contribute to an easier understanding of the entire price movement in the future.

As anticipated, the market flow has temporarily moved upward from its initial downward bedding (Fig. 9.7 on p. 154). In spite of this, the down-sloping trend is more evident than ever. We have purposely refrained from drawing the second warning line (WL-2) of the major pitchfork in order to ensure better market flow visibility.

The minor pitchfork continues to optimally describe the market flow in its down-sloping deluge (Fig 9.8 on p. 154). The upper warning lines of the minor pitchfork serve as a symmetry

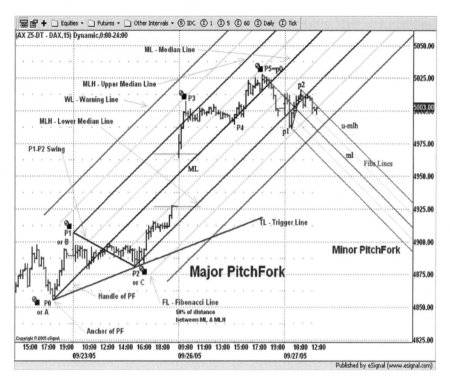

Figure 9.5   Using a new PF to describe a reversal (cont.) (Courtesy of www.pitchforktrader.com)

Figure 9.6   Using a new PF to describe a reversal (cont.) (Courtesy of www.pitchforktrader.com)

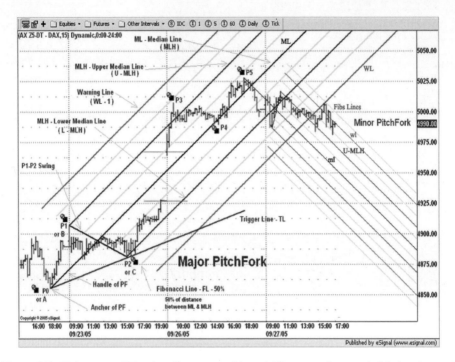

Figure 9.7 Using a new PF to describe a reversal (cont.) (Courtesy of www.pitchforktrader.com)

Figure 9.8 Using a new PF to describe a reversal (cont.) (Courtesy of www.pitchforktrader.com)

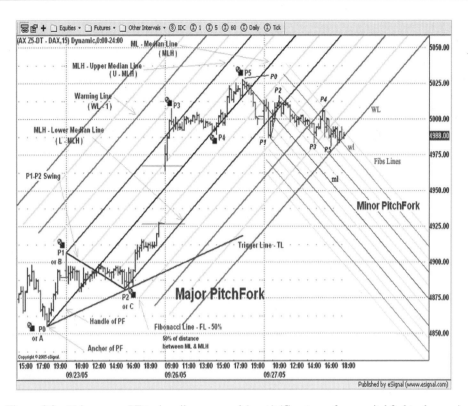

Figure 9.9   Using a new PF to describe a reversal (cont.) (Courtesy of www.pitchforktrader.com)

axis. The market has chosen to glide effortlessly through the channel formed by the first and second upper Fibonacci lines, just outside the minor pitchfork.

The market flow in Fig. 9.9 seems to be temporarily halted by the warning line WL-2. It has already been tested four times, in conjunction with the confluence of the warning lines (WL-2 and wl) of both pitchforks. Even if the bias is not obvious at the moment, the matter will be settled by the next two or three bars.

The market flow depicted in Fig. 9.10 seems to have decided it wants a lesser trending slope, getting out of the initial minor pitchfork and having an anchor at the P5 level. The drawing of a second minor pitchfork (the Schiff pitchfork – see Chapter 10) will describe the more recent market much better. Its median line (ml) will serve as a borderline between the up or down bias.

We removed the Schiff minor pitchfork from Fig. 9.11 (on p. 157) for visibility reasons. We are constantly aware of the need not to overcrowd the chart. (Remember: as the market develops, go with it! Update the developing patterns to better illustrate the market progression, remove or add those indispensable chart clues. Keep your workplace (the chart) clean – the health of your decisions depends on it!)

The presence of the Schiff minor pitchfork would have been very advantageous if the market had continued to progress in a lesser downward slope, as when it was drawn. But, instead, the market attempts an up-sloping trend and halts the drop for the moment. Multiple tests of the second warning line (WL-2) of the major pitchfork will be significant.

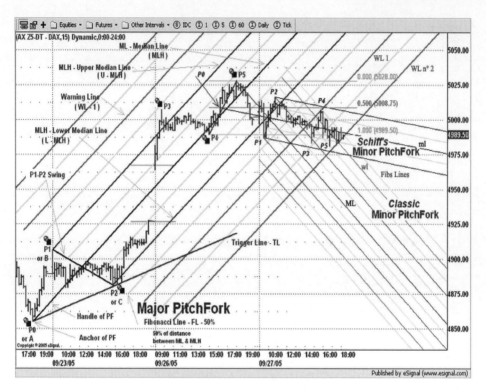

Figure 9.10   Using a new PF to describe a reversal (cont.) (Courtesy of www.pitchforktrader.com)

The market flow was embedded in the chart (Fig. 9.12 on p. 158) by three pitchforks:

- The first pitchfork, having the ML1, encloses the entire market, and almost forces the flow to take the lower channel formed by the ML1 and its lower ML.
- The second pitchfork (ML2) was drawn in the expectation that the market will take an up-sloping bias, which it does not, at least for the moment. We will see below that this pitchfork pattern results in a temporary up-sloping failure.
- The third pitchfork (ML3) is designed and drawn for a down-sloping bias.

In spite of drawing all three pitchforks we are not yet sufficiently ready to enter a low-risk high-probability trade. But . . . we have set up the context and followed the market in its local turbulence.

Careful observation of this labyrinth of lines and pitchforks reveals the following:

- The lower median line of the first pitchfork makes a strong and successful trigger line for pitchfork no. 2.
- The recent market (three bars behind) pierces it three times, zooming through but always closing above it.
- The last market bar is a perfect inside bar which, together with the piercing and closing above the line, gives a strong indication that an up-swing reversal is in the making.

Figure 9.11   Using a new PF to describe a reversal (cont.) (Courtesy of www.pitchforktrader.com)

If we are wrong, and the market breaks down the trigger line, then the Hagopian rule (Section 6.2) will come into effect, and the trigger line will be converted into a Hagopian line. The practical lesson here is: 'Always follow the failure!'

In order to get an even clearer insight (Fig. 9.13), we have decided to draw the almost invisible local market rectangles, defined by at least four price touches, two each on a resistance and the supporting horizontal trend lines respectively. They are described below by:

- A parallel line drawn through the highest high (P01), forming the upper border of rectangle no. 1.
- A parallel line through the p02 of the ML3 pitchfork, constituting the upper border of rectangle no. 0 (named the *inceptive rectangle*).

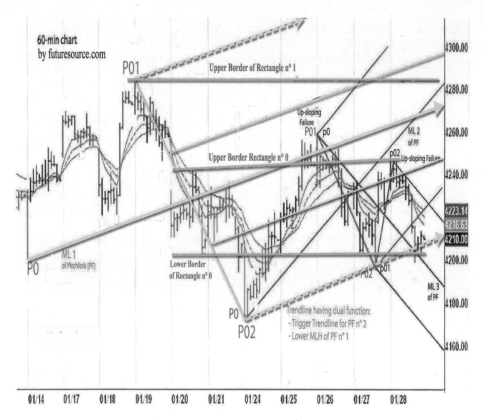

Figure 9.12   Three pitchforks embedding market flow (Courtesy of www.pitchforktrader.com)

• A projected parallel line drawn through the penultimate low of the P01−P02 swing at the 4205 level, forming the lower border of rectangle no. 0. The market validates rectangle no. 0 with at least seven touches. The up-sloping failure (p02 pivot) takes place exactly on the upper border of this inceptive rectangle.

With the help of a low-risk initial stop loss, under the low of the last piercing bar (at the 4198 level), we can enter the market with a prearranged long entry just above the high of the bar before last (level 4214).

The minimum objective target should be the upper border of the inceptive rectangle (at the 4248 level), where the first half of the trade will be exited. There is a strong probability that the market inertia will swing all the way up to the upper border of rectangle no. 1 (at the 4283 level). Now, looking back, we realize that the initial labyrinth was not really such a mess of lines and pitchforks!

A whole chapter is dedicated to the relationship between pitchforks and rectangles (see Volume III, in preparation).

Conclusion: I hope that the above study has convinced you that a seemingly random market can be transformed into a highly organized context, ready to give up — albeit with much effort and patience from the trader's part — low-risk high-probability trade opportunities.

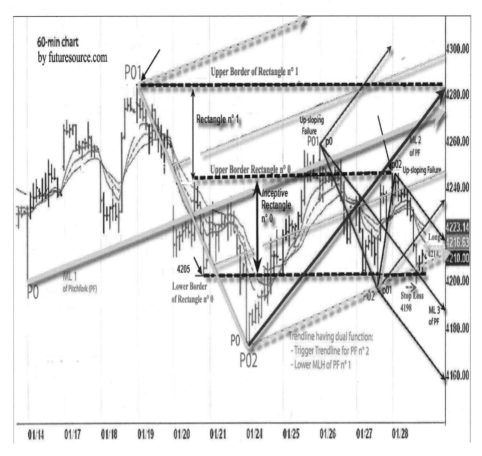

Figure 9.13   Drawing local market rectangles (Courtesy of www.pitchforktrader.com)

9.5   KEY LEARNING POINTS

- Get ready to accept the multiple pitchforks concept, which many traders think is too complicated.
- Apply the concept in a timed, organized and, especially, a sequential manner.
- Track the pattern of chained multiple pitchforks, or that of a global context major pitchfork (on the same or a different time frame) embedding multiple minor pitchforks.
- Follow closely these nuts-and-bolts techniques: double channelling, the magnet-like power of the ML, confluence zones with their energy-building clusters, classic components of an entry (piercing, testing, retesting and zooming) and multiple time-frame pitchforks.
- In spite of the crowded appearance, do not hesitate to use a second, third, or even a fourth pitchfork (especially from a different time frame); it might be the clue to your low-risk high-probability trades.
- Look for rectangles, which are almost invisible to most traders.
- Keep a continuous and vigilant watch on market developments through the use of multiple pitchforks and other chart formations (trend lines, rectangles, etc.).

- Update the patterns to improve the illustration of the market progression.
- Try not to overcrowd the chart!
- 'Always follow the failure!' It might trigger your initiative! Remember, it is one of the inceptive factors of low-risk high-probability trades.

Ensure that you have understood the concept of transforming an initial seemingly random market into a highly organized market environment. Do not hesitate to go over and over the charts, as many times as necessary! Sheer effort and willpower are the prerequisites of the consistent trader! And remember, not everybody is capable of doing it . . . It takes guts!

10
Schiff Pitchforks and Affiliates

This chapter looks at the construction, market integration and dynamics of the Schiff pitchfork. The Schiff pitchfork is the 'missing link' – it is an efficient substitute for the traditional pitchfork when the latter cannot be drawn for whatever reason.

10.1 DEFINITION

Jerome Schiff, a student of Dr Alan Andrews, invented the Schiff pitchfork. It became clear that a new tool was needed when the three pivots necessary to draw a more traditional pitchfork could not be found. The set-up choice of three pivots was replaced with a substitute: two pivots and the midpoint of a preceding swing. The purpose of this innovative pitchfork structure remains the same: to find the optimal description of the market flow.

The Schiff pitchfork was originally named the *Schiff median line*, and was sometimes called the *modified* or the *50% median line*. We have settled for calling it the 'Schiff pitchfork'.

The construction of the Schiff pitchfork is performed in three steps:

1. First, we look for the logical direction of the market flow context: not only the direction of the trend but also its slope. In the event that the trend is at its beginning (see Fig. 10.2), and we want to follow its future development with a Schiff pitchfork, we will have to wait until the first correction. This technique can be applied to either an up or a down new trend.
2. Second, on the new trend we try to find a swing whose high and low can be used as the P1 and P2 pivots. We mark the midpoint of the P1–P2 swing, preferably by using the charting program's Fibonacci tool.
3. Third, we try to construct the anchor of this pitchfork at the midpoint of the last swing of the just-terminated trend, opposing the ongoing correction pattern. Once again, this can be calculated through the Fibonacci tool.

A question arises: When should the Schiff pitchfork be used? Several instances are described below:

- when the traditional pitchfork pattern cannot be drawn because it is not possible to detect either the anchor (P0), the P1 or the P2;
- at the reversal's low or high, in order to optimally describe the ensuing trend;

•   when a trading range is in progress, or we are in an energy-building rectangle, whether or not the minor pitchforks are used.

The best way to begin when drawing any pitchfork is to study the context and see what type of major pitchfork (Schiff or traditional) will *optimally describe the market flow*. The same judgment should be made when drawing a minor pitchfork to enclose the local market. It is important always to have this purpose in mind, and to make it part of the daily routine.

10.2   CONSTRUCTING THE SCHIFF PITCHFORK

The chart in Fig. 10.1 is now set to construct a Schiff pitchfork. We are at the end of a down-sloping trend; the midpoint (P0) of the last swing (A−B) will create the anchor for the Schiff pitchfork.

As we have seen, the Fibonacci tool was used to calculate the midpoint of both swings (A−B and P01−P02). The market begins an up-sloping correction pattern from the B reversal pivot, the lowest low. The P01 reversal pivot terminates the first impulsive swing of the new trend. The first correction (P01−P02 swing) is complete. The P02 reversal pivot is ready to continue the third swing of the correction pattern, which is also its second impulsive swing.

Figure 10.1   Constructing a Schiff pitchfork (Courtesy of www.pitchforktrader.com)

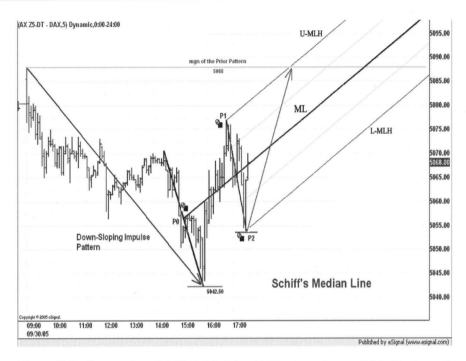

Figure 10.2   Constructing a Schiff pitchfork (cont.) (Courtesy of www.pitchforktrader.com)

The P0-P1-P2 Schiff pitchfork is now ready to describe the market. The next market movements will tell how well this structure will perform. Within a second bar rising from the P2 pivot (Fig. 10.2), the market reaches the median line, and closes right on it. It is the first confirmation that this is the right pivot to use.

After some sideways activity (Fig. 10.3) the market shoots straight up towards the median line, which is serving both as a symmetry axis and also as support and resistance. The target objective is attained (the confluence of 5088 resistance and the median line). Now we can say with certainty that using the Schiff pitchfork was the best option.

Figure 10.4 (on p. 165) shows a version of the Schiff pitchfork which exploits the presence of the up-gap. The trader expects a very substantial up-sloping trend because the gap is there.

The construction of the pitchfork is classic. The median line (ML) optimally describes the market flow: multiple tests, a retest, a piercing and a channel formation with upper median line (U-MLH).

10.3   THE EFFICIENCY OF THE SCHIFF PITCHFORK: 1

Anchor: midpoint of 1st swing *after* P5 reversal of upward trend

In Fig. 10.5 (on p. 166), we construct a Schiff pitchfork which, once the present sideways movement is terminated, will eventually describe a down-sloping market. The midpoint P0 (5011.75 level) is set, as also are the P1 and P2 levels. Now we are ready to join the midpoint P0 (located on the first swing after the P5 reversal) to the midpoint of the P1−P2 swing

Figure 10.3   Constructing a Schiff pitchfork (cont.) (Courtesy of www.pitchforktrader.com)

(Fig. 10.6 on p. 166). Thus we obtain the Schiff median line. We see once again the importance of the Fibonacci tools in locating both midpoints. The Schiff median line is drawn (Fig. 10.6). As mentioned, we are anticipating a down-sloping trend.

In Fig. 10.7 (on p. 167), the Schiff minor pitchfork perfectly describes the local market flow. It is in the process of leaving the major pitchfork's main body area, the zone delimited by the upper and lower median lines.

Even though it has temporarily left the main body, the Schiff pitchfork (Fig. 10.8 on p. 167) is faithful to the down-sloping description of the local market flow.

Drawing the upper Fibonacci lines of the Schiff pitchfork (Fig. 10.9 on p. 168) emphasizes the confluence zone with the warning line (WL-1) of the major pitchfork. Thus we can see the quality of the interactions for both pitchforks. This intersecting zone behaves like a catalysing factor for the continuing down-sloping trend. The two highs in the confluence zone resemble mirror bars.

Figure 10.10 (on p. 168) shows the market flow effortlessly continuing its down-sloping course. The channelling between warning lines w1 and w2 seems to have embedded the local market (Fig. 10.11 on p. 169). Warning line 2 (WL-2) of the major pitchfork represents a vigorous support. The stopping power of the sliding parallel lines (PH) is causing a real up-sloping failure (Fig. 10.12 on p. 169). The minimum price objective is the Schiff median line (ml).

The market flow (Fig. 10.13 on p. 170) seems to have found the ideal channel through which to glide, formed by the upper median line and the inner Fibonacci line of the Schiff minor pitchfork.

The market flow abruptly changes to an upward direction (Fig. 10.14 on p. 170), but it is vigorously halted by a second sliding parallel line (PH-2), the cousin of PH-1. The last bar seems to be cornered between the two. As with the sliding parallel line PH, the warning line WL-2 of the major pitchfork is empowered by the market flow to closely protect for any downward sliding.

Figure 10.4   Exploiting the up-gap (Courtesy of www.pitchforktrader.com)

Figure 10.15 (on p. 171) is essentially the same as Fig. 10.14, but with different set-up lines. The purpose is to reveal whether the upper Fibonacci lines of the Schiff pitchfork have or not the power to halt the trend. After a huge bar, the market closes right on the Fibonacci lines. Please note that the anchor (P0) of the Schiff pitchfork in Fig. 10.15 is the midpoint P0 of the first swing (P5–P6 swing) located after the P5 reversal (5028 level) of the up-sloping trend.

10.4   EFFICIENCY OF SCHIFF PITCHFORK: 2

Anchor: midpoint of 1st swing *before* P5 reversal of upward trend

All the previous charts (Figs. 10.1–10.15) used the anchor P0 (5011 level) as the midpoint of the first swing (P5–P6 swing) after the P5 reversal (5028 level). In Fig. 10.16 (on p. 171) we have

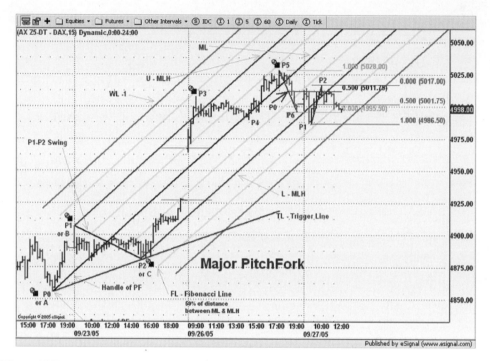

Figure 10.5   Schiff pitchfork describing a down-sloping market (Courtesy of www.pitchforktrader.com)

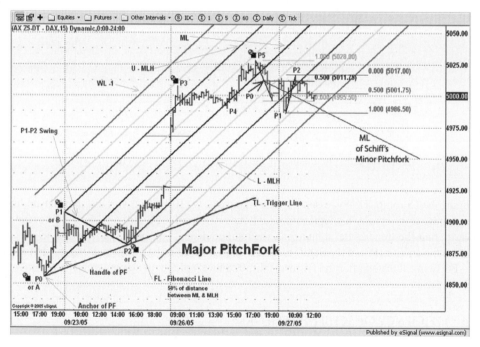

Figure 10.6   Schiff pitchfork describing a down-sloping market (cont.)
(Courtesy of www.pitchforktrader.com)

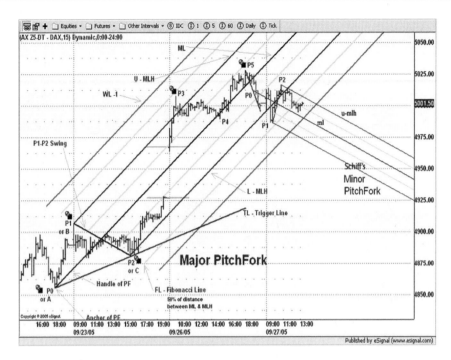

Figure 10.7 Schiff pitchfork describing a down-sloping market (cont.)
(Courtesy of www.pitchforktrader.com)

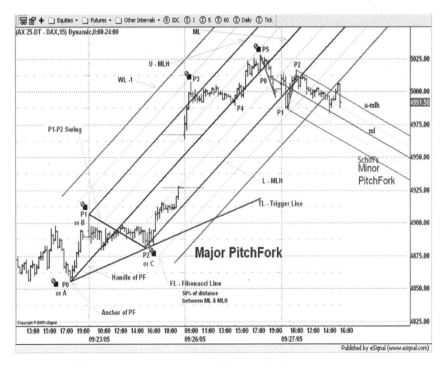

Figure 10.8 Schiff pitchfork describing a down-sloping market (cont.)
(Courtesy of www.pitchforktrader.com)

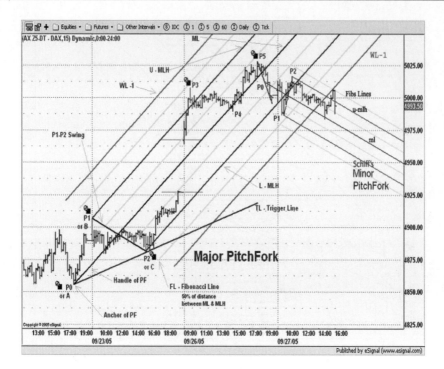

Figure 10.9 Schiff pitchfork describing a down-sloping market (cont.)
(Courtesy of www.pitchforktrader.com)

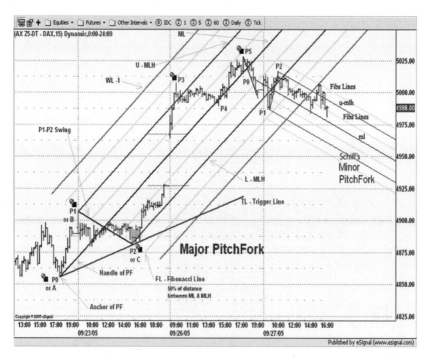

Figure 10.10 Schiff pitchfork describing a down-sloping market (cont.)
(Courtesy of www.pitchforktrader.com)

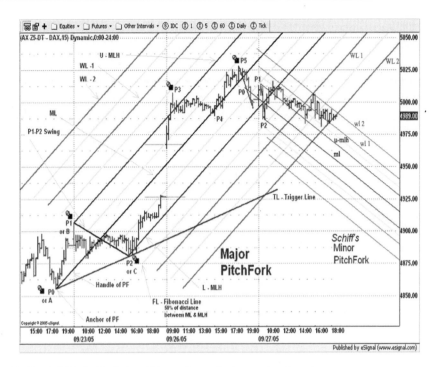

Figure 10.11 Schiff pitchfork describing a down-sloping market (cont.)
(Courtesy of www.pitchforktrader.com)

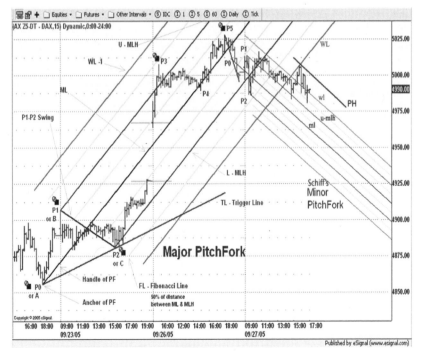

Figure 10.12 Schiff pitchfork describing a down-sloping market (cont.)
(Courtesy of www.pitchforktrader.com)

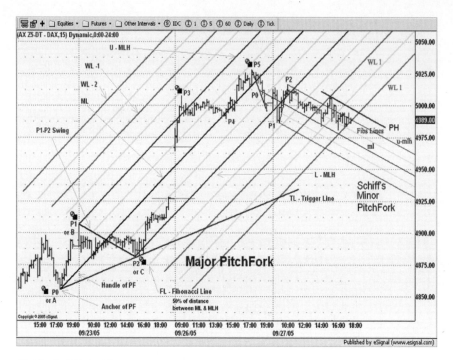

Figure 10.13 Schiff pitchfork describing a down-sloping market (cont.)
(Courtesy of www.pitchforktrader.com)

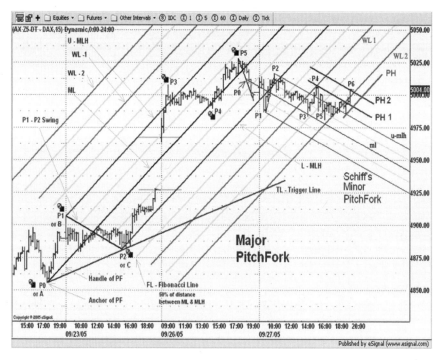

Figure 10.14 Schiff pitchfork describing a down-sloping market (cont.)
(Courtesy of www.pitchforktrader.com)

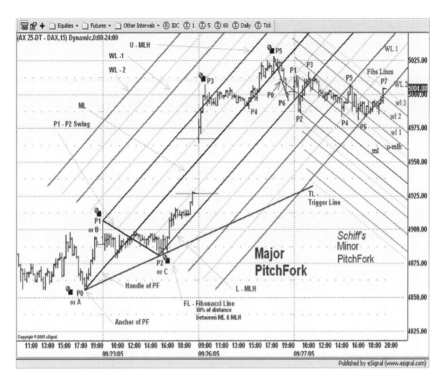

Figure 10.15 Schiff pitchfork describing a down-sloping market (cont.)
(Courtesy of www.pitchforktrader.com)

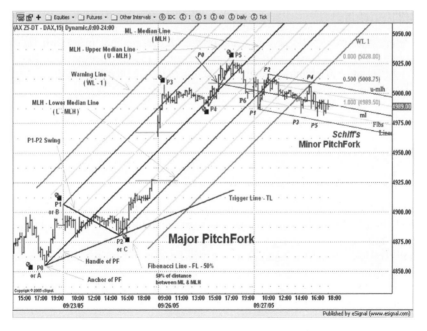

Figure 10.16 First swing midpoint used as an anchor before the highest high reversal
(Courtesy of www.pitchforktrader.com)

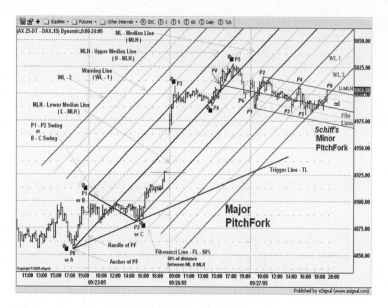

Figure 10.17   First swing midpoint used as an anchor before the highest high reversal (cont.)
(Courtesy of www.pitchforktrader.com)

constructed another version of the Schiff pitchfork by using the midpoint (5008.75 level) of the
first swing (P4−P5 swing) *before* the P5 reversal (5028 level) and then analyzing the differences.
As can be seen, the market flow is much closer to the median line of the new Schiff pitchfork
version. This serves as an excellent testing and symmetry axis.

The market flow is well stabilized within the body of the new Schiff pitchfork shown in
Fig. 10.17. The p6 pivot (5004 level) is just on the upper median line (U-MLH); the same
level on the first version of the Schiff pitchfork version (marked pivot no. 7 in Fig. 10.15) is
near warning line no. 3 of its minor pitchfork. We conclude that the latter version of the Schiff
pitchfork is much more optimal in describing the market flow.

10.5   THE T-PITCHFORK

Anchor: midpoint of A−B virtual swing *before* P1−P2 swing

A pitchfork constructed using an anchor (P0) at the midpoint of an A−B virtual swing is called
a *T-pitchfork* (Fig. 10.18). To our knowledge, this type of pitchfork is unique and has never been
described before.

The choice of the AB virtual segment will set the orientation of the future median line. It
goes without saying that the only reason that it counts is to be able to optimally describe the
ongoing market flow. The advantage of the T-pitchfork over the Schiff pitchfork is its early
influence when a new down-sloping trend is developing, which at the moment has built only the
first down-sloping impulsive swing. We do not have to wait for its correction in order to draw its
corresponding Schiff pitchfork.

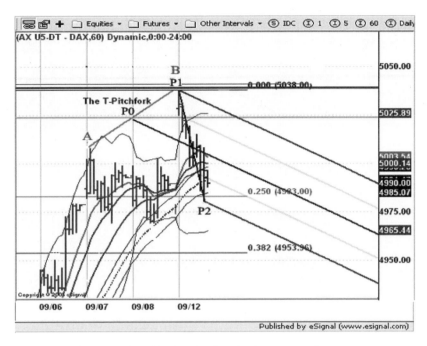

Figure 10.18 T-pitchfork using the midpoint of a virtual swing as an anchor
(Courtesy of www.pitchforktrader.com)

The 15-min chart in Fig. 10.19 represents the terrain for the construction of another T-pitchfork. We want to emphasize and better describe the local market flow, which has just bounced off the sliding parallel line (PH-1). We can see that the ML, the L-MLH and the inner lower Fibonacci line have been retained from the upper time frame (30-min chart). We frequently use this technique because of its strong halting power on the operational time frame (15-min chart).

With the A−B virtual swing selected, opposite the P1−P2 swing, we calculate its midpoint (P0) with the help of the Fibonacci tool (Fig. 10.20). We construct the median line by linking the P0 with the midpoint of the P1−P2 swing. Note that the median line of the new T-pitchfork is perfectly parallel to the local market flow, which bounces up from PH-1, rising along its lower median line (not labelled).

If we switch to a bigger (30-min) time frame, we realize that there is a choice of two pitchforks: either a traditional one (Fig. 10.21 on p. 175) or a T-pitchfork (Fig. 10.22 on p. 175). We will study both to see which one retains the most optimal description of the market flow. The traditional pitchfork uses the P0 pivot, the penultimate pivot of the down-sloping trend. We have intentionally transgressed the rule on how to number pivots for pitchfork construction (High-Low-High or Low-High-Low, respectively P0-P1-P2), because we consider that the anchor should always be labelled P0, being the origin of the pattern. If we had respected this rule, in Fig. 10.21 we would draw the pivotal anchor as the market P1 pivot, instead of P0, in the sequence P0-P1-P2.

Compare the T-pitchfork in Fig. 10.22 with the traditional pitchfork shown in Fig. 10.21. We immediately observe that the market flow is better described, because the median line has a better parallelism with the trend. Here the Fibonacci lines realize their full significance: the internal lower ones (50% Fibs) play an optimal symmetry axis, and the external lower ones (150% Fibs) are tested several times.

Figure 10.19   Constructing a T-pitchfork on a 15-min chart (Courtesy of www.pitchforktrader.com)

Figure 10.20   Calculating the midpoint using the Fibonacci tool (Courtesy of www.pitchforktrader.com)

Figure 10.21   Traditional pitchfork on a 30-min frame (Courtesy of www.pitchforktrader.com)

Figure 10.22   T-pitchfork on a 30-min frame (Courtesy of www.pitchforktrader.com)

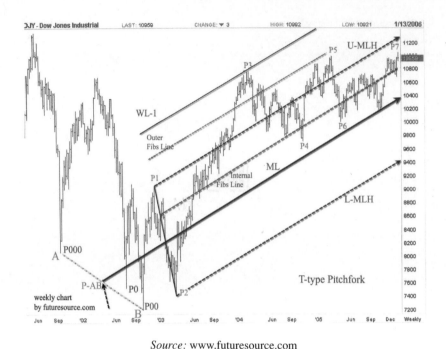

Source: www.futuresource.com
Figure 10.23   T-pitchfork on a weekly chart (Courtesy of www.pitchforktrader.com)

The weekly chart in Fig. 10.23 is optimally described by a T-pitchfork: its median line has a very ergonomic and synchronous parallelism with the trend, and the market flow continuously glides above the ML — typical up-sloping trend behaviour.

Compare the Schiff pitchfork in the weekly chart shown in Fig. 10.24 with the T-pitchfork in Fig. 10.23. We observe also in Fig. 10.24 that each pitchfork almost identically describes the market flow context, each having its own cruising channel. We also note that the T-pitchfork's ML was tested and retested twice while the Schiff's ML was not tested. From the point of view of the test and retest entry technique, we prefer to use the T-pitchfork.

10.6   THE 'HYBRID' PITCHFORK

'Suspended' anchor and P1−P2 swing of the pitchfork born out of A/R Lines

The 'hybrid' pitchfork was mentioned briefly in Chapter 3. The Action/Reaction Line (which was also briefly mentioned and which is treated in detail in Chapter 11) is the parent of the median line. Its Center Line can be perfectly assimilated with the median line of any pitchfork. The multiple tests of the ML shown in Fig. 10.25 substantially validate its choice in the process of optimally describing the market flow.

The Action Line reveals the down-sloping failure (5090 area level) and converts the internal lower 50% Fibonacci lines and, later, the up-sloping median line (ML) into Hagopian lines. The Reaction Line here performs the function of a price objective line, once the market price transgresses the median line zone. A 'hybrid' pitchfork is a result of the Action/Reaction Lines set-up.

Source: www.futuresource.com

Figure 10.24 Schiff pitchfork in a weekly chart (Courtesy of www.pitchforktrader.com)

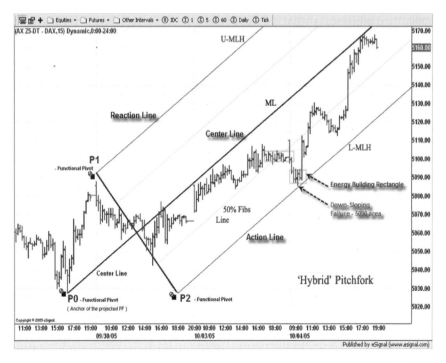

Figure 10.25 'Suspended' but functional P1 and P2 virtual pivots (Courtesy of www.pitchforktrader.com)

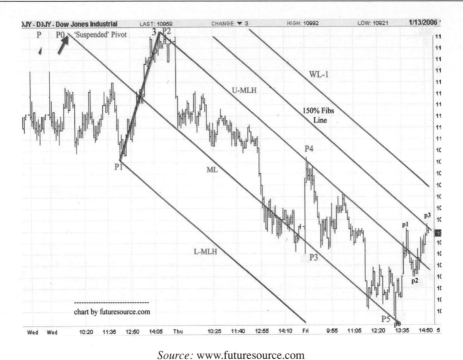

Source: www.futuresource.com

Figure 10.26 'Suspended' P0 virtual pivot but physical P1 and P2 pivots
(Courtesy of www.pitchforktrader.com)

The particulars of the 'hybrid' pitchfork are as follows.

• It may or may not have a 'suspended' anchor. In Fig. 10.26, the anchor of the 'hybrid' pitchfork is 'suspended', taking the location of the P0 virtual pivot.

• P1 and P2 may be also 'suspended' or have the same location as physical pivots. The 'hybrid' pitchfork in Fig. 10.26 has P1 and P2 physical pivots.

• Its construction is carried out progressively, as soon as the Action, Reaction and Center Lines are drawn. The usual chronological order of this phenomenon is as follows:

  (i) Draw an Action Line which faithfully describes the context of the market flow. It can be identified with the upper or the lower median line.

  (ii) Match the Center Line with the parallel Action Line. Remember that it should test at least one (and ideally several) pivot. As we have already specified, the Center Line will perfectly identify with the median line (ML).

  (iii) Complete the pattern by drawing the Reaction Line, which corresponds with one of the upper or lower median lines, and is usually reserved to use later.

Figure 10.27 is the same as Fig. 10.26. We wanted to show the integration of a 'hybrid' pitchfork in the real-time trenches of trading.

The pattern in Fig. 10.28 (on p. 180) closely resembles that of the reverse mini-median line treated in Chapter 4. But this time it is a 'hybrid' pitchfork born out of an Action/Reaction Lines set-up, which optimally describes the down-sloping market flow. The market has focused its gliding bed in the channel formed by the Center Line (median line) and the Action Line (upper median line).

Figure 10.27 Integrating a 'hybrid' pitchfork in real-time trading (Courtesy of www.pitchforktrader.com)

10.7 THE REVERSE PITCHFORK: BUILDING THE FUTURE

Past pitchfork projecting the near future

The reverse pitchfork is not frequently used because it is little known, in spite of its efficiency. It is a great help in revealing an oncoming reversal, a failure or, alternatively, a continuation movement of the market price. It covers the immediate and the intermediate past periods and then it synchronizes with the immediate and intermediate future market movements. It has the magic-like property of projecting futures moves. We will enhance this projecting move potential while using:

- the sliding parallel lines (most frequently used);
- the warning lines;
- the bearish or bullish divergence of the Momentum indicators in regard to the market price (see Volume II, in preparation).

We begin to consider constructing a reverse pitchfork right after the weight of evidence has confirmed the trend reversal (P2 pivot). We have set up the P0-P1-P2 backward-looking pitchfork sequence (Fig. 10.29), which is ready to project into the future the inherent market vibration ratios of the immediate past. We have drawn the first level of the lower warning line, delineated by the two arrows. This measured height can lead the market momentum far into the future.

Figure 10.28 'Hybrid' born out of an Action/Reaction Lines set-up
(Courtesy of www.pitchforktrader.com)

Source: www.prorealtime.com
Figure 10.29 Constructing a reverse pitchfork (Courtesy of www.pitchforktrader.com)

Source: www.prorealtime.com
Figure 10.30   Testing and retesting the warning line (Courtesy of www.pitchforktrader.com)

The market flow did exactly what was expected (Fig. 10.30), testing and retesting warning line 1 (WL-01). The downward momentum is strongly indicated, betrayed by the huge down bars, having the close at their lowest extremity. Our chosen measured height really does influence the current movement, even if it was created months ago. This is the magic of the market... Who says that the markets are random?

The market jumps warning line 2 (WL-02), only to come right back to test and retest it (Fig. 10.31). Then it continues its course toward the WL-03. It looks as though the down-sloping momentum will be ferocious.

Indeed (Fig. 10.32), warning line 3 is reached after the market flow changes direction and makes a reversal, right in the middle of the space between WL-02 and WL-03. WL-03 serves as a symmetry axis and also as support and resistance in the testing process. The WL-03 touching zone resembles that of the WL-01. It looks like the market flow is directed towards the WL-03 for a last retest.

By scrutinizing the warning line zones (Fig. 10.33 on p. 183) we can see that the measured height is still in operation, giving the opportunity for the warning lines to play either a symmetry axis or a testing function. So far it is 10 months since we first used the reverse pitchfork, and the initial measured height is not only valid but is still going strong.

In Fig. 10.34 (on p. 183), we reach the present day (February 2006) and the market is still obedient to the initial measured move, which is one year old.

We strongly recommend that you routinely use the reverse pitchfork every time a reversal is in view, combined with all the integrated factors that are treated in detail in Volume II.

Conclusion: We cannot iterate too strongly this important message:

I hope that the above study has convinced you that a seemingly random market can be transformed into a highly organized context, ready to give up — albeit with much effort and patience from the trader's part — low-risk high-probability trade opportunities.

Figure 10.31   Reverse pitchfork and warning lines (Courtesy of www.pitchforktrader.com)

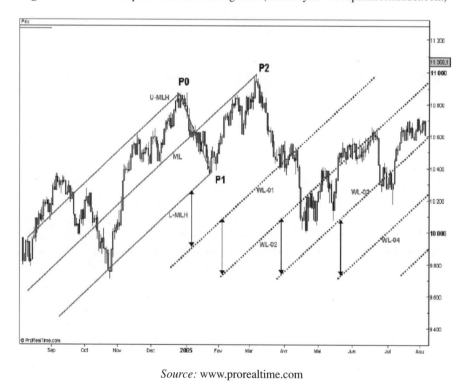

Figure 10.32   Reverse pitchfork and warning lines (cont.) (Courtesy of www.pitchforktrader.com)

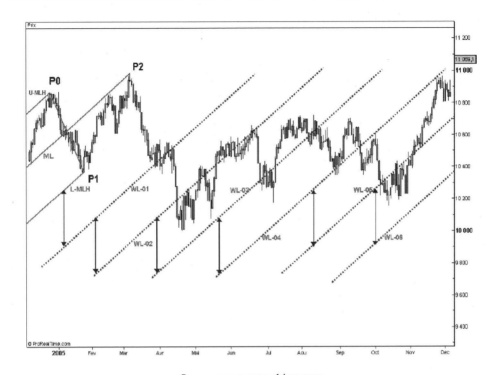

Source: www.prorealtime.com
Figure 10.33   Reverse pitchfork and warning lines (cont.) (Courtesy of www.pitchforktrader.com)

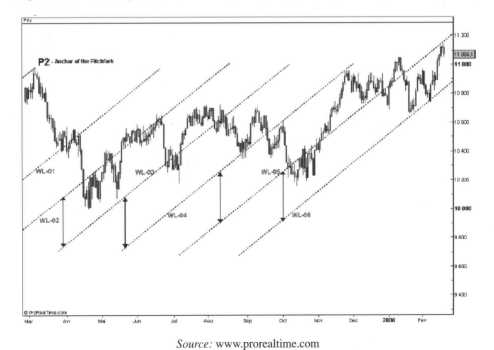

Source: www.prorealtime.com
Figure 10.34   Reverse pitchfork and warning lines (cont.) (Courtesy of www.pitchforktrader.com)

10.8   KEY LEARNING POINTS

- Remember that when there is no possibility of drawing a traditional pitchfork, the Schiff pitchfork can be drawn as an alternative.
- Don't neglect the precious assistance that Fibonacci tools give when calculating the midpoints of the two swings.
- Keep in mind Version 1 of the Schiff pitchfork. It is drawn from the midpoint (P0) of the first swing after the trend reversal (P5, P7, P9 or P11) and the opposing midpoint of the P1−P2 swing belonging to the ongoing trend.
- Keep in mind Version 2 as an alternative. Some Schiff pitchforks are drawn from the midpoint (P0) of the first swing before the trend reversal (P5, P7, P9 or P11) and the opposing midpoint of the P1−P2 swing belonging to the current trend.
- The purposes of Version 2 are multiple, e.g. the creation of confluences or the replacement of a traditional (or the Version 1 Schiff) pitchfork.
- Stay continuously focused on other types of pitchfork that you can use instead: the T-pitchfork (having a virtual anchor), the 'hybrid' pitchfork (born out of the A/R Line set-up) and the reverse pitchfork.
- Whenever the chart shows an incoming reversal, a predisposed failure or a continuation of a trend, use the reverse pitchfork; it will project its measured height into the future, which can last for months.

11
Action and Reaction Lines

The concept of Action and Reaction Lines is not frequently used by traders. If you browse through the Technical Analysis literature you can see that this topic has seldom been addressed. The first person to mention it was Roger Babson, followed by Dr Alan Andrews. Both of them practised this particular technique with huge success, making profits of millions of dollars.

11.1 DEFINITION AND HISTORICAL FOUNDATION

The efficiency of Action and Reaction Lines is based on Newtonian principles. Sir Isaac Newton (1642–1727) claimed that: 'Truth is ever to be found in simplicity, and not in the multiplicity and confusion of things.' His genius marked not only the 17th century but also the future of mankind. In his works, he stated:

> Geometry is founded in mechanical practice, and is nothing but a part of the universal mechanics . . . the description of right lines and circles, upon which geometry is founded, belongs to mechanics. Geometry doesn't teach us (how) to draw these lines, but requires them to be drawn.

He focused mainly on topics related to gravity, elastic force, levitating phenomena, the resistance of fluids and attractive or impulsive forces. In his main book *Principia* (1687) he covered the three laws of motion. Newton's 3rd Law (Action and Reaction Principle) states:

For every Action there is an equal and opposite Reaction.

Where there are two bodies, A and B, when the former (A) exercises an action on the latter (B) with an *Action* F_{AB} force, then body B exercises on A an equal and an opposite directed F_{BA} force called *Reaction*. This principle is illustrated in Fig. 11.1.

- Action and Reaction forces are always equal and opposite in direction.
- Action and Reaction forces can't be added (compounded) because each is applied to different bodies.
- Mathematically, $\overrightarrow{F_{AB}} = -\overrightarrow{F_{BA}}$. The arrows signify the vectorial character of each force, defined by magnitude and direction. These two forces are equal in magnitude but opposite in direction.

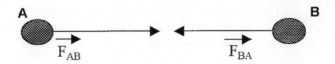

Figure 11.1   Action and Reaction principle

11.2   COMPREHENSION AND BUILD-UP

The Egyptians probably used the first Action and Reaction devices around 4000 BC as they built the pyramids (see Appendix I: Historical Basis); it seems that they discovered the Action/Reaction Principle well ahead of Europeans. Let us try to explain how we can adapt the three steps of this mechanism to the trading environment of the third millennium:

1.   *Action Phase*: The multiple composite forces of the market flow create a dominant vectorial force having its strength in the most optimal process for describing the market, illustrated by the Action Line (AL).

2.   *Equilibrium Phase*: This is represented by the Center Line (CL), which also dictates the shift of the direction of the market force vectors. It coordinates the projection of the exhaustion and restoration of the market flow's kinetic energy around cluster zones. The dynamics of the market price around this trend line will temporarily create oscillatory movements illustrated by a sinusoidal curve, travelling from one side of the trend line to another whilst at the same time piercing, zooming, testing or retesting it. In this way, the Center Line becomes the vital element in the trader's comprehension of market flow movements, in making trading decisions and in his practice of the ever-present money management technique. A pitchfork's median line is nothing more than a specialized application of the Center Line of the A&R Line set-up.

3.   *Reaction Phase*: This is a component of the newly-created market flow embedding process, having the Center Line encapsulated by the Reaction and Action Lines, each mirroring the other. This reaction phase is revealed and expressed by the Reaction Line (RL), which usually borders and may or may not contain the impulse of the vectorial forces implemented by the Center Line's measurement. The origin of these impulses comes mostly from the Action Line Zone.

11.3   CHARACTERISTICS AND FUNCTION

The Action and Reaction Principle has withstood the test of time and, more than 300 years later, the resulting structure – classical mechanics – is everywhere: in the financial markets, in business, and in our everyday life.

We now know that Action and Reaction Lines represent vectorial forces. The dictionary defines the word 'vector' as:

> *A quantity that has magnitude and direction and that is commonly represented by a direct line segment whose length represents the magnitude and whose orientation in space represents the direction; broadly, an element of a vector space.*[1]

---

[1] Merriam-Webster's Collegiate Dictionary, 10th edition, 2002

We know from our high-school days that every force carries a certain degree of energy. What better channel to carry this kinetic energy of the market flow than the structure created by the Action and Reaction Lines? They carry the market flow energy through the time−price virtual space, showing where the market could modify its kinetic energy status via:

- an energy-building rectangle or cluster, which will help the price restore its energy, and then break out from this zone with renewed momentum; or
- an entire energy exhaustion process provoking a reversal with an ensuing counter-trend movement;
- an intersection of multiple vectorial forces called a *confluence*, which promptly halts most of the kinetic forces. The greater the number of the forces that form the confluence, the stronger its halting power (for more details, see Chapter 15);
- the formation of huge bars, having 2−4 multiples of the Average True Range[2] (ATR) which will encase all the kinetic energy of the local market flow in a highly-charged movement, ready to break through the energy field at high speed.

11.4   FOUNDATION AND DEVELOPMENT

We have seen that the A&R Lines set-up is the parent of the median line (ML) concept; in other words the ML is a specific example of an A&R Lines set-up. Once this is accepted, we can go further and note that the Center Line can be not only a median line, but also a traditional or even an unorthodox trend line. The construction of this set up is described in detail in Figs. 11.2−11.7. Whichever type of trend line it represents, the Center Line:

- carries the market flow energy measurement, precisely the same tasks as performed by the median line of a pitchfork: the exhaustion or restoration of the market flow energy; the search for confluences using multiple trend lines; the projections of the bigger time frames trend lines on the operational time frame; and many others;
- is carried by multi-point structures, many more than the two points of the median line of a pitchfork (the P0 anchor and the midpoint of the P1−P2 swing). This element enhances the capabilities of describing the markets: the more numerous the birthing pivots of the Center Line, the more faithful the process of identifying the most optimal market flow embedding, the landmark of our trading decisions;
- has a specific timing in its construction compared with that of a pitchfork's median line or of Action and Reaction Lines.
    - The Center Line is usually drawn with the assistance of more than two pivots. Its trajectory can be anywhere: above the market, below the market, or through the market. It never respects market prices because it traverses the market, camouflaged among the numerous valleys and peaks.
    - It is not drawn using any midpoints of the swings.
    - It doesn't have to be drawn first, like the median line of a pitchfork. It can be drawn after the Action and/or Reaction Lines (however, in some specific cases it has to be the first line drawn in the A&R Lines set-up).

---

[2] ATR is the larger of either the distance between the current day's high and low, or the current day's high or low and yesterday's close.

- has a triple function when the trader wants to monitor market activity and which he must always keep in mind when employing this technique; it monitors:
  - the immediate or the intermediate past market flow;
  - the current market activity;
  - the price projection into the immediate and intermediate future.

11.5   CONSTRUCTING TRADITIONAL ACTION AND REACTION LINES

When the trader wants to use the A&R Lines, his ability to optimally construct this set-up can lead to a highly profitable trade. It all starts with context, as mentioned above. This format helps to crystallize the general context, and then puts an emphasis on the turbulence of the local market, which is under the influence of the contextual factor. We cannot say too many times that the best tool to capture the market's peregrinations is pivot analysis.

Looking at the chart in Fig. 11.2, we can count eight pivots, labelled 0 to 7. The market is up-sloping, probably ready for a reversal. Here the A&R Lines play a very efficient role in

Figure 11.2   A traditional A&R Lines set-up (Courtesy of www.pitchforktrader.com)

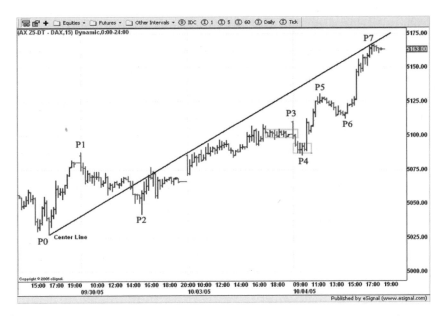

Figure 11.3 Plausible choice of position for the Center Line (Courtesy of www.pitchforktrader.com)

identifying the precise moment when the reversal will occur. This tool is conceived to:

- reveal the immediate future market movement if we believe that the reversal is imminent (as in this case study); and
- pursue the development of the trend in order to either enter the trade or, if already in, to scale in or out (progressively adding or exiting trading units).

The most plausible choice of position for the Center Line (Fig. 11.3) is obtained by linking the extreme pivots (from P0 to P7) because of the behaviour of the market price while the trend is developing: numerous trend line touches; several tests and retests; and a zoom and retest. Finally, we can see that the market flow switches its path from above to below the Center Line but, in spite of this, has safeguarded its up-sloping direction. We conclude by saying that this choice of Center Line optimally describes the market flow in its trend's development, especially in the way it mimics and parallels the trend line.

The Action Line is drawn after the market price breaks out of the P4 pivot rectangle zone. The Center Line attracts the market price once again, creating the P7 pivot (Fig. 11.4).

The Reaction Line perfectly mirrors the Action Line (Fig. 11.5). It is used when the market flow once again goes above the Center Line, toward the higher price objectives.

Once the A&R Lines are constructed, we can see that the pattern closely resembles a 'hybrid' pitchfork (see Section 10.6). Born out of this A&R Lines format, the pitchfork takes the 'hybrid' name because of its possible 'suspended' features: P1 and P2 pivots and anchor. On Fig. 11.6 (on p. 191) we have two 'suspended' but functional pivots (P1 and P2), and a 'non-suspended' pivotal (P0) anchor.

Looking at the Dow Jones Industrial Index chart in Fig. 11.7 (on p. 191), we observe that the P0 to P5 pivots have already been selected and the Action Line drawn, being aligned on the

Figure 11.4   Creating the P7 pivot (Courtesy of www.pitchforktrader.com)

Figure 11.5   Reaction Line mirrors the Action Line (Courtesy of www.pitchforktrader.com)

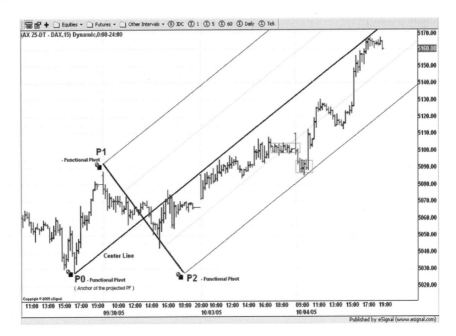

Figure 11.6 A&R Lines set-up closely resembles a 'hybrid' pitchfork
(Courtesy of www.pitchforktrader.com)

Source: www.futuresource.com

Figure 11.7 A&R Lines set-up on a Dow Jones Industrial Index chart
(Courtesy of www.pitchforktrader.com)

Figure 11.8   Center Line is creating a real symmetry axis (Courtesy of www.pitchforktrader.com)

P0-P2-P4 pivotal direction. The purpose of using this specific set of A&R Lines is to detect the exact moment when the current up-sloping trend reverses, and to prepare an eventual short trade once the breakout takes place.

Drawing the Center Line (Fig. 11.8) joins the P1 and P5 pivots. It appears that a real symmetry axis is thus created, separating the up and the down sections of the market flow

Drawing a parallel trend line through the P3 pivot to the Center Line establishes the Reaction Line (Fig. 11.9). We are now prepared for trading in both directions. Because of the steep slope of the trend and because the terminal pivot is no. 5, we expect a reversal with a strong down-sloping movement.

11.6   CONSTRUCTING GAP A&R LINES: IMAGE MIRRORING TECHNIQUE

The Center Line (which has been drawn through the gap), describes the down-sloping trend in Fig. 11.10. During its construction we linked the P0 pivot (the highest high) with the midpoint (50%) of the gap at 4962 level; Fibonacci tools were used. Once this trend line is drawn, we are not surprised to see that it optimally describes the market flow; with numerous trend line touches and an almost perfect symmetry axis which balances the market flow from above to beneath the trend line, in a pendulum-like, oscillatory movement. All this has been done in such a synchronous manner that the trend has preserved its initial down-sloping direction.

Source: www.futuresource.com

Figure 11.9   Establishing the Reaction Line (Courtesy of www.pitchforktrader.com)

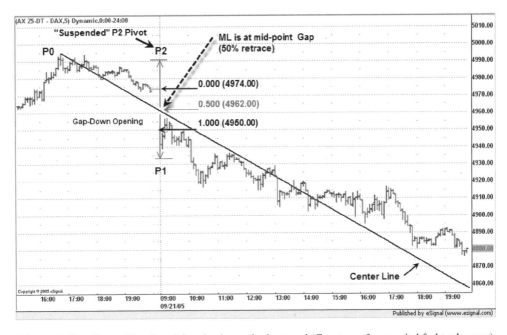

Figure 11.10   Center Line describing the down-sloping trend (Courtesy of www.pitchforktrader.com)

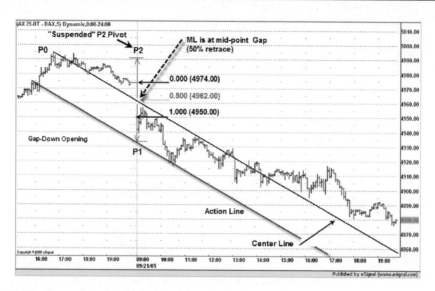

Figure 11.11 Center & Action Lines describing the down-sloping trend
(Courtesy of www.pitchforktrader.com)

Once the exact locations of the P1 and P2 pivots have been established (compare with Fig. 11.9), the position of the Action and Reaction Lines in regard to the Center Line (Fig. 11.11) seems quite obvious.

11.6.1   Image Mirroring Technique

The Action Line of Fig. 11.11 was constructed as follows.

- First, we calculated the distance between the midpoint of the gap (4962 level) and the P1 pivot location. This measure can be performed with the Fibonacci tools and used later for the construction of the Reaction Line, through the Image Mirroring Technique (see Fig. 11.12).
- Second, we have drawn a parallel trend line to the Center Line through the P1 Cartesian coordinates location, thus obtaining the Action Line.

The *Image Mirroring Technique* is of the utmost importance in the construction of the Reaction Line in Fig. 11.12. First, with the help of Fibonacci tools, we calculate the exact P2 pivot Cartesian coordinates location, creating a 'suspended' P2 pivot by using the already measured distance – P1 to gap's midpoint. Second, we extrapolate this measure above the Center Line. Third, we draw a parallel trend line to the Center Line through the P2's Cartesian coordinates location; the Reaction Line is thus constructed. This A&R Lines study automatically brings up the comparison with a *gap median line* (see Chapter 12).

11.7   A&R LINES AND THE PRICE TRANSLATION ACROSS THE MARKET SLOTS

The A&R Lines in Fig. 11.13 have been drawn to enclose the up-sloping trend. The market flow optimally travels through the channel formed by the Center Line and the lower 50% Fib line,

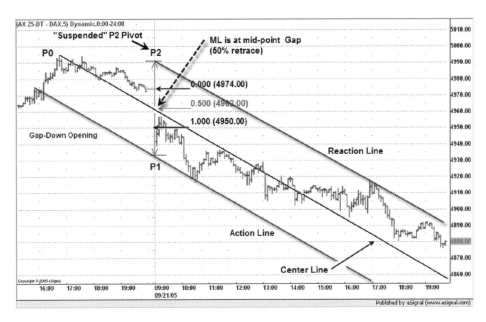

Figure 11.12   Using the Image Mirroring Technique to construct a Reaction Line
(Courtesy of www.pitchforktrader.com)

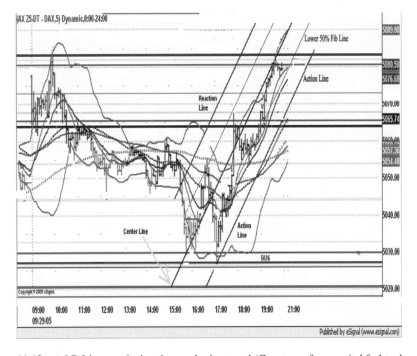

Figure 11.13   A&R Lines enclosing the up-sloping trend (Courtesy of www.pitchforktrader.com)

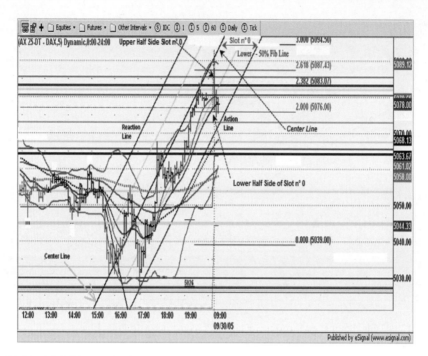

Figure 11.14   A&R Lines enclosing the up-sloping trend (cont.) (Courtesy of www.pitchforktrader.com)

just above the Action Line. The market closes at the 5080 level, being halted by a strong old gap level.

During the first 15 minutes of the opening period, the market makes a tentative upward move to break the old gap's resistance at the 5080 level (Fig. 11.14). The first huge bar has managed to upwardly pierce this strong level, but closes beneath it. The second and third opening bars are leading towards a down-sloping tendency, looking like a possible reversal.

The market flow has emerged from the channel formed by the Center Line and the lower 50% Fib line (upper half of slot no. 0), towards a lower slot space formed by the same lower 50% Fib line and the Action Line (lower half of slot no. 0). The transition from an upper-left half space slot to the lower-right half space slot (in relation to the Center Line) usually confirms a change of market tendency. The first 30 minutes of the opening will confirm whether or not this scenario is correct.

As we expected, the first 30 minutes of the chart in Fig. 11.15 set the tone for a down-sloping morning, or even predict the trend for the whole day. The translation of the market flow from the left upper slot to the right lower slot, in relation to the Center Line, is carried out in a continuous down-sloping movement, from the morning's high at the 5088 level to the midday's low at the 5056 level. This three-hour movement has the merit of illustrating the mechanism of the market price translation across the slots, from the initial slot no. 0, contiguous to the Center Line, to the Sliding Parallel Line (PH) situated within slot no. 3. The PH vigorously halts the market flow just before reaching Action Line 3. The close of the last bar is near its high, revealing a potential down-sloping failure.

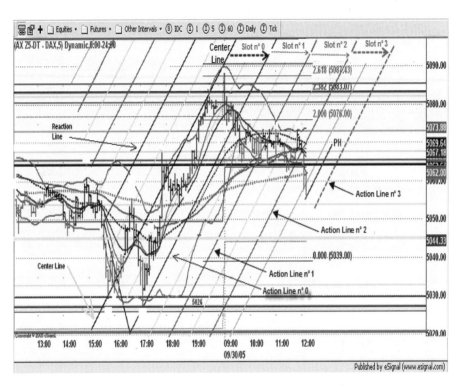

Figure 11.15   A&R Lines enclosing the up-sloping trend (cont.) (Courtesy of www.pitchforktrader.com)

11.8   CONSTRUCTING DOUBLE A&R LINES: CRISS-CROSS PATTERN TECHNIQUE

We have chosen this A&R Criss-cross Pattern Technique (like a sort of market mapping), through the dispersion mechanism of the Action & Reaction Lines around the Center Line, in order to study its influence on the outcome of the entry and on the potential results of the whole trade.

Its conclusiveness depends on the varying degrees of kinetic energy carried across the market flow by these three sets of trend lines throughout the selected 60-min time frame chart (see Fig. 11.16). The selection of their trajectory, including the choice of the pivots, becomes paramount in our quest for low-risk high-probability trades.

As we can see in Fig. 11.16, the P0 to P5 pivots have been selected and labelled. The 8-times-tested Center Line has been drawn. In this case, our goal is to study the two A&R Line constructions having the same Center Line, with the expectation of a reversal. By using it together with the Hagopian Rule, it will greatly help us to pinpoint the place and time of our trade entry.

Action Line 1 is constructed by drawing a trend line parallel to the Center Line, through the P5 pivot (Fig. 11.17).

The Reaction Line shown in Fig. 11.18 (on p. 199) mirrors the Action Line with regard to the Center Line. Its use will be very profitable once the market flow reversal begins. The Hagopian Rule will convert this Reaction Line into a Hagopian Line once the up-sloping failure in P5 is confirmed (see Chapter 6). The A&R Lines set-up 1 has been constructed in the following order: first the Center Line, then the Action Line and finally the Reaction Line.

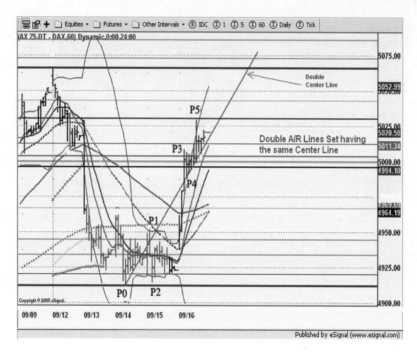

Figure 11.16   Double A&R Line construction (Courtesy of www.pitchforktrader.com)

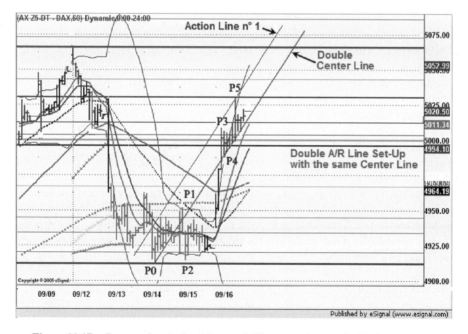

Figure 11.17   Constructing Action Line no. 1 (Courtesy of www.pitchforktrader.com)

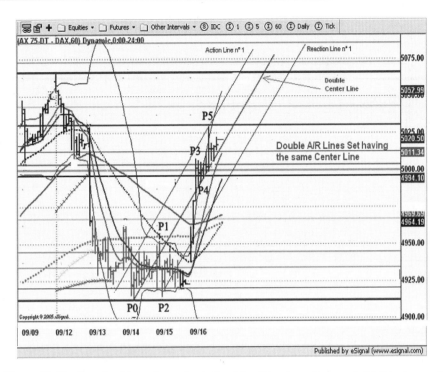

Figure 11.18   Reaction Line mirrors the Action Line (Courtesy of www.pitchforktrader.com)

To study the A&R Lines set-up 2 in Fig. 11.19, we have chosen the same 8-times-tested Center Line. Action Line 2 is constructed by drawing the tangent to the curvature inflexion of the two intersected/joint moving averages, a lower parallel trend line to the Center Line, through the Cartesian coordinates of the second higher low where the P0 pivot was the lowest low (reversal point) and the P2 pivot the first higher low.

Reaction Line 2 mirrors Action Line 2, in respect to the same Center Line (Fig. 11.20).

- The A&R Lines set-up 2 was constructed in the same order as the A&R Lines set-up 1 (first the Center Line, then the Action Line and finally the Reaction Line), although the two Action Lines (nos 1 and 2) are not on the same side of the Center Line; the same is true for the two Reaction Lines. These two sets of lines do not form a concomitant symmetry in relation to the Center Line; each side contains an Action and a Reaction Line from a different A&R Lines construction. We have deliberately chosen this type of A&R Criss-cross Pattern Technique in order to study its influence on the outcome of an entry and the potential results of the whole trade.

- Action Line 2 was constructed by tangentially drawing a line to the curvature inflexion of the two-intersected/joint moving averages.

In order to better understand this A&R Criss-cross Pattern Technique, we have purposely drawn the dual combination of the two different Action Lines, each on a different side of the Center Line (Fig. 11.21 on p. 201). Thus, we have created a better description of the current market flow, which freely travels upward through the channel formed by the Center Line and Action Line no. 1. The market rests for three bars, and is now ready to proceed either upward (having Action

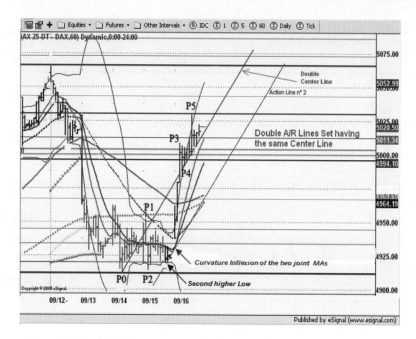

Figure 11.19 A&R Lines set-up no. 2 (Courtesy of www.pitchforktrader.com)

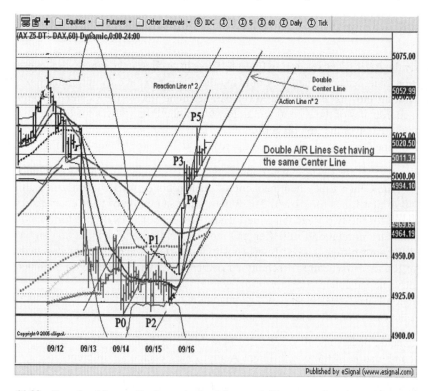

Figure 11.20 Reaction Line no. 2 mirrors Action Line no. 2 (Courtesy of www.pitchforktrader.com)

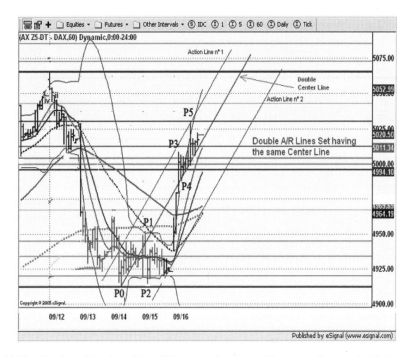

Figure 11.21 Dual combination of the different Action Lines (Courtesy of www.pitchforktrader.com)

Line no. 1 as an objective) or downward, dropping like a stone into deep waters. The latter movement will take Action Line no. 2 as its primary target. The numerous (eight) tests on the Center Line denote a strong support pleading for the continuation of the up-trend, but both the steep slope of the two moving averages and the P0–P5 labelling announce a vigorous market reversal.

Our two set-ups are now complete (Fig. 11.22) and we are ready for the market to make its next move. What will it be: a trend continuation or a fall into the abyss?

As we partially expected (see Fig. 11.23) the market drops twice its usual daily ATR (120 points worth about $3600), as a result of the political and economic instability provoked by Sunday's German election (09/18/05).

This study about the German election will cultivate our taste for *expecting the unexpected*. It will be much more profitable if, prior to our incoming German Dax Index trading day, we pay more attention to our preparation, such as looking at the status of the fundamentals: Nikkei 225, S&P 500, crude oil, Euro/US dollar and the German Bund.

Also you must take into consideration those unpredictable events which occur so frequently in our modern times: an exacerbation of ongoing conflict (such as in Iraq), acts of terrorism, natural catastrophes and, of course, the results of national elections.

Going back to Fig. 11.23, we deliberately showed it without the double A&R Lines construction. Even though it is clear that the market drop is significant, it is perhaps not as clear how a trader should have behaved at the following times:

- before the gap day;
- during the gap's day (the opening period, the morning or the whole day); and
- during the days following the gap.

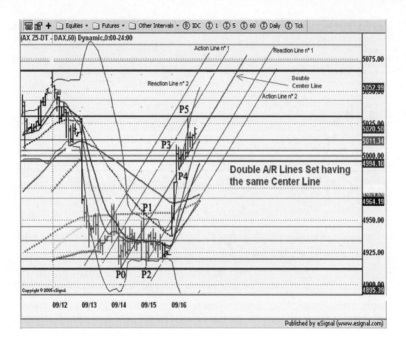

Figure 11.22   Two complete set-ups (Courtesy of www.pitchforktrader.com)

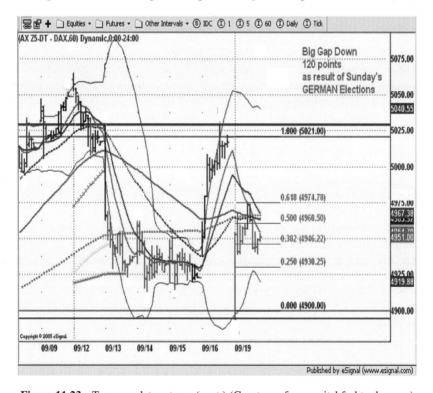

Figure 11.23   Two complete set-ups (cont.) (Courtesy of www.pitchforktrader.com)

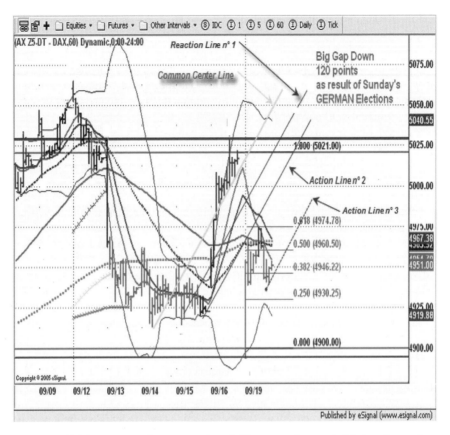

Figure 11.24   Two complete set-ups (cont.) (Courtesy of www.pitchforktrader.com)

The experienced trader would have been getting the most out of this situation (tailor-made to illustrate 'expect the unexpected'), yielding well above average profits for the trader.

Figure 11.24 is identical to Fig. 11.23, but most of the essential trend lines are already drawn. We can more clearly observe the behaviour of the market flow, and adopt the trader's attitude in an optimal manner. In spite of the huge down gap, the opening 60-mins bar retraces more than 38.2% but less than 50%.

The second opening bar climbs all the way up to the Action/Reaction Line 2, creating an almost 55% retracement. With these high-powered movements complete, the market flow enters a sideways phase, varying between the 30% and the 62% retracement zone within a rectangle. This rectangle is formed, and the last low leans against the newly-constructed Action Line no. 3.

We were earlier talking about 'getting the most out of this situation (tailor-made to illustrate 'expect the unexpected'), yielding well above average profits for the trader'. The astute trader would have thoroughly analyzed this complex trading situation, in a progressively evolving manner with several time-related aspects in mind:

- The previous day, in the *pre-close phase*, he would have noticed the equal probability chances for a next day morning trade: either a long or a short trade (refer to the text describing Fig. 11.21). I do not usually recommend entering in pre-close and staying with the market overnight (and even less over the weekend), but I must confess that there are times when it is really worth taking the risk. That Friday (09/16/05) was one of those days…!

• The pre-opening phase (refer to the text describing Fig. 11.23) emphasizes the usefulness of intensive pre-open preparation, in this case finding out who won the German elections; it was already Monday morning (09/19/05). Therefore, we could have gathered some substantiated information well ahead of the market opening and had fuller understanding of the imminent market drop situation.

• The opening bar reveals the immensity of the gap (twice the ATR) and instantly informs us of the hyper-extended volatility ('rubber band'-like phenomenon). It is not only normal but also very profitable to enter against the gap, right at the opening level of 4900, with a consistent number of multiple trading units because:

  – the market has a strong probability to revert to mean, with a strong retracement potential beyond the 50% level. It actually reached the 61.8% value (4974 level) six hours later;

  – this trade was made even more optimal by the extremely low risk of only 5 Dax points (125 euros/contract); the day's low was at the 4895 level;

  – we don't have this great opportunity very often, so the trader must be aware of them and select and apply the correct techniques. In short, the profitable reward/risk ratios are:

    a) **9** for an objective target of 38.2% retracement, calculated by dividing the reward (4946 minus 4900) by the risk (5 points) – the formula is [(4946 − 4900)/5]

    b) **12** for an objective target of 50.0% retracement – the formula is [(4960 − 4900)/5]

    c) **15** for an objective target of 61.8% retracement – the formula is [(4975 − 4900)/5].

• During the day's activity, once the 62% retracement area was reached (4974.75 level), it is almost certain that the market players will be tired after 6−7 hours of excitement, and that a sideways market activity will ensue. The sideways trader takes great pleasure here, making at least one trade profit of 20−25 Dax points/contract.

• In the post-gap trading days, in spite of the huge gap, the German Dax 30 Index does not deserve to get stuck at these low levels. It was only a matter of political context. Within five days, the industrious German stock market completely fills the huge gap, thus reaching the 5021 level once again.

Note: So far, on this 60-mins time frame, we have noticed that the market is guided by the main Fibonacci ratios: 0.382, 0.500, and 0.618.

Figure 11.25 differs from Fig. 11.24 simply by the presence of Reaction Line no. 2. It is very useful to become familiar with how well the market flow movements are regulated by the latter line, which serves as an authentic symmetry axis in spite of the dramatic and painful movements of the huge gap.

Conclusion: The efficiency of this type of Action and Reaction Lines dispersion, through the A&R Criss-cross Pattern Technique, has been fully proved.

11.9   CONSTRUCTING DOUBLE A&R LINES: SYMMETRICAL PATTERN TECHNIQUE

Figure 11.26 is the first of a series (Figs. 11.26−11.29) in which we try to illustrate another method of dispersing Action and Reaction Lines around the Center Line, but this time on 5-min

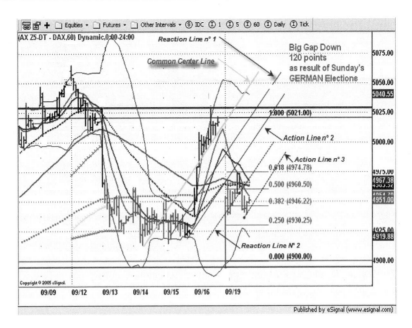

Figure 11.25   Two complete set-ups (cont.) (Courtesy of www.pitchforktrader.com)

time-frame charts. Like the A&R Criss-cross Pattern Technique, the *A&R Symmetrical Pattern Technique* has a double set of A&R Lines, but differs in that both the Action Lines are on one side of the Center Line, and both Reaction Lines are on the other. We have purposely modified the previous technique in our search for the low-risk high-probability trades.

Once we have selected the pivots (Fig. 11.26), the position of the Center Line becomes clear. It appears to optimally describe the market flow, showing numerous tests, an ergonomic role as

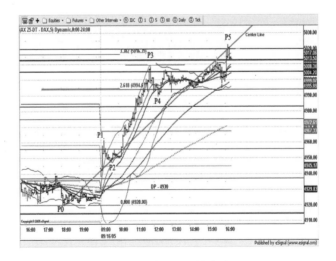

Figure 11.26   Developing the A&R Symmetrical Pattern Technique
(Courtesy of www.pitchforktrader.com)

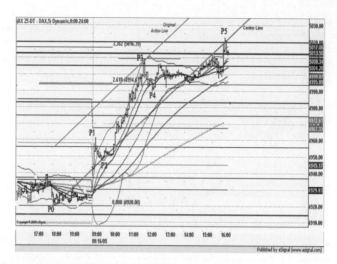

Figure 11.27 Developing the A&R Symmetrical Pattern Technique (cont.)
(Courtesy of www.pitchforktrader.com)

a symmetry axis and a logical labelling of the pivots from P0 to P5, all within the development
of the up-sloping trend.

Drawing a line parallel to the Center Line (Fig. 11.27) through the P3 pivot constructs the
Action Line of the first A&R Lines set-up, labelled on the chart as the *Original Action Line*.

In Fig. 11.28, the drawing of the double A&R Lines is complete with a double set of trend
lines gravitating around the common Center Line. The flow of the local market (the most recent

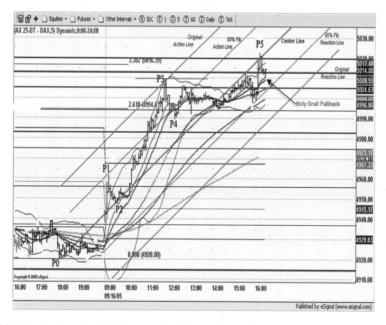

Figure 11.28 Developing the A&R Symmetrical Pattern Technique (cont.)
(Courtesy of www.pitchforktrader.com)

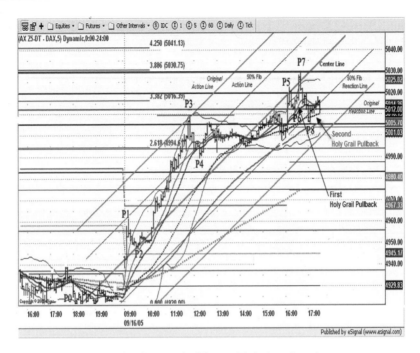

Figure 11.29   Developing the A&R Symmetrical Pattern Technique (cont.)
(Courtesy of www.pitchforktrader.com)

activity) travels along the channel created by the Center Line and the 50% Fib Reaction Line. Observe the 'Holy Grail' pullback just after the P5 pivot, leaning on the double moving averages, giving away the secret of the trend continuation. In the event that this continuation materializes, the pivots' labelling will also continue to P6, P7 or even to P9.

As we anticipated, the 'Holy Grail' pullback reveals the secret of the trend continuation (Fig. 11.29). The P7 pivot point is reached, the P8 pivot point is just terminated, and the P9 pivot point might be in progress if the ongoing up-trend continues. The market flow rides exactly on top of the 50% Fib Reaction Line, after it has tested it several times. A second 'Holy Grail' pullback is in progress, leaning on the bigger moving average.

Conclusion: The A&R Symmetrical Pattern Technique reveals another optimal way of detecting the low-risk high-probability trade.

11.10   PRE-CLOSE BREAKING-UP/DOWN TREND LINES

As can be imagined from the title, this section covers the opening period of trading through the trend lines' breaking-out process; it is a rather difficult task for the apprentice trader, but fairly workable for the experienced trader.

Figure 11.30 does not actually illustrate the A&R Lines, which are discussed and drawn in Section 11.11. However, we will see their great contribution to this kind of opening trading method, which reveals the low-risk high-probability opportunities. To our knowledge these studies have never before been published, and we are glad to share our research with our readers.

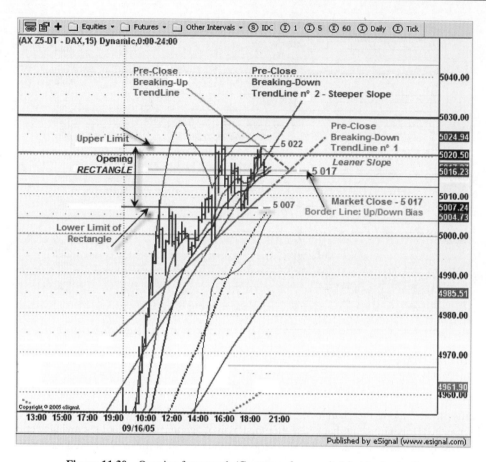

Figure 11.30   Opening framework (Courtesy of www.pitchforktrader.com)

11.10.1   Preparing the Structural and Functional Framework of Tomorrow's Opening

A thorough survey of the 15-min chart shown in Fig. 11.30 reveals the main features of the upcoming day. It is a kind of opening framework, prepared in advance and in detail, right after the close of the day's market.

- The *slant trend line* detects the probable breaking-out of the opening movements, formed in this case by three trend lines: one up and two down, the latter having two different degrees of trending slopes.
- The *horizontal trend line* forms a pre-close rectangle, composed of upper and lower horizontal limits. If the rectangle had been taller, we would have also drawn its midpoint line, with the help of the Fibonacci tools. This did not happen because, in this study, the rectangle's height was only 15 Dax points (about $440), instead of the usual minimal 20 Dax points value.
- The *border line guarantor* sanctions the location of the border of the day's market, in regard to projecting tomorrow's up/down market's bias. Its market level can be the close

of the day, or the symmetrical level of a chart pattern formation. (Many other choices are possible; this list is not exhaustive.)

- It could be the *bisector* or the *apex horizontal line* in a symmetrical triangle; this is just what has happened in our case study.
- In an ascending/descending rectangular triangle, it could be the *upper level of the upper/lower trend line opposing the hypotenuse.*
- It could be the *midpoint line* (50%), rather like a median line, between the upper and the lower rectangle's limits in a rectangle.
- It could be the *median line* in a pitchfork structure.
- It could be the *horizontally-oriented bisector* which separates the upper and lower sides of the rhomboid structure in a diamond chart formation.

Ideally, for the location of the borderline level, we prefer a cluster zone which has a stronger influence on market price behaviour when it reaches the confluence zone (cluster area). Once again, this is our case today because the apex trend line practically coincides with the day's close at 5017 level.

Conclusion: Only when we have properly resolved the structural and functional framework of tomorrow's opening constituted by the three factors (slant, horizontal TLs and border guarantor), will we really be ready to apply the A&R Lines in order to enhance the opening trading potential (see Section 11.10.2).

11.10.2   Synergy of A&R Lines and Pre-Close Breaking-out Trend Lines

We are now prepared to let the market come to us, whatever its bias will be. The break-out of the already-prepared trend lines will be sufficient to guide us in executing the entry, but insufficient to optimally manage the trade. First, we have to decide what the objective target(s) is (are) and, second, we have to decide what attitude we are going to take about the money management, the ultimate factor of a trade's profitability.

Once we have understood the opening layout (slant, horizontal TLs and border guarantor), let us go further in our understanding of a trade's management, and construct the best A&R Line set-up for this type of pre-close environment.

On Fig. 11.31 we have first drawn the P0 to P5 pivots and then the Center Line which joins the P0 and the P6 pivots. This trend line seems to optimally describe the market flow through its numerous touches: 14 between the P0 and P1 pivots, and five between the P4 and P6 pivots. These are good credentials for a Center or a Median Line and, as a result, we choose it as our only pre-close breaking-down trend line. Finally, we have also drawn the pre-close breaking-up trend line; the simplified structural opening framework is almost complete.

In Fig. 11.32, drawing a parallel trend line through the P3 pivot creates the Action Line of this set-up. The high of the spike above it creates the P5 pivot and motivates us to build an outer sliding parallel trend line above it, and its corresponding inner sliding parallel trend line; we have thus created an overlapping of two channels of almost equal width, which optimally describe the market.

The construction of a parallel trend line (through the Image Mirroring Technique) of the Action Line in relation to the Center Line creates the Reaction Line, completing the current A&R Line set-up (Fig. 11.33 on p. 211). This Reaction Line (no. 0) constitutes our minimum price objective in the event of a down-sloping market movement.

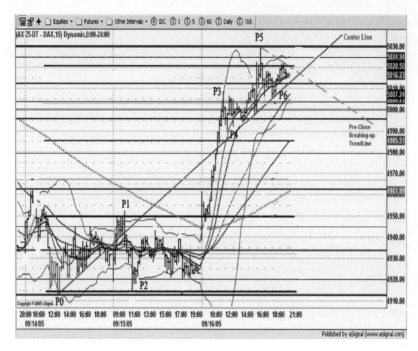

Figure 11.31   Simplified structural opening framework (Courtesy of www.pitchforktrader.com)

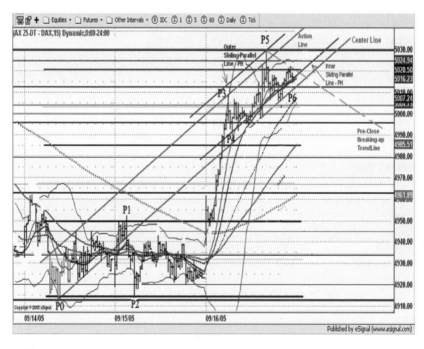

Figure 11.32   Creating the Action Line (Courtesy of www.pitchforktrader.com)

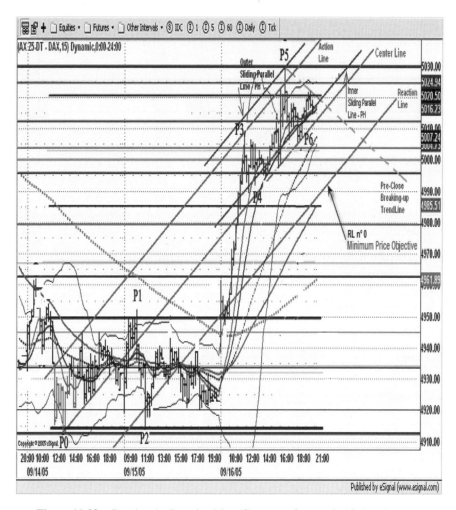

Figure 11.33   Creating the Reaction Line (Courtesy of www.pitchforktrader.com)

If a stronger down-sloping momentum takes place, either as a result of market internals or to some sort of human action, the market price could roll down to the lower price objective levels: first the classic at Reaction Line no. 1, and then to Reaction Line no. 2 or even Reaction Line no. 3 (Fig. 11.34).

As we anticipated, the market has fallen markedly from its previous close at 5017 level to the 4900 opening level (Fig. 11.34). After a very short down excursion of 5 Dax points (1 point is about $30), and while in the process of making the day's lowest low (4895 level), the market price takes a deep breath, restoring its kinetic energy, and suddenly starts to retrace upwards.

Here come into play the dynamics of the preponderant role of the Center Line and that of the four Reaction Lines (nos 0–3). In Fig. 11.34 the Center Line illustrates a textbook example of a downward break-out. The concept of 'the final indicator is a tried and tested trend line' does not work here because of the strength of the humanly-driven events which are causing the huge gap. When one of these strong lines is tested many times by the market price, it will usually increase the strength of its halting power.

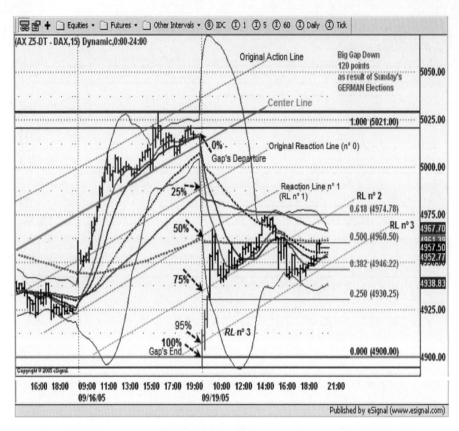

Figure 11.34   Single Center Line implicating two Reaction Lines (Courtesy of www.pitchforktrader.com)

In this case, the huge down gap has created a hyper-extended movement which, from the money management point of view, can only be managed by the systematized structure of the multiple Reaction Lines levels. Their specific layout will monitor the development of the downtrend precisely. The market's recovery (*a correction move*) to the initial market level of 5021 will enhance this energy-restoring phenomenon. This remediation process ensures the *before the event* market flow homeostasis.[3]

In brief, the multiple Reaction Lines (RLs) have had very specific roles during the hyper-extended down gap and its upward recovery.

- The original RL no. 0 slices the downward gap exactly into one quarter, at the 25% level.
- RL no.1 splits the downward gap into two quarters, close to the 50% percentage (47% to be exact). It also serves as an impregnable fortress of resistance at the morning's high 4968 level, blocking the highly-charged upward retracement for over five hours. In addition, it constitutes the upper border of the channel formed with RL no. 2, used by the market flow to reach the 61.8% retracement (4975 level).
- RL no. 2 divides the downward gap at the three quarter (75%) level. It faithfully serves as the lower border of the above-mentioned channel in which the market price travels for

---

[3] Homeostasis: a relatively stable state of equilibrium or a tendency toward such a state between the different but interdependent elements of a group (*Merriam-Webster's Collegiate Dictionary*, 10th Edition)

over six hours. With RL no. 3, it also forms the upper border of a lower channel, where the market flow will travel upward the whole afternoon, until the close of day.

• RL no. 3 almost encases the downward gap at the 95% level. It faithfully serves as the lower border of the above-mentioned lower channel, into the end-of-day close. The huge downward tails of the first and second opening bars just pierce RL no. 3, and then they both close in their bar's upper quarter, just above RL no. 3.

An *aggressive* entry would be right at the opening 4900 level, once the market reverses from its lowest low of 4895. The trader will use a tiny stop loss at the same low location. There is also an excellent *conservative* opportunity, once the market reverses and travels upward, above the close of its first bar (4911 level). The trade will take place above RL no. 3 (Fig. 11.34).

So far, on this 15-min time frame, we have noticed that the market is guided by the *Gann ratios*: 0.25, 0.50, 0.75 and 1.00. (We ought to add here: Never neglect their halves and eighths.)

Figure 11.35 illustrates the first element responsible for a well-executed, successful opening trade. Once the market price closes above it, RL no. 3 serves as a landmark in the reversal process. It not only signals the timing for the conservative entry, at the 4911 level, but also offers

Figure 11.35   First element of a well-executed, successful opening trade
(Courtesy of www.pitchforktrader.com)

a very convenient stop loss for an unusually large profit. RL 3 also serves as a second landmark, in that:

- through its first pullback, it confirms the validity of the conservative entry, once the market travels above the close of the opening 15-min bar;
- at the same time, it offers to the trader a very successful first scale-in trade entry level through its pullback's termination, when the market price reaches the high of the opening 15-min bar (4918 level). This is very clearly seen on a lower time frame (Fig. 11.35).

Conclusion: The contribution of RL no. 3 to the trade's profitability represents a very important portion, compared with that of its associates. It constitutes a real edge in the process of entering this huge down gap trade.

11.11   THE STRAIGHT PIVOT ALIGNMENT PITCHFORK

To our knowledge the study in this section will greatly help the trader to distinguish between the A&R lines and the pitchforks.

Scrutinizing Fig. 11.36, we can see that an A&R Lines construction is overlapping a P0-P1-P2 pitchfork-like structure. This is a rather interesting kind of 'parenthood', or should we

Figure 11.36   Overlapping A&R Lines set-up with a P0-P1-P2-like pitchfork structure (Courtesy of www.pitchforktrader.com)

say 'brotherhood'? ('Parenthood' illustrates the supremacy of the A&R Lines over this kind of pitchfork, and 'brotherhood' compares the two structures at the same level, and highlights the inter-dependent nature of the relationship.) The straight P0-P1-P2 alignment pitchfork depicted in Fig. 11.36 differs from the traditional pitchfork by several parameters:

- The P0-P1-P2 pivots are all aligned within the swing's trend line, just before the reversal.
- The anchor (P0) is located within the P1-P0-P2 swing, rather than on the preceding P1–P2 swing, as is the case with the traditional pitchfork. We note that the anchor, here calculated with the Fibonacci tools, is identical with the midpoint of the P1–P2 swing.
- The median line links the P0 pivot and the P3 pivot, rather than joining the P0 pivot and the midpoint of the P1–P2 swing, as is the case with the traditional pitchfork.

Once these differing parameters have been explained we conclude that, in spite of their structural differences, both structures function in the same way, without any one structure having rank over the other.

Before closing this chapter we would like to emphasize the importance of studying the market in modules in a multiple time-frame mode, as we did in these sections:

- Section 11.8: study of 60-min time frame charts;
- Section 11.9: study of 5-min time frame charts;
- Section 11.10: study of 15-min time frame charts.

11.12   KEY LEARNING POINTS

- In this chapter we *only* treated the price aspect of the A&R lines. The time aspect (cycle-related) is developed in Volume III (in preparation).
- The major role of the A&R Lines is as a vehicle for the flow of market energy through the time-price virtual space, indicating the minimal and the maximal zones prone to a reversal, acceleration, or a market consolidation.
- Keep in mind the different pitchforks closely associated with the A&R Lines: the 'hybrid' or 'suspended' pitchfork, and the straight pivots alignment pitchfork.
- The Image Mirroring Technique is invaluable every time we construct the A/R lines set-up with regard to the Center Line.
- The market price translation across the slots is a simple but very efficient method of detecting an early trend change and is closely related to the up/down failure concept.
- Don't neglect the tip about constructing an Action or a Reaction Line by tangentially drawing the curvature inflexion of the two-intersected/joint moving averages.
- In order to enhance the efficiency of the A&R Lines concept, master the methodology of the double A&R Lines set-ups (the A&R Criss-cross and A&R Symmetrical Pattern Techniques).
- Assimilate and cultivate the 'expect the unexpected' concept. Always prepare prior to the next day's trading.
- Make the pre-close breaking-out trend lines a reality in your trading and as part of your everyday routine through the use of the triad: slant TLs, horizontal TLs and border guarantor.

- The Reaction Line is invaluable when efficiently executing a trade. Make full use of it.
- Make a special effort to study the market in modules, to help crystallize your comprehension of the multiple time frames concept and the search for the market obeying ratios: Fibonacci's, Gann's or Dow's. They might differ from one time frame to another. These ratios will be described in detail in Volumes II and III (in preparation).

12
The Gap Median Line

Even although it seems inconceivable, many inexperienced traders do not use gap median lines in their trading. Why? Well ... it is a barrier embedded in our psychological reasoning. A gap is seen as an interruption that perturbs the wellbeing of a trend's development flow. Moreover, it is true to say that trading the gap necessitates a real understanding of the pre-market situation and also a full comprehension of the opening gap scene which, most of the time, can predict the future behaviour of the market flow.

The gap median line is a great help in obtaining consistency. Once the trader becomes familiar with it and other pitchfork parallels, he/she should implement a daily routine in the search for low-risk high-probability trades.

12.1 DEFINITION

The gap median line is no different in construction than the median line of a traditional pitchfork. It needs the same three pivots: the anchoring pivot (P0), and the classic midpoint of the P1–P2 swing. As the name suggests, the difference between the two lines comes in the process of selecting the set of three pivots which ultimately give birth to the gap median line:

- The anchor (P0) of a gap median line is usually situated within the gap's immediate environment:
  - on the high, the low or the midpoint of the gap location;
  - on the close level (yesterday's last bar) or the open level (today's opening bar) of the gap.

  We will see in Volumes II and III that the anchor can be calculated more precisely through the advanced study of Fibonacci, Gann and Dow ratios.
- The P1–P2 swing is usually located right at the beginning of the ongoing trend, when the first swing is terminated. Sometimes, the trader uses the second or even the third post-gap swing.
- The gap median line is obtained by linking the P0 pivot with the midpoint of the P1–P2 swing.

The only – and therefore the most important – criterion in selecting the three pivots with the corresponding swing midpoint is to match the gap median line with the trend's direction.

Optimally the gap median line should serve as a symmetry axis in order to do its best in describing the market flow (see Chapter 3).

In this chapter we will describe the different versions of gap median line, taking into account a variable location of all three P0-P1-P2 pivots.

12.2   BUILDING THE PITCHFORK WITH A GAP MEDIAN LINE

12.2.1   Version 1: Anchor (P0) Located at Open Level of Today's Opening Bar

As we can see in Fig. 12.1, the choice of the P0 pivot is at the open level of the first bar (the high of the gap). The second swing after the gap's inception was chosen as the P1–P2 swing. Once we link the P0 and the midpoint of the P1–P2 swing, we will obtain the gap median line (ML). We notice right away the symmetrical parallelism of the ML with the trend's direction, which has ensured the optimal description of the market flow.

Figure 12.1   Obtaining the gap median line (Courtesy of www.pitchforktrader.com)

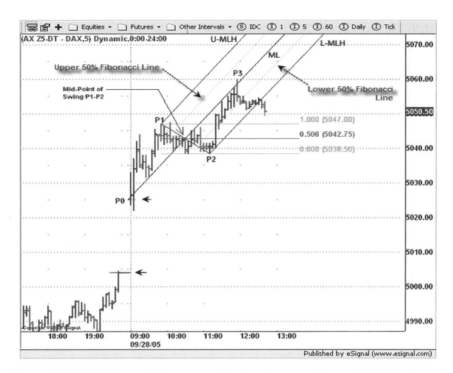

Figure 12.2   Pitchfork containing a gap median line (Courtesy of www.pitchforktrader.com)

The construction of the pitchfork containing a gap median line has been completed (Fig. 12.2). The upper and lower 50% Fibonacci lines have also been drawn. We can see that the market flow travels for a while through the narrow channel formed by the ML and the lower Fibonacci line, terminating the creation of the P3 pivot. After this big reversal bar with its close in the lower third, the market starts its translation to the right and to lower levels. It looks like the reversal has well and truly begun. After testing and retesting the lower median line (L-MLH) the market decides to continue its down-sloping movement.

The market continues to crawl downward in the process of translating its average kinetic energy across the market slots, from left to right (Fig. 12.3).

In Figs 12.4 (on p. 221) and 12.5 (on p. 222) we switch to a higher time frame (60-min), in order to reveal the overall market context. We notice that the gap median line serves as an adequate symmetry axis, optimally describing the market's trend. Even if the P01 and P02 pivots' Cartesian coordinates are not the same as those on the 5-min chart and the anchor has the same pivot location (P0), the commonality principle is fully respected. This principle establishes that specific events, tools and attributes are valid across the time frames and/or across the different markets.

Figure 12.5 is identical to Fig. 12.4, except that we have used Fibonacci tools to construct a different type of pitchfork, the Schiff pitchfork (see Chapter 10). Compared to the gap median line of Fig. 12.3, its median line joins the P0 pivot and the midpoint of the P01–P02 swing, i.e.:

*   a different P0 pivot (midpoint of the gap opposing swing);
*   the same P01–P02 swing, thus the same midpoint;
*   a 10° clockwise rotated median line, drawn above the gap.

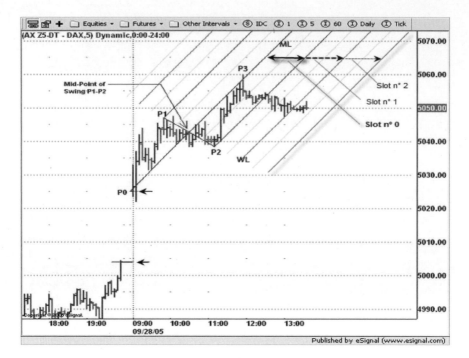

Figure 12.3 Translating the average kinetic energy across the market slots
(Courtesy of www.pitchforktrader.com)

If we scrutinize Figs 12.4 and 12.5 we note that they are both optimally describing the market flow, and that the median line on the 60-min chart is located beneath the market flow. We prefer this time frame and this type of ML because of the bigger market context visibility, and also because the market flow is above rather than beneath the ML; the magnet-like power of the ML is much greater than that of its parallels.

12.2.2 Version 2: Anchor (P0) Located at the Midpoint of the Gap

On the 15-min chart shown in Fig. 12.6 (on p. 223) we have used the midpoint of the gap as the anchor (P0) of the gap median line. We observe that the ML has been frequently tested, and actually the market sits on it, after a test and a slight pierce. The big reversal bar, with its close in the lower third and the P5 labelling has given a clue that there will be a reversal

12.2.3 Version 3: Anchor (P0) Located at the Close Level of Yesterday's Closing Bar

In Fig. 12.7 (on p. 223), we are looking at the same chart as that illustrated in Fig. 12.1, but this time we have constructed a gap median line by using the close level of yesterday's last bar as the anchor (P0) of the same P1–P2 swing.

After completing the pitchfork in Fig. 12.8 (on p. 224) with a gap median line, anchored at the gap's low, we can see that the market flow is climbing through the channel formed by the lower 50% Fib line and the L-MLH. The market price has just completed a retest of the latter.

Figure 12.4 Overall market context in a 60-min time frame (Courtesy of www.pitchforktrader.com)

At first sight, Fig. 12.9 (on p. 224) closely resembles Fig. 12.3. However, if we look more closely we can see that the price translations across the L-MLH and the warning lines (WLs) are much more visible, thus more tradable.

12.2.4   Version 4: Anchor (P0) Located Outside the Gap, P1–P2 Swing Gap's Measure (Down-Sloping Market)

The gap median line in Fig. 12.10 (on p. 225) has its specificities:

* the anchor (P0) is located outside the gap, but close to it;
* the P1 and P2 pivots are located respectively at the high and the low of the gap, thus measuring the gap's height;

Figure 12.5 Adding a Schiff pitchfork to the overall market context
(Courtesy of www.pitchforktrader.com)

- the midpoint of the P1–P2 swing coincides with the high of the opening bar and the midpoint gap, better visualized in Fig. 12.11 (on p. 225);
- the gap median line's parallelism with the down-sloping trend line is almost perfect.

As we observe in Fig. 12.11, this type of gap median line crosses the gap's height right at its midpoint. Thus, the market flow is optimally described:

- frequent tests of the gap median line, which performs a faithful symmetry axis;
- three touches of the L-MLH;
- six touches of the U-MLH;
- perfect parallelism of the gap median line with the trend line of the global market flow. Its context is profitably revealed to the trader.

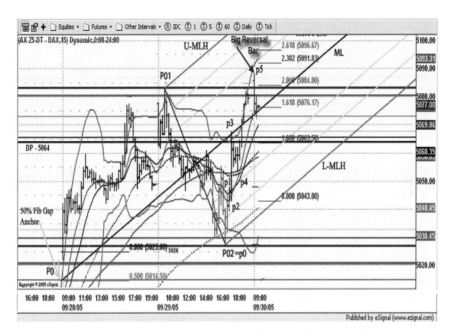

Figure 12.6   Midpoint gap anchor of a pitchfork (Courtesy of www.pitchforktrader.com)

Figure 12.7   Gap median line: using yesterday's close as anchor (Courtesy of www.pitchforktrader.com)

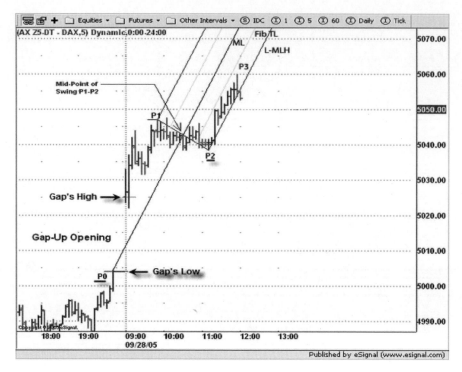

Figure 12.8 Gap median line: using yesterday's close as anchor (cont.)
(Courtesy of www.pitchforktrader.com)

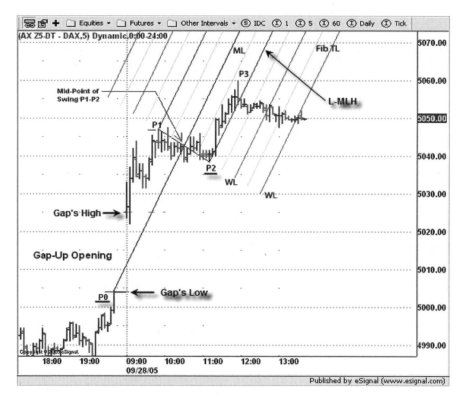

Figure 12.9 Gap median line: multiple price translations (Courtesy of www.pitchforktrader.com)

Figure 12.10 Specificities of the gap median line (Courtesy of www.pitchforktrader.com)

Figure 12.11 Gap ML crosses the gap's height at the midpoint (Courtesy of www.pitchforktrader.com)

Figure 12.12 Projecting the market outburst through the gap measure technique
(Courtesy of www.pitchforktrader.com)

Another substantial argument in favour of this type of gap median line (see Fig. 12.12) is its
ability to measure the market outburst through the intermediary of the gap measure technique.
This aspect of measuring the gap's projections into the future is treated in detail in Volume II
(in preparation).

12.2.5 Version 5: Anchor (P0) Located Outside the Gap, P1–P2 Swing Gap's Measure (Initial Sideways Market)

We will now treat the same gap median line concept on a sideways chart formation (Fig. 12.13).
Looking at the pivotal layout in this chart, we determine that we are in a non-trending market.
By linking the P0 and P2 pivots we obtain a horizontal resistance, limiting the upside potential
of the market flow, and by joining the P00 and the P1 pivots we get a horizontal market support,

Figure 12.13 Gap median line on a sideways formation (Courtesy of www.pitchforktrader.com)

ready to halt its down-sloping tendency. The two horizontal lines create a breakout layout, very useful for trading decisions. On analyzing this layout again, at first sight we are ready to trade this sideways market. However, we will see that this is not the only possibility.

The gap median line concept will help us to consider the situation in a completely different way than most other traders. How? The intra-rectangle location of the up-sloping gap and the double tops formed by the P0 and P2 pivots have created an urgent need for the market gap to be filled as soon as possible, even if it takes several days. This is an idiosyncratic parameter applicable to any type of market having a high degree of liquidity. It acts like the attracting functionality of the median line and its parallels. We can add that any horizontal parallel lines drawn from the gap's open, close, low or high will take the shape of a virtual citadel, blocking efforts whenever the market tries to break them.

In Fig. 12.14, we are in the process of building a gap median line using the Fibonacci tools. The gap median line will link the P0 pivot with the midpoint of the P1–P2 swing, which is also the gap's height, so is indispensable in applying the gap measure technique.

Once the pitchfork is completed (Fig. 12.15), we can see that the current market initially seems to have a sideways bias but, in reality, it also presents a down-sloping tendency. Without the gap median line, this would not have been visible. The 75% Fibonacci line has already been tested five times. This leads us to believe that there is an imminent move (within 1 to 3 bars time period), with the high probability of a down-trend and also a less probable up-sloping swing.

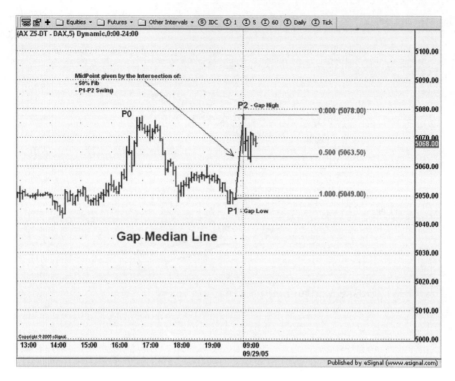

Figure 12.14 Building a gap median line with Fibonacci tools (Courtesy of www.pitchforktrader.com)

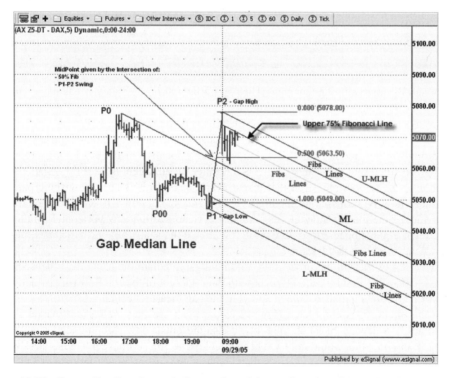

Figure 12.15 Gap median line: down-sloping market tendency (Courtesy of www.pitchforktrader.com)

Figure 12.16   Gap median line: down-sloping market tendency & external Fibs lines
(Courtesy of www.pitchforktrader.com)

By now we have observed that the P0-P2-P00-P1 rectangle-like structure has been punctured and halted by the external Fibs lines. In spite of the two outside closes of the mirror bar structure, the following bar (the last bar on the chart of Fig. 12.16, which is not yet closed) fluctuates under the P0–P2 resistance line before it definitively closes beneath it in its lower quarter.

Could it be a false breakout, or rather a pullback, which will ensure the continuation of the ongoing up-trend? Remember that false breakouts are composed of:

• the throwbacks (price returns to the breakout point and even lower, within a few bars of being halted while dropping towards the opposite extremity line – here the P00–P1 support line);
• the bull trap (impersonates the precise throwbacks that will drop beyond the support line, farther into the underneath area). On the chart shown in Fig. 12.16, we rather plead for the bull trap situation because of the mirror bar structure. Most traders will believe in a new up-swing.

(Although it seems that we have diverted somewhat from the gap median line discussion, I firmly believe that it was worth the detour, especially when one realizes that the throwbacks and bull

Figure 12.17   Bull trap illustrated by a pitchfork (Courtesy of www.pitchforktrader.com)

traps represent about 25% of all breakouts, with the former happening more than twice as often as the latter.)

Next (Fig. 12.17), the original sideways-looking market drops like a stone, catching the traders in the bull trap all the way down to the 5027 lowest low, from a breaking point at the 5078 level. The down-sloping market flow is steady, balancing from one side of the upper median line to the other. If we had drawn its movements, we would have obtained an almost perfect oscillatory dynamic curve. The down-oriented momentum is pretty constant in its strength even though the market price tries a weak up-trend swing, but it reverses properly after testing the upper warning line (WL).

Finally (Fig. 12.18), the market approaches the first upper warning line (WL-1) once more, resulting in an acceleration process with a prior test and retest. This sudden move is expressed by a single huge bar move of 18 points, more than three times the value of the ATRs (Average

Figure 12.18   Climbing the ladder of warning lines (Courtesy of www.pitchforktrader.com)

True Range of MA(21) where MA = Moving Average) on this time frame. This unusually high bar links WL-1 and WL-2, testing the WL-2 in the process.

Once across WL-1, exhausted by this highly-charged move, the market flow restores its up-sloping energy by cruising along a slightly inclined down-sloping channel, right beneath the WL-2. The price breaks up through WL-2 with enough stored-up momentum to get the market flow all the way up to the WL-3 frontier, in an organized manner. Once again the market flow recharges its stock of energy, and makes a last up-move, closing the day right on the External Fibonacci Line no. 4, half-way between the WL-3 and WL-4 (not shown).

Now ... Look again at the above chart, think for a minute, and see where you would put the most optimal minor pitchfork after the close of the 5080.50 level. The answer is just one chart away, where Fig. 12.19 presents one of the best choices. At this stage of studying the book, there should be no problem in drawing a minor pitchfork optimally describing the local market flow!

The chart in Fig. 12.20 resembles Fig. 12.19 in that it is the same 5-min time frame, but showing a different market day. This is a textbook example of building, studying and using the technique of the gap median line. We will let the reader analyze it in the same way as with the prior chart. Once this is done, please proceed to the next chart (Fig. 12.21 on p. 233) to study

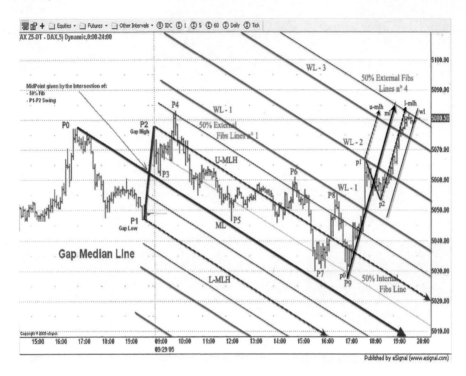

Figure 12.19 Climbing the ladder of warning lines (cont.) (Courtesy of www.pitchforktrader.com)

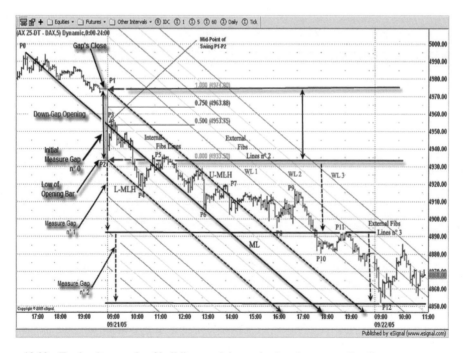

Figure 12.20 Textbook example of building, studying and using the gap median line (Courtesy of www.pitchforktrader.com)

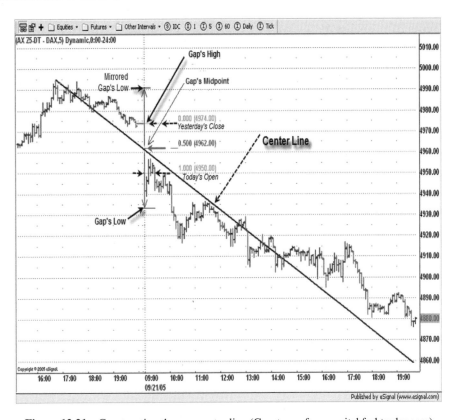

Figure 12.21   Constructing the gap center line (Courtesy of www.pitchforktrader.com)

the Action and Reaction Lines set-up, through the gap center line (that valiant parent of the pitchfork's gap median line).

Version 7: Similarity with a Gap Median Line

Once all the facets of the gap median line are understood, let us now study its intricacy with the Center Line of the A&R Lines (see Chapter 11).

The construction of the gap Center Line, shown in Figs 12.21–12.23, uses yesterday's high and the midpoint of the gap at the 4962 level. Its drawing reveals the degree of market description, which is directly dependent on the selection of the pivots supporting the Center Line, with their intrinsic consequences:

- the numerous price touching points, confirming its magnet-like power;
- the symmetry axis function role;
- the parallelism with the down-sloping trend line, thus revealing the context of the entire market on this time frame.

We have prepared the drawing of the Action and Reaction Lines, where we calculated the Cartesian coordinates of the low of the gap and also its mirrored coordinates, in relation to the Center Line (see Fig. 12.21).

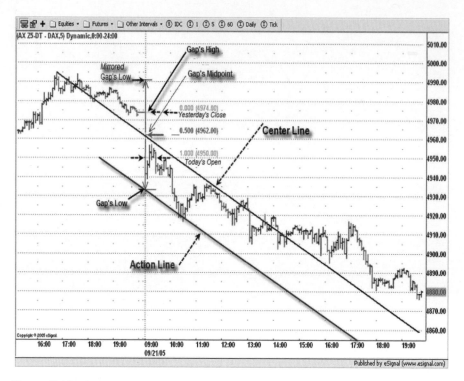

Figure 12.22   Constructing the gap center line (cont.) (Courtesy of www.pitchforktrader.com)

The Action Line (AL) is easily obtained (Fig. 12.22) by drawing a parallel trend line to the Center Line, through the low of the gap.

We can see in Fig. 12.23 that the Center Line has optimally described the market flow, based on: the number of touches, the symmetry function and the degree of parallelism with the whole market trend line. The Reaction Line here is a parallel trend line going through the mirrored low of the gap, in relation to the Center Line.

Now let us examine in depth the comprehensiveness of the gap Center Line and analyze the A&R Lines set-up completed in Fig. 12.23:

- The Center Line (CL) optimally describes the market flow.
- The Action Line has been tested five times. It also assisted the market to reverse towards the Center Line (the 'return to mean' phenomenon – see Glossary).
- The Reaction Line (RL) has also been frequently tested, and twice has deflected the market flow downward to the mean (CL). In the context of this A&R Lines set-up, we must not forget to mention the indispensable role taken by the Reaction Line in the process of entering the trade when the market flow burst out of the current A&R Lines set-up. (This was treated in detail in Section 11.10.)

The last illustration (Fig. 12.24) of this section will remind the reader that symmetry is a main feature in interpreting the market flow. We know already that the A&R line construction is the parent of the pitchfork. In Fig. 12.24 the A&R Lines give birth to a derived P0-P1-P2 pitchfork, having a 'suspended' pivot (P2).

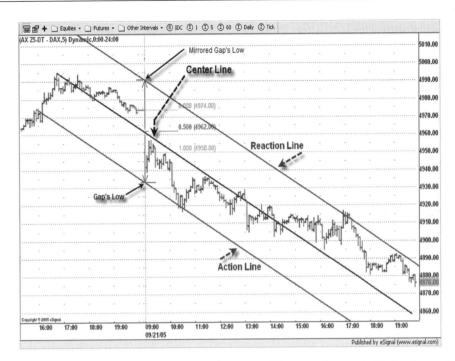

Figure 12.23   Constructing the gap center line (cont.) (Courtesy of www.pitchforktrader.com)

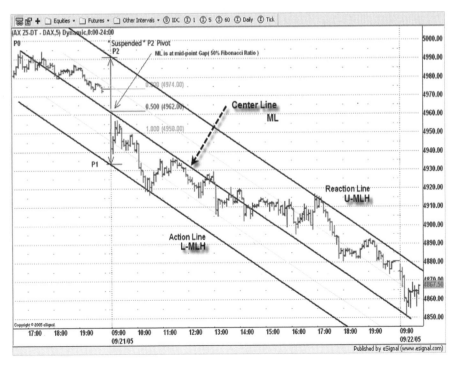

Figure 12.24   Symmetry is a main feature in interpreting the market flow
(Courtesy of www.pitchforktrader.com)

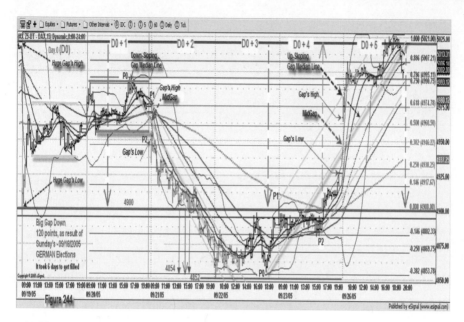

Figure 12.25   Illustration of creation of a huge down-sloping gap (Courtesy of www.pitchforktrader.com)

All the elements of these structures can be intricately connected so that they can build up highly interdependent phenomena. Shall we say synergy,[1] or perhaps the medical word commensalism[2] is more suitable?

12.3   MULTIPLE GAP MEDIAN LINES AND OTHER CHART PATTERNS

We are now able to interpret the consequences of a gap median line on the market flow. But, what happens when the market flow necessitates multiple gap median lines? Or, even more complex, how would you proceed when the market price makes a huge gap, and you have to understand the intricacies of different chart patterns during the gap-filling period?

Well . . . ! Let us take one subject at a time, and employ the Technique of Module Learning so that our procedure is to:

- first, divide the gap-filling interval into multiple modules; and
- second, once you have drawn a conclusion for each individual module, assemble the parameters that will enable the best trading decisions. Do not forget to integrate the conclusions of the study of the immediate pre-gap interval with those of the post-gap filling period. It is nothing more nor less than the old saying: 'Analyze, synthesize and finally decide!'

We take as a study chart Fig. 12.25, which illustrates the creation of a huge down-sloping gap taking place over the weekend. The ascending steps fill the gap, ending the turbulent behaviour between its creation and ending.

---

[1] Synergy: a mutually advantageous conjunction or compatibility of distinct elements, *Merriam-Webster's Collegiate Dictionary*, 10th edition.
[2] Commensalism: two organisms which live together, neither bearing a parasitic relation to the other, without harm or prejudice to either but with one or both members deriving benefit. *Stedman's Medical Dictionary*, 23rd edition.

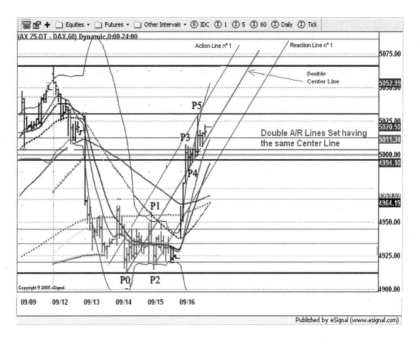

Figure 12.26 First four days preceding the gap in Fig. 12.25 (Courtesy of www.pitchforktrader.com)

As we have mentioned, this double daily ATR (Average True Range) gap is a rare event in the history of trading the German Dax 30 Index. The full responsibility for this major event can be attributed to the results of the German Elections during the weekend of 17 and 18 September 2005.

12.3.1 Pre-gap Period

Our first module (Fig. 12.26) shows the pre-gap period which is composed of four days: a three-day energy-restoring consolidation period followed by a pre-gap day (16 September 2005) fully occupied with the up-sloping trend development. The trend is visualized on the right side of the chart, having the following characteristics:

- a very steep slope, above 45°, nearly at the 55° angle;
- a very visible line, with labelled P0 to P5 pivots;
- does not terminate its upward potential. The pre-gap day's close is at the 5017 level, and the five-day-old high has not yet been taken (about the 5066 level).

12.3.2 First Day Gap Period (D0)

- The size of this huge gap is, as we have said, two daily ATRs.
- The open is exactly at the 4900 level. (We always say that the majority of traders love those levels exactly numbered in hundreds, fifties or tens.) The market does the trader a great favour because, after the opening, the price falls even lower to 4895 before reverting to the mean, and all this within the first 3-min bar (refer back to Chapter 11, Fig. 11.36).
- Once it takes off, the price evolves with an almost vertical slope, straight to its 50%–61.8% retracement zone, within only five 15-min bars time period (see Figs 12.25 and 12.27).

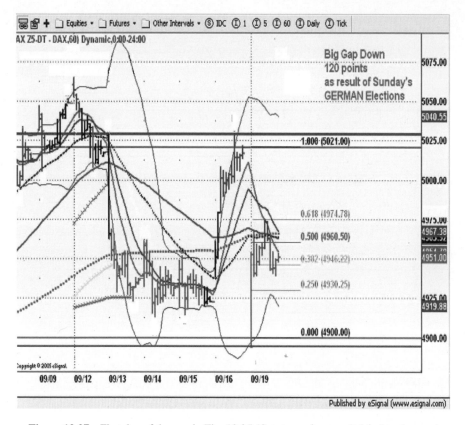

Figure 12.27   First day of the gap in Fig. 12.25 (Courtesy of www.pitchforktrader.com)

- The golden ratio location of 61.8% (4974.50) is attained at exactly 15:00 CET (30 minutes before the opening of the NYSE).
- The rest of the day the price fluctuates in a trading range of 30%–62% retracement zone (see rectangle on D0 interval on Fig. 12.25).

12.3.3   Second Day Gap Period (D0 + 1)

This constitutes another trading range, but this time higher, between the 50%–78.6% retracement zone.

Once again, the Fibonacci level at 78.6% (which, together with the 88.6% point, I call the *Despair Return Point*) halts the market flow at exactly the 4995 level. Follow these Fibonacci ratios levels by looking at the right side of the chart illustrated in Fig. 12.25.

Prior to the final huge, gap-filling momentum, reaching these levels was the last chance where a Fibonacci location could be taken into consideration for a possible downward reversal (*correction of a correction*). Above these levels, the reversal process would be invalidated. The reversal at the 78.6% level is a signal that the market will reverse towards the main support of the gap (4900 level), before having a second gap-filling attempt. This level could be considered as the locus (P0) of a future pitchfork anchor, given its psychological importance.

12.3.4 Third Day Period (D0 + 2)

The third day period not only continues the down-sloping momentum begun at the 78.6% reversal point, but also adds to its strength (Fig. 12.25). The presence of the down-gap has favoured our planned median line, so we draw it from the 78.6% anchor through the midpoint of the day's down-gap. This ML has now become a *gap median line*, with greater tendencies than those of the traditional median line. Very quickly we notice that this gap median line gives an optimal description of the market flow:

- numerous touching points;
- a fully-imitated parallelism with that of the down-sloping trend line; and, of course,
- a textbook example of its symmetry axis function.

Once the gap median line has been drawn, it should be closely followed until the termination of the down-trend. The upper gap median line will be the landmark of a definite up-sloping reversal. We *expect* a very strong support at the 4900 level, with a possible strong bounce... But the *reality* may be quite different! As we always say: Let the market come to you. Don't be impetuous and try to anticipate its movement but, instead, always be ready to react to its unexpected behaviour!

In other words: Always expect the unexpected!

Under the influence of the US markets, one hour after the NYSE opening the German Dax 30 market flow not only breaches the 4900 level, but also drops even lower to the 4875 level, closing a few points above.

12.3.5 Fourth Day Period (D0 + 3)

During the first 30 minutes, the market drops even lower, bottoming at the 4850 level. Then it is confined to a trading range all day, being held under the huge gap's opening level of 4900. It is important to note that we have used *negative Fibonacci ratios* (see the right side of the chart in Fig. 12.25), which have the power of revealing the degree of the market drop, under the initial huge gap's opening. With this hyper-extended market, we can already start looking for the equivalent of the 78.6% location (see Section 12.3.3), to be used as the anchoring point (P0) of the future up-sloping pitchfork. This will guide the market flow to a very probable 100% filling of the huge gap which is already 4 days old. We scrutinize two possible locations, which could become the anchor location of the awaited pitchfork:

- the approximate $(-)$ 38.2% location (4850 level) impersonating the lowest low so far; and,
- the exact $(-)$ 38.2% location (4854 level) representing the first higher low.

Even if these two points have price Cartesian coordinates only four points apart, the selection of either will greatly affect the future pitchfork's median line slope, even if we use the same midpoint of the same P1–P2 swing. Anyhow, during this phase it is too early to make any choices. We will have to wait for the breakout of the 4900 level, and the creation of an up-gap or a significant swing.

12.3.6   Fifth Day Period (D0 + 4)

This period is predominated by a fairly narrow trading range (4882 to 4900), about 18 points, which represents less than 50% of a normal daily ATR of 54 Dax points (1 point is equal to approximately $30). Finally, around 17:00 CET (90 minutes after the NYSE opening) under the influence of the US markets, the market price finally breaches the 4900 level, with the help of a big bar. Within three hours, the market flow recovers almost a quarter (23.6%) of the lost battlefield, closing upwards at around the 4927 level. However, there are still another three-quarters to be recovered in order to completely fill the huge gap.

At this stage of the market development, we are able to observe that the 4854 level constitutes a better anchor (P0) position than the 4850 level. Once the P1 (high of the opening bar) and P2 (the terminal low of the day) pivots are chosen (Fig. 12.25), we have drawn the median line of the up-sloping pitchfork.

12.3.7   Sixth Day Period (D + 5)

This starts strongly, with a substantial up-gap of around 40 points from yesterday's close of 4927 to today's open of about 4967. And guess what . . . the median line drawn yesterday divides the gap just in half at the 4947 level. We can now relabel the up-sloping median line as a gap median line, which optimally describes the market flow's filling of the five-day-old huge gap.

The market price reaches the 88.6% retracement 5007 level, another mythical Fibonacci ratio, at the end of the first opening hour. Then it decides to trade during the next eight hours in a rather tight range of about 15 points. Once again, under the influence of the US markets, at 17:00 CET (90 minutes after the NYSE opening and the same time as yesterday's breaching of the 4900 level) it finally surges in two huge up-sloping bars and attains the initial level of 5021, completely filling the gap. After spending about two hours above this level, it suddenly returns underneath it, and makes the day's low at 4995 level, again the 78.6% mythical Fibonacci ratio.

Conclusion: After analyzing the filling of this huge gap, over a period of six trading days, we can now conclude that the choice of using the gap median line has greatly assisted us in our analysis, in order to trade this specific type of market. We could add that the selected 15-min and 60-min time frame charts were both more than adequate. The market closely obeys the Fibonacci ratios, especially those two mythical values of 78.6% and 88.6%, which many traders do not use with any frequency.

12.4   KEY LEARNING POINTS

- The gap median line should be the first tool to be used at the opening of the market. It can be prepared, or even drawn, into yesterday's pre-close. The potential anchor candidate (P0) is established for an up-sloping pitchfork at the low or at the immediate higher low of the immediate/intermediate pre-close past swing, for up-trends and vice versa for downtrends.
- Be prepared for the transformation of a traditional median line into a gap median line as soon as the day's gap is unlatched.
- Do not neglect to consider any other gap median line construction which utilizes the old highs or lows of the previous day, or even the day(s) before that.

- The building of a gap median line is based on an optimally selected P0, and also P1–P2 set of pivots. Its validity and adaptability are heavily dependent on this choice. The location of the anchor (P0) is mainly within the gap's close, open, high, low or its midpoint. It can be also selected within the predominant pivots of the gap's immediate environment, on condition that the median line traverses the territory of the gap.

- When trading intra-day, do not hesitate to search across higher time frames (30-min, 60-min, 120-min or even 240-min) to find the most visually dominant trend.

- With the risk of sounding trivial, you should routinely compare the position of the market flow in relation to the gap median line (or any median line), while performing the selection process. We prefer it when the market flow evolves above the median line rather than beneath it: the magnet-like power of the ML is much greater than that of its parallels.

- Whenever you are in the process of drawing a pattern across an opening, think of the similarities of an A&R Lines set-up and the gap median line.

- We cannot overemphasize the contribution of the Reaction Line to a trade's profitability. It represents a real landmark in the process of entering the trade.

- The kinematics of filling a gap represents a crucial factor in the process of learning to trade. It could become a real edge in your life as a trader if you practise this hard enough, by analyzing hundreds or even thousands of gap-filling charts. The gap is and remains a mysterious beast in the mind of most traders. So, once again ... you had better be prepared for the unexpected!

- As they say ... most people learn from trial and error. Try to take advantage of an event already experienced, and develop from this an everyday routine. Once a certain Fibonacci value keeps repeating in a certain time frame, especially the less frequent ones (78.6% or 88.6%) then learn to religiously trace and use them in the future, but only on that specific time frame where they apply. The same argument is valid for any other types of ratio.

- The gap median line concept is validated by the *commonality principle*, which establishes that specific tools and attributes are valid across the time frames and/or across the different types of markets.

Conclusion: Whenever the learning process challenges you, just remember and then apply the Technique of Module Learning. Even though it was first used around 1855–1860, it still represents the state-of-the-art learning process today.

13
Breakaway and Runaway Gaps

Gaps and their trading have always been a mystery for traders. Most intra-day traders know that the majority of gaps are filled within the same day or the following few days. Very few gaps remain unfilled, although when trading Futures and the front contract expires, the existing gap might remain unfilled. The gap's occurrence is due to internal or external factors that influence the market and upset the equilibrium.

13.1 DEFINITION

The definition of the gap is pretty simple because it is pretty conspicuous. The trader can't help automatically noticing this interruption to the market flow. Richard W. Schabacker, who traded during the 1930s (the same period as Roger W. Babson) is one of the most prominent founders of modern-day Technical Analysis. In his second book, *Technical Analysis and the Stock Market* (1932), he wrote:

> *Gap is a stretch of 'open water' between the price range of two successive trading days as pictorialized on our stock charts.*

The reality of the interruption to the market flow, given shape by the existence of the gap, makes us accept the gap's lower and higher limits as the close of the last bar and the next bar's open respectively.

Thus the definition of a gap on a daily chart is the *interval between yesterday's close and today's open*. It becomes vital for the trader to understand the gap's boundaries when he uses its height in his measuring techniques. In spite of this, it is always possible to consider the gap as a chart formation, having its limits between the gap's high and low. As we know, geometry and the market frequently form a harmonious symbiotic pattern, and the correct definition of the boundaries can make all the difference.

Richard W. Schabacker was aware of the Action and Reaction Principle, and he applied it, not only to explain the gap's mechanism, but also to his everyday successful trading. In his first book, *Stock Market Theory and Practice* (1930) he explained:

> *The laws of action and reaction account largely for still another technical chart tendency which is often valuable, especially in short-term trading. This is the formulae for covering gaps in chart trading. A chart gap or spread is a vertical gap, or open*

Figure 13.1   Gap context chart (Courtesy of www.pitchforktrader.com)

space, between one day's range and the next. . . The theory is that sooner or later the
stock will return and 'cover' this spread or gap. When the spread is not covered it is
almost always followed by a very long and profitable major movement in the direction
of the original spread.

The mystery of the gap will rapidly be solved when its foundation and development mechanisms are fully understood.

Now that we understand the definition of a gap, let us see how we can progress with the
learning process. In order to understand the gap, we invite you to carefully observe Fig. 13.1, on
which we have purposely omitted any drawings or markings, except the market price.

13.2   THE GAP CONTEXT AND THE SYSTEMATIZED VISUALIZATION TOOL

Before we go into the details of a gap, we must study the context in which it develops. By
looking at Fig. 13.1, from left to right we can easily see a series of interruptions in the market
flow. In order to capture the important details the best approach is to train us to scan them
systematically.

This simple tool of *systematized visualization* will immediately reveal that the whole chart
consists of several types of module which in turn create portions of the chart that optimally
describe the market. The first chart module, using the *swing distribution technique*, is the first

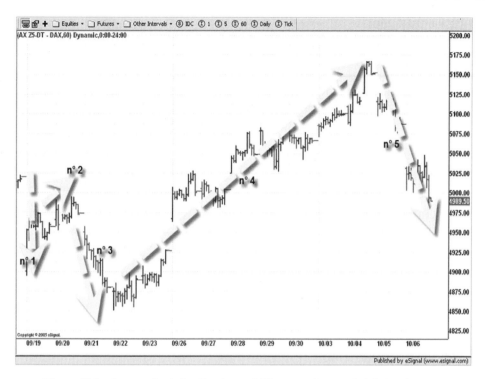

Figure 13.2   Systematized visualization tool (Courtesy of www.pitchforktrader.com)

element that will help the trader to fully understand the contextual concept. Starting from left to right, we see in Fig. 13.2:

1.   A large zigzag pattern composed of swings 1, 2 and 3, which leads the market flow in a down-sloping trend.
2.   A very strong up-sloping swing (no. 4), which has a steep 45° slope. It not only corrects the previous down-sloping zigzag trend but more than doubles its length.
3.   A zigzag pattern with a very steep (28°) slope composed of swing no. 5. It is dropping with the market flow so quickly and forcefully that the trader would expect the corrective move to retrace beyond the 100% value.

In Fig. 13.3 we continue to apply the tool of systematized visualization. Our second module uses the *territorial distribution technique*. The purpose is the same as above: to fully understand the contextual concept. This technique immediately reveals the whole market concept composed of three territories, from left to right:

- **Territory no. 1** encloses the three swings (see Fig. 13.2) whose trend has a predominant down bias, containing three gaps.
- **Territory no. 2** encases only one swing, which has an almost continuous up-sloping movement and five gaps.
- **Territory no. 3** has only one swing, which has the hard task of correcting the previous strong, lengthy swing. The corrective pattern, which has a roller-coaster momentum expressed by the swing's steep down slope, should be capable of accomplishing the

Figure 13.3 Territorial distribution technique to put the gaps into context
(Courtesy of www.pitchforktrader.com)

>   100% corrective task. The two gaps in this territory are of above-average size. They have
>   been created in order that the lowest level is reached as quickly as possible and shows
>   the momentum covering as much corrective ground as possible.

   Figure 13.4 clearly illustrates the two modules of the systematized visualization tool (swings
and territorial techniques).

13.3 GAP MECHANISMS: FOUNDATION AND DEVELOPMENT

By closely observing the three territories in Fig. 13.4, we notice that an entire array of gaps
have been created as the market flow goes through the process of consolidation. There are four
types of gap, with a total of 10 in all, and they are all highly visible. The four types of gap are:
common, breakaway, runaway and exhaustion. Each type of gap is now studied in the order of
its importance.

13.3.1 Common Gaps

Common gaps are visible in Fig. 13.5 (see the two gaps indicated by double arrows). Called
area or pattern gaps, they are the most common. However, they are almost useless for trading
purposes although the scalpers are sometimes interested in them. They are usually built within a
consolidation pattern, representing mostly local market reactions, because of their close proximity
to the upper/lower boundaries. The narrow swings accompanying this type of gap mean that no

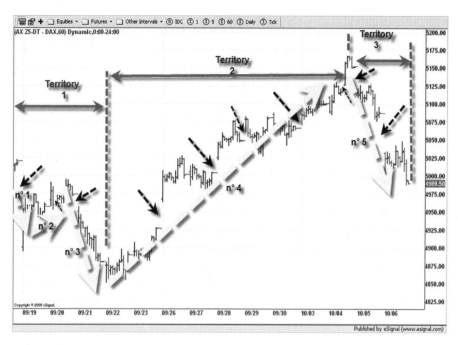

Figure 13.4 Combining the swing and territorial distribution techniques
(Courtesy of www.pitchforktrader.com)

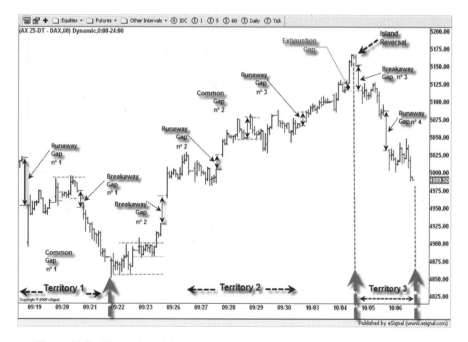

Figure 13.5 Illustration of four types of gap (Courtesy of www.pitchforktrader.com)

directional or strategic values are attributed to it. The characteristics of common gaps are easy to remember:

- They close very rapidly, mostly within a day.
- There are many common gaps within the development of a trend, in spite of the absence of any forecasting information.
- They do not have any definite price acceleration, unlike the other three types.
- Their evolving environment is constructed out of consolidation areas, mostly rectangles. In 1932, Richard W. Schabacker wrote that these gaps 'occur during active but nervous markets'.
- Although rectangles are the source of many common gaps, they can also occur in other types of continuation patterns, in triangles and also in reversal patterns. A trader seeing this type of gap within the development of an ongoing chart formation would look for a continuation pattern rather than a reversal.
- Its own volume is insignificant, but watch the decreasing volume of the ongoing pattern to which the common gap belongs.

13.3.2   Breakaway Gaps

This type of gap is considered one of the most important for several reasons.

- It remains open most of the time, although sometimes it is partially filled.
- It occurs much less frequently than the common gap, and is usually present at the beginning of a trend development.
- Its *raison d'être* is market acceleration which tells the trader that an ongoing trend is just beginning. It tells the trader that a very strong momentum is taking place with its ensuing trend development.
- Its starting blocks are mostly consolidation patterns, and usually each well-developed trend contains a single breakaway gap.
- It possesses a specific volatility triggering mechanism, because most breakaway gaps trigger other types of gap within the developing trend.
- Volume plays an important role in identifying this kind of gap, and also in determining its degree of highly charged momentum. A great tip is to expect the volume to only increase during or right after the first breaking bar.

13.3.3   Runaway Gaps

A runaway gap is less important than a breakaway gap; however, it can forecast the termination of the ongoing trend.

- Its closure is identical to that of the preceding gap; it stays open, though sometimes it can be partially closed.
- There are more runaway than breakaway gaps but fewer than common gaps.
- It does not have the strong jailbreak momentum potential of the breakaway gap, but it is strong enough to carry the other developing half of the ongoing trend until its termination.
- The inception nest is usually in the middle of the trend, and it is thus much appreciated by the astute trader for its forecasting ability.

- *Differential gap diagnosis*: each of the gaps following a breakaway gap must be carefully analyzed, especially if it is taller than its predecessor. This apparently trivial detail has vital implications when applying the gap measuring technique to establish the approximate termination level of the whole trend.
- The runaway gap shows a lesser degree of volume compared to the breakaway gap. The volume might even decrease if the breakout is oriented downward.

13.3.4   Exhaustion Gaps

As the name indicates, the exhaustion gap illustrates the degree that the price exhaustion will reach during the terminal part of the ongoing trend. Once correctly identified, this type of gap is a real blessing for the trader, because of its tremendous profit potential when trading the imminent reversal.

- It is the only gap that will be closed very shortly after its creation; the trader is on his way to enter a low-risk high-probability reversal trade.
- 'For every trend, one exhaustion gap' is the saying for this type of gap.
- Being at the end of the trend, the momentum is weak compared with the other types of gap. The same weakness is valid for volume.
- The exhaustion takes place at the end of the trend; the gap takes place just before the termination of the trend.
- *Differential gap diagnosis*: if the initial (breakaway) gap measuring values have not yet been reached in a reasonable manner, the diagnosis is that a continuation rather than an exhaustion gap is in development.
- At the end of the up-sloping trend the enthusiasm is no longer there. There are only a few buyers left, the demand diminishes and, by default, prices drop. The volume is less than that of the runaway gap, but still substantial.

13.4   ARRAY OF TRADABLE GAPS

The trading edge of the swings and territorial techniques has the merit of revealing that gaps are really known because of their locations in their chart context (see Fig. 13.6). After finding the gaps in the market flow, let us now try to understand the synergy between their morphology and trading potential. Are there any parallelisms or any similarities? We will study only those having a practical trading advantage in detail, and taking them one by one in their order of importance: breakaway gaps, runaway gaps and exhaustion gaps.

13.4.1   Trading the Breakaway Gap

Richard W. Schabacker describes the breakway gap in his first book, *Stock Market Theory and Practice* (1930):

> ... *It comes generally at a particular stage in the market formation and forecasts the beginning of a sharp, long and profitable movement in that direction. . . It follows the major formation, indicates the beginning of the major move previously forecast by the developing picture of the accumulation or distribution, and is very seldom covered.*

Figure 13.6 Structural study of the trend reveals the different types of gaps
(Courtesy of www.pitchforktrader.com)

And he continues: 'It may be used best to check up on the correctness of the previous analysis, and as the final signal to get aboard for the profitable excursion.'

Schabacker uses the term *seven cardinal formations* in order to define the common basic formation, representing the starting blocks of the breakaway gap:

- **Major accumulation patterns**: Head and Shoulder Bottom; Common Upward Turn; Triangular Bottom; Ascending Bottom; Double Bottom; Complex Bottom; Broadening Bottom.
- **Major distribution patterns**: Head and Shoulder Top; Common Downward Turn; Triangular Top; Descending Top; Double Top; Complex Top; Broadening Top.

Observing the 60-min chart in Fig. 13.7, we can easily see that the consolidation pattern has been completed with the breakout above its upper boundary, two bars before the day's close. This accumulation pattern could be the foundation of a future up-sloping trend, built on triple — if not quadruple — bottoms.

We can see that the lower border of the consolidation pattern has three touches and a slight piercing of the support level. The upper border has seven price touches. We can therefore consider this a very strong accumulation pattern (rectangle bottom). Continuing with our analysis, we notice that, after it has consolidated for seven bars, the market price breaks upwards with a first big bar, right underneath the higher boundary of the pattern.

After one narrow bar resting area (a sort of tiny pullback), the momentum continues with another big bar, closing the day almost at the high of the last bar of the day.

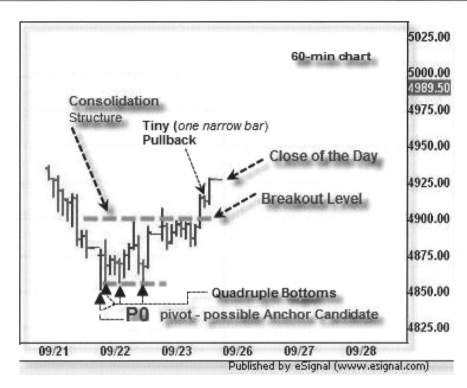

Figure 13.7   Strong accumulation pattern (Courtesy of www.pitchforktrader.com)

The volume of this consolidation pattern decreases from the moment the piercing bar (P0) is created. The fact that the price makes a false breakout above the upper boundary, and then persists with a seven-bar consolidation, right under the same upper boundary, convinces us that an up-sloping breakout is imminent. If that were the case, then our best choice for a future pitchfork anchor (P0) would be the lowest low, as illustrated in Fig. 13.7. We are prepared for the next market move of the market if it goes in the planned direction.

Moreover, knowing the importance of a gap median line in our trading, we are prepared for its drawing, waiting for the best location for the P1–P2 swing. Tomorrow's opening period will partially or entirely determine our gap opening strategy. We should not neglect the possibility of trading a lower time frame (5-min or 15-min).

In the event that the opening bar information is not reliable enough, we will wait patiently until at least the first opening half an hour, perhaps the whole morning/noon period, and sometimes even until the opening of the US market at 15:30 CET (09:30 US ET).

We would also like to utilize a higher time frame (60- or 120-min chart) in the construction of the gap median line, so that the P0-P1-P2 formation becomes bigger and longer. Once built, the gap median line is a very reliable tool for measuring the height of the trend and timing the termination of the trend.

The price bursts out like a rocket (Fig. 13.8) in an almost vertical slope, and forms the P1 pivot just one hour before the close of the day (09/26/05). The P2 pivot is drawn just the next day. Now, two days after the creation of the breakaway gap, our gap median line is completed and we are ready to get the most out of it. Our main objective is to closely verify whether it will

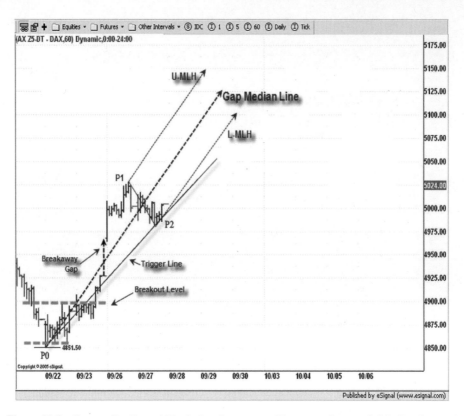

Figure 13.8   Gap median line within the breakaway gap (Courtesy of www.pitchforktrader.com)

or will not optimally describe the market flow. This will only be possible during the next day (Fig. 13.9).

Conclusion: To end this section we emphasize and enumerate the critical elements of breakaway gap trading:

- a legitimate major chart formation serving as launching base;
- a jailbreak manner of breaking off the chart formation;
- a decreasing volume during the major chart formation outweighed by an above-the-average volume at or even after the breaking point;
- a well-informed single or multiple choice selection (timed at the formation's end) of the best anchor candidate (P0) of the future gap median line (mostly at the lowest low in the up-trend), whether the P1 and P2 pivots are a few bars or even days apart; and
- a well-studied territory ahead of the gap, with key levels systematically catalogued. Thus the risk of the end run is fully avoided, and the market flow will develop its full trending potential.

The *end run* occurs when a perfectly healthy breakout is suddenly halted after a couple of huge bars swiftly reverse towards the breaking point. This usually happens because of poorly observed key levels (resistance and support – ahead of the gap) or very often due to the hidden but strong

Figure 13.9   Gap median line within the breakaway gap (cont.) (Courtesy of www.pitchforktrader.com)

levels. This topic is studied in detail in Volume II. The end run is not to be confused with the throwback or the bull trap!

13.4.2   Trading the Runaway Gap

Most of the time the breakaway gap has such an increased volatility that it stimulates the creation of multiple gaps in the continuing trend development. One of those gaps is the runaway gap, also called the *continuation* or *measuring* gap (Fig. 13.9).

This gap may be created out of a mini-consolidation taking place at the end of the first correction of the ongoing trend, which culminates with the creation of the P2 pivot. Its main characteristic is where it begins, in the midst of a high-momentum trend, thus revealing the approximate termination level of the trend through the measuring technique. Not only does it project the trend's termination but it also creates very strong key levels (gap's high, low and midpoint) that will greatly influence the market flow in a later corrective pattern phase.

Another great advantage of the runaway gap is that it will teach the inexperienced trader how to use the *scale-in technique* (adding-on to a present position), right after the gap's inception or, for more conservative traders, straight after the first pullback.

The scale-in, trigger-shy trader will apply this technique with confidence, because this type of gap is a perfect example of what buyers (in an up-trend) will use who are firmly in control of the market. Knowing that we are acting after the breakaway gap, which guarantees the inception of a healthy trend, will enhance this confidence. The scale-in entry, after a pullback, will double the trader's confidence and dramatically increase the profit of the trade.

Figure 13.9 illustrates the power of the runaway gap, which appears in this chart as the catalyst of the magnetic power of the gap median line. It literally propels the market price upwards like a rocket, testing the median line three times. We have also drawn in three *market slots*, labelled (−1), (+1) and (+2), from left to right, to help us visualize the concept of the market price translation across the slots. In this example, our first task is to monitor the development of the trend; our second is to detect any up/down-sloping failures.

We include Fig. 13.10 in order to illustrate the myriad gaps that take place in a well-developed trend. The gap median line is stronger than ever in optimally describing the market flow. The two warning lines (WL-1 and WL-2) constitute a real bedding for the up-sloping market flow. The sliding parallel line efficiently reveals a down-sloping failure, which greatly enhances the trader's comprehension of the trend's continuation.

We end this section with the wise words of Richard W. Schabacker, written over 70 years ago but just as applicable today:

> *A Continuation Gap may, in fact, be considered as only a specialized form of the Break-away Gap, or vice versa, since both indicate the rapid continuation of a movement. One occurs at the beginning of the movement and the other after it has started, and neither is covered for some time.*

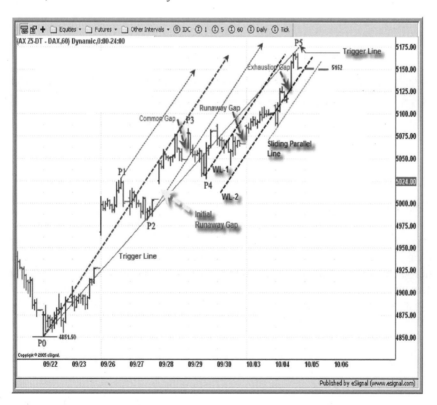

Figure 13.10 Myriad gaps in a well-developed trend (Courtesy of www.pitchforktrader.com)

13.4.3   Trading the Exhaustion Gap

The exhaustion gap is the easiest one to identify, especially when the trend is already rich in multiple gaps (Fig. 13.11). Schabacker wrote: 'It [the exhaustion gap] is the logical complement of the Gap series.'

Its action is characterized by a 'last gasp' of an already weakened trend before the imminent reversal (Fig. 13.11). It is one of the best signals that the highly-charged up-sloping momentum has been diluted and is now waning away. The trend's reversal is just around the corner. Once the market price makes its highest high (P5) with a three-mirror bar reversal encapsulating the middle inside bar, we can say that the exhaustion zone is almost complete. Its final culmination will be in effect when the price of the corrective pattern reaches the low of the bar that has opened the exhaustion gap.

The exhaustion gap is not always a reliable indicator of a major reversal. But one thing is certain: it will always signal a *possible* one. The trader should be aware that a steep corrective trend is not the rule after every reversal. The occurrence of a top/bottom consolidation, right after the one bar reversal or multiple bars reversal pattern, is always possible.

Before we close this section, let us verify the obedience of the market flow towards the gap median line. Scrutinizing Fig. 13.11, we observe that the market flow has been mostly up-sloping within the channel formed by the warning lines WL-1 and WL-2. The trigger line blocks the weakened momentum trend, forming the highest high (P5) so far. It is a textbook example of an up-sloping failure ready to reverse the main trend.

Figure 13.11   Exhaustion gap (Courtesy of www.pitchforktrader.com)

13.5   TRADING THE ISLAND REVERSAL

The exhaustion zone has naturally been converted into an *island reversal zone*, which is formed by an exhaustion gap on its upward slope and a breakaway gap on the other side (Fig. 13.12). The occurrence of the second gap definitely signals the existence of the exhaustion gap, especially when the ongoing market price drops all the way down under the low of the bar that opens it. Once the reversal is confirmed, a new median line is required. The p0 pivot is quickly identified with the highest high (P5) and the search for the p1 and p2 pivots is systematically launched. So far we have already selected the first two new pivots. The island reversal often indicates the end of an intermediate move, and is much better visualized on a higher time frame.

The influence of the gap median line is still going strong. The close of the 36 Dax points breakaway gap's low bar lands exactly on the third warning line (WL-3). One question arises, however: Should we abandon the current gap median line when the new p0-p1-p2 pitchfork is constructed? Well, I would not agree with this! But... let the market come to us, and decide for us.

As we anticipated (Fig. 13.13), the market has decided to obey the initial gap median line. Its down-sloping momentum is very strong, this time creating a 56 Dax points runaway gap.

After so much turbulence, the market should consolidate for a moment (for at least a few bars). Once again, the market flow prefers the initial gap median line, halting exactly on the 50%

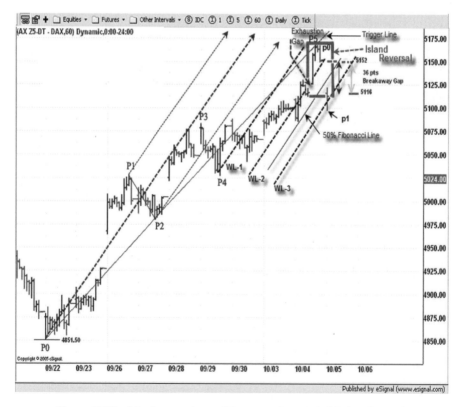

Figure 13.12   Island reversal zone (Courtesy of www.pitchforktrader.com)

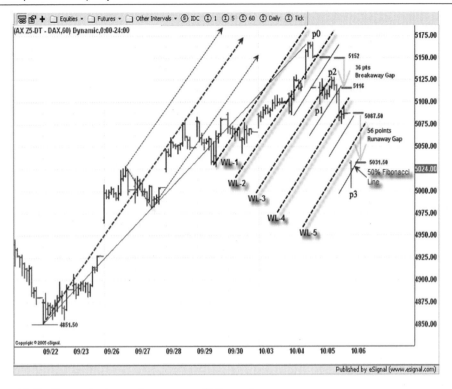

Figure 13.13   Down-sloping market creates a 56 Dax point runaway gap
(Courtesy of www.pitchforktrader.com)

Fibonacci line of the channel formed by the fifth warning line (WL-5) and the sixth warning line
(WL-6, not drawn).

13.6   GAP TRADING: GAP MEDIAN LINE VERSUS A&R LINES

The chart in Fig. 13.14 will greatly help us to understand how to time our entries and exits by
using either a gap median line, which has been so useful up to now, or an Action and Reaction
Lines set-up.

The question now arises: Which chart structure would be the most useful, the former or the
latter? We invite the reader to evaluate the two methods already described and come up with the
right answer!

Figure 13.15 is identical to Fig. 13.14 except that supplementary Reaction Lines 2 and 3 have
been added. Let us try to help with the homework given above.

When studying the individual, synergetic or differing characteristics of the gap median line
and A&R Lines, the trader should first have a global view (the context) and then come down to
the local market flow level. Try to analyze the territory covered by each method, in spite of the
crowded chart. You can first draw both techniques on the trading chart for a temporary study,
and then select the best. Also look for failures or confluences for both patterns: first individually
and then in an overlapping drawing.

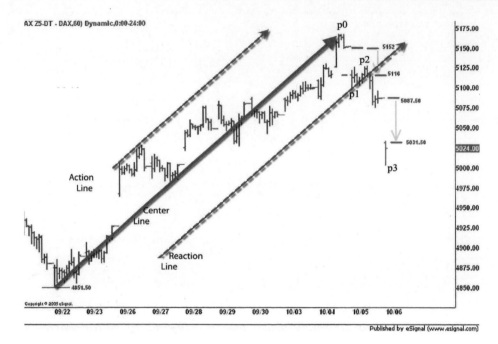

Figure 13.14 Timing entries and exits: gap median line vs. A&R Lines
(Courtesy of www.pitchforktrader.com)

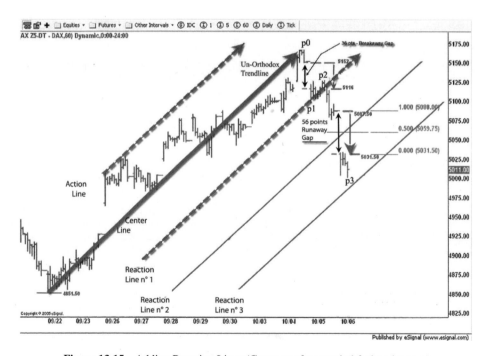

Figure 13.15 Adding Reaction Lines (Courtesy of www.pitchforktrader.com)

13.7 KEY LEARNING POINTS

- Always use the *swings* and the *territorial techniques* when a gap occurs out of a possible array of gaps, especially when it has a jailbreak behaviour. These are important modules in the systematized visualization tool.
- Consider *any* inceptive chart formation as a possible source of an imminent breakaway gap.
- The complete array of the gap's characteristics include its: closure, size, degree of presence/absence within the trend, volume during the first bar and aftermath and degree of acceleration.
- Recall in a few words the identification footprint of each type of gap: common (*change signal*), breaking away (*strong trend signal*), continuation (*ensures momentum's inertia*) and exhaustion (*termination and reversal possible signal*). Be aware that a gap can always introduce one or more other gaps.
- Professional traders say that to know and understand about gaps, and to master all four types, is one of the hardest things to acquire, but doing so results in a very profitable edge.
- The measuring technique should be a trading routine when a gap has occurred. The drawing of the gap's dimensions should be systematically done.
- Even if these techniques are very well performed, there will be no efficient trading results unless you take into consideration the territory ahead of the gap, in such a way that the key levels are systematically catalogued. Thus, the risk of the end run is fully avoided, and the market flow will develop according to its full trending potential.

Conclusion: We conclude this chapter of the professional trader's Knowledge Curve with the words of Richard W. Schabacker, from his 1932 book *Technical Analysis and Stock Market Profits*:

> The Common Gap indicates only changes, generally within a congestion area; the Breakaway denotes the beginning of a strong trend; the Continuation Gap promises the rapid continuation of such a trend; and the Exhaustion Gap suggests the completion of the movement and an early reversal.

14
Fibonacci Price Lines

Fibonacci price and time analysis is one of the most profitable techniques in contemporary trading. No serious trader nowadays would imagine trading without it. In this chapter we will only talk about the price aspect of this technique. Fibonacci Time Lines analysis is dealt with in Volume III.

We certainly do not believe in magic, but our experience and the whole trading literature leads us to believe in superior powers which often represent an advanced degree of predictive potential. More often than not, the novice trader will be astonished how the market obeys these Fibonacci price or time levels.

14.1 DEFINITION AND BRIEF HISTORICAL BASIS

Merriam-Webster's Collegiate Dictionary (10th edition), defines the Fibonacci numbers as follows:

> *An integer [number] in the infinite sequence 1, 1, 2, 3, 5, 8, 13, 21, 34, 55, 89, 144... of which the first two terms are 1 and 1 and each succeeding term is the sum of the two immediately preceding.*

Fibonacci was the son (*filius*) of Bonacci and was therefore known as *filius Bonacci*, which eventually was abbreviated to become Fibonacci. Born sometime during the 1170s (his exact birth date is not known), he became one of the 13th century's most famous mathematicians. He frequently travelled to North Africa, first as a child accompanying his customs officer father, and later as a scholar, with a special interest in studying the mathematics of the pyramids. He discovered that the relationship between the height and the base of the pyramid is 61.8% (see Table 14.1). His well-known book *Liber Abacci* (Book of Calculation) was written just after a sojourn in Egypt. It has the incommensurable merit of introducing the decimal system to Europe, known nowadays as the Hindu-Arabic system.

Once this sequence (series) of numbers is defined, the most important element of their use is their ratios. In the first instance we would say that the ratios obtained by dividing any number of the series by the next higher one will constitute another infinite sequence. In reality, the further we go with the dividing operation, the closer we get to the 0.618 Golden Ratio (see Table 14.1).

Table 14.1   Golden Ratio ($phi = 0.618$)

No	Ratio	No	Ratio
1	–	89	0.617978
1	–	144	0.618056
2	–	233	0.618026
3	0.666667	377	0.618037
5	0.600000	610	0.618033
8	0.625000	987	0.618034
13	0.615385	1597	0.618034
21	0.619048	2584	0.618034
34	0.617647	4181	0.618034
55	0.618182	6765	0.618034

14.2   PRICE FIBONACCI TOOLS

As mentioned before, the Fibonacci ratio techniques, and their graphic expression through the *horizontal and oblique lines*, are tools that should be fully practised in today's markets and it would be true to say that every astute trader uses them. Over the years, traders have noticed that certain Fibonacci ratios predominate and have more applicability than others:

- for retracement (counter-trend) purposes: 0.146, 0.236, 0.382, 0.500, 0.618, 0.786, 0.886;
- for projecting logical price objectives: 1.00, 1.146, 1.236, 1.272, 1.382, 1.500, 1.618, 2.000, 2.618, 4.236 and 6.85.

During the daily trading routine, traders keep a few Fibonacci ratios in mind. This happens naturally when they have acquired an in-depth knowledge of the behaviour of most of their trading securities. The following ratios are very commonly used:

- retracements: 0.382, 0.500, and 0.618;
- projecting logical objectives: 1.618, 2.000, 2.618, 4.236 and 6.85 for projecting logical objectives.

Essentially, the Fibonacci tool is used for measuring retracements of a developing trend or, alternatively, the trend's projected objectives and targets. This is easily done by measuring the distance between the extreme points of the following:

- retracement (its high and then its low);
- first swing (its low and then its high) of the ongoing trend;

and then the corresponding Fibonacci ratios applying to their values.

Nowadays, traders are very spoiled compared with their colleagues of the pre-computer era as most software chart packages have a Fibonacci tool as a standard feature. The trader should only select the most applicable Fibonacci ratios for his particular type of market and then apply it properly whatever the behaviour of the market at that precise moment, whether an inceptive counter-trend, or an extended trend which has its origin at the beginning of the first swing.

Let us continue with mastering the application of the Fibonacci tool.

There are many ways in which these ratios can be applied, but most are not systematic in their use. As a result, traders experience rather erratic values, very difficult to interpret, and especially challenging to utilize to gain a real edge. We have chosen the systematized classification practised by Robert C. Miner in his very practical and educational book, *Dynamic Trading*.

14.2.1 Retracements

There are two types of retracement:

1. *Internal retracements* (less than 100%), which illustrate the percentage retracement of the prior swing, in the process of building a correction (23.6, 38.2, 50.0, 61.8 and 78.6%).
2. *External retracements* (greater than 100%), which illustrate the percentage retracement of the prior swing, in the process of building a counter-trend (123.6, 127.2, 161.8, 200.0, 261.8 and 423.6%).

The daily chart in Fig. 14.1 illustrates the calculation of the *internal* price retracements of the current market flow. After the huge, highly-charged, upward momentum is stopped short by the warning line (WL-3), the market flow quickly retraces: first to a 23.6% retracement within the reversal bar (point C-1), then a 38.2% retracement within the first 4 bars (point C-2), and finally to a 50% level at point C. These Fibonacci ratios are applied to the height of the A–B swing. Each ratio value has been subtracted from the highest high value (point B at 364.75).

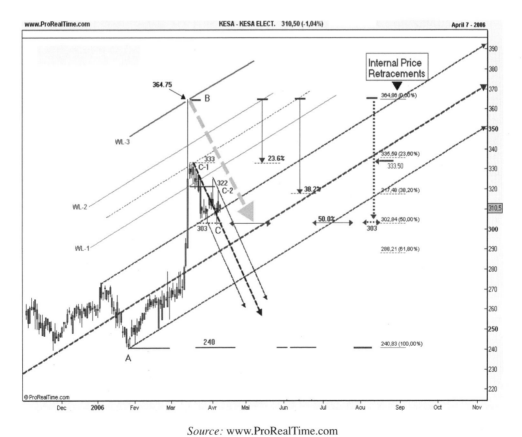

Source: www.ProRealTime.com

Figure 14.1   Calculating the internal price retracements (Courtesy of www.pitchforktrader.com)

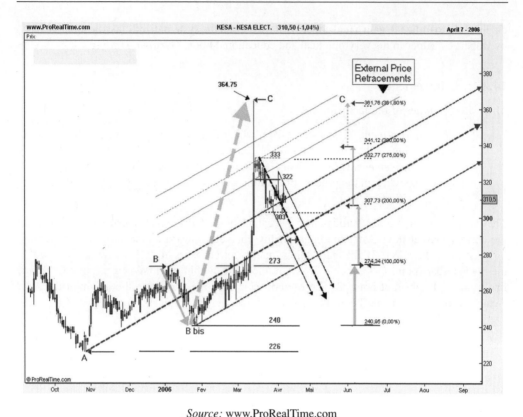

Source: www.ProRealTime.com

Figure 14.2 Calculating the external price retracements (Courtesy of www.pitchforktrader.com)

The daily chart in Fig. 14.2 illustrates the calculation of the *external* price retracements of the market flow. In spite of the fact that many traders cannot really visualize or readily understand the extra 100% retracements, we have applied the corresponding Fibonacci ratios to the *B−B bis* swing. The Fibonacci ratios have been applied to the B−B bis swing's height, and then added to the 100% ratio level at the 273 level.

We notice that the huge upward momentum provokes an up-sloping swing halted at the 364.75 level, which coincides with a 361.80% value increase at point C (361.76 level).

14.2.2   Alternate Price Projections

We illustrate the price projection percentage(s) of past alternate swing(s) – swings versus swings and counter-trends versus counter-trends – as the name indicates. The measuring (ongoing) and the measured (prior) swings must be in the same direction as the ongoing market flow, thus respecting the alternate principle. This topic is studied in detail in Volume II (in preparation). The projected values will indicate the possible termination levels of the current developing swing.

The most commonly used projection percentage values are: 61.8, 100.0, 161.8, 200.0, 261.8, 423.6 and 685%.

Figure 14.3 shows the method of applying Fibonacci ratios to obtain the alternate price projections. Once the selected ratios have been established, we take the vertical measure of

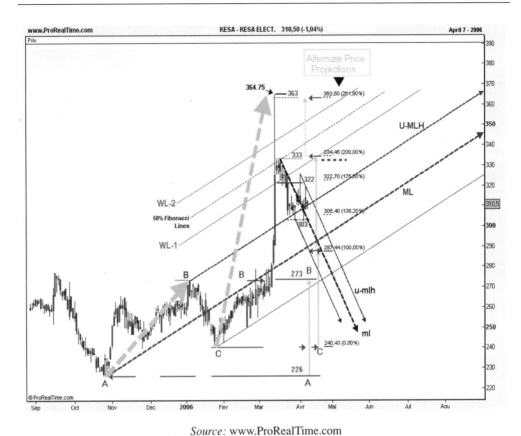

Source: www.ProRealTime.com

Figure 14.3 Applying Fibonacci ratios to obtain the alternate price projections (Courtesy of www.pitchforktrader.com)

the A−B swing and project it upwards from point C. The merit of this type of calculation is that it respects the alternate principle, which is at the base of the market flow for swings and counter-trend moves. Due to the market's strong momentum, the ongoing swing has become hyper-extended, reaching the 261.80% ratio of the prior A−B swing at 363.50 level, next to the highest high at 364.75.

14.2.3 Price Expansions

First, we should say that these price expansions complement the two preceding techniques and are used only to confirm them. They illustrate the price expansion percentage of the same swing(s), in the direction of the current trend, especially applied to the inceptive swing.

The most commonly used percentage values are: 61.8, 100.0, 161.8, 200.0, 261.8, 423.6 and 685%.

The chart in Fig. 14.4 shows the price expansion method. As the name indicates this tool expands the momentum of the initial A−B swing, thus finding its possible exhaustion location. In Fig. 14.4, the strong up-sloping momentum pushes the market price beyond the 161.8% ratio value, being halted at 364.75 level, just 1.75 points off the 188.60% ratio value at 363.0.

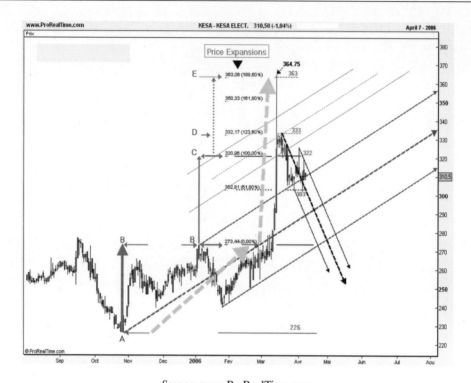

Source: www.ProRealTime.com
Figure 14.4   Price expansion method (Courtesy of www.pitchforktrader.com)

14.3   FIBONACCI PRICE RATIO (HORIZONTAL) LINES: CASE STUDIES

German Dax Index Charts

The chart in Fig. 14.5 illustrates the calculation of the internal price retracements applied to the terminated upward B−A swing. The market is firstly attracted and then halted by the median line.

The chart in Fig. 14.6 uses the internal price retracements applied to the A−C sub-swing of the down-sloping B−C swing. The market flow manages to retrace to the 50%−61.8% zone levels.

We apply the external price retracements technique (the market price travels from point C to point D) to the B−C swing (Fig. 14.7 on p. 268). The highly-charged, upward-sloping, hyper-extended C−D swing has burst all the way up to the 3.00 ratio level at 4575 (a 300% increase of the B−C measured swing). The market flow has suddenly been halted, just on the warning line (WL-6) at the 4575 level. Once again, the peak of the measured C−D swing (3.0 ratio at 4576.75 level) has almost coincided with the highest high at the 4575 level (point D).

Figure 14.8 (on p. 269) illustrates three different types of price ratio techniques: alternate price projections, internal price retracements on a prior swing and an internal price retracement on a huge bar:

1.   The *alternate price projections* (the price travelling from point C to point D) are using the measured A−B swing in order to reveal the termination level of the measured C−D swing. The development of the latter has led the price all the way up to the 4576.50 level, very close to the 2.00 Fibonacci ratio at 4582.75 (a 200% increase of the initial swing).

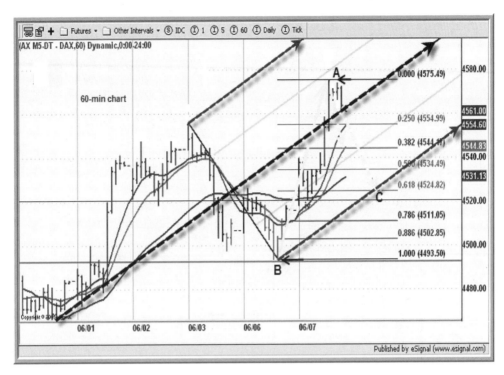

Figure 14.5   Calculating the internal price retracements (cont.) (Courtesy of www.pitchforktrader.com)

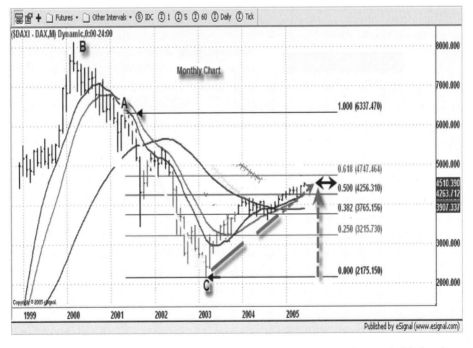

Figure 14.6   Calculating the internal price retracements (cont.) (Courtesy of www.pitchforktrader.com)

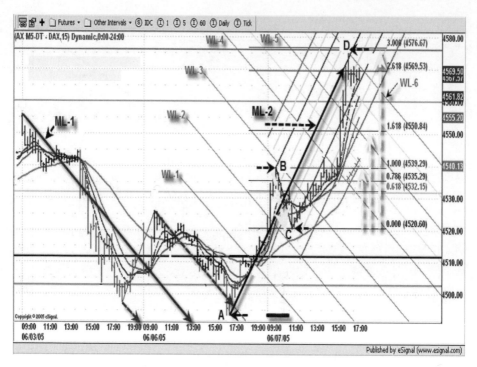

Figure 14.7 Calculating the external price retracements (cont.) (Courtesy of www.pitchforktrader.com)

2. The *internal price retracements* (the price will probably travel from point D to point F) are applied to the upward C−D swing. The main Fibonacci ratio values are in place and the reversals will most probably commence at those values.

3. The *internal price retracements* (the price will probably travel from point D to point E) are applied on the tallest (D−E) bar. We have divided the bar's height into thirds, in order to monitor the zone in which the market price will prefer to move.

As long as the market price does not breach the 50% Fibonacci ratio at the 4548 level, we are still in an up-trend. This technique is very efficient when the market is ready for a reversal or to create an inside bar, as in our case.

Figure 14.9 illustrates two types of price ratio techniques − external price retracements and internal price retracements − applied to the prior swing.

1. The external price retracements (the price has travelled from point C to point D) are using the measured B−C swing to reveal the termination level of the advancing C−D swing. The development of this swing has led the price all the way up to the 4575 level, very close to the 3.00 Fibonacci ratio at 4576.50 level (a 300% increase of the initial B−C swing).

2. The internal price retracements (the price will probably travel from point D to point E) are applied to the upwards F−D swing, which is a sub-swing of the bigger A−D swing. The main Fibonacci ratios values are in place and the reversal has already started. We are targeting the 38.2% retracement ratio (point E).

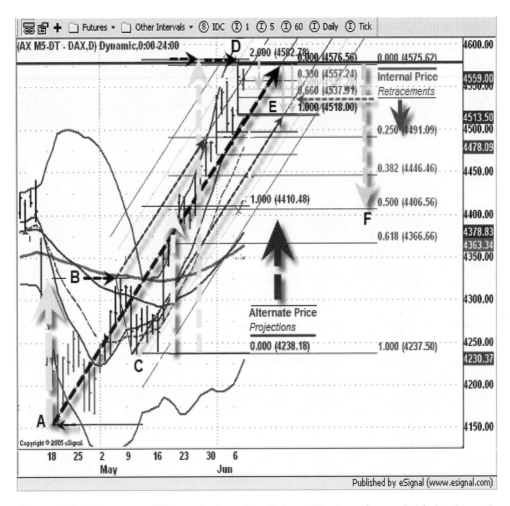

Figure 14.8   Three types of Fibonacci price ratio techniques (Courtesy of www.pitchforktrader.com)

14.4   DYNAMICS OF INTEGRATION: PITCHFORK AND FIBONACCI PRICE RATIO (HORIZONTAL) LINES

S&P 500 e-mini and German Dax Index Charts

In this section, we will try to show the applicability of the Fibonacci price ratios' horizontal lines to the development of a traditional pitchfork (see Figs 14.10−14.16).

Once the market has created the P0, P1 and P2 pivots, we can draw our traditional pitchfork (Fig. 4.10 on p. 271). The first time we apply these ratios is to measure the extent of the P2 pivot retracement into the P1−P0 swing zone. The value of this intrusion will give the trader a great edge concerning the future potential of the developing trend. The internal price retracement technique

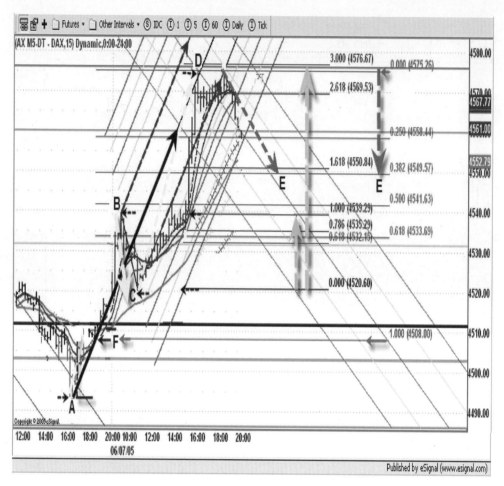

Figure 14.9   Two types of Fibonacci price ratio techniques (Courtesy of www.pitchforktrader.com)

reveals a 50% retracement, which corroborates the working hypothesis that the incoming trend will have an average-to-high development potential. In addition we notice:

- The 23.6% to 38.2% retracement zone is forecasting the potential to explode.
- The 50% to 61.8% retracement zone is labelling a weak trend potential. The 'to be or not to be' principle of a retracement versus a full reversal is classically known to be located at the 100% retracement level. However, the real borderline of this retrace/reversal transition is situated in the 78.6% to 88.6% retracement zone. We affectionately call these two rare but very ergonomic ratios the *Despair Return Points*. There is a high probability that the initial retracement will end up as a full reversal movement, behind the 88.6% retracement level.

Delving deeper into this topic, we have applied the alternate price projections technique in order to evaluate the possible development of the P2–P3 swing, in comparison to its prior alternate

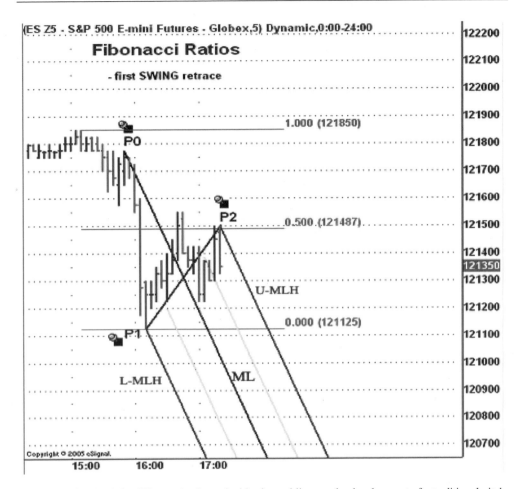

(ES Z5 - S&P 500 E-mini Futures - Globex,5) Dynamic,0:00-24:00

Fibonacci Ratios

- first SWING retrace

PO

1.000 (121850)

P2
0.500 (121487)

U-MLH

0.000 (121125)

P1

L-MLH   ML

Copyright © 2005 eSignal.

15:00   16:00   17:00

122200
122100
122000
121900
121800
121700
121600
121500
121400
121350
121300
121200
121100
121000
120900
120800
120700

Figure 14.10 Applying Fibonacci price ratios' horizontal lines to the development of a traditional pitch-fork (Courtesy of www.pitchforktrader.com)

P0–P1 swing. At this stage of the trend's development (see Fig. 14.11) we notice that the size of the P2–P3 swing matches that of the P0–P1 swing – a 100% projection.

Considering the 50% value of the P2 retracement (see Fig. 14.10), our ongoing trend should have been catalogued as an average-to-high-level development. Its inner potential will carry the market price to at least a 161.8% (1.618 ratio) projection of the initial P0–P1 swing around the 1203 level.

We also notice the strong magnet-like power of the median line (ML), guaranteeing the optimal market flow description by the current choice of pivots embedding the developing of the down-sloping pitchfork.

The big bar's down-sloping trend (Fig. 14.12 on p. 273) does not yet get to the 161.8% projection (around 1203), but reaches the 138.2% level, where it reverses, creating the P3 pivot. So far, the retracement process develops in two stages: first at the 50% level, and second at the 62% ratio at the 1212 level.

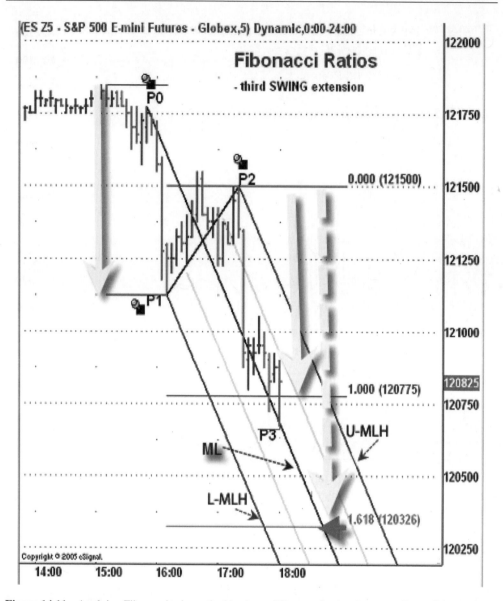

Figure 14.11 Applying Fibonacci price ratios' horizontal lines to the development of a traditional pitch-fork (cont.) (Courtesy of www.pitchforktrader.com)

The market price is stumbling upwards during two time bars to the upper median line before continuing its upward retracement towards the 62% zone. The creation of the P4 pivot is achieved by the market flow halt, provoked by the strong resistance of the upper external 50% Fibs line. This freshly-created P4 pivot could be the starting point of a reversal, which will continue the initial down-sloping trend.

The ES chart (Fig. 14.13 on p. 274) illustrates the market hesitation in a sideways formation, right under the 61.8% ratio retracement level, but not under the 50% level, in spite of the last

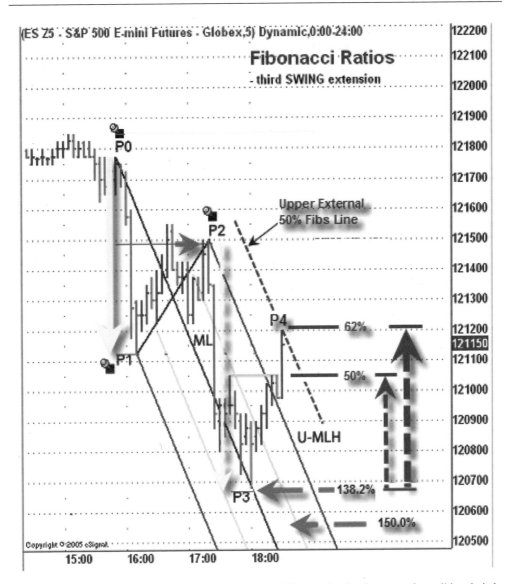

Figure 14.12 Applying Fibonacci price ratios' horizontal lines to the development of a traditional pitchfork (cont.) (Courtesy of www.pitchforktrader.com)

piercing. We should be alert to the fact that if the price breaks the 50% ratio support level, it will probably head for the fifth down-sloping swing. 1210.50 is a very strong level (50%), which so far has been tested six times by the market flow. (The final values of retracement levels can be seen in Fig. 14.15 on p. 275.)

The 50% ratio level first plays a resistance role and, later, becomes a strong obstacle (Fig. 14.13). The market is probably awaiting the US afternoon news, at 20:30 CET (14:30 US ET). It will make all the difference between an up or a down afternoon market. Remember that the 50% ratio Fibonacci level coincides with the 50% Gann level.

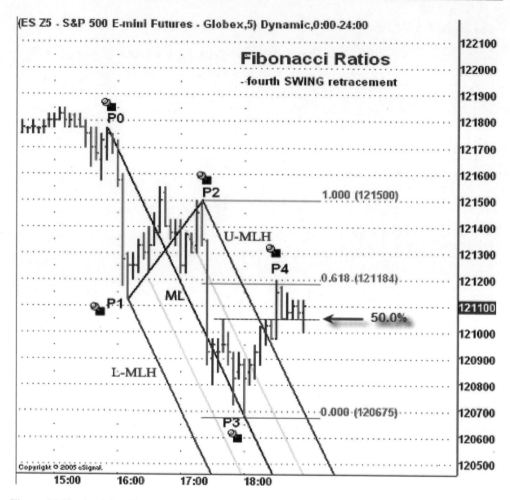

Figure 14.13 Applying Fibonacci price ratios' horizontal lines to the development of a traditional pitch-fork (cont.) (Courtesy of www.pitchforktrader.com)

By looking very carefully at the day's close and also at the opening of the following day (seen in Fig. 14.15), we will gather all the information we need concerning this emphatic borderline: nine times tested as a support line, three piercings and two closes beneath the line.

Before it definitely breaches downwards, the market retraces as long as it can to the 88.6% ratio retracement level, one of our mythical Fibonacci levels that I call the Despair Return Point.

Applying the alternate price projections technique (Fig. 14.14) to the P0–P1 measured swing (the first alternate before the previous), we are now ready to study the development of the P4–P5 swing (the fifth swing). We could also have taken the P2–P3 swing (the last alternate projection) or the entire P0–P3 alternate swing as a measured swing.

Our anticipation was correct (Fig. 14.15). The market flow drops like a stone from the height of the Despair Return Point (our 88.6% ratio level at 1214.25) into deep waters, to exactly the 2.00 ratio (200% increase of the measured swing).

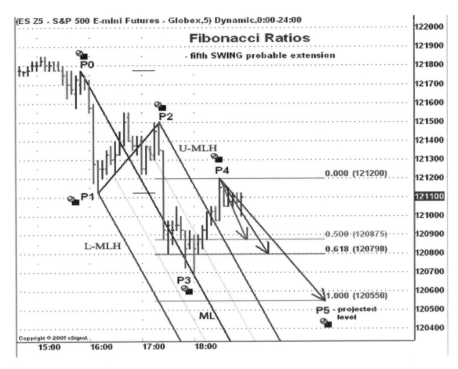

Figure 14.14 Applying Fibonacci price ratios' horizontal lines to the development of a traditional pitchfork (cont.) (Courtesy of www.pitchforktrader.com)

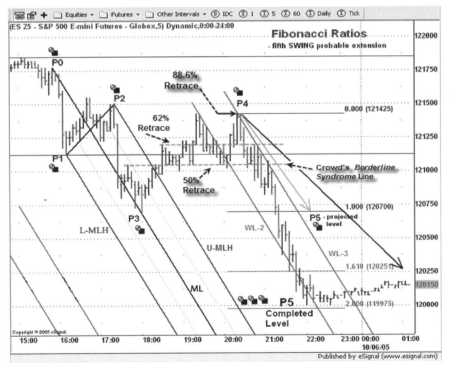

Figure 14.15 Applying Fibonacci price ratios' horizontal lines to the development of a traditional pitchfork (cont.) (Courtesy of www.pitchforktrader.com)

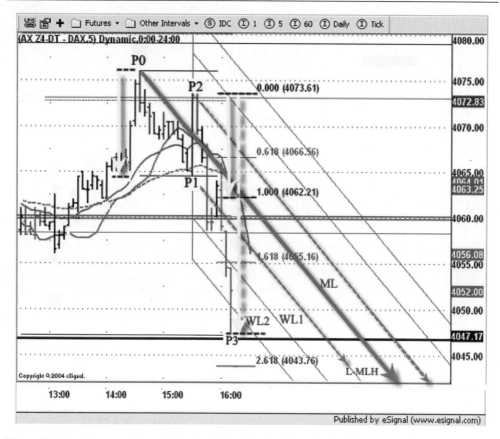

Figure 14.16   Alternate price projection technique in relation to the pitchfork
(Courtesy of www.pitchforktrader.com)

Figure 14.16 emphasizes the alternate price projection concept, in relation to the P0-P1-P2 pitchfork's main body and its boundaries.

Once again, in Fig. 14.17, the alternate price projection technique demonstrates its efficient and profitable features as a reliable trading tool.

14.5   DYNAMICS OF INTEGRATION: PITCHFORK AND FIBONACCI PRICE RATIO (OBLIQUE) LINES

German Dax Index Charts

In this section, we will try to show the applicability of the Fibonacci price ratios' oblique lines to the development of a traditional pitchfork (from Figs 14.18–14.23).

These Fib lines are nothing but parallel lines to the median line of a pitchfork, through the well-defined Fibonacci ratio levels (Fig. 14.18 on p. 278). Within the pitchfork, the most-used Fibonacci ratio level is 50%, followed by the 38.2% and 61.8% ratio levels. Outside the pitchfork's main body, the most-used ratio is again the 50%, followed by the 23.6% (equivalent of Gann's 25%), and the 61.8% level.

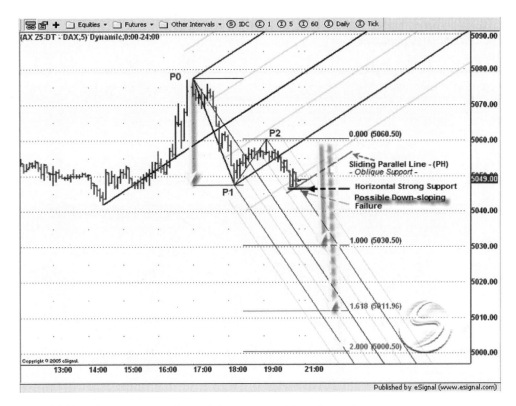

Figure 14.17 Alternate price project technique as a reliable trading tool
(Courtesy of www.pitchforktrader.com)

One thing is sure: the taller the height of the pitchfork's P0—P1 swing, the larger the separating ML and U-MLH distances, and the wider the inter-spaces between the Fib lines.

The Fib lines within the body of the main pitchfork are labelled *internal* or *inner* lines (lower and higher, meaning below or above the ML) and those located outside are labelled *external* or *outer* lines (lower and higher, meaning below or above the pitchfork's ML).

The Fibonacci annotations on Fig. 14.19 (on p. 279) are 50%, 150%, 250% and 275%; they are positioned and calculated in relation to the median line (equivalent of 0% Fib line), to the lower median line (100% Fib line), and so on. The first warning line (WL-1) would be the equivalent of the 200% Fib line, and so on. On Fig. 14.19 we can see that the market flow has been cruising upwards through the channel formed by the warning line (WL-1) and the Fib lines (250% and 275% ratios).

The Fib lines are part of the mapping context, assisting the trader to efficiently localize the market flow in order to optimally describe it (Fig. 14.20 on p. 279). It is a great tool, which completes the action of other median line parallels.

The trader must play the role of a maestro, i.e., manage a whole orchestra of players (management of market participants whose psyche is expressed by Fig. 14.21 on p. 280) with as sparse a selection of tools as possible. The lack of tools is a necessity here. There is no place for asynchrony or for overcrowding the well-oiled process of decision-making or chart drawings. Necessity dictates the type and number of tools employed, at any specific moment in time. The Fibonacci lines in Fig. 14.21 illustrate a very efficient down-sloping market flow channel formed by the 50% and 125% Fib lines.

Figure 14.18   Applying Fibonacci price ratios' oblique lines to the development of a traditional pitchfork (Courtesy of www.pitchforktrader.com)

As a standard procedure (see Fig. 14.22), the trader should always draw the 50% Fib line, expecting the market development to implicate further Fib lines. At the risk of overcrowding it, always keep on the chart the Fibonacci line that is the most tested, re-tested or broken out by the market price. Don't forget the adage: An old resistance may become a new support line. It might save your shirt!

When the market consolidates at the top (Fig. 14.23 on p. 281) do not ask for anyone else's opinion. Just do your work and let the market come to you! But watch out ... you must be prepared for it:

- Draw a double biased pitchfork set-up (one for each of the scenarios).
- Apply the Fibonacci tool in both directions: the double alternate price projections in the case of the current trend continuation, and the internal price retracements for a probable retracement of the market flow.
- Apply the Fibonacci ratio lines to the pitchfork covered by the immediate action of the market's trading range (the up-sloping one, in this case). The Fib lines of the other pitchfork will be drawn *only* if the market should reverse and drop beyond the borderline bias at 5040 level.

Figure 14.19 Applying Fibonacci price ratios' oblique lines to the development of a traditional pitchfork (cont.) (Courtesy of www.pitchforktrader.com)

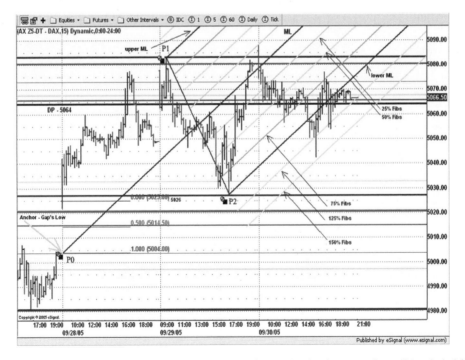

Figure 14.20 Applying Fibonacci price ratios' oblique lines to the development of a traditional pitchfork (cont.) (Courtesy of www.pitchforktrader.com)

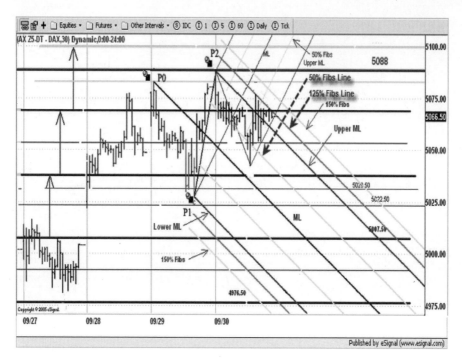

Figure 14.21 Applying Fibonacci price ratios' oblique lines to the development of a traditional pitchfork (cont.) (Courtesy of www.pitchforktrader.com)

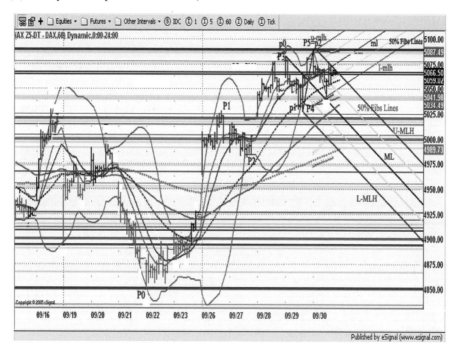

Figure 14.22 Applying Fibonacci price ratios' oblique lines to the development of a traditional pitchfork (cont.) (Courtesy of www.pitchforktrader.com)

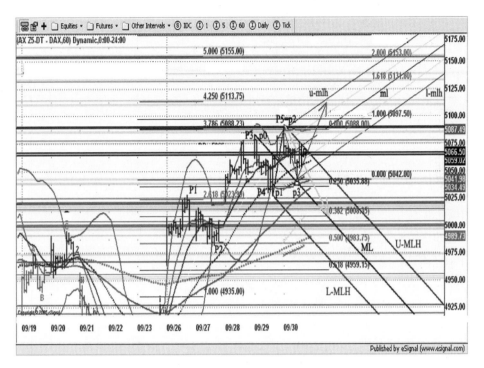

Figure 14.23   Applying Fibonacci price ratios' oblique lines to the development of a traditional pitchfork (cont.) (Courtesy of www.pitchforktrader.com)

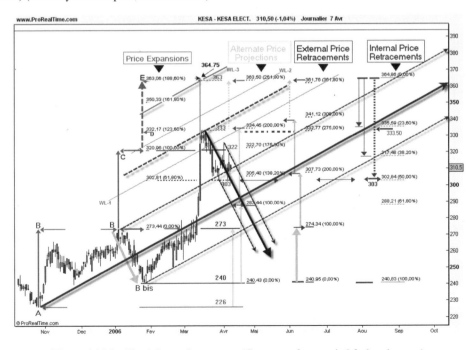

Figure 14.24   Obtaining a cluster zone (Courtesy of www.pitchforktrader.com)

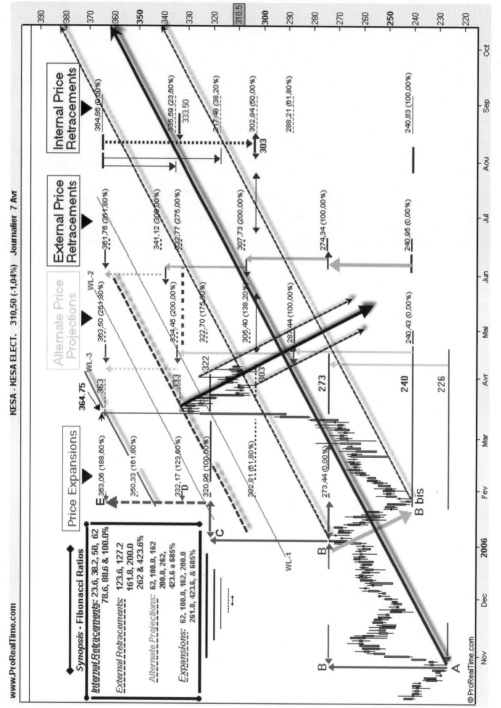

Figure 14.25 Anticipating the market by using Fibonacci tools (Courtesy of www.pitchforktrader.com)

Like they say: Keep the work place (chart) clean!

Conclusion: At the same time, the trader can also use multiple alternate or mixed swings (Fig. 14.24 on p. 281). The outcome of these multiple projections can reveal multi-layer levels, contiguous, superimposed or very close to each other. A cluster zone is then obtained, which has a very high probability of imposing its law on current market flow: a reversal, acceleration or a simple consolidation.

14.6   KEY LEARNING POINTS

- If there is a trading secret, it is to learn how to anticipate market movements, by using the Fibonacci tools (Fig. 14.25), but ... don't forget: Let the market come to you! Thus, the rigorous follow-up of the market's meanderings will naturally guide you to making the best trading decisions.

- Master all four techniques: internal and external price retracements, alternate price and expansion projections (Fig. 14.25). Do not forget that the latter only has a confirming role.

- Do not overload your mind and your chart with all the Fibonacci ratio numbers. Constantly practise your market, learn its habits, and later on, after a couple of thousand charts, you will know not only the behaviour of the market flow, but also the most significant ratios, including the adequate Despair Return Points!

- Whenever these techniques are applied, do not neglect to take into consideration multiple swings, in such a way that the outcome will easily create a cluster zone strong enough to impose its law on the market flow. Apply these tools also to: the last significant trending bar (top/bottom), the opening gap, the rectangle-type consolidation within trend's development, the consolidation area at the top/bottom, and so on.

- Even if these techniques are very well performed, there will be no efficient trading results unless you take into consideration the territory ahead of the gap/market, in such a way that the key levels are systematically catalogued. Thus, the risk of the end run is fully avoided, and the market flow will develop its full trending potential.

- Keep in mind the concept of the borderline syndrome for the crowd's psyche, concerning the bias decision-making.

- Do not forget to use the Fibonacci lines rigorously as an integral part of the mapping context. As we said: play the role of a maestro!

Conclusion: Knowing that the pitchfork is one of the most efficient techniques to optimally describe the market, we can say that its symbiosis and synergy with the Fibonacci tools will greatly enhance the process of finding the low-risk high-probability trades.

15
Confluences

Although essentially they are only graphical signs, confluences contribute markedly to a trade's potential, and are at least as efficient as the Fibonacci lines. Sometimes one cannot see things because they are too obvious. The same may happen with confluences. But one thing is sure — if you do not know how to make them clear on the naked chart, their usefulness will remain hidden.

15.1 DEFINITION AND FUNCTION

The word 'confluence' is defined in the dictionary[1] as 'a coming or flowing together, meeting, or gathering at one point'. From our point of view, the exact meaning is the intersection of two lines, whatever their direction: horizontal with oblique (and vice versa), or simply the intersection of two or more oblique trend lines. They mostly belong to the median line parallels of two or more different pitchforks (major vs major, major vs minor, or minor vs minor pitchforks). However, even though the confluences of these trend lines offer many low-risk high-probability trades, we should not neglect the panoply of other lines, such as: Fibonacci lines, old high/low levels, high/low/midpoint levels in old or recent gaps, and so on.

Once these confluences are efficiently defined, let us proceed to their detailed description. Defined as an intersection, the confluence zone (point) is the meeting point of multiple vectorial forces of the market, which promptly halts most of its kinetic movements. The more numerous the forces, the stronger the confluence's halting power will be.

Important: We consider a confluence valid *only* if the price bars either cross the intersection zone (point) or are very near, no further away than 1–3 bars.

However, there are situations when the trespassing market price might accelerate its pace or even temporarily halt in order to create a consolidation before its next movement. The trader should always look for more than two trend line intersections, thus ensuring a solid confluence point.

The procedure for implementing a confluence comprises several steps:

1. First, ensure that you totally understand the context of the market flow, and that the existing pitchforks optimally describe not only the context, but also the local market.

---

[1] Merriam-Webster's Collegiate Dictionary, 10th Edition.

2. Second, analyze the energy status of the current market flow, revealing whether the market is trending or not and, if it is, in which energy stage and level it is situated. In other words, you need to know whether or not the market still has sufficient energy to pursue the ongoing trend.

3. Third, draw both a major and a minor pitchfork. If required, also determine the different trend lines with a view to drawing an adequate confluence point or the confluence zone (multi-layer trend line intersection).

One very important thing in this context is the timing of the price projection route towards the confluence, what we call the *timing trajectory of the confluence*. We might have a shorter or a longer choice, especially in the case of two or more confluences located on the same horizontal target zone. Reaching each of them is a question of timing (the time necessary to reach the confluence level), which does not depend on the trader but rather on the market. As we like to say: Let the market come to you... but be prepared for any of these three scenarios: trending movements up, down and sideways. The more precise these intersecting zones are, the better the halting power of the confluence.

15.2 DOUBLE LINE INTERSECTION CONFLUENCES: CASE STUDIES

German Dax and S&P 500 e-mini Index Charts

Building the right confluences is based on drawing a pitchfork that optimally describes the market flow and adequate trend lines (see Fig. 15.1).

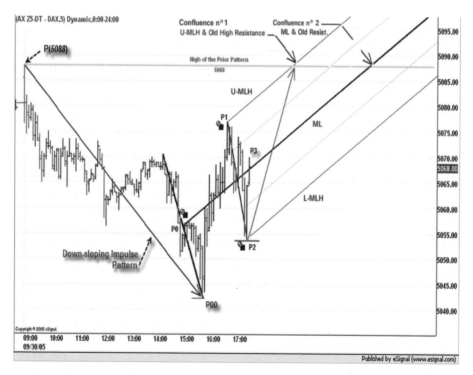

Figure 15.1   Building correct confluences is based on the drawing of a pitchfork
(Courtesy of www.pitchforktrader.com)

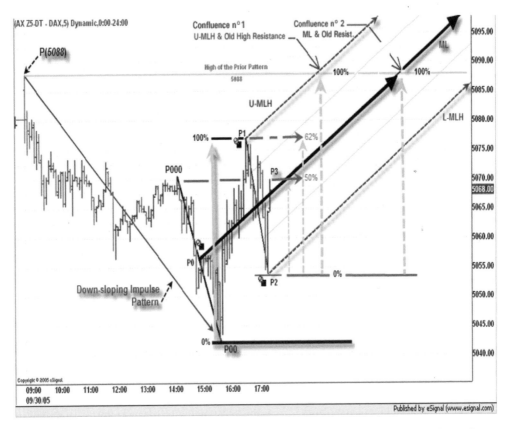

Figure 15.2 Energy status of the ongoing correction (Courtesy of www.pitchforktrader.com)

The market context illustrated in Fig. 15.1 is an ongoing correction (P00–P3 zigzagging swing) of the previous down-sloping trend terminated by the P00 pivot. Analysis of the energy status of the ongoing correction (P2–P3 move) reveals that its current momentum is in a strong developing stage (Fig. 15.2). To evaluate its strength or weakness, we take the following steps.

1.   We closely observe the market context and the local market (most recent swing and bars). In this case, the last swing is composed of two huge bars, and the market has every chance to further correct the entire previous down-sloping impulse pattern, at least for a few bars, or it may even reach the 100% correction level at 5088.

2.   Once this observation is complete, we project the Fibonacci ratio lines, taking as an initial move the P00–P1 swing. We can now apply the four Fibonacci techniques as discussed in Chapter 14. For the sake of simplicity, we have applied only the alternate price projections method, which will project the measured P00–P1 swing to reach the 5088 level of resistance. The value of this level seems to match, not only from a confluence point of view, but also from a cluster point of view (see Figs 15.15 and 15.16).

3.   However, this whole market development observation could be useless if we neglect the end run concept, which we cannot stress enough should be an essential part of the daily routine. Even if these techniques are very well performed, there will be no

efficient trading results unless the trader takes into consideration the territory ahead of the market price, in such a way that the key levels are systematically catalogued. Thus, the risk of the end run (a sudden market reversal to a breaking point, after a short-lived breakout) is fully avoided, and the market flow develops to its full trending potential.

The scrutiny of the market field projected ahead in the expected direction reveals several end run potential risk locations (see Figs. 15.2 and 15.3):

- the 50% Fibonacci ratio level (P3 pivot) applied to the P00—P1 alternate measured swing and projected upwards from the P2 pivot location;
- the approximate 62% correction level of the P(5088)—P00 down-sloping impulse pattern at P1 level; and
- the 5088 level resistance (last high), which coincides with the 100% Fibonacci level of the fully corrected P(5088)—P00 down-sloping impulse pattern.

All these potential end run levels can either:

a) temporarily halt the market in order to consolidate (under a resistance or they may form a horizontal channelling); or
b) first they halt the market flow permanently and then later they reverse it, if they have exhausted their up-sloping kinetic energy.

The drawing of a major P0-P1-P2 Schiff pitchfork and important trend lines constitute the next step. We notice that the last high is within the limits of the daily trading range and within the reach of an eventually strong up-sloping movement. Thus we logically believe that the level of 5088 could be reached by the end-of-day, or at the latest by tomorrow morning, especially if the opening is stimulated by an exacerbation of the fundamentals overnight: S&P500, Nikkei 225, Crude Oil, Euro/US Dollar and so on.

The trajectory timing of the confluence concept is fully realized here (Fig. 15.2). Once we have drawn the resistance from the last high, at the 5088 level, we automatically get two confluences:

a) first, an intersection of this resistance line with the upper median line (U-MLH); and
b) second, another intersection formed by the same resistance line, but this time with the median line of the P0-P1-P2 pitchfork.

Looking at both of them, a question arises! If the 5088 level is attained, which confluence will be hit — number one or number two? Not that we really have to know, but we should be prepared for the right confluence! Who knows, an add-on trade (*scale in*) is always around the corner or, alternatively, a reversal can change the course of the actual market stream.

The required time (number of bars) that is needed to reach the most probable confluence can be calculated well in advance. For this purpose, we apply the projecting Average True Range [ATR (21)] technique, which is routinely used when the trader wants to project his/her minimum price objective. You will find a more detailed discussion of this topic in Chapter 19.

As we anticipated (Fig. 15.3), the market flow does not jump straight to the confluence level. The Fibonacci ratio (23.6%, 38%, 50% and 62%) resistances do their work efficiently, to such an extent that a main horizontal channel is formed between the 38% and 50% Fibonacci ratio levels for over two hours into the close of the day. The opening of the next day is very strong and the market flow bursts open, like a virtual jailbreak. The huge gap's height is almost three times the

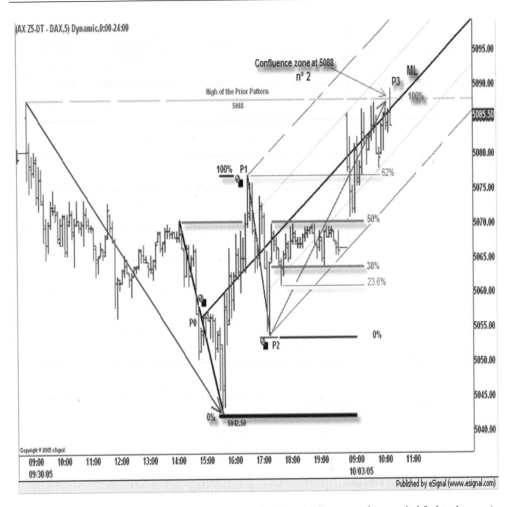

Figure 15.3 Energy status of the ongoing correction (cont.) (Courtesy of www.pitchforktrader.com)

width of the 38−50% Fibonacci ratio channel. Before the morning is over (around 10:45 CET), the market reaches the confluence zone no. 2 at the 5088 level.

Conclusion: Finally, what appears to be a double layer confluence has become a triple one, because the revealed resistance materializes at the 100% Fibonacci ratio level. Thus, our confluence becomes stronger and more respectable, in spite of the erratic movements caused by the local market price turbulence which is ready to reverse or to explode at any time.

15.3 MULTI-LEVEL LINE INTERSECTION CONFLUENCES: CASE STUDIES

S&P 500 e-mini and Dow e-mini Charts

The multi-level confluences in Fig. 15.4 show very strong support potential, in spite of the turbulence of the local market. Confluence no. 1 is a triple layer intersection formed by the trigger line (TL) of the P0-P1-P2 pitchfork, the warning line (WL-02) of the same pitchfork,

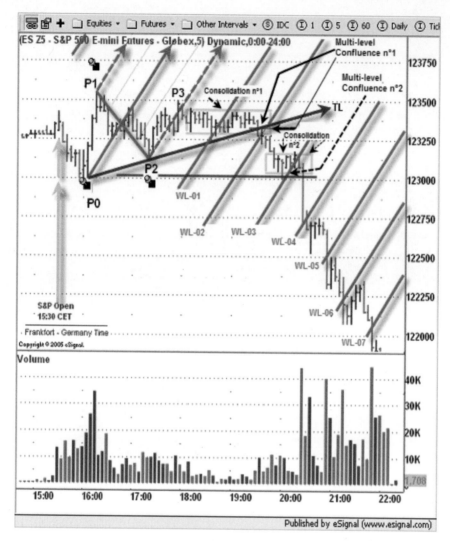

Figure 15.4   Multi-level confluences (Courtesy of www.pitchforktrader.com)

and the lower border of consolidation no. 1. As we can see, the market tests this border line several times until it reaches the confluence point, where it zooms through, tests it, and then retests it for the last time, on its way down.

Confluence no. 2 is also a triple layer intersection formed by the P0 resistance line at 1230 level, the warning line (WL-03) and the lower border of consolidation no. 2. We notice the multiple bar consolidation no. 2 with the market touching its lower borderline several times (Fig. 15.4). When it reaches confluence point no. 2, the price zooms through downwards, without looking back. The market flow drop is maintained for several hours, until the close of the day.

Figure 15.5 illustrates two multi-level confluences, each of them composed of three trend lines. The first confluence is situated at the 10960 level and is composed of a horizontal resistance line of two previous highs, the upper border of a symmetrical triangle and the 50% Fibonacci ratio line of the up-sloping pitchfork. The second confluence is located at the 11455 level, and

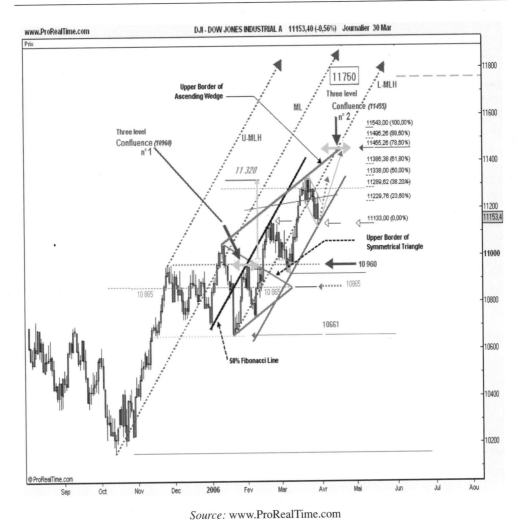

Source: www.ProRealTime.com

Figure 15.5   Two multi-level confluences (Courtesy of www.pitchforktrader.com)

is a three-line intersection of the upper border of the ascending wedge[2], the lower median line (L-MLH) and the 78.6% Fibonacci ratio level.

15.4   MULTI-ZONE CONFLUENCES WITH MULTI-LEVEL LINE INTERSECTIONS: CASE STUDIES

Vodaphone (FTSE 100) Charts

As we have already mentioned, the confluence must be drawn well in advance (see Fig. 15.6). The market flow could stop dead, accelerate or make a sideways move when approaching the confluence zone. The three confluences at the 125.15, 133 and 139 levels become obvious when we have studied the field ahead of the market. It goes without saying that there could be other

---

[2] Wedge – a chart formation having the shape of converging straight lines either slope up or slope down.

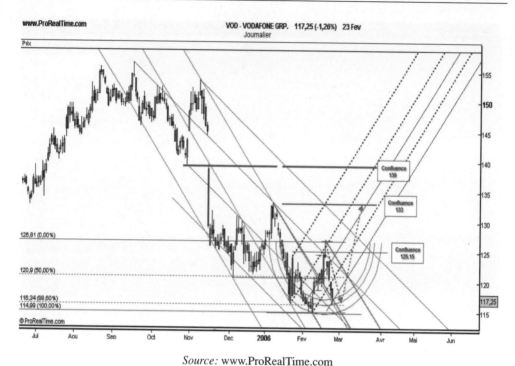

Source: www.ProRealTime.com

Figure 15.6   Triple pitchforks and Fibonacci arcs (Courtesy of www.pitchforktrader.com)

choices. The three confluences marked in Fig. 15.6 have a similar composition, being formed of horizontal resistances, median lines and the associated lines of the three pitchforks, possibly also Fibonacci lines (not calculated and not shown).

Continuing our research (Fig. 15.7) we have located additional confluences. We have also drawn a more illustrative pitchfork for the local market, with a gap median line where the anchor is located exactly at the 50% Fibonacci ratio of the gap.

Adding an inside mini-median line (Fig. 15.8) to the already existing P0-P1-P2 major pitchfork will certainly greatly help the trader detect the hidden confluences, thus offering new trading opportunities. Finally, the study of the confluences would not be complete without the assistance of the Fibonacci ratios tools (Fig. 15.9 on p. 294).

15.5   CONFLUENCE VS CLUSTER

KESA (UK Stock) Charts

We have defined the confluence as the *intersection* of two or more trend lines, usually composed of median lines and their associates, the Fibonacci ratios lines, and any trend lines emanating from key levels of the immediate past of the market activity. The more numerous the lines participating in a confluence, the stronger its stopping power will be. A three-line intersection has more opportunities to stop the market flow than a two-line intersection. All these trend lines have a *criss-cross structure*, made of horizontal and oblique trend lines.

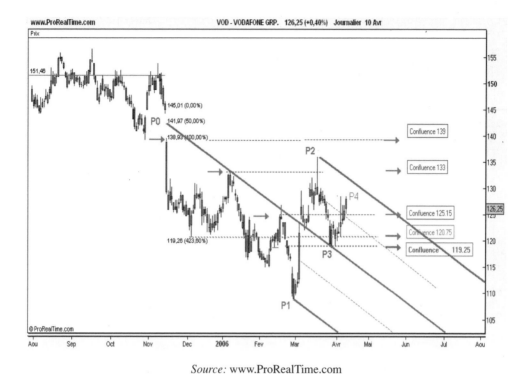

Source: www.ProRealTime.com

Figure 15.7   Locating additional confluences (Courtesy of www.pitchforktrader.com)

Source: www.ProRealTime.com

Figure 15.8   Adding an inside mini-median line (Courtesy of www.pitchforktrader.com)

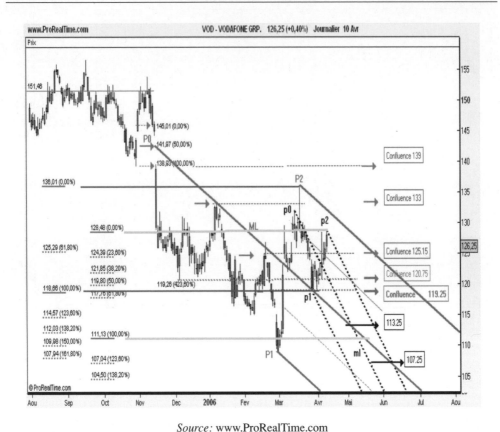

Figure 15.9   Adding the Fibonacci ratios (Courtesy of www.pitchforktrader.com)

The cluster is usually formed when the market builds a very *narrow and/or overlapping zone*, where multiple trend lines are either superimposed, contiguous or in close proximity to each other. Again, the more numerous they are, the stronger the characteristics of the cluster will be. The cluster differs from the confluence because it is not an intersection of horizontal and oblique lines, but rather a parallel line structure formed of various horizontal lines which are more or less overlapping.

Let us continue with our study of the differences between the confluence and the cluster concepts, using Figs. 15.10–15.16, and Table 15.1.

Figure 15.10 illustrates the building of a two-level confluence using the 273 level resistance and the median line of the A-B-C pitchfork. The AB and BC swings have been drawn in order to use the Fibonacci tools if the breakout above point D materializes. We have multiple reasons to believe in an imminent breakout.

- A wide range consolidation between the 226 and 273 levels.
- A narrow range consolidation (265 and 273 levels) – smaller than a quarter of the wider consolidation – located right under the proposed breaking out D point. The presence of a narrow height consolidation within a wider one emphasizes the probability of an imminent breakout. The resistance location under the 273 level, and the fact that is situated in the upper quarter of the wide consolidation, enhances this probability even

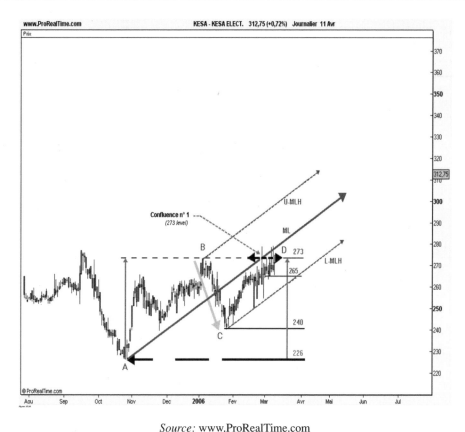

Source: www.ProRealTime.com

Figure 15.10   Building a two-level confluence (Courtesy of www.pitchforktrader.com)

more. The narrower the bars of the trading range, the more probable the eventuality of an imminent breakout will be.
- A probable inceptive up-sloping trend generated at the A pivot anchor of the pitchfork,
- An up-trending channel formed by the L-MLH and the ML, having the most current market flow in its upper half.

The great strength of the 273 level resistance line is expressed by the multi-point touches of the local market (Fig. 15.10) and also by the presence of two preceding tops (mid September 2005 and beginning of January 2006). This true resistance landmark has, for almost a year, strongly resisted all laborious piercing and breaking attacks caused by the market turbulence.

One thing is almost sure! Should the market flow succeed in breaching this dam-like landmark, there will be a strong outburst, with huge bars, the only way of invading a long-infallible citadel.

As we anticipated, the market flow has escaped (Fig. 15.11) from the double range consolidation, plainly shown by the two huge bars. There will certainly follow additional volatile bars, because of the lengthy attack period of the now breached 273 level resistance. With the initial swings in place we are immediately ready to apply all four Fibonacci ratio techniques.

The huge amount of unlocked kinetic energy encapsulated within the dam-like market structure propels the price sky high, to more than twice its initial wide consolidation (Fig. 15.12).

Once we apply the three Fibonacci techniques for determining the market value projections and expansions, we obtain five levels of confluence (details in Fig. 15.13 on p. 297).

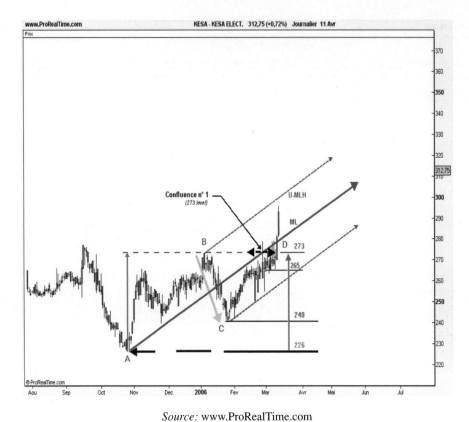

Source: www.ProRealTime.com

Figure 15.11   Market flow escape (Courtesy of www.pitchforktrader.com)

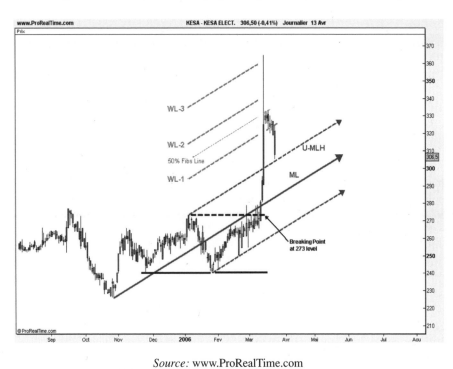

Source: www.ProRealTime.com

Figure 15.12   Kinetic energy propels the price sky high (Courtesy of www.pitchforktrader.com)

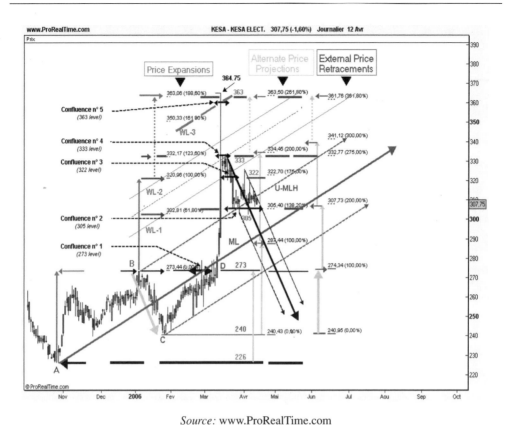

Source: www.ProRealTime.com
Figure 15.13   Five levels of confluence (Courtesy of www.pitchforktrader.com)

Once the market flow retraces from its short-lived top at the 364.75 level (Fig. 15.14) we apply the indispensable internal retracement Fibonacci tool with the concomitant creation of a minor pitchfork. Thus the local market is better described within the general context already revealed by the major pitchfork. Out of the five choices already obtained by the Fibonacci tools (Fig. 15.13), three are calculated by applying the internal price retracement technique (Fig. 15.14).

In order to have a general view of all possible confluences (remember the dictum 'Think globally and act locally!'), we have systematized (Fig. 15.15 on p. 299) the results of the four Fibonacci ratios techniques, and therefore have obtained five confluences, each having their own degree of halting power.

Figure 15.16 (on p. 299) gives a charting synopsis of the total number of clusters obtained either through the use of the four Fibonacci tools or by searching for key levels. Thus we have obtained a global view of clusters which perfectly synchronizes with the confluence levels.

In order to improve our understanding of the cluster concept, in Table 15.1 we have analyzed in detail the characteristics of the clusters drawn in Fig. 15.16. We notice that there are five 2–4 multi-level clusters with a cluster zone width representing 0.33% to 1.60%. The tighter the percentage, the more efficient the cluster will be.

Conclusion: Instead of being symbiotically and systematically used as part of the daily routine, confluences and clusters are too often neglected or badly used by the novice trader. They are both excellent and prolific tools in our search for low-risk high-probability trades.

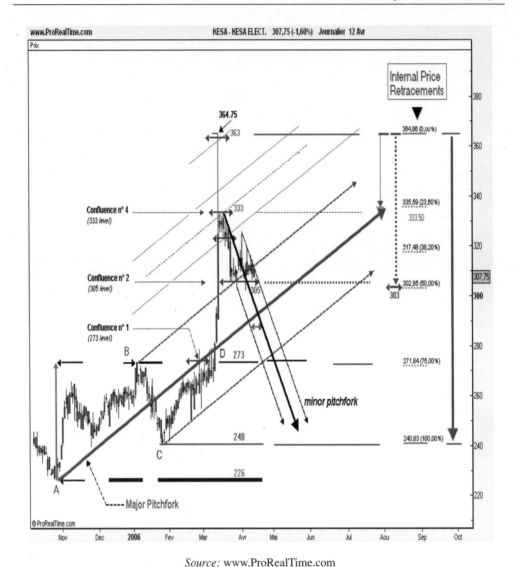

Figure 15.14   Applying the internal retracement Fibonacci tool on dual pitchforks
(Courtesy of www.pitchforktrader.com)

15.6   KEY LEARNING POINTS

Even if the confluences seem to be highly visible on our charts, it is not so obvious how to use
them successfully because most traders do not have the necessary experience to unveil the entire
panoply of the hidden trend lines.

- Do not forget that even if the confluences have a specific power to halt the market flow
  in its tracks, especially when they are multi-leveled, we should not ignore the possibility
  of an acceleration through or a consolidation.

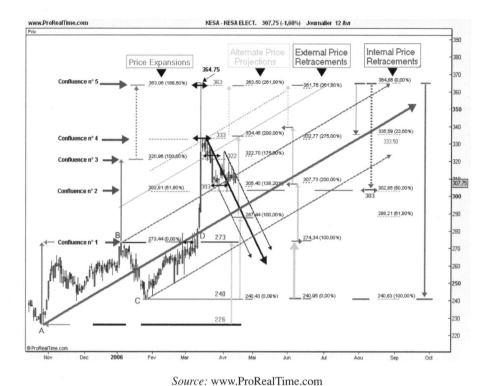

Source: www.ProRealTime.com

Figure 15.15 Results of four Fibonacci ratios leading to the creation of five confluences (Courtesy of www.pitchforktrader.com)

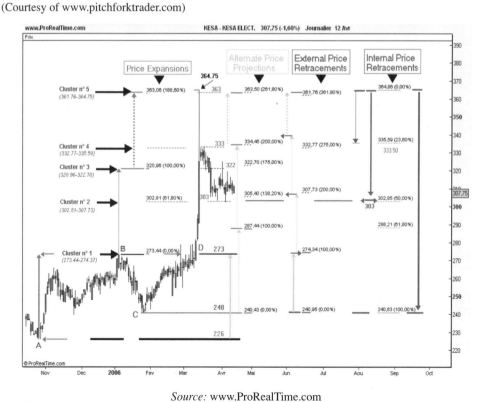

Source: www.ProRealTime.com

Figure 15.16 Global view of clusters (Courtesy of www.pitchforktrader.com)

Table 15.1 Characteristics of clusters

Cluster no	1	2	3	4	5
Zone's High	274.34	307.73	322.70	335.59	364.75
Zone's Low	273.44	302.81	320.81	332.77	361.76
Width	0.90	4.92	1.89	2.82	2.99
Percentage	0.33%	1.60%	0.59%	0.84%	0.82%
Zone's Midpoint	*273*	*303*	*322*	*333*	*364*
Zone's Layers	2	4	2	3	3

Source: www.pitchforktrader.com

- The procedure for managing a confluence is composed of the following triad: understanding the context, energy status analysis of the current market flow, and the drawing of the confluences. The timing trajectory of the confluence, well in advance of the market flow development, is the trading landmark. The intersecting point calculations are usually done with the help of the projecting ATR(21) technique. The contribution of the confluences to the profit potential of the trade will be greatly enhanced by taking into account the end run concept.
- Confluences and clusters can be used in an excellent symbiotic relationship, with one enhancing the stopping power of the other. The intricacy of a minor pitchfork within the major pitchfork on the same or higher time frame constitutes an integral part of the confluence/cluster duo practice.

All these techniques are highly workable when the trader remembers the saying 'Think globally and act locally'. There are few techniques more efficient than a systematized view of the context, landmarked by confluences and clusters and all this drawn on a neat chart.

16
Mirror Bars

Out of the multitude of reversal patterns, in this chapter we will treat only the mirror bars. We consider them to be very efficient patterns which offer a great opportunity for successful trading. Their optimal use will greatly assist the trader in his quest for low-risk high-probability trades. In order to be consistent, the trader has to behave rather like a hunter, searching for the trails on the trading grounds which will reveal the vital clues and lead him to the trade. In this search, we can detect two or multiple bar patterns which will signal the degree of exhaustion of an ongoing trend: *mirror bars* and *energy building clusters* (rectangles). The former topic is treated here and the latter in Chapter 17.

16.1 DEFINITION AND FUNCTION

The mirror bar pattern is classically formed from two bars of almost identical size, with the second bar listed as a reversal bar. Its characteristics are very suitable for trading because it reveals the exhaustion of the entire preceding trend. There may be three or even four bars of almost identical size in a row. The middle bar(s) can play the role of an inside bar, and their presence greatly enhances the reversing power of the entire pattern (Fig. 16.4).

An in-depth study of this pattern will reveal its positive reversal characteristics:

- The steeper the preceding trend's slope, the stronger the potential reversal will be.
- The higher the close of the first bar (preferably in its upper quarter, as near as possible to its high), the stronger the reversal probability will become; the close must be in the direction of the ongoing trend (see Fig. 16.5).
- The opening of the second bar could be very near to the close of the first bar. We notice that the lower the close of the second bar (preferably in its lowest quarter, as near as possible to its low), the more probable the reversal will become; the close must be moving opposite to the direction of the ongoing trend.
- The smaller and more numerous the mirror bars, the more likely the reversal. It is one of the ideal patterns where the market flow is able to restore its kinetic energy.

Where there are two huge bars, the probability of a reversal is dramatically improved. The first of these gaps represents the last gasp of the terminating exhausted trend, with the second huge bar representing the newly restored kinetic energy of the market. The reversal might be very sharp and is often accompanied by an enormous volume of traded transactions (usually known simply as 'volume'). When the size of these bars goes beyond the length of the three ATRs -Average True Range of the last 21-bar period, the trader should expect a *propagating sharp retracement*, which can be just around the corner before the countertrend develops. We affectionately call it the 'propagating pullback' because of its synergetic function in continuing the propagation of the restored kinetic energy. It greatly contributes to the start of the new trend.

The momentum that creates huge mirror bars is often so strong that it induces a runaway gap; especially after the sharp retracement occurs which will greatly contribute to the enhancement of the countertrend's kinetic energy storage.

- The smaller the inside bar (within the three or four mirror bar pattern), the stronger the development of the reversal signal.
- The exact time frame where the mirror bars are located has its own importance. The higher the time frame, the more probable that a reversal will come into being.

This pattern is not only used for reversals but also has its indispensable place in money management strategy. It can be successfully used as an initial stop loss or as a trailing stop location. To the trader, its sudden appearance will indicate a highly probable trade entry, with a well-chosen ergonomic stop loss just above/below the mirror bars for a corresponding short/long trade. There is more information on these topics in Chapter 19.

16.2   MIRROR BARS: CASE STUDIES

German Dax and S&P500 e-mini Index Charts

By looking at the trend line in Fig. 16.1, straight away we notice some of the characteristics of the mirror bar pattern mentioned above.

- A strong and consistent up-sloping trend line, with an inclination of about 30°.
- A triple bar pattern having a classic distribution of the open/close duo within the pattern:
  - the *close* of the first bar overlaps with its high at the 5167 level;
  - the *open* of the second bar is at the same level as the close of the first bar; this is identical with the open of the third bar. Notice that the middle bar is an extremely small bar, and is classified as an inside bar;
  - the third bar of the pattern has an open which coincides with the close of the inside bar, indicating a very strong level of indecision by the crowd. And, finally, the close of this third bar coincides with the low of the bar, revealing that the crowd has already taken its selling decision;
  - a narrow range, three-bar pattern is strongly indicating a high-velocity incoming momentum if the reversal is going to materialize. It does not foretell its future direction.

When in doubt about the trend's termination, draw an unorthodox line through the market, linking the lowest low and the highest high of the trend. It's a great visual tool!

As we anticipated, the market price stores enough down-sloping kinetic energy to gap down (Fig. 16.2 on p. 304). Instead of dropping like a stone, the market has decided to restore its kinetic energy and perform another trading range, having the double height of the initial top narrow range composed of the top triple bars.

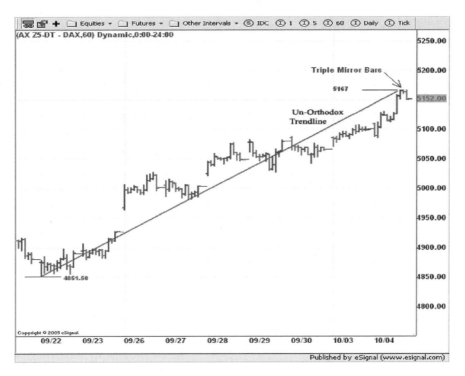

Figure 16.1   Characteristics of the mirror bar pattern (Courtesy of www.pitchforktrader.com)

Consolidation no. 1 and the ensuing pullback revitalizes the kinetic energy of the market flow (Fig. 16.3 on p. 305), bringing about a second gap almost double the size of the first. Before dropping further the price will rest for a while, creating consolidation no. 2.

If we take a global look at the market flow (Fig. 16.4 on p. 305) we realize that there are numerous double and triple mirror bars, each pattern having its own degree of halting power. The essential point to note here is the need to search for the supplementary factors, the reversal's catalysts that frequently accompany the mirror bar pattern. The unorthodox trend line is the visual tool that enhances the trend's presence.

The double deck narrow consolidation (Fig. 16.5 on p. 306) situated at the trend's top, is one of the strongest reversal patterns, especially when it is composed of seven narrow bars (NR7). The research work carried out on the NR4 and NR7 by Toby Crabel has plainly proved this (see his 1990 book *Day Trading with Short Term Price Patterns and Opening Breakout*).

As mentioned above, the advent of huge mirror bars (Fig. 16.6 on p. 306) is one of the few patterns that indicate a highly imminent reversal, the guarantor of a low-risk high-probability trade. Scrutinizing the mirror bars in Fig. 16.6, we note that, besides their more-than-double ATR, the open of the second bar is superimposed on the close of the first bar, and its close is contiguous, almost superimposed, on its high. There is a very high probability of a strong reversal.

The Fibonacci tool is very helpful here, indicated by the starting blocks of the second huge reversal bar. Not only does its open precisely coincide with the close of the first bar, but this unified open/close duo is laid out exactly on the 61.8% Fibonacci ratio location at 5056 German Dax level.

Figure 16.2   Multiple mirror bars (Courtesy of www.pitchforktrader.com)

Figure 16.7 (on p. 307) goes into more detail about the occurrence and development of the mirror bar pattern. As we can see, even if the two reversal bars are not exactly equal in height, the close of the first bar coincides with the open of the second bar, which has its close in its upper quarter. Even if it does not belong to the mirror bar pattern, the third bar greatly enhances the reversal by its height and its close, which is nearing the bar's high. It seems that the pattern's momentum is well revitalized, ready to invade the higher 'Plains Plateau' (otherwise the higher-price tablelands, the land of green grass grazing profit).

In spite of these two huge, consecutive upwards bars (nos 2 and 3), we caution the trader to expect a pullback in the very near future. Our own name for it is the 'reverberant pullback' because of its synergetic function in reverberating (continuing propagation) the restored kinetic energy, not only in confirming the reversal but also in greatly contributing to the inception of the new trend. However, we caution that frequently this pullback may occur by itself or accompanied by other pullbacks or even by a greater or narrower trading range.

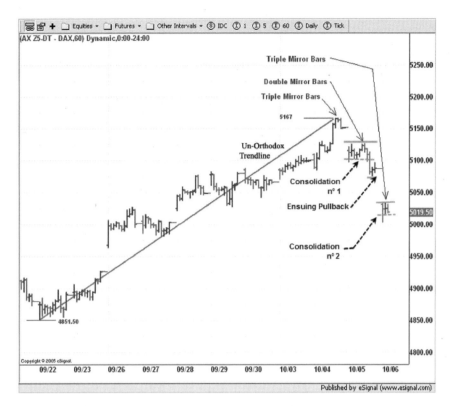

Figure 16.3   Consolidation and pullback process creates a second gap
(Courtesy of www.pitchforktrader.com)

Figure 16.4   Global look at the market flow with double and triple mirror bars
(Courtesy of www.pitchforktrader.com)

Figure 16.5 Strong reversal pattern: the double deck narrow consolidation
(Courtesy of www.pitchforktrader.com)

Figure 16.6 Huge mirror bars indicate a very probable reversal (Courtesy of www.pitchforktrader.com)

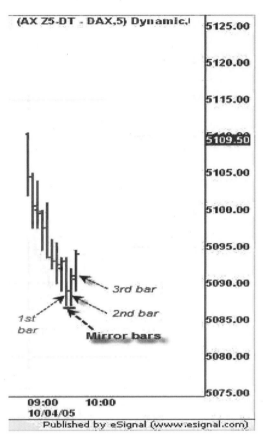

Figure 16.7 Origination and development of the mirror bar pattern
(Courtesy of www.pitchforktrader.com)

As we anticipated, the mirror bar pattern has developed a trading range (Fig. 16.8). It is bordered at the top by another mirror bar pattern (point B), and at the bottom by the initial mirror bar pattern (point A) associated with a piercing bar (point C). This fairly complex pattern could be the nucleus of a kinetic energy-building process that will catapult the market price all the way up to the last high (point F). One question naturally arises: If the accumulative process of the consolidation range restores sufficient kinetic energy, causing the market flow to explode, how high will it move? Or, in other words: How high is high?

The answer to this question is straightforward. The minimum price objective is the 100% projected height of the initial consolidation. However, we have frequently seen projected values between 200% and 400%.

Comparing Figs 16.8 and 16.9 (on p. 309), it is easy to see the sideways progression of the ongoing trading range. The piercing bar (point C) of the lower boundary retraces its close in the upper half, thus creating a long downward tail which witnesses the lost battle by the bears. As frequently happens in this case, the market flow creates a second consolidation formed by the parallels to points D and E, within the pre-existing trading range (bound by the two sets of mirror bars at points A and B).

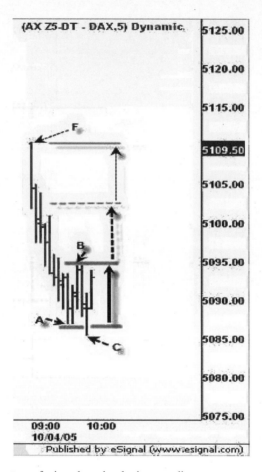

Figure 16.8 Complex pattern of mirror bars developing a trading range
(Courtesy of www.pitchforktrader.com)

This double-decker consolidation pattern has accumulated a tremendous amount of kinetic energy during its 13 bar length, and is now ready to explode the price upwards towards the 'Plains Plateau', the land of green grass grazing profit.

The mirror bars located at point E constitute the real starting blocks of this virtual price explosion, functioning as a price catapult. The move is so intense that it goes beyond the highest high (point F) in a swing of only three bars, more than five ATRs away. By the same token, it has evolved more than 200% of the initial measure consolidation height.

16.3 MIRROR BARS AND THEIR PITCHFORK APPLICABILITY: CASE STUDIES

German Dax Index and S&P 500 e-mini Charts

In the first part of this chapter, we learned the characteristics of the mirror bar patterns. Let us pursue the process of understanding them, and examine their applicability to the pitchfork (Figs 16.10–16.14).

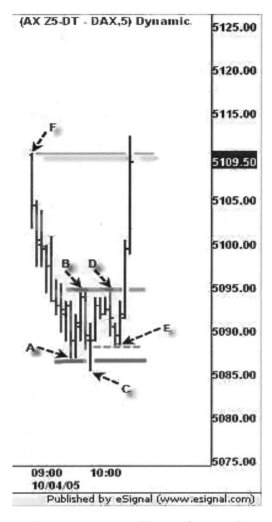

Figure 16.9 Ongoing trading range progresses sideways (Courtesy of www.pitchforktrader.com)

The mirror bar pattern plays an extremely important role in selecting both the originating P0-P1-P2 pivots and the neighbouring pivots (P4 to P7) which constitute the working framework of the developing pitchfork. The daily search for mirror bars, both on the main trading time frame and also on higher time-frame charts, will greatly enhance the optimal building of a workable pitchfork. Preferably it should be done as a matter of routine before the opening. In Fig. 16.10, the P2, P3 and P4 pivots of the P0-P1-P2 traditional pitchfork are all formed of mirror bars.

The chart in Fig. 16.11 (on p. 311) shows two sets of triple mirror bars: the higher reversal level P0 pivot and the lower halt location P3 pivot. The former has the power of reversing the prior trend, and the latter is just halting the market flow in the process of correcting the ongoing down-sloping trend.

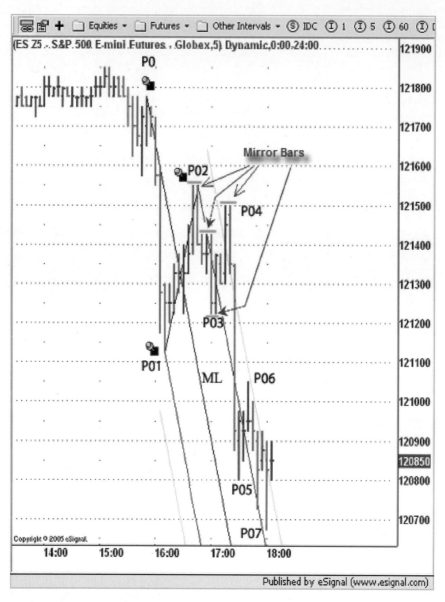

Figure 16.10 Mirror bars forming the pivots of a traditional pitchfork
(Courtesy of www.pitchforktrader.com)

As we can see in Fig. 16.12, there is a synergy between the up-sloping major pitchfork and the down-sloping minor pitchfork, creating a competitive edge for the trader:

- enhancement of the halting power of the triple mirror bars (P3 pivot level);
- creation of a very visible and efficient confluence formed by the horizontal support of the P3 pivot, the sliding parallel line (PH) and the upper median line (u-mlh) of the minor down-sloping pitchfork;
- the choice of applying the Fibonacci ratios tools and creating further confluence zones.

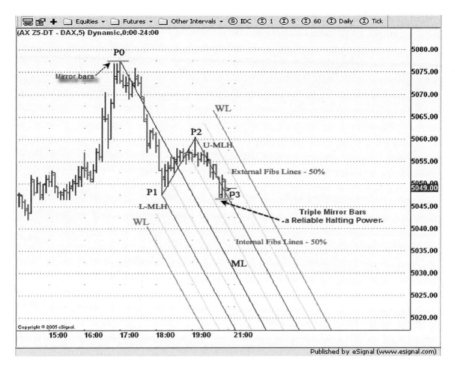

Figure 16.11   Two sets of triple mirror bars (Courtesy of www.pitchforktrader.com)

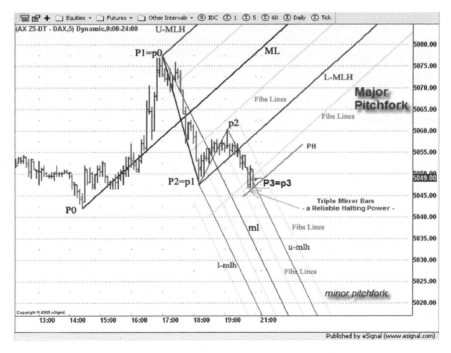

Figure 16.12   Example of the synergy between the major and minor pitchforks and the mirror bar pattern (Courtesy of www.pitchforktrader.com)

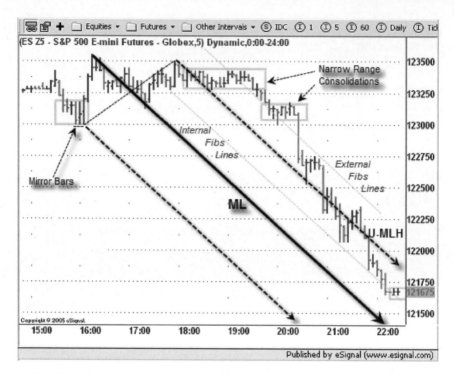

Figure 16.13 Mirror bars used collectively in a trading range consolidation
(Courtesy of www.pitchforktrader.com)

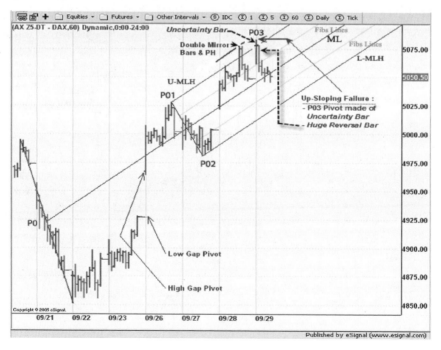

Figure 16.14 Role of the mirror bar in creating short trade opportunities
(Courtesy of www.pitchforktrader.com)

The chart illustrated in Fig. 16.13 shows the power of the mirror bars when used not only individually with their strong reversing or temporary halting powers, but also collectively as a component of a trading range consolidation.

Figure 16.14 wonderfully illustrates the role of the mirror bar set-up in full synergy with a double pattern top (an uncertainty bar and a big reversal bar), thus creating an up-sloping failure at P03 pivot level. This situation gives the trader two great short-trade opportunities: one under the low of the second bar of the mirror bar (trade no. 1) and the second under the low of the uncertainty bar (trade no. 2).

These two trades can be considered not only as two unrelated trades (1 and 2), but also as a single trade, where the first entry (1) is the entry for the main trade, and the second (2) is purely an add-on order, surely confirming the highly-profitable short trade. Related or not, the two trades have in common the initial stop loss location situated just above the double mirror bars.

Conclusion: In spite of its extraordinary quality as a power to reverse a well-developed trend and as a temporary halting landmark of a vigorous trend while initiating a corrective movement, the mirror bar pattern is no less valuable when used in a money management strategy as well as an initial stop loss or applied as an optimal trailing stop.

16.4 KEY LEARNING POINTS

- Mirror bars are faithful witnesses to a trend's exhaustion. They are implicated in reversals, temporary trend halts and money management strategies.
- Any mirror bar analysis encompasses: the prior trend's slope (better visualized with an unorthodox trend line); the open/close duo; the type and number of bars within the pattern; and the routine mirror bar search in at least three time frames.
- Mirror bars go hand-in-hand with the narrow inside bars and their narrow trading range (NR4 & NR7) or, alternatively, the volatile bars with their 'reverberant pullback' followed by a possible consolidation just before the virtual jailbreak towards the highest high.
- The reliability of the mirror bar as a trading tool is greatly enhanced by a synergetic association with the pitchfork tool.

17
Energy-Building Rectangles

The management of the energy exhaustion and acceleration processes of the market flow is a scarce topic in our trading literature. We believe that this is an omission because most energy-related profitable trades are easily identified after the trader has sufficiently trained his eye.

17.1 DEFINITION AND FUNCTION

Energy is the essence of movement, however and wherever it is displayed: physiologically, as in the human body, or financially, as displayed in the markets. The user is seldom aware of this energy and rarely does he actively try to master it. Most of the time, the events and routine of the day consume the necessary energy without the participant being conscious of what is going on. Extreme energy-consuming situations, such as *exhaustion* (almost total consumption) or *exacerbation* (high quantity consumed in a very short period of time), will force the participant to consider the regulatory mechanism of energy management.

Understanding the dynamics of energy consumption is one of the basic requirements of the trading process. Moreover, understanding it fully is what makes the difference between an experienced and a novice trader. With regard to extreme fluctuating energy situations, we can say that the market movements are responsible for the energy consumption cycle characterized by the following two points.

1.   *Exhaustion* represents the lowest energy level, which will be restored in an ergonomic rhythm so that the market flow will be partially or totally revitalized, ready to continue the trend's development. The trader should be aware that this mechanism couldn't be forced nor readily influenced. It occurs as and when the market judges that it is necessary.
2.   Most of the time, *exacerbation* occurs in a virtual jailbreak manner; expressed by a few big bars, each with a height of 2–4 times the Average True Range – ATR(21). The slope of the trend is over 60°. The huge liberated energy will be tremendous but of short duration, and a reversal or an associated consolidation will be imminent.

Market fluctuations can also develop more gradually, reaching the highest energy level through a milder acceleration process. It is most probable that they will be guided by a 40–60° sloping channel. In this case, the size of the bar will be just above the value of one ATR(21). All chart formations are more-or-less energy related in their developmental stages.

It is difficult to identify the energy-building rectangle at the start of its development. It is defined as a rectangular pattern which has a minimum of two touches on each boundary line that forms its upper and lower limits (see Fig. 17.1). In a breakout energy pattern, a rectangle can also be identified by having three touching points, with the fourth counted as the breakout point. Of all the energy-related chart formations the energy-building rectangle is the one most frequently encountered. Its characteristics can be interdependent and widely diversified:

- *Location*: The location can be anywhere on the trending or sideways pattern: a small bar range forming a pullback within a trend; a small bar range within the ascending and/or descending swings of a consolidation; a rectangle within a rectangle; a big rectangle chart formation with a reversal role at the end of the trend, etc.
- *Height and width*: The height and the width dictate the strength of energy-building rectangles. Their morphology will act as:
  - a real magnet; or as
  - a halting brick wall; or as
  - the starting block, a virtual catapult of the market price.

  The modulation of the market flow turbulence becomes the highest priority.
- *Internal structure*: The internal structure plays an important role and is dependent on the distribution of the closes of the four touching boundary bars. The study of alternate closes can confirm, first, the pattern and, second, the continuation (or not) of the rectangle pattern. Close observation will certainly help detect the creation of a breakout which will release the energy. In order to better visualize the alternate closes, draw a series of linking segments from one close to the next. Most of the time, there is a signal at the end of a narrow bar energy-building rectangle which informs the trader that the pattern will be terminated.
- *Measuring technique*: The measuring technique is not well known but it represents a real competitive edge for the experienced trader. The procedure is very simple. Measure the height of the pattern, which is price dependent, and project it vertically from the lower/upper boundary in order to obtain the measuring upwards/downwards projection (see Fig. 17.9). We can also measure the width of the pattern as a horizontal distance (segment), and project it vertically from the lower/upper boundary in order to obtain the most probable measuring upwards/downwards projection.
- *Count technique*: Another practically unknown method is called the count technique. It consists of literally counting the number of bars which make up the consolidation pattern. The trader should expect the same number value at the end of the trend as at the breaking point, just above the upper boundary for an upward projection and vice versa for a downward projection. For example, expect at least an eight-bar trend after an eight-bar consolidation rectangle.
- *Market future direction*: It is almost impossible to forecast the future direction of the market after the energy-building structure is in place. However, by using certain confirming factors such as higher time frames, momentum and volume indicators, Elliott waves and others, the canny trader can pretty well anticipate the most probable direction.

And anyway . . . the last word belongs to the pre-selected, initial stop-loss location which will validate or invalidate the entry depending on the pre-established individual risk tolerance of each trader.

17.2 MICRO AND MACRO ASPECTS OF ENERGY-BUILDING RECTANGLES: CASE STUDIES

S&P 500 e-mini, German Dax Index and FTSE Stock Charts

Figure 17.1 illustrates the micro aspect of an energy-building rectangle which has already created six touching points during the night's ES session. The sixth bar is an inside bar that announces a possible reversal towards the opposite boundary (lower border). We are looking for a breakout trade at the opening of the S&P 500 at 15:30 CET (09:30 ET US). Two very important factors must be considered:

1.   The night ES chart is used mostly as a guide for inter-market analysis when trading the German Dax Futures. We watch the ES pre-opening reactions after the 08:00 ET US news (14:00 CET), almost 90 minutes before the S&P 500 opening (see the rectangle labelled 1 through 6 on Fig. 17.1). Thus we expect a strong breakout within the first S&P

Figure 17.1   Micro aspect of an energy-building rectangle on a night ES chart (Courtesy of www.pitchforktrader.com)

500 opening hour. The afternoon Dax will closely follow the moves of the S&P 500. The usual operational time frame is 15-min, but lower time frame charts (ES and Dax) are often referred to in order to pinpoint an eventual entry.

2.   We watch the night ES chart as an inter-market decision factor but, more often than not, the trade will be performed on a 15-min German Dax Futures chart.

Figure 17.2 shows a similar breakout-type trade through the use of the 1-2-3-4 energy-building rectangle. The first clue to a very probable up-side reversal is the formation of the mirror bar

Figure 17.2   Break-out trade through a 1-2-3-4 touches energy-building rectangle
(Courtesy of www.pitchforktrader.com)

(marked 5 on the chart), which will become the origin of the breakout. We can see the upper boundary has been penetrated through the breaking point by a huge bar belonging to a series of bars showing accelerated momentum. It has built a strong kinetic energy during its trading range sojourn (14 bars). The duration of the up-sloping trend, very close to its highest high, is composed of 15 bars, if we count the breaking point bar, and only 14 without it.

Here again in Fig. 17.3 can be seen the same breakout-type trade, awaiting the opening of the S&P 500 market. The energy-building rectangle revitalizes the market flow dynamics, and initiates an upwards move by almost three initial height projections before returning to the initial

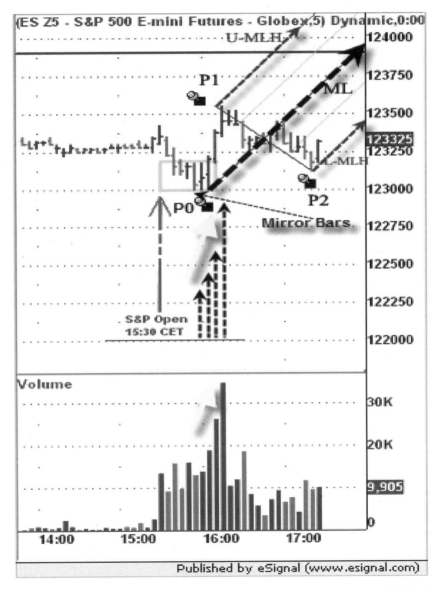

Figure 17.3 Break-out trade at the opening of the S&P 500 market (Courtesy of www.pitchforktrader.com)

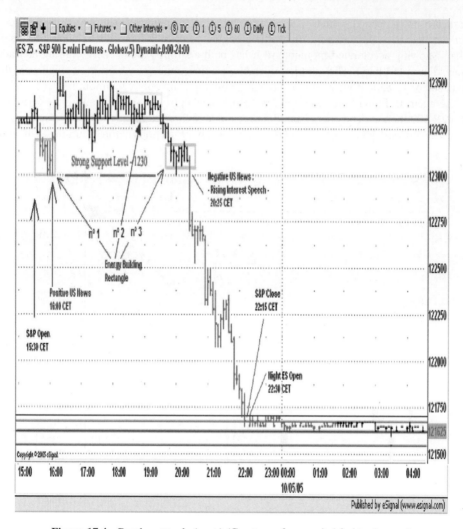

Figure 17.4 Break-out trade (cont.) (Courtesy of www.pitchforktrader.com)

rectangular zone. Please see the continuation of this chart in Figs 17.4 and 17.5. The building of the mirror and the breaking bar is well sustained by a gradually increasing heavy volume.

After this initial upwards projection, done immediately at the S&P 500 opening, the market flow continues sideways for more than three hours (Fig. 17.4). Around 20:00 CET (14:00 ET US) it drops to the same zone as that of the S&P 500 opening energy-building rectangle. It is halted at its lower boundary at the 1230 level, in the expectation of the 20:25 CET (14:25 ET US) speech by Alan Greenspan (then Chairman of the Board of Governors of the Federal Reserve). More and more tight energy-building rectangles are built, this time with much stronger restored energy. They represent a perfect graphical expression of the mental reflection of the crowd anxiously awaiting the news. As the news is bad, the market drops eleven times the height of the initial energy-building rectangle no. 3 situated just above the 1230 level. Right after the announcement of rising interest rates, we note that the market price drop is fierce and quick.

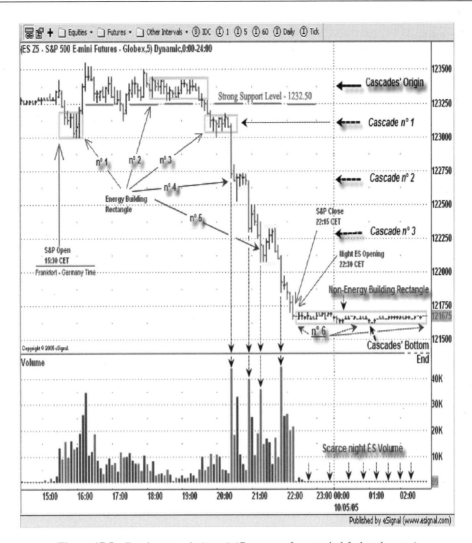

Figure 17.5   Break-out trade (cont.) (Courtesy of www.pitchforktrader.com)

Looking at the chart in Fig. 17.5, which is similar to Fig. 17.6, we notice that the huge drop was not only due to the energy build-up in trading ranges 2 and 3. Another two energy build-up rectangles (4 and 5) have also contributed greatly to the enhancement of the down-sloping momentum. The peculiarity of these narrow bar ranges is not only their own formation process but also their Cartesian distribution within the down-sloping intangible time–price space, in an almost perfect series of virtual cascades (Fig. 17.5). It is the inverse of the ladder-like structure which takes place in an up-sloping market (refer to Fig. 17.9).

Important: The narrow range rectangle (6) is not an energy-building pattern, in spite of its narrow bar range outlook. It is created only by the low overnight activity of the night ES limited volume. It starts with the close of today's S&P 500 day session and ends at the opening of the next day's S&P 500 session.

Figure 17.6   Double deck energy-building rectangles (Courtesy of www.pitchforktrader.com)

The double deck rectangles (numbers 1 and 2) in Fig. 17.6 have greatly contributed to the strength of the market flow energy. Although the energy of the preceding trend has propelled the price up to the 5110 level zone, it now has to stop and consolidate its kinetic energy. Its partially exhausted energy reserve is greatly revitalized when the market flow has to temporarily break its 35° ascending slope and create the double deck energy building rectangles.

The second energy pattern (no. 2) is very likely to be developed, due to the very strong support in the 5090 zone. Remember this double deck energy-building pattern is very often the prelude to a strong trend continuation.

Once again, we stress the fact that looking for the energy build-up rectangles will greatly improve your trading results. Make it a daily routine. And don't forget to check the multiple time frames as well!

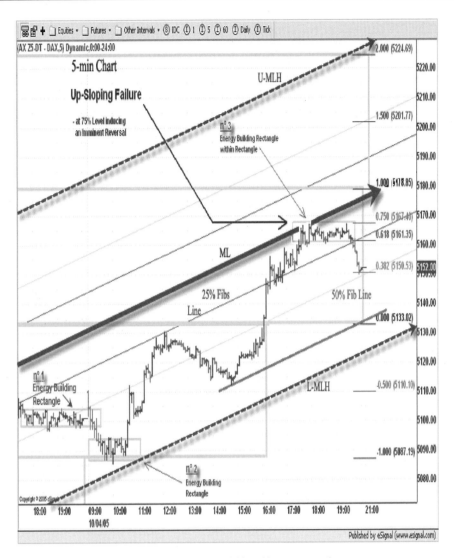

Figure 17.7 Power of energy-building rectangles within a bigger rectangle
(Courtesy of www.pitchforktrader.com)

Figure 17.7 illustrates the power of energy-building rectangles (1, 2 amd 3) within a bigger
rectangle (a pattern within a pattern). The energy exhaustion of the up-sloping trend, and the
energy build-up of a counter-trend momentum through the formation of the narrow rectangle
(no. 3), reveal the up-sloping failure (5161−5167 zone).

Once again, this technique provides a competitive and profitable edge to the trader. The use of
the Fibonacci ratios technique greatly enhances the visibility and comprehension of this specific
pattern of behaviour.

Figure 17.8 illustrates the development of the up-sloping trend from P0 to P7 pivots. It is
scattered with multiple energy-building rectangles, either as an originating zone (no. 1) or as

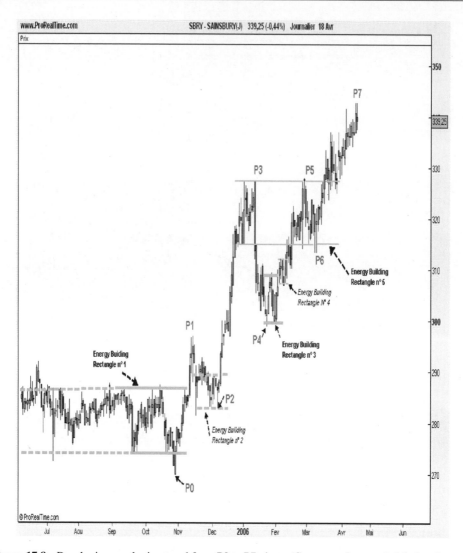

Figure 17.8   Developing up-sloping trend from P0 to P7 pivots (Courtesy of www.pitchforktrader.com)

pullback patterns (numbers 2, 3, 4, and 5). It is abundantly clear that they are the hallmarks of the trend's development, from inception to development to termination.

17.3   MEASURING TECHNIQUES AND ENERGY-BUILDING RECTANGLES: CASE STUDIES

German Dax Index Charts

The left side of the chart in Fig. 17.9 is scattered with four narrow bar ranges going from NR4 to NR7 (seven narrow range bars), which represent a ladder-like up-trending structure from the P0

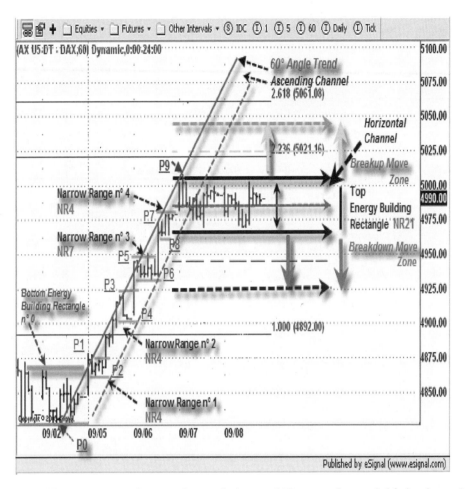

Figure 17.9 'Broken arrow' aspect of an up-sloping trend (Courtesy of www.pitchforktrader.com)

to P9 pivots. It is the inverse of the cascade-like trend structure (refer to Fig. 17.5) which takes place in a down-sloping market.

The peculiarity of this market is not the multitude of its narrow range bars but rather the 'broken arrow' aspect of the up-sloping trend. The market flow has flown like an arrow from a bow, from the bottoming energy-building rectangle (no. 0) whose lowest point is the P0 pivot, to the highest high (P9 pivot). This ladder-like channel in a 60° slope guides this almost perpendicular ascension. When it reaches the P9 pivot level, the halting power of the three bar reversal pattern abruptly breaks the slope, which goes from a 60° angle to a zero ground level angle. It is as if the market flow has been hit by a high-speed train so that the up-sloping arrow is broken into two portions around the 5000 price level, again the multiple zeros key number levels.

Now the horizontal channel (0° angle) encapsulates the local market flow within its upper and lower boundaries, practising the same ladder-like structure, but this time oriented horizontally. Perhaps we should describe it as *horizontal zigzagging*?

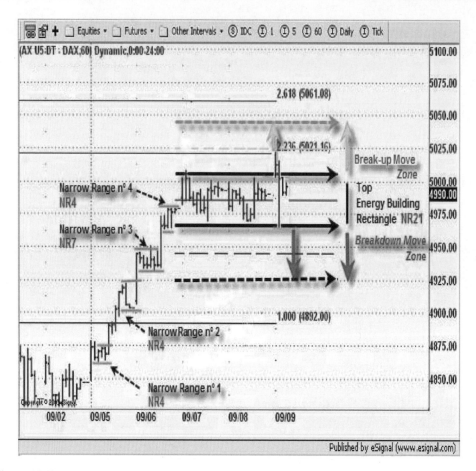

Figure 17.10   Dual trending characteristics of the initial energy-building rectangle
(Courtesy of www.pitchforktrader.com)

The measuring technique illustrated in Fig. 17.9 is not well known, in spite of its great and fairly consistent potential for profit. Every time that a sideways market is initiated, the astute trader routinely applies this technique in upward and downward projections, thus creating a dual breakout zone. When the breakout is initiated, the multiple projections will keep track of the developing trend, assisting the trader in the decision-making process. Do not ignore the opposite projections, because they could assist you over and over again. As the old adage says: An old resistance can always become a new support and vice versa!

Figure 17.9 has optimally prepared us for the imminent breakout of the market flow. Figure 17.10 illustrates its bursting out and immediate development. After the first bar of the upwards false breakout, the second huge bar first completely reverses and then entirely traverses the height of the energy-building rectangle, testing its lower boundary. Then, attracted by the magnet-like power, it closes just below the upper boundary. The following two narrow range bars are sheltered right under the wing of the top energy-building rectangle, probably starting a new narrow trading range within the upper half of this top rectangle.

17.4 MAPPING THE CONTEXT AND LOCAL MARKET: CASE STUDIES

German Dax Index Charts

There is nothing more stressful than a 'naked' chart. A trader's task is to choose the most appropriate tools for his type of market which are optimally suited to his personality traits. After the choice of tools, the most difficult part of the task is to apply them successfully and consistently.

Apart from money management and the knowledge of one's psychology, it is the tactics of trade management which highlight the difference between a novice trader and the experienced trader of five years' standing. Even if it seems obvious to say so, trading is an art which consists of not only adding the most efficient tools to the 'naked' chart, but also in applying and managing them most effectively.

In the hands of a skilful trader the energy-related patterns can make all the difference. He will certainly know how to integrate these energy-building patterns with other techniques, in a harmonious synergy (Fig. 17.11):

- measuring techniques (market reaches 338% projection);
- unorthodox and traditional trend lines;
- trend lines including the pivotal (P0-P4 and P2-P4) lines;
- confluence (between the ML and the unorthodox trend line at the 4400 level);
- median lines and associate lines;

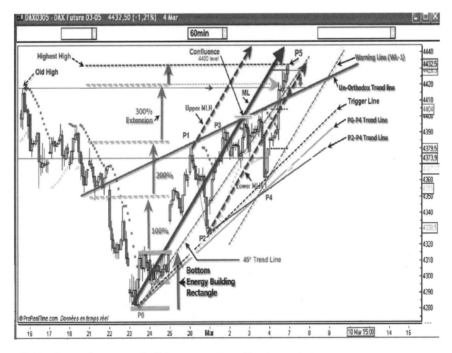

Figure 17.11 Integrating energy-building rectangles with other techniques (Courtesy of www.pitchforktrader.com)

- detection of key levels as part of the everyday routine;
- most adequate time frames for intra-day trading (15-min and 60-min charts);
- 45° angle trend line.

Conclusion: The trader is only a player of his markets, but in his mind he should aspire to perform as well as the accomplished musician who has left behind the mere mechanics of music making after becoming an artist in his field.

Many are selected, but only a few elected!

17.5 KEY LEARNING POINTS

- Learn how to detect the energy-building patterns and you will acquire a competitive edge.
- Be aware of the two main components of the energy consumption cycle successfully applied to the market flow: exhaustion and exacerbation.
- When screening the charts for these energy patterns be aware of their main influential characteristics: location, height, width, internal structure, measuring and the confirming direction factors.
- Watch the volume when you expect a breakout. It could be completely absent in a down-trend or exploding in an up-trend, at the breaking-point timing location or the next one or two bars. Otherwise expect a false breakout.
- The trading technique of awaiting news is for the experienced trader, who is capable of keeping the pre-arranged stops, and mastering the re-entries.
- Be aware of the cascade and ladder-like trend structures and take advantage of them.
- Always keep searching for confirming factors before you take the final decision.
- Remember that the energy-building patterns are the hallmarks of a trend's development, from inception to development through to its termination.
- And at the risk of repetition, remember the saying: An old resistance can always become a new support and vice versa!

18
The Pitchforks' Journey Through Multiple Time Frames

If we had to define in a single word the multiple time frame concept, it would be *cross-referencing*, which is described by the Merriam-Webster Collegiate Dictionary as: 'a notation or direction at one place to pertinent information in another place'. This term is slightly modified for financial markets, because in defining the time frame concept the word 'place' is replaced by the expression 'time environment location'. It is true to say that the price analysis of an upper time frame chart may have a stronger impact on the trade's outcome than using only the price study of the operational time frame.

18.1 DEFINITION AND FUNCTION

A time frame is defined as a unit of time utilized in the process of charting a security. It can vary from the smallest (a *tick*) to the longest time frame (a *year*). For short-term trading we primarily use the 15-min and 60-min operational charts.

In this chapter we will explore the synergy between the upper time frame pitchforks and the lower time frame median lines. We can usually rely on the strong magnetic attraction of the median lines of a higher time frame, which halt the market flow cold on the lower time frame. The upper time frames (daily, weekly and monthly) are only consulted initially; especially during the pre-open, in order to find the dominant trend which will guide our decisions. We also initially use the lower time frames, such as the 5-min or 3-min charts, in order to pinpoint our entries and exits, when they are not prearranged. The difficulty in understanding and using multiple time frames, illustrated by the lack of literature about the subject, is only natural and results from the complexity of the topic and our in-born conditioned behaviour. Cynthia A. Kase, a well-known teacher and trader, wrote a great book titled *Trading with the Odds*, which I warmly recommend. In the chapter called 'Freedom from Time and Space with Universal Bars', she quotes and interprets the research of Einstein:

> *Einstein maintains that our conceptions of time and space derive from our own human experience, the frame of reference that results from our empirical observations. This frame of reference is highly subjective. Our perceptions are limited to those we can easily comprehend using the five senses with which we examine the world ... Our universe is*

both infinite and limited. Freeing our minds from preconceived notions of reality allows us to grasp larger concepts. We live in an infinite universe that is limited only by our own perceptions of it ... This ability to imagine concepts beyond our perceived reality is what has made mankind's intellectual progress possible.

To see a time frame as a portion of another time frame is not easy; it requires imagination, creativity and training but is not impossible to accomplish. The time and effort spent during the learning process will be more than compensated by the reward of acquiring a hard-to-get competitive edge. Thus the trader will be able to quickly spot the dominant trend, so useful in the current short-term, competitive trading environment.

18.2 MULTIPLE TIME FRAMES AND FRACTAL GEOMETRY

The best way to get to grips with this concept is by understanding fractals, but don't worry, we do not intend to go into a detailed study.

If we want to measure the perimeter of the Mediterranean coast of Southern France using a 50-metre measuring unit, we will undoubtedly miss a number of details. By diminishing the measuring value and using a much smaller unit, we will increase the accuracy of the measurement by several degrees, thus obtaining a plethora of details. This is a classic example of an infinite choice measuring a unit in a finite space.

Benoit B. Mandelbrot first studied this phenomenon in the early 1960s. He described this new concept as applied to the financial markets in his 1997 revolutionary book entitled *Fractals and Scaling in Finance*. He created from scratch the science of fractal geometry, which is the only tool for studying complex systems such as analyzing the roughness of jagged edges. He named these highly irregular natural forms or complex events as *fractional dimensions*, shortened to *fractals*. They remain constant through magnification, and this constancy explains why in the financial markets, whatever the time frame used, we always get the same pattern formations in charts of various time frames. A set of Russian dolls perfectly describes this phenomenon: a big doll holds a smaller one, which contains an even smaller one, and so on. This repetitive containing process can continue to infinity. The *Brownian movements*, another complex chaotic process having dynamic fractional dimension characteristics, illustrate the fractal behaviour of the matter at the microscopic scale.[1]

18.3 MULTIPLE TIME FRAMES AND PHOTOGRAPHS FROM SPACE: AN ANALOGY

In order to better grasp the concept of multiple time frames, let us offer a visual and practical analogy using a series of satellite shots from space. The common denominator of this comparison will be to find the best results that will assist the pedestrian or the trader to optimally accomplish their individual tasks: better street orientation and optimal intra-day chart use, respectively. This will motivate us to strive as efficiently as possible to obtain the most appropriate outcome. Our objectives are precisely defined, as follows:

a)   to optimize a pedestrian's orientation in a crowded city, and
b)   to find the optimal market trend through the various time frames in such a way that the operational chart offers the best trading opportunity.

---

[1] Merriam-Webster's Collegiate Dictionary, 10th Edition defines the Brownian movements as 'a random movement of microscopic particles'.

Once these objectives are defined, let us proceed as follows:

1. In the first case, we study satellite observations of our planet progressively taken from a high altitude to street level.
2. In the second case, we study the market charts of the Brownian-type price movements throughout the financial market time frames.

The second objective in fact has the same logic as the first, which we hope will make it easier to understand. During this study you might feel rather overwhelmed as a result of the abundance of detail. However, do not forget the main aim of the exercise – to maximize efficiency. This study will assist us to efficiently capture low-risk high-probability trades and, once the solution of the second objective is found, it will become a daily trading routine.

Our satellite study is about helping a pedestrian find his way in the streets of a crowded city. We have chosen the area between Brooklyn Bridge and Battery Park in Manhattan Island, in downtown New York City. After reaching this first objective we will then compare it with the second, issued from the financial markets.

Let us start by comparing each of the seven altitude levels:

1. *7300 miles* is the highest (1st) altitude. First we have to find the Western hemisphere in order to locate the Northern American Continent. No signs of terrestrial civilization can be observed from this altitude – Earth looks like an uninhabited planet, a globe spinning in space. We can take a step back and see how an entity (our studied region/city/residential area) fits within another entity (the terrestrial globe). Going even further, we note that our planet belongs to yet another entity (the solar system), which on this occasion is not only terrestrial, and is defined as a group of planets, classified as telluric. Besides sharing the same density and silicate composition, they occupy a specific time–space system, having the sun in the center. So far, we have an entity within an entity within another entity.

    By analogy, let us consider this highest altitude level as corresponding with the *monthly time frame*, which is one of the highest time-measure units used in financial market charts (see Fig. 18.4). Higher time frames such as quarters and years are not used in trading.

2. *2200 miles* is the second highest altitude. The Eastern coastline appears as a sinuous curve, bordering the western limits of the Atlantic Ocean. The cities are just beginning to be visible. Let this second highest altitude level correspond to the *weekly time frame*, as used in financial market charts (Fig.18.7).

3. *22 miles* is the third highest altitude. We have zoomed in on the Eastern American coastline. The western limits of the Atlantic Ocean skim along the Eastern American coast, drawing even more sinuous contours. On this scale we can clearly see the separation between New Jersey and New York, and locate Manhattan Island in the New York Metropolitan area. The overall visibility is distinct but we cannot yet see the buildings or the streets of Manhattan. The different bridges take the shape of tiny links. By analogy, we will consider this third altitude level as corresponding to the *daily time frame* used in financial market charts (Fig. 18.10).

4. *34200 feet, around 6 miles* is the fourth highest altitude. We have once again zoomed down into the Eastern coastline – we are three times closer than in the previous image. The Hudson River Bay appears in all its splendour. The visibility has greatly improved and we can even see the wakes left by the boats battling against the current of the river on its way to the Atlantic Ocean. The buildings and streets cannot yet be seen in any detail

but we are getting a more accurate impression of the city. We can now almost measure the lengthy arch of the Brooklyn Bridge. We continue our analogy and make this fourth highest altitude level correspond to the *hourly time frame* of the trading charts (Fig.18.13).

5. *7800 feet, about 1.5 miles* is the fifth highest altitude. The Hudson Bay is magnified four times compared to the previous image. The city visibility has greatly improved, and we can distinctly see the southern contours of Manhattan Island, the buildings and the streets as well as the almost perfect contours of the docks. The boundaries of our objective, the territory between Brooklyn Bridge and Battery Park, are clearly defined. We have almost reached our objective of optimizting the pedestrian's orientation in the crowded streets of Southern Manhattan. Even though we can now easily find our way through the streets, we are still not able to participate in the everyday life of the city's residents. (But on the other hand, this is not really our purpose.) Once again, by analogy, let us consider this third highest level as corresponding to the *30-minute time frame* used in trading charts (Fig. 18.15).

6. *2000 feet, about a third of a mile* is the sixth highest altitude. Again the image is magnified four times greater than the previous image. The visibility has greatly improved; we can distinctly see Southern Manhattan Island, not just the buildings, but even the big air-conditioning ventilators on the roofs. The streets are full of tiny cars and the greenness of Battery Park looks very inviting. We are now closer to the everyday life of the city's residents. We have almost terminated the analogy and will consider this level as corresponding to the 15-minute time frame used in trading charts (Fig. 18.18).

7. *200 feet level, less than quarter of a mile*, is the lowest (7th) altitude. This last visual is ten times greater than the previous one. We now enter everyday life: we can see people walking on the streets, distinguish the buses from the cars, and can almost distinguish the make of each car. It is like looking down from a 20-storey building. The visibility is at its best compared with all the previous satellite snapshots. We have almost come 'down to earth'. We are now even closer to the everyday life of people, but we cannot yet be part of their group. This will only be possible when we reach the ground. We will terminate our analogy at this stage, considering this level corresponds to the *1-minute time frame* used in trading charts (as this time frame is almost never used in intra-day trading, except for scalping, it is not illustrated).

We have purposely given more importance to the description of the different altitude levels than to the description of the corresponding time frames. Thus, we have emphasized the practical aspect of the first objective, extrapolating it to the understanding of the second objective, which is harder to grasp. A detailed study of the intricacy of multiple time frames will follow later in this chapter.

Given our first objective of finding the best orientation for pedestrians in a crowded city, one question arises: Which altitude level(s) will help the pedestrians reach their destination, in the shortest amount of time, with a minimum of effort?

We have noticed that the satellite snapshots at levels 4, 5 and 6 would be the optimal candidates to achieve our objective:

•   Level 4 brings us into the region in which we are interested. The boundaries of this picture introduce the idea of a *closing-in* on the neighbouring geographical area, compared with the *closing-out* which characterizes the higher altitude snapshots. Remember the comparison with the *hourly time frame* chart, already described.

•   Level 5 illustrates layout of the local streets with an optimal visualization of the limits of our territorial objective. It seems that with this satellite snapshot, it will be hard to get lost in the defined area; an east-side up-town walk will get you to the Brooklyn Bridge, and Battery Park is fully visible on the southern side of the Manhattan Island. Remember the comparison with the *30-minute time frame* chart.

- Level 6 is a greatly magnified image which concentrates only on the Battery Park area, which represents our departure point towards Brooklyn Bridge. It is the equivalent of detecting the exact location of a trade entry, as soon as the trend is revealed through an analytical study. Remember the comparison with the *15-minute time frame* chart.

Conclusion: Out of the seven altitude levels it seems that no. 5 is the optimal choice to accomplish our task. We have realized that in order to guide the pedestrian through the streets of Southern Manhattan, our task will be greatly improved (time and effort saved) if we have the most appropriate tools to assist us in:

- first, finding the best mapping of our action;
- then defining the departure and arrival zones;
- planning the route, even if it is only a few miles (speed, duration, halts, quantifying the risk of getting lost);
- and finally, we must ensure that the mobile phone is fully operational, just in case . . . Always expect the unexpected!

Now we will apply the same technique to finding the most appropriate time frame in our search for the low-risk high-probability trades.

18.4 GLOBAL BEHAVIOUR

No market is an island. No market trades on a single time frame only. In spite of this, most of the investors or traders use only a single time frame chart in their trading practice. When you think about the complexity and difficulty of understanding the fractals, it seems fairly logical to utilize multiple time frames.

A market is a continuous phenomenon in which hundreds of thousands of participants contribute through their supply or demand transactions. Most of them think that a single time frame is sufficient. But . . . is it efficient?

Let us see how all this will help us to better understand the market behaviour; how to detect not only the building blocks of a chart pattern, but also to untangle the numerous interactions among multiple time frames.

If we look at two charts of the same market which do not show the time frames, we cannot tell the difference between a 30-minute and a 60-minute chart. If we take two unlabelled time frames which are more distant, like a 60-min and a daily chart, we notice that one of them can be a portion of the other. Thus the containing daily chart gives a macro view of the market, and the contained 60-min chart reveals the micro level, in other words, the turbulence of the local market.

18.4.1 Six Rules for Multiple Time Frames

Robert Krausz, a well-known trader and prolific writer, has dedicated a great deal of his work to the study of multiple time frames. Whatever trading programs he has conceived, his six rules are constant:

1. Every time frame has its own structure.
2. Higher time frames overrule lower time frames.

3.   Prices in the lower time frame structure tend to respect the energy points of the higher time frame structure.
4.   The energy points of support/resistance created by the higher time frame's vibration (prices) can be validated by the action of the lower time periods.
5.   The trend created by the next time period enables the definition of the tradable trend.
6.   What appears to be chaos in one time period can be orderly in another time period.

These rules should guide us throughout the process of understanding multiple time frames. If we want to make a shorter checklist, more practical for everyday short-term trading, we can note that the multiple time frames are mainly used for:

- trend analysis, especially detecting the dominant trend;
- revealing the turning points;
- setting the logical price objectives.

18.4.2   Dominant Trend

As mentioned earlier, the monthly, weekly and daily time frames are considered the most useful in short-term trading, especially intra-day trading. In order to grasp the concept of 'a trend within a trend', the trader should look at a minimum of three time frames: the operational time frame, the one above and the one below.

Going under the operational time frame will lead the trader into the fuzziness of the lower time frame market noise. The deeper we go, the noisier the market becomes. Going above the operational time frame, and the improved visibility and the up- and down-sloping zigzags of the swings will reveal the hidden trend. We would like to emphasize that the 'broken-arrow' trend line should be always be considered as a consolidation until the weight of evidence convinces us that the trend has ended. We should also be aware that it is possible for one time frame to be in one trend, and another time frame in a different trend. All this is only the natural behaviour of the market. For example, we may have:

- An up-trend on the daily chart and a down-trend on the 60-min chart. This is normal, because the lower time frame only corrects the higher time frame's trend; it is a corrective pattern belonging to the higher time frame trending pattern.
- An up-trend on the daily chart and also an up-trend on the 60-min chart. This time, the trending swing on the lower time frame is nothing but a portion of the developing trending swing of the upper time frame.

We can continue with infinite examples, due to the abundance of the fractal(s) within fractals, in other words, the swing(s) within swings or pattern(s) within patterns. If we think for a minute, the adage 'Trend is your friend, till the end' is only common sense.

We know that the market moves out of a sideways consolidation, trending upwards, only if the bulls (demand) overcome the bears (supply) and vice versa for a down-sloping movement. The consolidation is only an energy-building rectangle of the birthing trend or, if the trend is already developed, it will represent the 'breathing areas', with the last one called the 'gasping rectangle'. It is always a question of building energy.

Does this mean that the trader should be able to identify the trend in its own operational time frame or only on the upper time frame? Well, the answer is not easy because of the complexity of the interrelationships between the multiple time frames.

One thing is sure, though! We should identify the most dominant trend, in other words, find out who is in control: the bulls or the bears. Knowing that the operational time frame is only a portion of the upper time frame, it is only common sense to go and look for the dominant trend in the upper time frame.

All canny traders live by the principle, 'Who is in control?' at all times. This vigilance will not only help to trade with the trend but will also help us to be in phase with the moment when the turning points start to be implemented. In a specific time frame, a complete trend is made up of five swings: three in the direction of the trend, and two that will correct the first and the third swing respectively. Once this pattern formation is terminated, it will be followed by its entire correction, which will include only three swings, usually forming a zigzag pattern or else a sideways or triangular chart formation. Most of the time, these pattern formations obey the Fibonacci ratio tools (see Chapter 14).

18.4.3   Tools to Reveal the Dominant Trend

One last question before we go into the detail of each time frame. How do we know which trend is the dominant one? We gave some idea in the above paragraph. Let us develop this concept and go into detail.

Staircase concept: where the market flow takes the form of a wooden staircase that terminates on the upper floors. Every floor is a virtual energy consolidation structure that will greatly help the trend to continue.

Zigzagging technique: a very visual method, revealing the orientation of each swing participating in the trend's development or in its post-termination correction. By linking the lowest low and the highest high of each swing, we create the swing's trend line. If we continue for all the swings, our trend will be as visible as a skyscraper against the summer sky. This technique deserves a great deal of attention because it not only reveals the hidden trend, but also efficiently and prolifically allows an easier application of the Fibonacci tools. Moreover, it will help the trader anticipate the slope of the developing swing (see Figs 18.1, 18.2 and 18.3). To my mind, this technique is one of the more profitable and at the same time one of the least used by the majority of traders.

Trough analysis: an up-trend is defined by higher highs and higher lows, and vice versa for a down-trend. The rule is not only full of common sense but also very efficient because it enables the trader to link these pivots (highs with highs and lows with lows), thus creating the traditional channel lines. The embedded market flow is thus revealed. I stress the fact that both highs and lows must be higher than the preceding ones, respectively. As we know a trend continues until the weight of evidence negates it.

The strength of a trend is directly proportional to the degree of the separating distance between the troughs. The larger this distance, the stronger the trend becomes, and vice versa. If the trend makes a lower high, it means that it is still developing. If the trend makes a lower high and a lower low, only then is it terminated.

Momentum indicators: as we know a trend is momentum-dependent. If they are properly used the indicators will enhance the visualization of the trend's inception, development and termination. Momentum indicators are treated in detail in Volume II (in preparation) but we mention the use of the Momentum (8), OSC (5,34) and OSC (5,17), and RSI (13).

18.5 MONTHLY TIME FRAME

In order to firmly grasp the multiple time frame concept, the most important is to understand that all price behaviours are specific within the context of their own time unit. First we will treat each one individually, describing their specific characteristics, and second, we will compare these features to help us determine the most optimal time frame for intra-day trading purposes.

The term *higher time frame* describes a size-related relationship with a lower time frame, the former about four to six times the trading span of the latter. In our case, the lower time frame will be the weekly time frame; a month contains on average 4.3 weeks.

Keep in mind that the higher the time frames the stronger the signal of trending or reversal. For intra-day trading, the monthly time frame has the strongest influence. Remember and practise it . . . it is a competitive edge! The monthly time frame offers the longest period for studying the market trading process. It describes more than 15 years of market activity. For investing or for the purpose of studying, the quarterly and annual time frames are also important. If we trade mostly futures, we use only the cash index for plotting these charts due to the short-lived nature of the futures contracts.

In order to study the monthly chart (see Figs 18.4 and 18.5), the procedure is as follows:

1.   Calculate the time span of the chart (around 20 years),

2.   Use the zigzag technique to reveal the camouflaged trend, which will greatly influence the trading decisions on the operational intra-day time frame.

3.   Evaluate the degree of different swing slopes related to the zigzag formations.

4.   Identify the major highs/lows, which will have a tremendous impact on the market flow of the lower time frames, especially on the operational intra-day time frame. The highest high and the lowest low levels of the monthly time frame are real milestones, and will always have the most dominant role and the greatest importance for traders, compared with all the other lower time frames. The areas above or below them are very difficult zones to break in to; it is the portion of the chart, right under a possible top, where through the process of distribution the rectangular market flow will consolidate, and either explode upwards or simply drop like a stone.

5.   Mark your pivots and keep track of them. Always compare them with those of the lower time frames. When a common pivot is created, it takes on real importance. The more the pivot belongs to multiple time frames, the more it will dominate the market flow. It will represent the ideal candidate for the pivotal anchor of a contextual pitchfork or for a minor pivot describing the local market.

6.   Be aware of the size of an Average True Range – ATR(21). Compare the bars among them to reveal the type of volatility that will dominate the monthly chart,

7.   Look for any seasonality features, especially at the beginning or end of the year,

8.   Scrutinize the type of bars that the market uses at turning points; it will give away the turning behaviour of this time frame market, even though it will not be constant through the time,

9.   Check the levels at which the market is making the turns, and observe any preferences towards whole numbers, tenths, fifties, hundreds or thousands.

10.   Apply Fibonacci ratios to see which are the most appropriate for this type of time frame.

In Volume II (in preparation), we describe the use of indicators to detect the presence and development of the trend. For the moment, we will only mention the dual moving averages, RSI(13), and OSC(5,34).

The monthly time frame is the *only* chart which has the ability to assess the general long-term trend for the trader.

18.6   WEEKLY TIME FRAME

This time frame is second in command. As with the monthly time frame, the trader should only plot the cash index charts corresponding to the traded securities. The weekly time frame is four times smaller than the monthly and it covers a time span four times shorter, between three and five years. This is fundamental, as we know that a business cycle averages four years.

The characteristics of the weekly time frame (see Fig. 18.7) are very similar to those previously described, whilst noting that it is dependent on the monthly time frame. This time frame offers the second longest period of market study, four years on average compared with the 20-year life span of the monthly time frame. The shorter time span is closer to the length of our trading period; thus not only does it carry several years of market memory but it also influences the lower time frames that are described below.

Among your other tasks, keep track of the trend's zigzagging direction, the common pivots (created so far), and the key resistance/support levels which are the closest to our current trading environment. The best thing would be to have a written checklist, including the monthly chart's main points which fluctuate in time, which you should update periodically. It will make all the difference between you being a novice or a consistent trader. Even if you take only a glance at it . . . every day!

The weekly and daily time frames will be the charts most used in our everyday routine to assess the intermediate and a portion of the long-term trend.

18.7   DAILY TIME FRAME

The daily time frame is one of the most familiar higher time frames but few traders use it, in spite of its advantages. If the intra-day trader had to choose only one of the upper time frames, this would be the one. Its characteristics are similar to those of the weekly and monthly time frames, but with the advantage of being closer to the current market flow, thus best influencing the intra-day trading. Most of the time it covers the last twelve months of the market. It only covers a quarter of the business cycle, but with the advantage of being the most current time period. The inter-time frame analysis will integrate the daily time frame in the context of the weekly and monthly time frame. Therefore, we know where we are situated in the context of the whole business cycle. This represents a very competitive edge for the trader, especially if it is studied in tandem with the inter-market analysis.

Our vigilant pre-market observations of the daily time frame will reveal the intermediate term trend in all its splendour (see Fig. 18.10).

Once again, as for the weekly time frame, keep track of the daily trend's zigzag direction, the common pivots (coincident daily, weekly and monthly pivots) and the key resistance/support levels created so far, in all three time frames. Again, the best method would be to have a written daily checklist, which is updated every morning. Also keep track of the trend of each time frame described so far. The best trades are done when all three time frames are aligned. Whenever you have a *mixed market* situation (bullish monthly chart, bearish weekly chart and bearish daily chart) stop and think for a minute. Analyze the long term and the intermediate trends before taking any decisions for intra-day trading. The magic word for all the market movement is *coordination* among the multiple time frames. And most of the time, their synergy is not far away! It is an art to find the path of least resistance, and the multiple time frames will greatly assist you.

We attach great importance to the *close* of a bar, whatever the time frame is, but especially on the daily chart. The next day's bias could be revealed by the exact location of the close with regard to the bar's body, divided in thirds and quarters. There is also the *80/20 rule* (see the Excel spreadsheet in Appendix II). It proclaims that if the market closes in its daily bar's upper 80−100 percent, the next day will have an up-trending morning if not an up-sloping day. On the contrary, if the market closes in its daily bar's lower 0−20 percent, the next day will be a downtrend morning, if not a down day. In short:

- the nearer the close is to the top of the daily bar, the more probable a next up-sloping day;
- the nearer the close is to the bottom of the daily bar, the more probable a next down-sloping day.

However, all this said, we have to proceed with caution. The last word of this 80/20 rule is dictated by the exact position of the closing daily bar within the current daily trend. It is one thing if the daily trend has just started, and another thing if it is near its top, especially if we have one or multiple confirmation factors. This reminds me of a rule regarding trading bars: never act on a single bar signal unless you have first studied the context of the market. An uncertainty bar (open equal to close) located in the middle of a swing within a consolidation means strictly nothing, but located at the top/bottom of a long trend may be a sign of weakness or even a reversal.

18.8   OPERATIONAL TIME FRAME: THE 60-MINUTE TIME FRAME

We have finally arrived at the operational time frame(s). When trading index futures, the most-used time frames are 60-min and 15-min charts, very seldom the 30-min chart (see Figs 18.13, 18.15, and 18.18). If trading currencies, the most utilized are 120-min and 240-min charts. These time frames belong to the short-term trading kingdom, our battleground. They offer a more accurate picture of the immediate upper time frame buying or selling pressure. The time span is 6−8 weeks for the 60-min chart and 1−2 weeks for the 15-min chart. It all depends on the length of the strongest trend pertaining to the market security. Ideally, the trader should choose an operational time frame time span that surpasses by 20% the longest trend detected so far in its own market. The swings on the 60-min charts have a classic tendency to temporarily interrupt the upper time frame trend, through the correction process. Moreover, it will allow a greater visibility of the different magnified meanders of the same upper time frame trend. An alignment of the two time frames would be optimal for a low-risk high-probability trade.

The advantages of using these short-term time frames are multiple:

- nearness to our current price market, in spite of a greater market noise development, through the whipsaws;
- possibility of a detailed study of the local market, and immediate decision making;
- rigorous follow-up of the current trend over several days;
- immediate detection of resistance/support level;
- utilization of the intimacy of the opening gaps, which will have a great impact on the market behaviour for the morning or even entire day;
- accurate study of the contextual market flow, especially when embedded through a regression channel, which also pertains to a higher time frame channelling;
- first hour movement information, which could lead the market until the afternoon or even until the day's end, thus giving the trader a real competitive edge.

Lower time frames, like the 5-min or even 3-min, are exclusively used to pinpoint the entries or exits on the 60-minute or 15-minute charts.

Conclusion: The multiple time frame concept offers a real and enviable edge in the modern highly competitive trading environment. If we had to summarize the concept in a few sentences, we would probably note the following:

- Use the 60-min or 15-min operational charts for intra-day trading.
- Always trade in the direction of the overall daily trend; otherwise do not take the trade. There is always another trade, even sooner than you think! Better to lose an opportunity than your shirt!
- If already in, and the higher time frame is again aligned with the lower time frame, do not hesitate to add on another trading unit (scale in).
- Be aware of the resistances/supports levels of all the time frames, ahead of the market price, and you will not be the victim of the end run event!

So far in this chapter, we have purposely not concentrated on the inter-relationships between the multiple time frames and pitchforks. These and their practical aspects are described in the next section.

18.9   MULTIPLE TIME FRAMES AND PITCHFORKS: PRACTICAL ASPECTS

S&P 500 and Dow Index Charts

18.9.1   Zigzagging Technique

The zigzagging technique is a highly visual and efficient method of revealing the orientation of each swing contributing to the trend's development or to its post-termination entire correction. By linking the lowest low and the highest high of each swing, we create the swing's trend line. If we continue to do this for all the swings, our zigzagging trend will not only be visible, but will dominate the entire chart view (Figs 18.2 and 18.3).

Close observation of the chart in Fig. 18.1 reveals the six-month daily trend (since mid-October 2005), from pivot P0 level until the 1280 level. In order to verify whether the trend will or will not

Source: ProRealTime.com
Figure 18.1   Example of a zigzagging trend (Courtesy of www.pitchforktrader.com)

continue further, until it reaches our anticipated pivot F, we apply the zigzagging technique. The second part of the chart (since January 2006) shows the market flow embedded in an ascending wedge-like structure with every chance of reaching the 1325 level, the highest high of the chart. The pivot 'e' at the 1280 level could function as a real price catapult, oriented towards the final target. We suspect that the e−F swing will probably be composed of three smaller zigzag swings.

Once the trend ends, it is very probable that the counter-trend will have enough down-sloping momentum to drop to the 1245 level.

As anticipated (Fig. 18.2), we have established the swing trends, and the whole trend is not only very visible but we can also project its termination. In projecting the last e−F swing, we use the same slope as that of the preceding alternate c−D swing. As we suspected, the last e−F swing is composed of three smaller swings: e−E, E−f and the terminal f−F, in progress. The 1325 level seems to be a Fibonacci ratio cluster (78.6% and 61.8%).

Source: ProRealTime.com

Figure 18.2   Projecting the termination of the trend (Courtesy of www.pitchforktrader.com)

It seems (Fig. 18.3) that the market has reached its top and, as anticipated, is at the 78.6% Fibs cluster level, at the 1325 level. In order to pinpoint the limits of the ongoing correction, we have drawn two pitchforks, in our search for confluences. Fibonacci retracements were also applied.

18.9.2   Pitchforks on Monthly Charts

In the monthly chart shown in Fig. 18.4, we have applied our first tools: the zigzagging technique and pivot labelling. It seems that the monthly market flow is struggling to reach the highest top.

By applying the pitchfork technique (Fig.18.5 on p. 343) we have not only confirmed the trend's up-sloping direction, but have also embedded the market flow between the 50% Fibs lower line and the median line of the contextual pitchfork. This monthly channelling will be very useful when trading the lower time frames

The bordered rectangle on the monthly chart shown in Fig. 18.6 (on p. 343) delineates the time period of the weekly chart time span (described below). The dominant weekly trend can clearly be seen.

18.9.3   Pitchforks on Weekly Charts

The weekly chart (Fig. 18.7 on p. 344) contains the overall zigzagging of the market flow, the pivot labelling and the markings of the common pivots of the two time frames (P00=P2). On

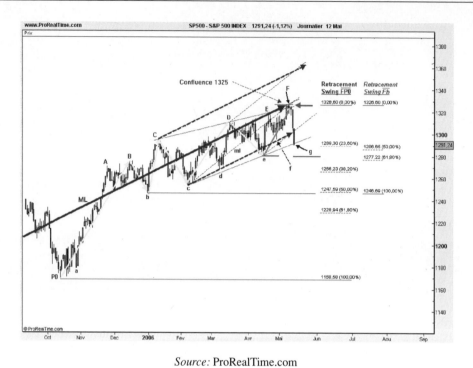

Source: ProRealTime.com

Figure 18.3   Two pitchforks in search of confluences (Courtesy of www.pitchforktrader.com)

Source: futuresource.com

Figure 18.4   Applying the zigzagging technique and pivot labelling
(Courtesy of www.pitchforktrader.com)

Source: futuresource.com
Figure 18.5   Applying the pitchfork technique (Courtesy of www.pitchforktrader.com)

Source: futuresource.com
Figure 18.6   Delineating the time period of the weekly chart time span
(Courtesy of www.pitchforktrader.com)

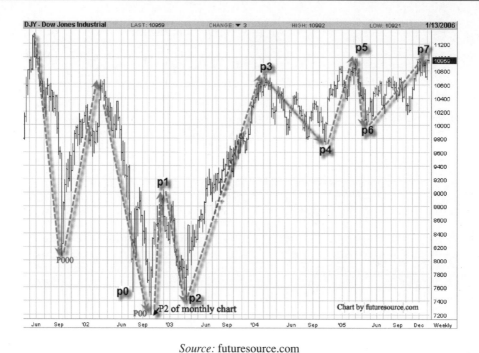

Figure 18.7   Contextual weekly chart: an overall zigzagging of the market flow
(Courtesy of www.pitchforktrader.com)

the left side of the chart we have also selected the three pivots (P000, p0 and P00), which are potential anchor candidates for drawing the conceptual pitchfork (see below).

Figure 18.8 illustrates which, out of the three tentative drawings, promises to be the best anchor candidate (p0) for building the pitchfork which optimally describes the market flow. In the trend's development, the market price ascends obliquely from left to right, from the upper median line to the first warning line (WL-1).

The bordered rectangle on the monthly chart shown in Fig. 18.9 delineates the time period of the daily chart time span (see Section 18.9.4). Thus the corresponding daily time frame is visualized here.

18.9.4   Pitchforks on Daily Charts

In the daily chart shown in Fig. 18.10 (on p. 346), we have applied our main tools for revealing the market trend: the zigzagging technique, the pitchfork technique and pivot labelling. It seems that the up-sloping daily market flow is still channelling between the median line and upper median line of the contextual pitchfork.

In order to optimize the description of the local market flow even better (Fig. 18.11 on p. 346), we have added the Action and Reaction Lines technique. We note that the market just escapes from Center Line's magnet-like attraction and is actually dropping to the Reaction Line, probably to the confluence of the Reaction Line and the median line of the contextual P0-P1-P2 pitchfork.

The bordered rectangle on the daily chart (Fig.18.12 on p. 347) delineates the time period of the 60-min chart time span, described below. The dominant 60-min chart trend is actually being

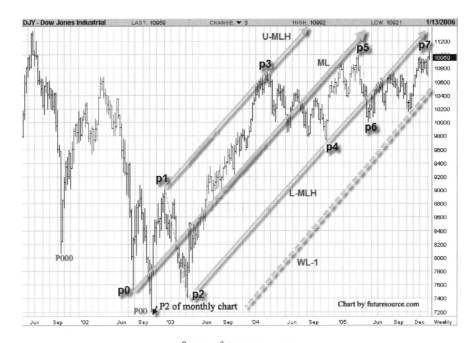

Source: futuresource.com

Figure 18.8 Best anchor candidate for building the pitchfork (Courtesy of www.pitchforktrader.com)

Source: futuresource.com

Figure 18.9 Delineating the time period of the daily chart time span
(Courtesy of www.pitchforktrader.com)

Figure 18.10   Applying the tools to reveal the market trend: zigzagging technique, pitchfork, and pivot labelling (Courtesy of www.pitchforktrader.com)

Figure 18.11   Adding the Action and Reaction lines (Courtesy of www.pitchforktrader.com)

Source: futuresource.com
Figure 18.12   Showing the time period of the 60-min chart on the daily chart
(Courtesy of www.pitchforktrader.com)

corrected on this daily chart. The common pivots belonging to the multiple time frames (the monthly and the weekly time frames) are visible: P5, P6 and P7.

18.9.5   Pitchforks on 60-min Charts

The 60-min chart seen in Fig. 18.13 represents the usual operational time frame. We have applied our main tools to reveal the market trend: pitchfork technique and common pivot labelling. It seems that the up-sloping market flow, which started at the P2 pivot level (which is also the daily P4 pivot), is still channelling between the median line and the upper median line (U-MLH). The logical profit objective would be either the upper sliding parallel line (PH-01) or the upper median line (U-MLH). The 60-min chart movements are in sync with the monthly, weekly and daily up-sloping biases.

The bordered rectangle on the 60-min chart (Fig. 18.14) delineates the time period of the 30-min chart. If we had chosen to use the 30-min chart as our operational time frame, we could now see that its dominant trend is actually being corrected, and the probability of the entire trend continuing is high.

18.9.6   Pitchforks on 30-min Charts

In the 30-min chart in Fig. 18.15 (on p. 349), we have applied only the common pivot labelling. The direction of the trend is obvious. It seems that the up-sloping market flow is being currently corrected and the price has not yet dropped below the 78.6% Fibonacci retracement level, the ultimate point of non-return.

Source: futuresource.com
Figure 18.13   Using the 60-min chart as the usual operational time frame
(Courtesy of www.pitchforktrader.com)

Source: futuresource.com
Figure 18.14   Delineating the 30-min time frame on a 60-min chart
(Courtesy of www.pitchforktrader.com)

Source: futuresource.com

Figure 18.15   Applying the common pivot labelling on a 30-min chart
(Courtesy of www.pitchforktrader.com)

Although at first glance it appears that the market is in an up-trend, drawing the contextual pitchfork (Fig. 18.16) brings a real edge in pinpointing the market flow's next move. An immediate up-swing towards the 50% Fibonacci line will probably test it and then consolidate on it. The restored energy newly acquired during the consolidation will shoot the price to the upper median line.

If we had chosen a 30-min chart in Fig. 18.17 as our operational time frame, we would now see that its dominant trend is actually being corrected. There is a high probability that the entire trend will continue.

18.9.7   Pitchforks on 15-min Charts

If we decide to use an even smaller time frame, this time a 15-min chart (Fig. 18.18 on p. 351), we have the advantage of better observing the local market flow movements and smaller size stop losses, but the disadvantage of the increased market noise. The common pivot labelling is in place.

The upper time frame (30-min chart) pitchfork median line and its lower median line can be seen at work on the 15-min chart shown in Fig. 18.19 (on p. 351). They fully optimize the embedding of the market flow. The context of the market flow is efficiently described, and locally, on the extreme right upper part of the chart, we can see the small ascending channel precisely correcting the last swing, illustrated by the descending channel.

We have arrived at the end of this chapter, which has described the world of market movements, from the highest time frame move (monthly) down to a 15-min chart time-frame turbulence. The

Source: futuresource.com

Figure 18.16 Adding the pitchfork emphasizes the next move of the market flow
(Courtesy of www.pitchforktrader.com)

Source: futuresource.com

Figure 18.17 Using the 30-min chart as the operational time frame
(Courtesy of www.pitchforktrader.com)

Source: futuresource.com

Figure 18.18 Using a 15-min time frame to observe local market flow
(Courtesy of www.pitchforktrader.com).

Source: futuresource.com

Figure 18.19 Upper and lower median lines at work on a 15-min chart
(Courtesy of www.pitchforktrader.com)

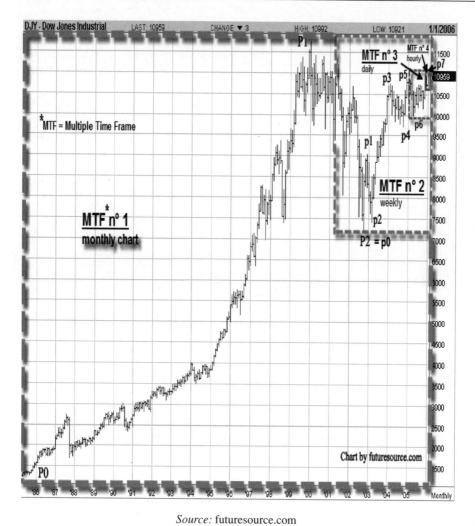

Source: futuresource.com
Figure 18.20 A multiple time frame: the higher time frames containing the lower time frames (Courtesy of www.pitchforktrader.com)

chart in Fig. 18.20, where the zooming varies from a monthly to an hourly time frame, plainly reveals the market time frame intricacy. It resembles the Russian dolls structure, the higher time frame containing the lower time frame. It also resembles the satellite levels that optimally helped the pedestrians achieve their objective.

Conclusion: As a trader, you are only a player of the markets. But like the professional piano player, you will have to not only choose the most appropriate tools (as few as possible) and be forced to depend on them, but must also tune them frequently in order to get the best out of them and achieve the best performance.

And never forget . . . your survival is at stake every minute! The multiple time frame technique is one of the best out there that will keep you consistent.

18.10   KEY LEARNING POINTS

- As a daily routine, learn and practise using at least three time frames, with the operational one in the middle.
- Use the median lines of the upper time frames as trading guides for the operational time frame. They have a far better strength than the local ones.
- Remember that the best turning points are those confluences formed by the various multiple time frame trend lines. Their intricacies reflect the best guarantor of the high probability reversal confluences.
- Always search for the dominant trend. It always comes from upper time frames, but not necessarily the nearest one.
- Learn the four indispensable tools to detect the trend: pitchfork analysis, the zigzagging technique, trough analysis and momentum-related indicators. Try all of them, and select the one that you are at ease with.
- Don't think that you have to stay with the same operational time frame every day. Test the feasibility of the 60-min, 30-min or 15-min time frames every pre-open, and select the one that will best serve your purposes.
- One thing though. Once chosen, stay with it . . . at least for the day. Never change a winning horse! Or in other words, *if it ain't broke, don't fix it!*

Fractals are the stem of our lives. They are the basic chain with which nature has crafted everything. And most of all, there are no crowd tribulations that are not governed by fractals. Try to read about and assimilate the concept. It might save you money!

19

Case Studies and Money Management

19.1 ZOOM AND RETEST TECHNIQUE: AFTER A GERMAN DAX ENERGY BUILDING RECTANGLE

As we have learned so far, there are many parameters to be considered before a profitable trade can be made. Without an organized approach, we risk neglecting important points and failing our trades. Listed below, in a chronological order, are the different decision-making steps of our trading approach, described as practically as possible:

19.1.1 Spotting the Trade Opportunity

Finding low-risk high-probability *spotting trades* is a very systematic process for the experienced trader who will scan the various choices of the operational time frame charts: 60-min, 30-min, 15-min and (rarely) the 5-min chart. Most of the time, this trade preparation is done in the pre-open period.

Our goal is to detect candidates for low-risk high-probability trades. Once these opportunities are revealed, we use different techniques using all the recommended discipline, rigour and patience. One of these is the *zoom-and-retest technique* (Fig. 19.1), which is applied to German Dax and is our first case study.

19.1.2 Finding the Optimal Set-Up

As we have mentioned, we usually use the 15-min or 60-min charts as operational time frames. The lower time frames will usually only help the trader to pinpoint the optimal entries and exits. However, although the 5-min chart is rarely used, we have chosen to illustrate it now because of its obvious profitable potential (Fig. 19.1).

We have spotted this trade opportunity through the presence of a narrow-range consolidation which is currently building an energy-building rectangle. Consequently, we believe there will be a restoration of the energy dispensed during the down-sloping move (Fig. 19.1).

The height of the rectangle is as we like it: under two True Range Averages – ATR(21). The smaller and the longer the rectangle, the bigger the bursting potential at the breaking point, and the probability of a pullback is greatly diminished. It is very important to have the patience to

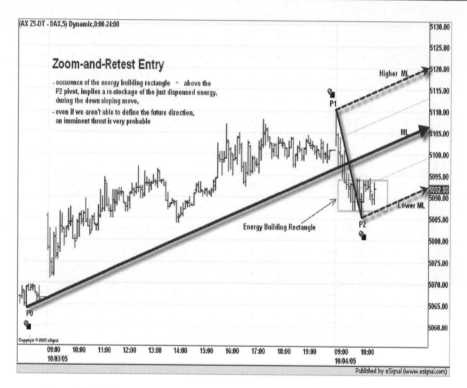

Figure 19.1 Zoom-and-retest technique (Courtesy of www.pitchforktrader.com)

wait and then verify if the rectangle is properly formed, having at least four touches! That is the case here!

This narrow rectangular formation is a very attractive proposition for breakout traders. But for us, it is nothing more than a 50% probability trade, due to the fact that the consolidation rectangle is perfectly level horizontally. Therefore, we cannot apply an alternative close pitchfork to clarify the probable market direction. So ... as this pattern is not our cup of tea, we will pass ... and wait for a probability opportunity of more than 50%, like the *zoom and test/retest set-up trades*. One thing is sure though − even if we do not know exactly in which direction the market will burst out, an imminent thrust is very probable.

19.1.3 Time Frame Alignment

We have ensured that the upper time frames (15-min and 60-min charts) are going in the same direction; they are both up-sloping.

19.1.4 Three-Pawn Technique: Triple Order Preparation and Trade Execution

We are now able to evaluate the trade precisely using the *three-pawn technique*. It is a 'to be or not to be' state, or a 'to make or not' entry decision. This technique consists of three progressive steps:

1. Find the most optimal entry and place the *first order*.
2. Look closely for the best stop loss location and then immediately enter a *stop order*, as soon as the entry order is executed. This is the second order.

3.   Find the most appropriate profit objective and then calculate the optimal *reward/risk ratio (R/R ratio)* which should not be under the value of 2.5. If this is the case, place the third order right after the stop loss order is working on the broker's waiting list. We take 2–2.5 R/R ratio trades seldom, and only if they have a high probability. Do not forget that our main purpose is capital preservation. There is always another opportunity, but only if you are still in possession of your capital. Our purpose is not to make any 'home runs' – we are only looking for low-risk high-probability trades.

Most of the time, these three trading orders (the three-pawn technique) are prearranged, established at the moment when the trade decision is made. In order to preserve capital, it is vital that, once they are in place, they are never changed. As this technique is so reliable, we have called it the *automatic trading mode*. It is one of the best remedies for the 'trigger-shy' syndrome. If only two orders are prearranged, we are in a *semi-automatic mode*. If none of the orders are prearranged, we are simply in a *manual mode*.

The three-pawn technique must be understood, learned and practised every day, with no exceptions. This requires discipline and patience:

*   *discipline*, in respecting the three rules one hundred percent, and
*   *patience*, in waiting for the entry order to be executed. Once this is done, the second and third rules will automatically follow, almost flawlessly. The trader must reach a high level of routine, and continuously check and double-check their decisions and actions, in such a way that the main task is preserved from everyday noise.

The trading life of a novice trader usually does not last more than three months because his main objective was not capital preservation. Those traders who have completely assimilated and rigorously used the three-pawn technique will be guaranteed consistent profits.

As we anticipated (Fig. 19.2), the market price zooms like an express train through the median line. We have no choice but to wait for our optimal set-up to come along. Patience here is the watchword. The first step, the zooming of the median line, has been accomplished.

Let us see if there is any testing or retesting of the median line. If there is, we will enter and target the upper median line. For a novice trader, the up-steaming momentum is a real signal to climb on the train and enter long right away. But like they say . . . Never run after the market. Let the market come to you.

The last bar on Fig. 19.3 is called an *inside bar*, because it is contained within the previous bar. It has a highly predictable reversing power. At this point we should prepare our trade, in case the market tests or retests the median line. If it does, first we will use a prearranged buy stop entry order at the 5103 level. As soon as this order is executed, we will make a second order, this time a sell stop order at the 5098 level, therefore establishing the stop loss at the low of the previous bar.

As we know, the third step of this technique is to place a prearranged exit for the logical profit objective. But before placing any orders, we have to establish the reward/risk ratio (R/R ratio). For that, we need the exact location of the exit level, calculated through the ATR technique.

The reward is calculated by projecting the ATR(21) toward our defined logical profit target, the U-MLH (Fig. 19.4 on p. 359). The ATR(21) for our time frame is five points. We start to build up ATR bars, taking as our first reference the highest third of the last market bar, followed by the upper thirds of each consecutive ATR bar, until we have progressively reached our target, the U-MLH. We note the intersecting value, and subtract 2–3 ticks to protect against a potentially risky situation, such as a reversal created by an up-sloping failure just in front of the upper median line. We should know by now that greed does not have a place in trading.

Figure 19.2   Market price breaks the median line (Courtesy of www.pitchforktrader.com)

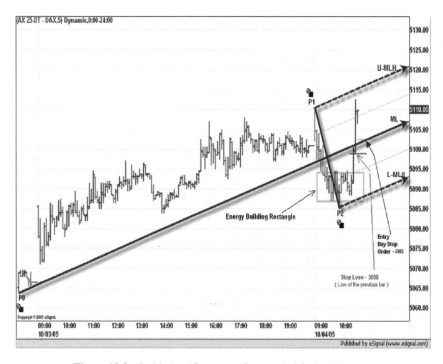

Figure 19.3   Inside bar (Courtesy of www.pitchforktrader.com)

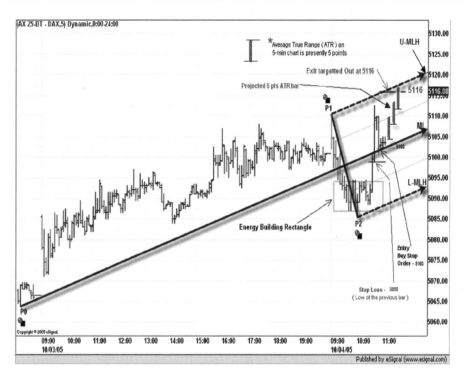

Figure 19.4 Projecting the Average True Range – ATR(21) (Courtesy of www.pitchforktrader.com)

Now we have finally reached our logical profit objective at the 5116 level. But before placing any orders, we have to establish the R/R ratio, and see if the value is above the usual 2.5 limit. We are able to calculate the reward/risk ratio (R/R ratio) as follows:

- *Reward* is 13 points: exit level (5116) minus entry level (5103);
- *Risk* is 5 points: entry level (5103) minus stop loss level (5098);
- *Reward/Risk* ratio is 2.6: 13 divided by 5 – our usual value.

Conclusion: The R/R ratio being acceptable, we can place our three prearranged orders.

19.1.5   The Profit and Loss Statement

Now that the trade has gone through, let us see its outcome:

- Per contract we have risked 5 Dax points representing €125 or about $150 (1 Dax point is worth 25 euros, about $30).
- The reward per contract pertaining to the R/R ratio of 2.6 is 13 Dax points, which is €325, about $400.
- The time spent in the trade was just 25 minutes.

The chart in Fig. 19.5 illustrates the final outcome of the market swing that we have just traded. Our targeted exit was at the 4116 level and the market has climbed all the way up to 5130.50. Theoretically, we have not taken advantage of the full up-steaming potential of the market, and we did not ring the cash register for the additional 14.5 Dax points. *Is this bad or good?*

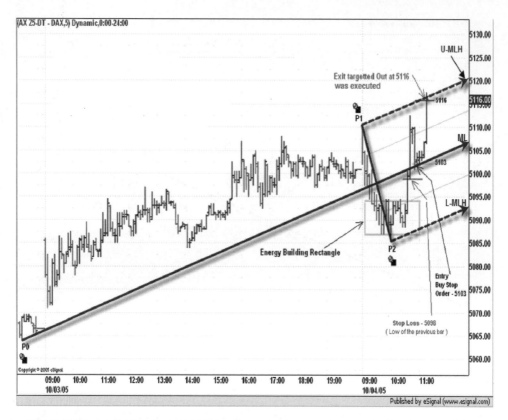

Figure 19.5 Market breaks through the projected level (Courtesy of www.pitchforktrader.com)

At this stage of our learning curve the result is more than enough. We did not lose any money. We have preserved our capital. And we are better prepared to progress and eventually reach a stage where the technique of acquiring those extra 14.5 points will be part of our trading arsenal!

19.1.6 A Trader's Journal: Keep Your Records Straight

Keeping your records straight is one of the most important actions in becoming a consistent trader. Trading is a business affair, and every business, profitable or not, keeps records . . . good records! It is the barometer of consistency, which will ask you the 'Whys' and tell you the 'Hows'. As the saying goes, you should always learn from history. Otherwise the risk is that history will repeat itself! The same is true for our trades. We should learn from our mistakes and tune-up good ideas, thus improving our tactics and profitability.

Write a journal of your trades. Yes, write − especially the main points − as soon as you have exited the trade, otherwise you risk forgetting the details. Whatever the outcome of the trade, good or bad, just do it! In the end, you will be happy to have the monthly trades' conclusions and be able to reference them again. Do not forget, we are eternal students of the markets . . . and happy to be!

19.1.7 Accuracy of the R/R Ratio Calculations

At every step of the trading process there is a need for mental reflection and accurate calculations. Most traders never go into the subtle and detailed subjects of considering and taking a risk! Let me ask you some quick questions, to illustrate my point:

- For a long trade, is it important to put the stop loss right at the low of the last bar, if we have chosen this type of coverage instead of buying puts?
- Or is it more important to drop your stop loss level 2−4 ticks, under the last bar's low, in order to be better sheltered from the whipsaws of the market noise? Do you think that you will be better protected this way?
- Do you think that the trader should establish their logical profit objective exactly at the intersection (Fig. 19.4) of the price bar with the upper median line?
- Isn't it better to allow a risk zone of 2−4 ticks, and set up your target below the intersection just in case of an unexpected up-sloping failure?

I sincerely hope that you see my point!

The most important point is not really how accurate the calculations are, but rather that you repeat them, using the same technique, every day, day after day − until, of course, you are on the right track! Thus, even if the probability does not increase over the pre-established *probability threshold* of the low-risk high-probability pitchfork-related trade, at least it will remain constant, allowing you to reside permanently in the green zone of *trading consistency*. If we align ourselves to this way of thinking, the result will be immediate: many small losses of pre-defined sizes and fairly frequent big profit trades. It is not important how much money you make; it is important how much you lose. We are in the business of capital preservation. Don't worry about the money, worry about respecting the trading rules . . . the money will come along automatically!

In Fig. 19.6, you can see that the market is right on time with our expectations. In only two bars, it not only reaches our targeted level at 5116, but also climbs over it.

Important: Once the trade ends, remember to cancel the initial stop loss at 5098. You should create a working method so at the end of each exited trade you automatically check that you have no working orders on the broker's waiting list.

I will restate, but only to give you something to reflect on, my earlier question regarding target attainment: Do you think that the trader should establish their logical profit objective exactly at the intersection of the price bar with the upper median line? Now, don't be in too much of a hurry to answer. Wait for more examples!

19.1.8 Conclusion

Looking back at this example of a trade, we can conclude the following:

- We fully respected the rules, especially those of the three-pawn technique.
- The reward is satisfactory, even if it does not represent a big win.
- We are not sore that we exited prematurely compared with the huge market swing, because it was planned this way.
- We can see that the zoom and retest technique has a high potential probability and that the pre-existence of an energy building rectangle enhances it.

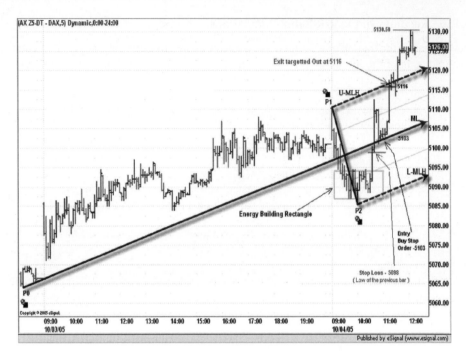

Figure 19.6 Final outcome of the market swing (Courtesy of www.pitchforktrader.com)

- For our future trading it will be very useful to note: the size of the huge swing, the size of the biggest bars, the excellent magnet-like power of the median line — in a word, any statistical element that can be used in our favour next time.

We will conclude this example of a zoom-and-retest trade by listing the main points of the trade:

1. spotting the trade opportunity
2. finding the optimal set-up
3. aligning the time frame
4. using the three-pawn technique: triple order preparation and trade execution
5. assessing the profit and loss statement
6. keeping your records straight.

Assimilate and practise these main points and respect their rules. It is one of the ways to achieve consistency in trading.

19.2 ZOOM-AND-TEST TECHNIQUE: ES ENERGY-BUILDING RECTANGLE AND TRIGGER LINE

19.2.1 Spotting the Trade Opportunity

Our second case study is the zoom-and-test technique as applied to the S&P 500 e-mini (ES) (Figs 19.7 and 19.8).

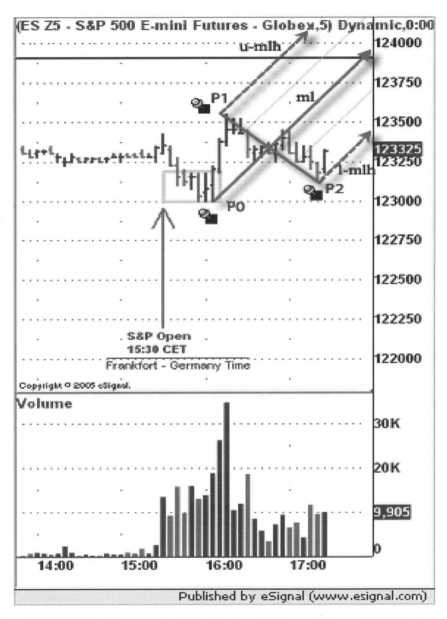

Figure 19.7 Selecting the most optimal chart for the trade (Courtesy of www.pitchforktrader.com)

After visually scanning the various operational time frame charts (60-min, 30-min, 15-min and 5-min), we have found an appropriate chart (Fig. 19.7). Our goal is to detect those charts representing low-risk high-probability trades. (As you have probably noticed, we have changed the trading futures, and moved on to an S&P 500 e-mini from German Dax futures. This should be done every time a trade opportunity is revealed. Another reason for doing it is there may be greater volatility in one market compared to another.)

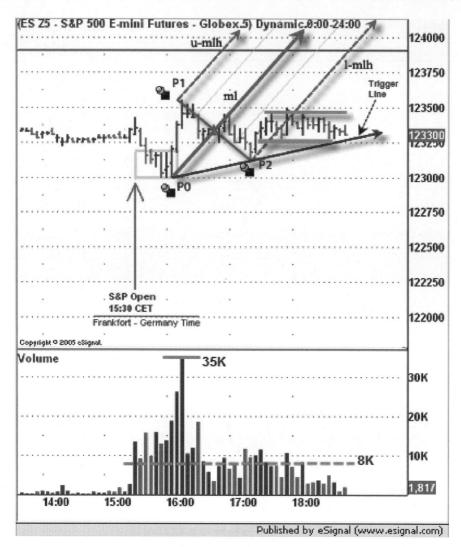

Figure 19.8 Narrow-range consolidation constructing an energy-building rectangle
(Courtesy of www.pitchforktrader.com)

19.2.2 Finding the Optimal Set-Up

We have spotted this trade opportunity because of the presence of a narrow-range consolidation just above the trigger line, which is currently constructing an energy-building rectangle. The immediate consequence will be to store the energy dispensed during the down-sloping move (Fig. 19.8).

As recommended in Section 19.1.6, we need to pay great attention to some of the statistics surrounding the immediate price market history. In Fig. 19.8, we can see that the first energy-building rectangle (containing the P0 pivotal anchor) has a huge volume (35K) at its breaking point, 4.38 times bigger than the average volume (8K). This information will be a great help when

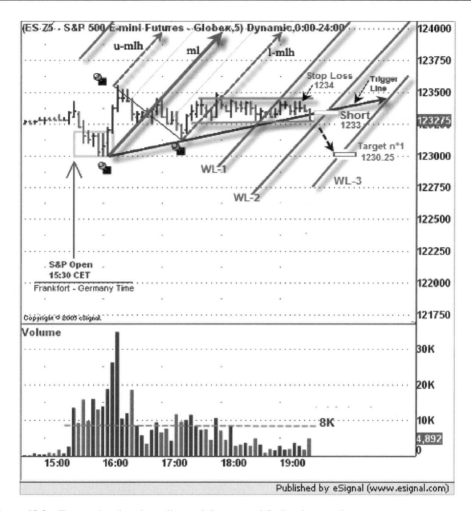

Figure 19.9 Trespassing the trigger line: a dainty morsel for breakout traders
(Courtesy of www.pitchforktrader.com)

the current rectangle (located above the trigger line) will propel the market price in whichever direction it will choose.

The narrow rectangular formation (Fig. 19.9), located just above the trigger line, is a real opportunity for breakout traders, like that of the preceding trade (Fig. 19.1). However, once again, for us this is nothing more than a 50% probability trade, due to the fact that the consolidation rectangle is levelled horizontally. Therefore, we cannot apply an alternative close pitchfork to reveal the probable market direction. So once again we will wait for an opportunity with a more than 50% probability, like the zoom-and-test/retest set-up trade.

Watch for the volume's behaviour, it could reveal great potential. Keep in mind that this market has an average volume value of 8000, on the 5-min time frame chart, with the probability of overtopping it at least four times!

The move through the trigger line (Fig. 19.9) represents the first part of the zoom-and-test/retest set-up trade. The enthusiasm of the market movement is short-lived, being stopped short by the current 1232.75 resistance, which coincides with the lower boundary of the current rectangle.

19.2.3   Time Frame Alignment

We have ensured that the upper time frames (15-min and 60-min charts) are in the same direction as the operational time frame: they are both down-sloping.

19.2.4   Three-Pawn Technique: Triple Order Preparation and Trade Execution

Now that the zoom is accomplished (Fig. 19.9), let us consider the following trade where there is a test or retest of the trigger line (TL):

- *Sell stop entry* at 1233 – test or retest after zoom move.
- Initial stop loss: *buy stop* at 1234, just above the last high (three bars earlier).
- First logical profit objective (target 1): *buy stop* at 1230.25 – just a tick over the confluence of the 1230 resistance (old low) and the warning line (WL-3).

Due to the length and the narrowness of the consolidation, it seems that the trade has a high potential. Therefore, we will consider two trading units:

a)   The first that exits at target level no 1.
b)   The second that will trail out through the open market. Who knows, we might get a free ride and trade with the market's own money.

But before placing any orders, we have to establish the reward/risk ratio, and see if its value is above the 2.5 usual limits. Let us calculate the R/R ratio for this probable short trade:

- *Reward* is 2.75 ES points: entry level (1233) minus target level no. 1 (1230.25).
- *Risk* is 1.00 ES points: stop loss level (1234) minus entry level (1233).
- *Reward/risk ratio*: 2.75 (2.75 divided by 1), our usual value.

Conclusion: The R/R ratio is acceptable, and we can place our three pre-arranged orders.

19.2.5   Trade Progression

The market flow did exactly as we anticipated (Fig. 19.10) and tested the trigger line, right after the zooming. Thus, the entry order is executed and we have entered the short trade.

Finally, the market reached the first target at the 1230.25 level. We have exited from our prearranged first trading unit, making as planned a gain of 2.75 ES points. The second trading unit is still in the market. We have changed its protection, from the initial stop loss at the 1234 level to the break-even point at the 1233 level. Now we are trading with the market's money, having a free ride. Whatever happens now, we will not lose any money, except for paying the broker's fees.

Now we are following the market flow very closely, because we have switched to semi-automatic pilot, compared with the automatic pilot mode of the prearranged three orders. The trading of the second unit implies that the profit optimization entirely depends on the trader's skill to snug the trailing stop(s) as loosely as possible, not to be burnt-out by the whipsaws, but tightly enough to allow an optimal profit.

As the situation is presented in Fig. 19.11, the market flow is consolidating again, right on the warning line (WL-3). The range is narrow and consistent and a steaming move is imminent. It is very probable that the down trend will continue.

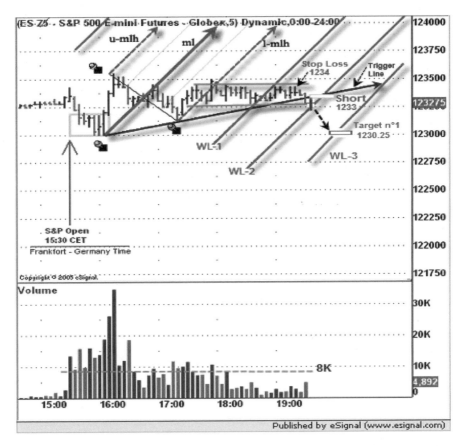

Figure 19.10   Market flow tested the trigger line (Courtesy of www.pitchforktrader.com)

As we anticipated, the market explodes (Fig. 19.12 on p. 369). Its volume has catapulted from an average of 8000 to 45000, a remarkable 563% increase. It is an even stronger move than that of the 16:00 CET (10:00 US ET), when the volume did not go over 35000. Such a volume surge reveals a very strong down-sloping momentum, and there is a very high probability it will continue, because even if the market wants to apply its brakes and reverse, it usually takes some time to fully reach the still status at the reversal point, just before changing direction.

One question is unavoidable: Will the down-sloping trend continue?

There is a very high probability that the down trend will pursue its course. Look closely at the last two bars and you can see that the market is very impatient to continue the down move.

- The huge down (penultimate) bar has:
  - the *open*, which is so close to the bar's high that it signals the exhaustion of the up-sloping momentum;
  - the *close*, which is so near to the bar's low that it reveals a consistent degree of down-momentum potential.

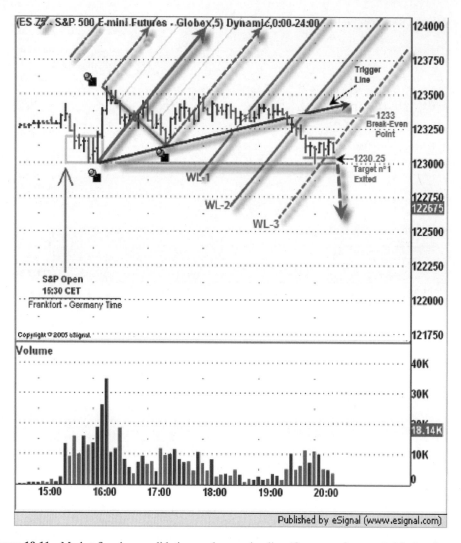

Figure 19.11   Market flow is consolidating on the warning line (Courtesy of www.pitchforktrader.com)

- The last market price bar (lowest bar) has:
  - retracements over the previous huge bar, which did not even reach the 23.6% Fibonacci ratio. This reveals the market's high degree of impatience to continue the down-sloping movement with the just-restored energy;
  - the close coincides with the bar's low, which represents a very high downward momentum.

The purpose of Fig. 19.13 (on p. 370) is only to emphasize the strong power of the contextual pitchfork's warning lines (WL-4). In spite of the market's tremendous down-sloping potential, this warning line halts the market flow cold, although probably only for a moment. We are trailing the market closely in our bid to preserve the maximum of our hard-earned money. The market

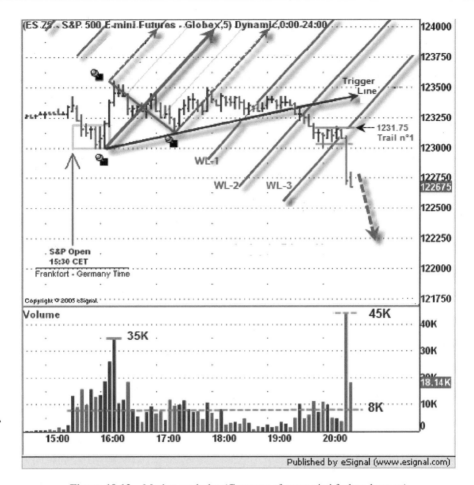

Figure 19.12 Market explodes (Courtesy of www.pitchforktrader.com)

has closed at 1226.75 level just below our trail no. 2 of 1228.25 level. We do not want to leave the money on the table for the market.

As we anticipated, the huge down-sloping momentum (Fig. 19.14 on p. 371) has brought the market flow all the way down to our fourth trailing stop at the 1221.75 level, thus exiting the second trade unit. Each time the market flow makes a new down swing, we snug the trail stop right on the top of the swing. The fourth trail bar is taken out by the market when bar no. 3 retraces over the high of bar no. 2. Therefore the trade has been terminated. (We should add that the choice of each trailing stop location was guided by the value of the ATR(21), which we have always taken into consideration. We have never accepted a trailing stop location with less than 1.00 ATR(21) value. A more comfortable trail-market price interdistance would be 1.5–2.50 ATRs(21).) As can now be seen, the fourth trailing stop was too close to the market, even respecting the above rules. In spite of this, and even if we did not take advantage of the entire downtrend potential, we are satisfied because we have achieved the trader's most vital mission: to preserve his capital. By respecting the rules, the trader overpowers his inclination to be greedy.

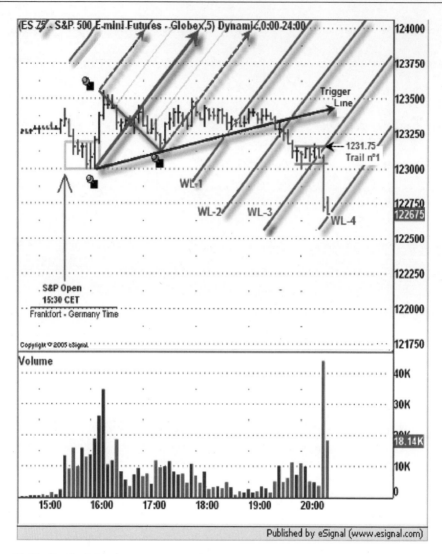

Figure 19.13 Emphasizing the strong power of the pitchfork's warning lines
(Courtesy of www.pitchforktrader.com)

In spite of our own critical acumen, assiduously noted in our trading journal, the second trading unit has travelled the market from level 1233.00 to level 1221.75, an 11.25 ES points per contract journey.

Before we end this example, let us underline the function of the pitchfork's parallel lines (the warning lines) and the role of the volume in propelling the market price, which most novice traders are not aware of. By closely observing the appropriate volume of the corresponding bar (Fig. 19.15 on p. 372), we can see the following market price events taking place right on these parallel lines:

> *Warning line 1*: Test, close on the WL with the bar's lower tail piercing it, followed by
> two retests with a small volume (half the average value of 8000).

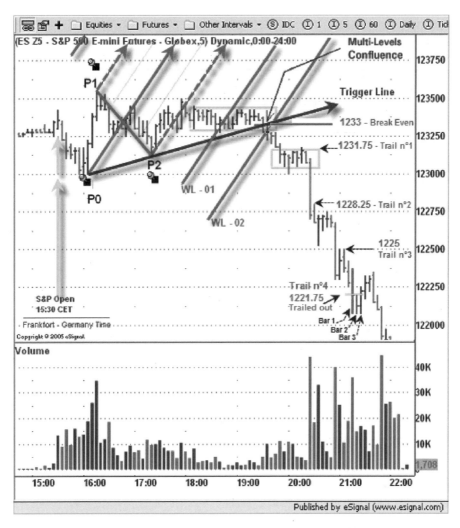

Figure 19.14   Cascade of trailing stops (Courtesy of www.pitchforktrader.com)

Warning line 2: Test and retest with a volume slightly over the average.

Warning line 3: Test, retest and piercing on its upper side, followed by a retest underneath with an average volume.

Warning line 4: Test with a huge volume (45K) and a zoom through with a big volume, almost 20K.

Warning line 5: A huge zoom bar with a huge volume (40K); the close of this bar is under the WL.

Warning line 6: A huge zoom bar with a huge volume (36K); the close of this bar is under the WL.

Warning line 7: A huge zoom bar having the biggest volume (46K), so far; the close of this bar is under the WL.

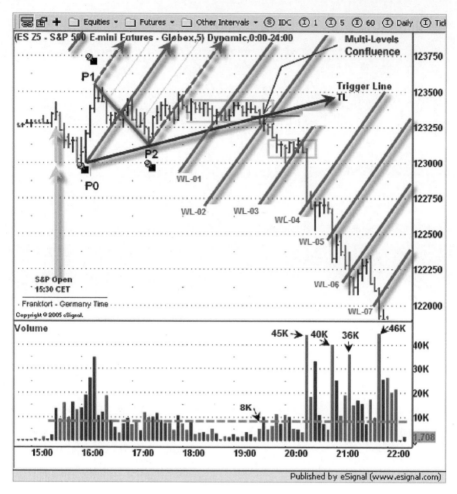

Figure 19.15 Emphasizing the function of the pitchfork's parallel lines
(Courtesy of www.pitchforktrader.com)

As you can see, a detailed study of the bars' sizes, their closes either above or below the warning lines, together with their degree of volume with regard to average value, could reveal the market behaviour, whatever its tendency: continuation or reversal.

19.2.6 Profit and Loss Statement

Now that the trade has been concluded let us see its outcome.

- We have taken double trading units: the first was traded on automatic pilot with three prearranged orders, and the second was traded following a semi-automatic pilot mode identical to the first except for the manual management of the trailing stops. We should emphasize that both units were governed by the three-pawn technique.
- Per contract we have risked one ES point representing $50.

- The reward pertaining to the R/R ratio of 2.75 initially calculated per contract was 2.75 ES points. By trading two separate units we have obtained the following results:
  - first trading unit per contract: the reward is 2.75 ES points, i.e., entry level (1233) minus target level 1 (1230.25);
  - second trading unit per contract: the reward is 11.25 ES points, i.e., entry level (1233) minus trail level 4 (1221.75)].

The total result per contract (both units) is 14 ES points: (2.75 + 11.25) − $700. The total time spent in the trade was one hour and 50 minutes.

19.2.7 A Trader's Journal: Keep Your Records Straight

We log the main topics in the journal, and also any unusual events or missing opportunities which have arisen either as a result of sticking to the rules or to new lessons pertaining to the learning curve. Let us proceed further.

- We fully respected the rules, especially the three-pawn technique rules.
- The reward is satisfactory, even if it does not represent a great win.
- We are not unhappy that we were trailed out prematurely compared with the continuation of the down-sloping market swing, because it was planned this way. We only respected the rules. Respecting them is our long-term advantage, the guarantors of consistency.
- We note that the zoom-and-test technique has a high potential probability and that the pre-existence of an energy-building rectangle enhances it.
- The inter-relationship between the bars' structure, their behaviour and the extreme variations of the volume, have enhanced our confidence in using them as confirmed parameters in order to reveal the market behaviour whatever its bias: continuation or reversal.
- The role of the pitchfork's warning lines was once more confirmed as a reliable tool in our trading arsenal.
- The trading of double units greatly enhances the P/L statement. In this particular trade, we have obtained 14 ES points instead of only 5.50 points (2 × 2.75), which represents an increase of 255%.
- Even if we usually use the 15-min chart as our operational trading time frame, we should not hesitate to scan all three time frames (60-min, 30-min and even 5-min). We never know where the opportunity is, so just have confidence in the rules and go hunting meticulously.
- This trade is a splendid example of really discovering the correlation between the size of the bars and the importance of the volume. Next time you can depend on it!

19.2.8 ATR and Money Management: New Lessons from This Trade

We have used the ATR value to tune in to the best market price/trail stop inter-distance.

As we have already mentioned, we have never accepted a trailing stop location less than 1.00 ATR value to the market. A more comfortable trail-market price inter-distance would be 1.5−2.5 ATRs. As the market progressed in our favour we have tightened the trailing stop to a minimum value of one ATR. We did not want to leave the money on the table for the market. As we expected, the market took out the fourth trailing stop, and the trade was terminated. However, the market has continued its down-sloping movement. The choice of this inter-distance can now reveal that it was too close to the market. Well, one questions arises: *What will be the best ATR to choose next time?*

In order to optimally answer this question, let us look more closely at the trading literature. Charles LeBeau and David W. Lucas were the first authors to describe the great importance of using ATRs in everyday trading. Their solid trading book, *Computer Analysis on the Futures Market*, is an excellent tool for measuring the market's volatility. When the ATR is lessened the volatility is low and an imminent explosion in the market price can be expected. On the other hand, if the ATR is big, then the volatility significantly increases and will have the necessity to revert to mean. Therefore, by using the measure of the most appropriate ATR value for stops, we will be in pace with the volatility of the market and eventually avoid a price whipsaw.

John Sweeney, a former editor of 'Technical Analysis of Stocks and Commodities', and the author of the highly appreciated technical book, *Campaign Trading: Tactics and Strategies to Exploit the Markets*, teaches the concept of *excursion analysis*, an indispensable method for trading markets. Sweeney's method is briefly described in Charles LeBeau's book as follows:

> *Hindsight can sometimes be a useful tool in determining stop points ... (Sweeney) has suggested measuring the maximum adverse price excursions of past winning trades to determine how wide a stop point would have been necessary to remain in all of the winning trades while eliminating the losers ... if you believe the future is likely to closely resemble the past, Sweeney's approach makes some sense and is probably better than most stop-setting methods we have observed.*

Now, let us try to answer our question, in order to know what our trading attitude will be next time. The ATR is one of the most optimal tools available to the trader. It takes into account the market volatility, which is the fundamental element of market movements. Ideally, the trader should also take into consideration the volume (i.e., the market price propelling factor), in such a way that our stops will be as close as possible to the market countermoves without the risk of being exited by the market noise.

19.2.9 Conclusion:

We believe that the future, especially the immediate one, resembles the immediate past as a result of human behaviour: the dominance of our immediate memory due to our inborn, genetically crafted character. There is no doubt in our mind that it is important to keep the stops outside the range of future randomness by utilizing the most appropriate ATRs of the immediate past. The best procedure would be to routinely prepare a weekly check-list for each of our favourite markets with the most optimal ATR values ranging from 1 to 2.5 ATRs. They will result from each market's individual hindsight. Detailed study will show the exact value of the volume coupled with its corresponding ATR. Thus, the trader will have the most efficient ATR-related stop tool, which is so necessary, at the crucial moment of the decisive price enhancement. As Steve Nison, a trader and prolific writer, says, 'To learn about the market, ask the market.'

19.3 ZOOM-AND-TEST (ENTRY) AND RETEST (ADD-ON) TECHNIQUE

German Dax Up-sloping Failure

19.3.1 Spotting the Trade Opportunity

Spotting low-risk high-probability trades is very a systematic process for the experienced trader who visually scans the various operational time frame charts: 60-min, 30-min, 15-min and, more rarely, the 5-min. Our goal is to detect potential candidates for low-risk high-probability trades. Once these opportunities are revealed, we will employ different techniques using all the recommended discipline, rigour and patience. One of these techniques is the zoom-and-retest technique (Fig. 19.19), which is applied to a German Dax up-sloping failure.

19.3.2 Finding the Optimal Set-up

In this trade, we have spotted triple up-sloping failures on 60-min, 30-min and 15-min operational charts (see Figs 19.16, 19.17 and 19.18). We have chosen the 60-min chart (Fig. 19.19) as our optimal operational trading time frame because of the better trend visualization, longer running profit and less market noise. The risk might be slightly higher but the profit is much more consistent.

19.3.3 Time Frame Alignment

We have noted that the upper time frames (weekly and daily charts) are both in the same up-sloping direction, but ready to be corrected. Then we have looked at the three lower time frames (60-, 30- and 15-min charts) to observe the local market movements, and to better pinpoint our entry. We notice that the corrections of the three up-sloping trends have already started. The 5169 level pivot is common for all the studied time frames: weekly, daily (not shown), 60-min, 30-min and 15-min charts.

The 60-min chart (Fig. 19.16) illustrates the beginning of a correction with a big down-bar closing right on the Center Line of the Action/Reaction Lines set up. The triple mirror pattern at the highest high (level 5169) is the guarantor of the reversal, and the beginning of a correction.

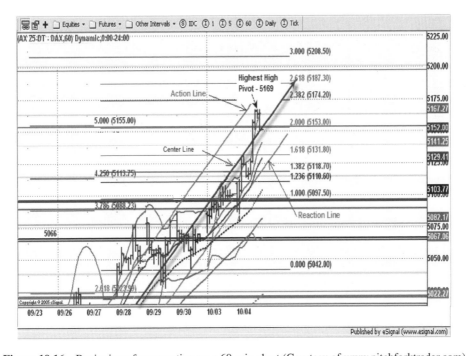

Figure 19.16   Beginning of a correction on a 60-min chart (Courtesy of www.pitchforktrader.com)

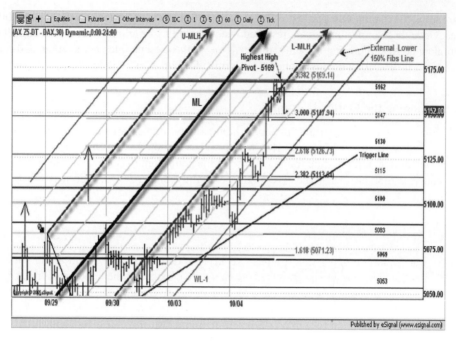

Figure 19.17   Beginning of a correction on a 30-min chart (Courtesy of www.pitchforktrader.com)

It is highly probable that the down move will continue, at least a few bars, with a highly charged momentum.

The 30-min chart in Fig. 19.17 illustrates the beginning of a correction. The market travels for a 6-bar duration on the lower median line, through a very narrow ascending channel, before being stopped dead at the 5169 resistance level. Then, it drops with a big downbar very close to the external lower 150% Fibonacci line. The triple mirror pattern at the highest high is the guarantor of the reversal, and the beginning of a significant correction. It is highly probable that the down move will continue, at least for a few bars, with a highly-charged momentum.

The 15-min chart in Fig. 19.18 illustrates the beginning of a correction. The very strong market travels almost vertically, making an eight-bar narrow range consolidation below the 5169 level. Then, it drops with a big down-bar, almost freely. The triple top pattern at the highest high is the guarantor of the reversal, and the beginning of a significant correction. It is highly probable that the down move will continue, at least for a few bars, with the same vigorous momentum.

19.3.4   Three-Pawn Technique: Triple Order Preparation and Trade Execution

In Fig.19.19, we can see that, as anticipated, the down move is continuing strongly and is creating a down gap, zooming through the upper median line of the ascending pitchfork. Now that the zoom is accomplished, let us consider the following trade, in the event of a test or retest of the upper median line (U-MLH):

- *Sell stop entry* at 5125: if test or retest, after zooming move.
- *Initial stop loss*: buy stop at 5129, just above the last high of the previous trend.

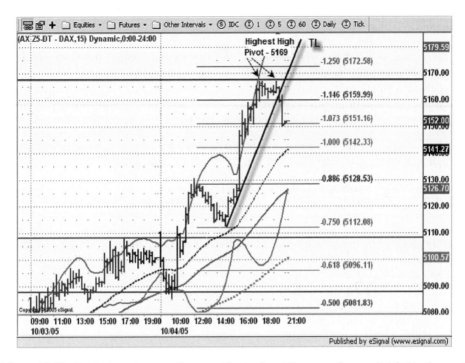

Figure 19.18 Beginning of a correction on a 15-min chart (Courtesy of www.pitchforktrader.com)

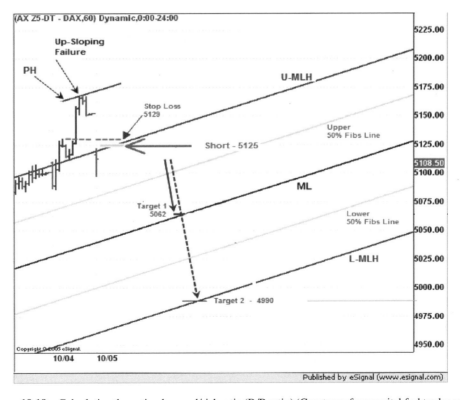

Figure 19.19 Calculating the optimal reward/risk ratio (R/R ratio) (Courtesy of www.pitchforktrader.com)

- *First logical profit objective* (target no. 1): buy stop at 5062 at the confluence of the market price with the median line (ML).
- *Second logical profit objective* (target no. 2): buy stop at 4990 at the intersection of the market price with the lower median line (L-MLH). The value of this target has been calculated using the ATRs technique (see Fig. 19.4).

Due to the size and location of the gap, which is probably a breakout gap, it seems that the trade has a high probability potential. Thus, we will consider two trading units:

a)   The first that will be exited at target 1 level no. 1; and
b)   the second that will be exited at target level no. 2. Who knows, we might be able to get a free ride and trade with the market's own money.

But before placing any orders, we have to establish the reward/risk ratio, and verify if the R/R ratio value is above/below our 2.5 usual limit. Let us now calculate the R/R ratio for this low-risk high-probability short trade. The calculation per contract will only be done with target no. 1. There will be no risk for target no. 2 because as soon as target no. 1 is attained, we will move the stop loss to the break-even point at 5125 level:

- *Reward* is 63 Dax points for target no. 1.
- *Risk* is 4 Dax points: stop loss level (5129) minus entry level (5125).
- *Reward/risk ratio* is 15.75: 63 divided by 4, an excellent value.

Conclusion: The R/R ratio being excellent, we will place our three prearranged orders.

19.3.5   Trade Progression

In Fig. 19.20, the second bar of the opening retraces just slightly over the upper median line, thus executing the entry order. The third opening bar (last one on the chart) has its close in its lower quarter, hinting towards a down-sloping move. We are confident in our progressing short trade, mainly because of the breakout gap and the down-zooming huge bar.

The market has started to develop a pullback with regard to the down move (Fig. 19.21). It is an excellent opportunity to *add on (scale in)* one trading unit. When adding, the trader should add on fewer units than the number of initial entry units. The standard value is 33% to a maximum of 50% of the number of the total entry units.

Therefore, we enter a pre-arranged add-on unit sell-stop order at the 5125 level. The same stop loss (5129 level) will be used as that of the initial entry, aiming for the same target no. 1. We now have two trading units initially entered and a third one as an add on, a total of three units. Two are exiting at target level 1, and the third at target level 2. The enormous potential of this trade requires more than one intra-day trading session, so we have decided to let the trade in overnight.

As anticipated, the next day the market drops further (Fig.19.22 on p. 380) with a huge gap of 55.5 Dax points. The market price not only reaches our target no. 1, it exceeds it. At the opening of the following day, we are still in the trade in spite of the prearranged buy stop at 5062 (target no. 1). Thus, we have to manually exit with two units, right at the opening bar (5032 level). We also move the stop of the remaining trading unit to the break-even level. We note that the occurrence of a second gap, usually called the *running gap*, gives another dimension to the already-consistent trade potential.

The 50% level of the running gap represents half the potential of the entire trend (see Chapter 13). The opening bar of the following day (Fig. 19.22) has a huge down tail, representing

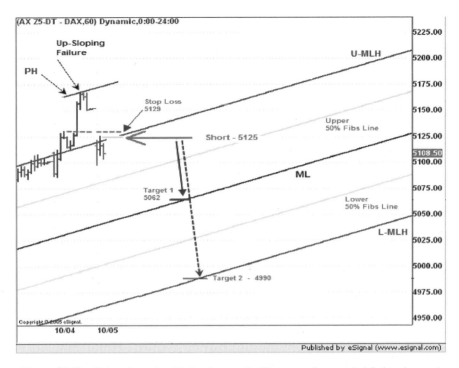

Figure 19.20 Going through with the short trade (Courtesy of www.pitchforktrader.com)

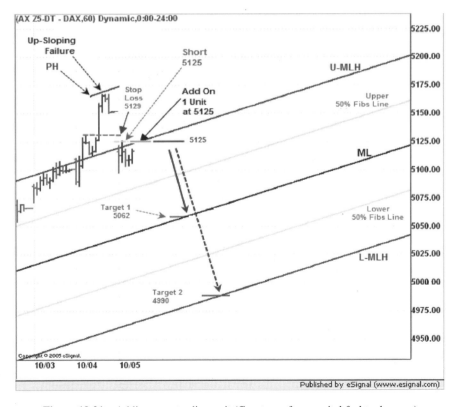

Figure 19.21 Adding-on a trading unit (Courtesy of www.pitchforktrader.com)

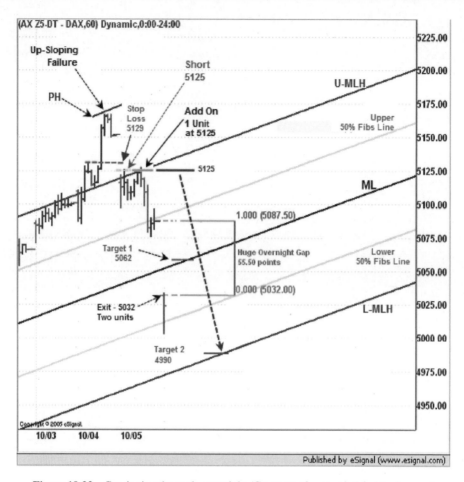

Figure 19.22 Continuing the trade overnight (Courtesy of www.pitchforktrader.com)

two-thirds of the body. It only signals a short break in the strong down-market drop, but it looks as if target no. 2 is very likely to be attained. This would be the moment to add on (scale in) another trading unit, because of the high probability of a good trade outcome.

Figure 19.23 illustrates our third (last) unit at the 4990 level (target no. 2) during the last hour of the day. Thus, our trade is terminated. We should emphasize here the merit of the prearranged exits, especially the second one, which helped us to get the most out of this trade. Without this, we would have not been able to optimally manage the trade.

19.3.6   Profit and Loss Statement

Now that the trade has been concluded let us see its outcome.

- We have taken three trading units, all of them traded on automatic pilot with prearranged orders, even if the market forced us to exit manually. We should emphasize that all three units were governed by the three-pawn technique.

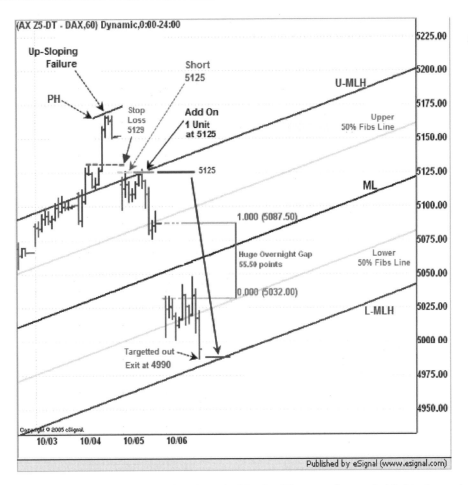

Figure 19.23 Targeting the last unit at the end of the day (Courtesy of www.pitchforktrader.com)

- Per contract we have risked four DAX points representing €100 ($127).
- The reward per contract pertaining to the R/R ratio of 15.75, initially calculated per contract, was 63 Dax points. As we know, we have traded three units: two at the initial entry and one add on. Their exits were as follows: two units at the 5032 level and the last at the 4990 level.

Therefore, we have obtained the following results:

1. For the two trading units, we have per contract a reward of 93 Dax points: entry level (5125) minus exit no. 1 level (5032).
2. For the third trading unit, we have per contract a reward of 135 Dax points: entry level (5125) minus exit no. 2 level (4990).

The total financial result per contract (all three units) is 321 Dax points (2 × 93 + 1 × 135) a total of €8025 ($10191). The total time spent in the trade was two days, from the second hourly bar of the first day to the last bar of the next day.

19.3.7   Trader's Journal: Keep Your Records Straight

We log in the main topics and also any unusual events or missing opportunities arising either from not respecting the rule or to new lessons arriving to the learning curve. Let us proceed further:

- We fully respected the rules, especially those of the three-pawn technique.
- The trade reward is excellent, with above-average results.
- We comfortably detected the first add-on opportunity which we traded. We also detected the second opportunity below the 5032 level, right at the opening of the second bar of the second day. We chose not to trade the latter because of the large stop loss that would be necessary.
- Once again, we realized the importance of identifying the types of gaps and their relationship with:
  - the median line and its contextual supporting pitchforks;
  - money management of the trade.
- We took note of the importance of scanning all five time frames in order to reveal a low-risk high-probability trade, thus giving us increased confidence in our tools and techniques. This is one of the best ways of treating and healing the trigger-shy syndrome.
- We noticed also the role of the failures, how to detect them and also the best way to trade them. Their concomitant occurrence in multiple time frames enhances the classic trade potential. Always look for them . . . they are great moneymakers!

19.4   ZOOM-AND-TEST TECHNIQUE: GERMAN DAX MEDIAN LINE

19.4.1   Spotting the Trade Opportunity

Spotting low-risk high-probability trades is a very systematic process for the experienced trader who will visually scan the various choices of the operational time frame charts: 60-min, 30-min, 15-min and (less frequently) the 5-min chart. Our goal is to detect possibilities for low-risk high-probability trades. Once these opportunities are revealed, we will employ different techniques using all the recommended disciplined rigour and patience. One such technique is the zoom-and-test of the median line of the pitchfork. It is one of the most powerful low-risk high-probability trades.

19.4.2   Finding the Optimal Set-up

In this trade, we have spotted a zoom through the median line of a contextual pitchfork in our preferred 15-min operational time frame chart (Fig. 19.25).

19.4.3   Time Frame Alignment

But first we turn to the 60-min chart (Fig. 19.24), and note that the upper time frame has made a double top, waiting for an imminent high-probability reversal around the 5080.50 level. Any new reversal bar will definitely confirm the reversal. If this happens, we will look for a low-risk high-probability trade using the zoom-and-test or retest technique of the nearest median line or its companions.

Figure 19.24   Imminent high probability reversal on a 60-min chart
(Courtesy of www.pitchforktrader.com)

19.4.4   Three Pawn Technique: Triple Order Preparation and Trade Execution

By observing the 15-min chart in Fig. 19.25, we note that the reversal took place, as anticipated in Fig. 19.24, expressed by a huge down-sloping zoomed bar the size of two ATRs. Now that the zoom is accomplished, let us consider the following trade, in the case of a test or retest of the median line (ML):

- *Sell stop entry at 5080*: if test or retest of the ML, after zooming move.
- *Initial stop loss*: buy stop at 5088, just above the last high of the previous trend.
- *First logical profit objective* (target no. 1): buy stop at 5064 at the confluence of the market price with the internal lower 50% Fibonacci line and the strong horizontal resistance at that level.
- *Second logical profit objective* (target no. 2): buy stop at 5057 at the intersection of the market price with the lower median line (L-MLH). The value of this target has been calculated using the ATRs technique (Fig. 19.4).

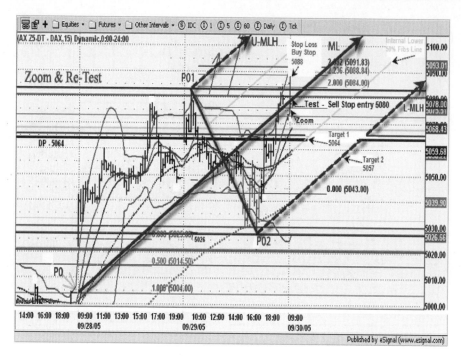

Figure 19.25   Reversal on a 15-min chart (Courtesy of www.pitchforktrader.com)

Due to the up-sloping failure situated at the highest high (5088 level), the huge downward bar, and the zooming of the median line, it seems that the trade has a high potential to succeed. Thus we will consider two trading units:

1.   The first that will exit at the level of target no. 1.
2.   The second that will exit at the level of target no. 2. Who knows, we might be able to get a free ride and trade with the market's own money.

But before placing any orders, we have to establish the R/R ratio, and verify whether its value is above or below our 2.5 limit. So now let us calculate the R/R ratio for this low-risk high-probability short trade. The calculation per contract will only be done for target no. 1. There will be no risk for target no. 2 because as soon as target no. 1 is attained, we will move the stop loss to the break-even point at the 5080 level.

- *Reward* is 16 Dax points for target no. 1: entry level (5080) minus target no. 1 (level 5064)
- *Risk* is 8 Dax points: stop loss level (5088) minus entry level (5080).
- *Reward/risk ratio* is 2: 16 divided by 8 – an acceptable value.

Conclusion: Even if the R/R ratio is under our usual value of 2.5, we will take the trade because of its low-risk high-probability and place our three prearranged orders.

In Fig. 19.26 the second bar of the opening retraces slightly, testing the median line, thus executing the entry order. Even if the next bar has its close in its lower quarter and almost reaches our target no. 1, we are confident in our progressing short trade, so we will stay in and respect

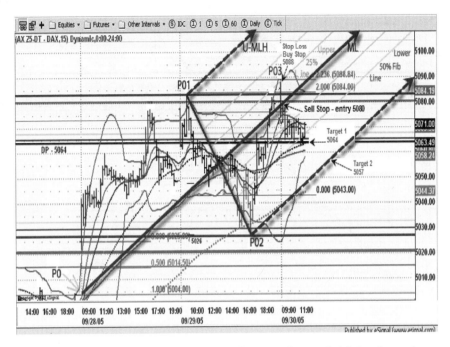

Figure 19.26   Executing the entry order (Courtesy of www.pitchforktrader.com)

the rules. The huge down-zooming bar and the test of the ML is the guarantor of a profitable outcome.

Finally, the seventh bar of the session pierces the 5064 resistance level, thus targetting our first trading unit. Immediately we change the location of the initial stop loss (5088 level) to the break-even level for the second trading unit, which is still in the market.

As we anticipated, the highly charged momentum pushes the market price lower, and targets our second trading unit (Fig. 19.27). The lower median line stopped the big exiting bar short. The next bar tests the L-MLH and closes in its upper quarter, leaving behind a virtual comet's tail. We are tempted to enter with a two unit add on. Thus, our trade is terminated and we are out with both trading units.

19.4.5   Profit and Loss Statement

Now that the trade has been concluded let us study its profit and loss statement.

We have taken two trading units, which were traded on automatic pilot with prearranged orders. Again, we should emphasize that the units were governed by the three-pawn technique. We have risked per contract only two DAX points representing €50 ($63.50). The reward per contract pertaining to the R/R ratio of 2.00, initially calculated per contract, was 16 Dax points. Therefore, we have obtained the following results:

*   For the first trading unit, we have a reward per contract of 16 Dax points: entry level (5080) minus exit level no. 1 (5064).
*   For the second trading unit, we have a reward per contract of 23 Dax points: entry level (5080) minus exit level no. 2 (5057).

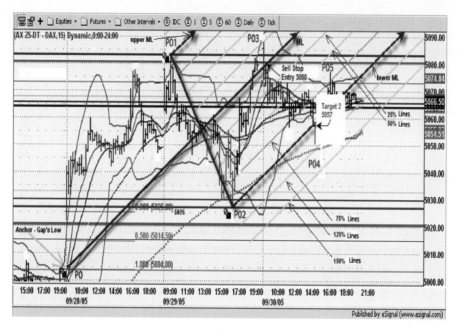

Figure 19.27   Trading with multiple trading units (Courtesy of www.pitchforktrader.com)

The total financial result per contract (both units) is 39 Dax points (16 + 23), a total of €975 ($1238). The total time spent in the trade was six hours.

19.4.6   Trader's Journal: Keep Your Records Straight

Log the main topics in the journal, and also any unusual events or missing opportunities arising either from a misuse of the rules, or to learning new lessons pertaining to the learning curve. Let us proceed.

- We fully respected the rules, especially those relating to discipline and patience, during the six-hour trade. We applied the three-pawn technique. The trade was executed in automatic control mode using the three prearranged orders.
- The trade reward is good, and many traders would consider it as achieving above-average profit results.
- Once again, we realized the importance of:
  - the median line and its contextual pitchforks;
  - the continuous management of the trade intimately coupled with money management.
- We would like to emphasize the role of the upper time frame (the 60-min chart in our example), which highlighted an imminent failure, better visualized and traded on the lower time frames.
- The role of basic technical analysis with the chart formations (double top in our example) took here its full importance (refer to Fig. 19.24).
- The occurrence and detection of the failure greatly enhances the classic trade potential. We will say it again: Always look for them — they are great money makers.

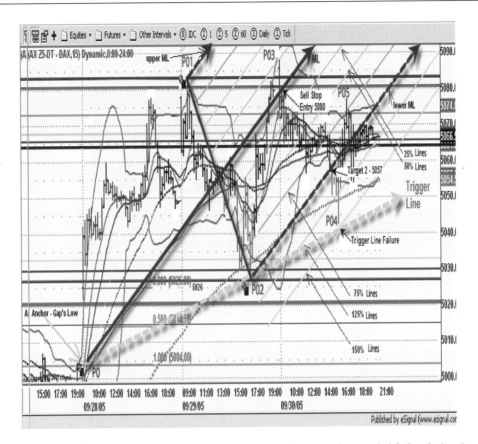

Figure 19.28   Market down-move, creating the P4 pivot (Courtesy of www.pitchforktrader.com)

The add-on trade that we were tempted to take, was liable to be executed right after the exiting bar of the second target. Now, after the event, as we study Fig. 19.28, we can see that the market did a good down-move almost touching the confluence of the trigger line and the external lower 150% Fibonacci line, thus creating the P04 pivot. We did not enter the trade because it was not part of our initial strategy. It is always better to lose an opportunity than suffer a financial loss.

19.5   BREAKOUT OF THE NARROW RANGE: GERMAN DAX MEDIAN LINE

19.5.1   Spotting the Trade Opportunity

Spotting low-risk high-probability trades is a very systematic process for the experienced trader who will visually scan the various choices of the operational time frame charts: 60-min, 30-min, 15-min and (less frequently) the 5-min chart. Our goal is to detect possibilities for low-risk high-probability trades. Once these opportunities are revealed, we will employ different techniques using all the recommended disciplined rigour and patience. One of these is the *breakout of a narrow range* situated on the median line of the pitchfork. It is one of the most powerful low-risk high-probability trades.

19.5.2   Finding the Optimal Set-up

In this trade, we have spotted a very probable breakout of a narrow range situated on the median line within a wider consolidation (a pattern within a pattern) in our preferred 15-min operational time frame chart.

Looking at Fig. 19.29, we can immediately see the small narrow-range formation where the local market price is virtually dancing on the median line of the contextual pitchfork. This small range consolidation has the advantage of being situated within a wider one, the a-b-c-d consolidation. A small narrow-range formation, right under the upper border of a wider consolidation, is prone to an imminent price explosion as a result of its intensive process of energy building. It is only a question of knowing the right direction.

Whenever this happens, the trader should always consider a low-risk high-probability trade in the direction of the upper time frame, in our case, the 60-min chart. We should be aware of a very probable pullback on the upper border within a 1−4 bar duration, right after the breakout. An even deeper pullback (throwback) could occur, right through this boundary. The preservation of the trader's capital requires a small stop loss, 2−4 ticks under the narrow range.

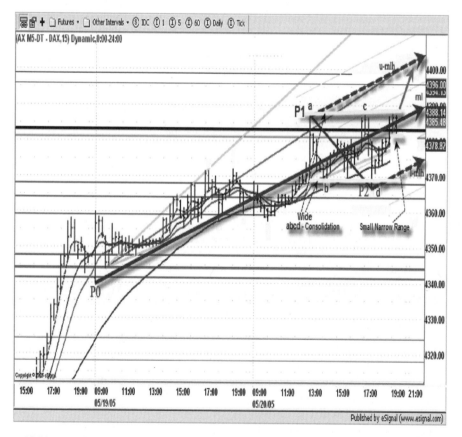

Figure 19.29   Small narrow range formation on a 15-min chart (Courtesy of www.pitchforktrader.com)

We selected this trade due to its small narrow range right on the median line within the wider consolidation and the up-trend of all time frames. Most of the time, this trade is a very profitable trade but its management, including the money management, should be treated with caution.

19.5.3 Time Frame Alignment

We notice that the upper time frames (daily and 60-min charts) both show the same up-sloping direction. Then we look at the three lower time frames (60-, 30- and 15-min charts) to observe the local market movements, and to eventually choose the optimal operational time frame and better pinpoint our entry. We notice the narrow trading range on the 15-min chart (Fig. 19.29).

19.5.4 Three-Pawn Technique: Triple Order Preparation and Trade Execution

On the 15-min chart in Fig. 19.30, we note that the small narrow-range formation situated on the median line is ready to explode. We will consider the following trade, in the case of a breakout from the median line.

- *Buy stop entry* at 4389 level.
- *Initial stop loss*: sell stop at 4382 just below the lower border of the small narrow range.

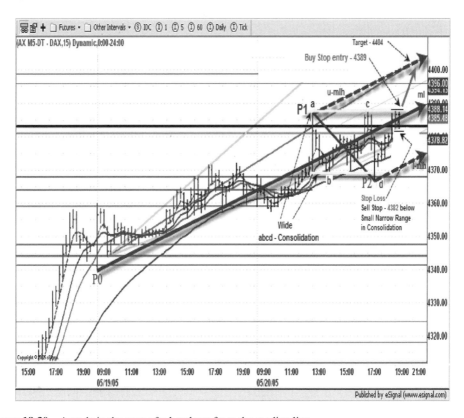

Figure 19.30 A trade in the case of a breakout from the median line
(Courtesy of www.pitchforktrader.com)

- *Logical profit objective*: sell stop at the 4404 level at the confluence of the market price with the upper median line of the contextual pitchfork. The value of this target has been calculated using the ATR technique (Fig. 19.4).

Due to the narrow range on the median line within the wider consolidation and the up-trend on all time frames, we believe that this trade has a high probability potential. Thus, we will consider three trading units exiting at the same time (target 4404). But before placing any orders, we have to establish the R/R ratio and verify if its value is above or below our 2.5 usual limit. Let us proceed and calculate the R/R ratio for this low-risk high-probability long trade:

- *Reward* is 15 Dax points: target level 4404 minus entry level 4389.
- *Risk* is 7 Dax points: entry level 4389 minus stop loss level 4382.
- *Reward/risk ratio* is 2.14: 15 divided by 7 – an acceptable value.

Conclusion: Even if the R/R ratio is under our usual value of 2.5, we will take the trade because of its low-risk high-probability and place our three prearranged orders.

As we anticipated, the market makes a virtual jail break (Fig. 19.31), closing its breaking-out bar just above the breaking line. The second bar almost tests the breaking line but goes on its way, closing in its upper quarter just above the higher internal 50% Fibonacci line.

We now have to take a decision: do we stay with the trade overnight? Due to the trade's high potential we decide to remain in. The closing bar of the day is small because of a strong resistance overhead, but still closes above the high of the preceding bar and above the Fibonacci line already mentioned.

As we anticipated, the next day the market climbs farther (Fig. 19.32 on p. 392) making a gap with an average size of 18 Dax points at the 4414 opening level. Not only does the market price reach our target, but also it exceeds it. At the opening of next day, we are still in the trade, in spite of the prearranged sell stop at the 4404 level (the trade's only target). We have to manually exit the trade during the opening bar (4415 level) with all three units. Thus, our trade is terminated.

19.5.5   Profit and Loss Statement

Now that the trade has been concluded let us see its outcome.

- We have taken three trading units, all of them traded on automatic pilot with prearranged orders, even if the market forces us to exit manually. We should emphasize that all three units were governed by the three-pawn technique.
- Per contract we have risked seven DAX points representing €175 ($222).
- The reward per contract pertaining to the R/R ratio of 2.14, calculated per contract, was 15 Dax points. The concomitant exit was manually done, at the 4415 level.

Therefore, we have obtained the following results: The trade has performed per contract a reward of 26 Dax points: exit level (4415) minus entry level (4389). The total financial result per contract (all three units) is 78 Dax points (3 units × 26) a total of €1950 ($2476). This is a classic example of an overnight trade, which in reality only lasted three bars: two pre-close and an opening bar.

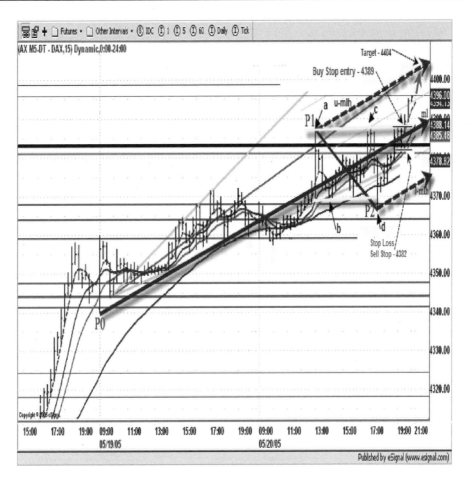

Figure 19.31 Strong market move guided by the median line (Courtesy of www.pitchforktrader.com)

19.5.6 Trader's Journal: Keep Your Records Straight

We log in the main topics and also any unusual events or missing opportunities arising either from not respecting the rule or new lessons adding to the learning curve. Let us proceed:

- We fully respected the rules, especially those relating to discipline and patience, during the trading period. We applied the three-pawn technique. The trade was executed in automatic mode using the three prearranged orders.
- The trade makes very good profit, as a result of the market's momentum and also our decision to trade three units.
- Once again, we realized the importance of:
  - the median line, its contextual pitchfork parallels and especially the power of a pattern within a pattern;
  - the trade management was continuously in automatic mode from the beginning of the trade. This not only relieves us from the psychological pressure but also avoids the trigger-shy syndrome.

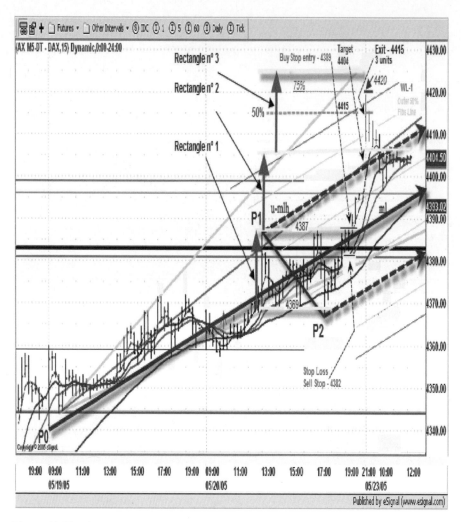

Figure 19.32   Continuing the trade the following day (Courtesy of www.pitchforktrader.com)

- The role of basic technical analysis with the chart formations (narrow range within a wide consolidation) shows its full importance here (Fig. 19.24).
- The exit, as you know by now, was done manually during the opening bar of the second day. You might wonder: why did we not stay in the long trade, after an eighteen Dax points up-gap, and eventually increase the trade's profit potential? The answer is simple. We have a strict rule: *never be tempted by unplanned actions*. We were already glad that the market opened in our direction. Greed will never get you anywhere during the trading life!

We will say a word about *ladder rectangles*, meaning a pile of rectangles, their power and also their role in detecting an up-sloping failure. A whole chapter is dedicated to the relationship between pitchforks and rectangles in Volume II (in preparation). Please read carefully the text under Fig. 19.33 in order to get a concise preview of the detailed explanation which will be given in the next volume.

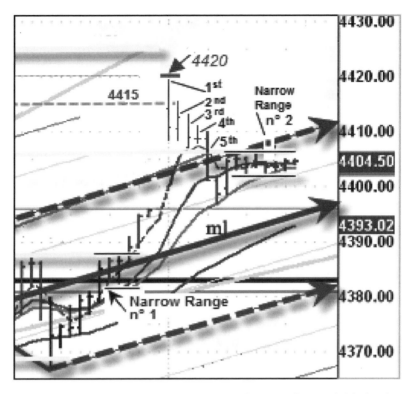

Figure 19.33 Magnified view of a trade's exit zone (Courtesy of www.pitchforktrader.com)

Figure 19.33 is a magnified view of a trade's exit zone. We can see that the first bar of the opening market makes a high at the 4420 level, which coincides with the 2.75 ratio projection of the initial wide consolidation. The narrow range no. 1 was the birthing nest of this huge move, which provoked the overnight gap.

The opening bar is a splendid example of a reversal bar, especially because of its close in the lower quarter. The array of regular down-sloping bar highs (1st to the 5th) emphasizes this reversal process. We can almost draw an optimal steep down-trend line linking all these progressive lower highs. By watching these bars carefully, the trader can understand that there is a high-probability of an imminent reversal.

We conclude this trade example by saying: *Who knows the past, preferably the immediate past, controls the future!*

This concept is very common in technical analysis. If you have any doubt, just look at the narrow range no. 2 located right under the upper border of the second projection of the initial wide consolidation and compare it with the narrow range no. 1. As you can see, it is more than three times longer and has range almost twice as narrow.

- Does it ring a bell, from the past, the immediate past?
- Will it have a wilder (more efficient) jailbreak thrust than the previous narrow-range rectangle?

I leave the heavy burden of getting the right answers to you − I am sure that future experience will provide you with them!

Appendices

Appendix I   Historical basis
Appendix II   The 80:20 percent rule
Appendix III Bibliography and references
Appendix IV Contents of Volumes II and III (in preparation)

APPENDIX I: HISTORICAL BASIS: USING THE CONCEPT OF THE PITCHFORK AS A TOOL

Ancient Egypt: 4000BC

(Courtesy of www.pitchforktrader.com)

1. **Equilibrium of up-move vectors**: There are two outer vectorial forces and an inner median (line) vectorial force. Each of these three vectors has their specific direction and magnitude. The thoroughly controlled unstable equilibrium will transport the stone blocks in the desired direction.

(Courtesy of www.pitchforktrader.com)

2.   **Up-rolling force vectors equilibrium**: Three parallel force vectors in synchrony.

(Courtesy of www.pitchforktrader.com)

3.   **Up-sloping forces at work**: An ingenious device offering a lesser degree of friction.

(Courtesy of www.pitchforktrader.com)

4.   **Action–reaction device**: The ingenious Egyptians seem to have discovered the Action/ Reaction principle, well ahead of Europeans. Let us try to explain the three steps of this mechanism:

- *Action phase*: the four workers create a dominant vectorial force, shifted to the right under the strict guidance of the foreman, here playing the role of the Center Line.
- *Equilibrium phase*: the fifth worker inserts the inclined wooden board under the granite block, and the foreman dictates the shift of the direction of force vectors.
- *Reaction phase*: once the foreman gives the signal to the workers, they will bring the granite block back in the opposite location to that of the action phase.

If plotted, the oscillatory movements of the granite slabs during the Action/ Equilibrium/Reaction phases will be a sinusoidal curve, travelling from one extremity to another, briefly going through the Center Line.

(Courtesy of www.pitchforktrader.com)

5.   Once the **global context** is defined, the Egyptians organize locally their pyramid-building task in synergy with their indigenous tools, which fully apply the Action/Reaction principle.

(Courtesy of www.pitchforktrader.com)

6.   The **over-balance** as a moving power: Again the three vectorial forces are searching for the equilibrium whose dynamics will help transport several tons of granite slab toward the top of the pyramid.

(Courtesy of www.pitchforktrader.com)

7.   The **ultimate confirmation** of a well-done job.

The 17th Century to Modern Times

At the end of the 17th century, Sir Isaac Newton (1642−1727) synthesized the works of Descartes, Kepler, Copernicus and Galileo, writing several books. His genius marked not only the 17th century but also the future of mankind. His Action and Reaction Principle is explained in Chapter 11.

Newton's work was a true keystone event in scientific development during the 17th century, and greatly influenced the work of several entrepreneurs during the 20th century.

Roger W. Babson (1875−1967)

In his late twenties, Babson became interested in what he then called '*the normal line*' principle, based on Newton's Action and Reaction Principle of his Third Law. His whole life was marked by his strong belief in the power of this law as applied to the financial market. And he was right. . . he made a fortune of more than $50 million. As a forecaster, he was one of the best. The 'Babson charts' were used in a New York magazine to forecast the October 1929 stock market crash, well ahead of the event.

Roger Babson truly enjoyed sharing his knowledge and his money with his peers: he promoted Technical Analysis by giving seminars, wrote over 45 books, founded Babson College and, at the age of 73, the Gravity Research Foundation. His charismatic character helped him to reach the very noble and enviable age of 93 years. He truly believed in common sense, self-control, imagination and integrity which, as we know, are the qualities of every consistent trader.

Dr Alan Hall Andrews

Being very passionate about Technical Analysis, the late Dr Alan H. Andrews attended Roger Babson's seminars about the Action and Reaction Newtonian Principle. In the early 1960s, he organized the essence of this concept in a 60-page course and sold it for $1500. Needless to say, this amount was rather stiff for those days, representing as it did a couple of months' salary for a professional worker. He named it the 'Action-Reaction Course' in acknowledgement of the contribution of Roger W. Babson to his learning curve. His work described the 'Median Line Method' − drawn median lines on the charts, having a resemblance to a fork − that became known in most of the charting programs as Andrews Pitchforks.

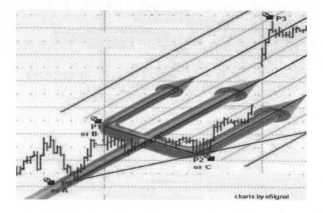

'... From the darkness of time the pitchfork becomes a state-of-the-art trading tool'

(Courtesy of www.pitchforktrader.com)

APPENDIX II: THE 80:20 PERCENT RULE

This Excel spreadsheet can be obtained from the author, Dr Mircea Dologa. Email: mircdologa@yahoo.com

80/20 Percent Rule

High	5,570.0
Low	5,558.0
Close	5,568.0

Note - Please fill in the values of High, Low & Close

Rule 80/20 Up				5,570.0	High
16.7%	**5,568.0**	high third			
2				5,566	
		mid third		**5,564**	**Mid**
		mid third			
10				5,562	
83.3%		lower third			**Low**
Rule 80/20 Down				5558.0	

Trading Range is **12**

Explanations of this Example:

16.7% is the distance Close-High (2 points)

83.3% is the distance Close-Low (10 points)

Length of trading range is 12 points

APPENDIX III: BIBLIOGRAPHY AND REFERENCES

1. Baron, Jonathan (2008). *Thinking and Deciding*. Cambridge University Press, NY, USA.
2. Crane, John (2000). *A Traders Handbook – The Reversal Phenomenon* 3rd ed. Tradenet Publishing Co., USA.
3. Crane, John (2003). *Advanced Swing Trading*. John Wiley & Sons Inc. NY, USA.
4. Dologa, M. (2005). 'Following the Median Line.' *Futures* (December).
5. Dologa, M. (2006). 'Integrated Pitchfork Analysis.' *The Traders Journal* (January/February).
6. Dologa, M. (2006). 'Trading Rectangles: Tactics and Money Management.' *Futures* (March).
7. Dologa, M. (2006). 'Preparing for Intra-day Trading.' *Your Trading Edge* (March/April).
8. Dologa, M. (2006). 'The Third Wave – Crowd Behavior and Elliott Waves, Part I.' *Stocks & Commodities* (May).
9. Dologa, M. (2006). 'Pragmatic Aspects of Trading Rectangles: A particular case of Dr Alan Andrews' Pitchfork?' *Technical Analyst* (May/June).
10. Dologa, M. (2006). 'Trading Life: The Quest for Best Intra-day Trading Tools.' *Your Trading Edge* (May/June 2006).
11. Dologa, M. (2006). 'Trading the Trend in Wave 3, Part II.' *Stocks & Commodities* (June).
12. Dologa, M. (2006). 'Short-Term Trading with A&R Lines.' *The Traders Journal* (June/July).
13. Dologa, M. (2006) 'The Third Wave, Part III.' *Stocks & Commodities* (September).
14. Dologa, M. (2006). 'Pre-Open Preparation of Dax Trading.' *Traders* (December).
15. Dologa, M. (2007). 'Trading the Dax Open.' *Technical Analyst* (January/February).
16. Edwards, Robert and Magee, John (2001). *Technical Analysis of Stock Trends*. CRC Press, Boca Raton, FL, USA.
17. E Signal Advanced GET Manual (2003). *The Tools, the Power and the Knowledge*. Hayward, CA, USA.
18. Fisher, Greg (2007). *Median Line Study*. www.Median-Line-Study.com.
19. Kase, Cynthia A. (1996). *Trading with the Odds*. McGraw-Hill, NY, USA.
20. Kirkpatrick II, D. Charles and Dahlquist, Julie R. (2007). *Technical Analysis*. FT Press, NY, USA.
21. LeBeau, Charles and Lucas, David W. (1992). *Technical Traders' Guide to Computer Analysis of the Futures Market*. McGraw-Hill, NY, USA.
22. Mandelbrot, Benoit (1997). *Fractals and Scaling in Finance*. Springer, NY, USA.
23. *Merriam-Webster's Collegiate Dictionary, 10th Edition* (2002). Merriam-Webster Inc, MA, USA.
24. Mikula, Patrick (2002). *The Best Trendline Methods of Alan Andrews and Five New Trendline Techniques*. Austin Financial Group, TX, USA.
25. Miner, Robert C. (1999). *Dynamic Trading*. Dynamic Traders Group, Inc., AZ, USA.
26. Morge, Timothy (2003). *Trading with the Median Line*. Blackthorne Capital, Inc., Aurora, IL, USA.
27. Morge, Timothy (2008). *Mapping the Markets*. Blackthorne Capital, Inc., Aurora, IL, USA.
28. Pring, Martin J. (2002). *Technical Analysis Explained*. McGraw-Hill, NY, USA.
29. Schabacker, Richard W. (1997). *Technical Analysis and Stock Market Profits*. Pearson Education Ltd, London, UK.
30. Schabacker, Richard, W. (1930). *Stock Market Theory and Practice*. Forbes Publishing Co., NY, USA.
31. *Steadman's Illustrated Medical Dictionary, 23rd Ed.* (1976). The Williams & Wilkins Company, MD, USA.
32. Sweeney, John (1996). *Campaign Trading*. John Wiley & Sons Inc., NY, USA.

APPENDIX IV: CONTENTS OF VOLUMES II AND III (IN PREPARATION)

Volume II Advanced Level

Introduction & Disclaimer

1. Context of the Trade
   Understanding of the time/price circumstances related to contextual and local market movements
2. Pre-open Preparation
   Key to understanding the outcome of the following day
3. News Trading: Overnight and intra-day unfolding
   Fuelling of morning and day's market movements
4. Inter-markets Analysis: Fundamentals of real-time use
   Roads to day's trading potential
5. Elliott Waves: Real-time and intermediate-term use – pitchfork intricacy
   Faithfully guided by the pitchforks, the Elliott waves reveal the direction and precise location of the price
6. Original Tools for Impulsive Pattern End: Diagnosis, kinetics and management
   Original tool research of trend-following traders
7. Channelling: Pathways in the sand or market move projections
   Excellent forecasting tool for profit targets
8. Variable Time/Price Location of Pitchfork's Anchor: Parallel trigger and P1-2 Fibs TLs
   Time–price related tool revealing the optimal market description by the traditional pitchfork
9. Variable Time/Price Location of the Anchor in the Schiff Pitchfork
   Time–price related tool detecting the optimal market description by the Schiff pitchfork
10. Fibonacci and Momentum Bar Counts Related to Pitchfork's Pivots
    Mapping momentum strength/weakness through bar counts and pivots
11. RSI and Pitchfork Synergism
    Discussing a poorly-understood synergistic tool – pitchforks applied to market and also to the RSI chart
12. Stochastics and Pitchfork Synergism
    Dual characteristics tool determining the trending and sideways markets
13. OSC(5,35) and Pitchfork Synergism
    Accredited tool for confirming or negating trends/reversals

Appendix I Price Fibonacci Ratios Technique Applied to Elliott Waves
Appendix II Reversal New Signals: Positive Reversal and Negative Reversals
Appendix III Key Level Mapping of the Operational Time-Frame Chart
Appendix IV Pre-Open Main Points
Appendix V Dax Pre-Open Trading Study
Appendix VI Miner's & Fisher's Calculated End-of-Wave 3
Appendix VII Miner's & Fisher's Calculations End-of-Wave W5
Appendix VIII Pivotal Bar Count Table
Appendix IX Types of Bar Count Numbers from 5 to 206
Appendix X Bar Count Grid
Appendix XI Three Pawn Technique

Volume III

Introduction & Disclaimer

1.   Bollinger and Keltner Bands: Pitchfork synergism
      Indispensable tool team of volatility trading
2.   Multiple Time Frame Floor Pivots and Mark Fisher Pivots
      Magical tool borrowed from the floor traders – pinpointing the market's price action
3.   Inceptive and Ladder-like Rectangles in Symbiosis with Pitchforks
      Two 'mal aimés' brothers, almost never working together
4.   Integration of Pitchforks in Very Profitable Chart Patterns
      An efficient tool poorly mastered by the crowd
5.   Synergy of Pitchforks and Fibonacci Time Ratios and Lucas Time Series
      Prolific projecting tool, wrongly labelled 'a hard to grasp concept'
6.   Breakaway and Runaway Gap Pitchforks: Observance, preparation and trading
      Highly profitable tool used by experienced traders unveiling the myth of gap trading
7.   Ellipses, Ladder-like Rectangles and Pitchforks
      Symbiosis and synergy in detecting breakouts
8.   Pitchforks Through the Multiple Time Frames
      Pitchforks' brotherhood tested by time-wise relationships
9.   Synergy of Pitchforks and Wolfe Waves
      Ergonomic tool for low-risk high-probability trades
10.   Synergy of Pitchforks and Jenkins' Circles
      Geometric tool for projecting pitchfork pivots – quantifying the 'time–price space'
11.   Gann Tools: Square of nine, % retracements, boxes, angles and pitchforks
      Apparently 'hard to grasp tools' revealing the endogenous cyclical nature of prices (S/R levels)
12.   Synergy of Pitchforks and Cycles
      Time-related relationships for optimal target projections
13.   Case Studies including Risk and Money Management
      Complete case descriptions: simple or pre-arranged entry, stop loss parsimony, targets, Reward/Risk ratios, trails, scale in, scale out, exits, nibbling and single/multiple trading units.

Appendices

EPILOGUE

We have arrived at the end of the book, exhausting the proposed material of our first volume. By now, you should be better prepared, and on your way to consistency in trading. I sincerely hope that we have given you the most useful topics to complete your trading arsenal. It is a real pleasure to be able to share my years of research with trading colleagues.

The second and third volumes at present in preparation (refer to Appendix) will offer more advanced material and will help you climb the ladder of professional trading in such a way that you will be able to trade for a living.

Please do not hesitate to e-mail your comments to me. Any questions are welcome!

We wish you . . . Good Trading!

Dr Mircea Dologa, MD, CTA
November 2008
Paris, France
mircdologa@yahoo.com
www.pitchforktrader.com

Glossary

A&R Lines Set-up.
Acronym for Action and Reaction Lines set-up.

Action and Reaction Line Set-up.
It represents vectorial forces implied in the market's movements which carry a certain degree of energy. The major role of the A&R Lines set-up is as a vehicle for the flow of market energy through the time-price virtual space, indicating the minimal and the maximal zones prone to a reversal, acceleration, or a market consolidation. The A&R Lines set-up is the parent of the median line concept (refer also to **Action Line, Reaction Line** and **Center Line**).

Action and Reaction Line Set-up Construction.
The trader closely observes the context of the market flow in his quest for a directional move, *already started or developing.* He will try to graphically cope with it. Once we have revealed the most optimal pivots, we can draw the Action Line, which is the trend line that firstly has been tested by the market flow.

The Center Line is usually drawn with the assistance of two or more pivots (see Fig. 11.3) and is meant to represent the direction of the market. Its trajectory can be ubiquitous: above, below, or through the market. It never respects market prices because it traverses the market, camouflaged among the numerous valleys and peaks.

The Center Line doesn't commonly have to be drawn first, *like the median line of a pitchfork does,* but in some specific cases it will be. Keep in mind that it can also be drawn after the Action and Reaction Lines have already formed the channel of the trending market.

The Action Line (see Fig. 11.4) is parallel to the Center Line through the corresponding pivots. When the Center Line is not yet drawn, then the trader will draw a two or more pivotal temporary trend line, which can become definitive, in the incipient market flow development.

The Reaction Line perfectly mirrors the Action Line (see Fig 11.5). It is used when the market flow goes above/below the Center Line or Action Line to the higher/lower price objectives.

Action Line.
The *action phase* of the market flow is graphically depicted by the Action Line. The multiple composite forces of the market flow create a dominant vectorial force having its strength in the most optimal process for describing the market, illustrated by the Action Line (AL).

Add-On.
See **Scale In.**

Aggressive Trade.
Whenever performing a trade, the trader can take bigger or smaller risks, which we say should be still within the trader's capital preservation potential. When the risk is increased with regard to trader's usual risk procedure, then the trade is qualified as aggressive.

It implies a better profitability and probably a higher frequency of the overall trades. But remember, the trade's risk is higher! See also **Conservative Trade.**

AL.
Acronym for Action Line.

Alternate Price Projection.
They are price projection percentages of past alternate swing(s) – *swings versus swings and counter-trends versus counter-trends* – as the name indicates. The measuring (*ongoing*) and the measured (*prior*) swings must be in the same direction as the ongoing market flow, thus respecting the alternate principle. The most commonly used projection percentage values are: 61.8, 100.0, 161.8, 200.0, 261.8, 423.6 and 685%.

Analysis Paralysis Syndrome.
This term represents the psychological aspect of decision taking inhibition. When a trader obscures the decisional tree of his trading plan then an inhibition of the triggering mechanism occurs, which will *temporarily paralyse* the trader in performing the trade.

Apex (of a Triangle).
This designates the level of triangle's converging lines.

Average True Range.
It is defined as the larger of either the distance between the current day's high and its low, or the current day's high or its low and yesterday's close.

ATR (21).
It designates an *Average True Range* calculated over a 21-bar period. It can be mostly calculated over a period of 5, 8, 13, 21 and 34 – which are Fibonacci numbers. Some traders use 14 because it is half of 28, that is 50% of a month, closely related to the moon cycle. We have a preference for the 21-bar period.

Why one number rather than the other? Well it's a question of habit, better knowing the market you trade and also of the time frame used. . . The best setting comes from experience on your particular markets.

Automatic Pilot Trading Mode.
When the three progressive trading orders, labelled the *three-pawn technique,* are *pre-arranged,* at the moment of the trade decision, then the trade is performed in *automatic pilot mode.* It is vital for the sake of capital preservation, that once they are established, they should *never* be changed. Due to the reliability and the automatism of this technique, we named it the *automatic pilot trading mode.* It is, one of the best remedies for the '*trigger-shy*' syndrome. See also **Three Pawn Technique.**

Bar Count.

The bars are counted in an up-trend and vice versa, in view of determining the end of the trend. More on this bar counting technique in our Volumes 2 and 3 (in preparation).

Breakaway Gap.

This type of gap is one of the most important because it signals the trader that an ongoing trend is just beginning. It remains open most of the time, although sometimes is only partially filled. Its starting blocks are mostly consolidation patterns and usually each well-developed trend contains a single breakaway gap.

Volume plays an important role in identifying this kind of gap and also in determining its degree of highly charged momentum. A great tip is to expect the volume to increase only during or right after the first breaking bar.

Break-Even Stop Loss.

It designates the *follow-up stop loss* of an ongoing profitable trade, which replaces the *initial stop loss*. The *break-even stop loss* is established when the market advanced in the trade's direction and is at 1.5 to 2.5 ATRs inter-distance. Its name tells the story. Its implementation will give the trader at least a *free ride* through the market!

Breakout (of a Trend Line).

The breakout efficiency of a trend line depends on the degree of its legitimacy, which in turn reveals the degree of fragility or strength of the trend. A bigger volume is needed to break a stronger trend line. The closing price of the bar penetrating the breaking trend line is a major clue of the breakout's efficiency. When the price closes two times in a row on the other side, in the direction of the trade, then it is very possible that the breakout will be definitive. *An efficient first time breakout is the exception, not the rule.*

The arithmetic confirmation of the breakout is valid when a certain arithmetic price limit percentage value is reached, away from the breaking point: a penetration of 1% for intra-day and a penetration of 3% for swing trading.

Breakout (False).

A *false breakout* occurs when the price returns, within a few bars, to the newly labelled support line (old resistance), in case of an up-trending move. Once it touches the support line it can either bounce away again in the direction of the trade or return to its departure point under the newly created support.

Bull Trap.

A *bull trap* is a version of the throwback described below, in which the price drops beyond the 100% retracement of the previous swing. See **Throwback.**

Center Line.

The *equilibrium phase* of the market flow is graphically expressed by the Center Line (CL), which also dictates the shift of the direction of the market force vectors. It coordinates the projection of the exhaustion and restoration of the market flow's kinetic energy around cluster zones. The dynamics of the market price around this trend line will temporarily create oscillatory movements illustrated by a sinusoidal curve, travelling from one side of the trend line to another whilst at the same time piercing, zooming, testing or retesting it. In this way, the Center Line becomes the vital element in the trader's comprehension of market flow movements, in making trading decisions and in his practice of the ever-present money management technique. A pitchfork's median line is nothing more than a specialized application of the Center Line of the A&R Line set-up.

CL.
Acronym for Center Line.

Cleanness.
Cleanness of the bars in a swing means that one has to evaluate their nature: the count, individual size and other bars' sizes, ATRs, down- versus up-bars, bars' location within the swing with their corresponding volumes, the reversal or continuation potential of the bars (volatile or *doji* or *hammer*, etc). This evaluation is essential in order to evaluate the pivot's efficiency at the end of the swing.

Cluster.
The price *cluster* has the characteristic of frequently halting the market, which we could compare with a *dam* blocking the rivers. It is usually formed when the market builds a very tight zone, where multiple trend lines are either superimposed, contiguous or in close proximity to each other. Again, as in the case of *confluences*, the more numerous they are, the stronger the blocking power of the *cluster* will be. The price *cluster* differs from the *confluence* because it is rather a very tight price zone formed by a parallel lines structure of various horizontal lines, which are more or less overlapping. By comparison, the *confluences* are an intersection of mostly slant lines but also of mixed oblique and horizontal lines.

We consider a cluster valid *only* if the width of the clustering zone is as narrow as possible. This narrowness limit is measured either in market points (*value*) or in market percentage or both. It all depends on the type of market and on the trader's trading habits. More details on this topic are depicted in our Volume 2 (*in preparation*).

One thing is almost sure! Should the market flow succeed in breaching this *dam-like landmark*, there will be a strong outburst, with huge bars, the only way of invading a long-infallible citadel.

Commensalisms.
This term is defined as '*two organisms which live together, neither bearing a parasitic relation to the other, without harm or prejudice to either but with one or both members deriving benefit*' (*Stedman's Medical Dictionary*, 23rd edition).

By analogy, we employ this term to illustrate that the elements of charting structures (*here A&R Lines set-up and pitchforks*) can be intricate so that they can build up highly inter-dependent phenomena.

Common Gap.
This type of gap is almost useless for trading purposes although the scalpers are sometimes interested in them. They are usually built within a consolidation pattern, representing mostly local market reactions due to their close proximity to the upper/lower boundaries of the consolidation pattern.

Commonality Principle.
It rules that the specific tools and attributes are valid across the time frames and/or across the different types of markets.

Confluence.
Defined as a gathering point, it is an intersection of multiple vectorial forces, which could promptly halt many of the kinetic forces. The greater the number and the impact of these forces, the stronger the halting power is. We can compare it with a rail road train depot towards which numerous tracks converge.

From our point of view, the exact meaning is the intersection of two lines, which may be horizontal with oblique or the intersection of two or more oblique trend lines. They mostly belong to the median line parallels of two or more different pitchforks (*major vs. major, major vs. minor, or minor vs. minor pitchforks*). We should not neglect the panoply of other lines, such as: Fibonacci ratio lines, old high/low levels, high/low/midpoint levels in old or recent gaps, and so on.

We consider a confluence valid *only* if the price bars either cross the intersection zone (*point*) or are very near, no further away than 1-3 bars.

Conservative Trade.
Whenever performing a trade, the trader can take bigger or smaller risks, which we say should be still within his capital preservation potential. When the risk is minimal with regard to trader's usual risk procedure, then the trade is qualified as conservative. It implies a lower profitability than the aggressive trade and probably a lower frequency of the overall trades. And remember, the trade's risk is lower! See also **Aggressive Trade**.

Context (of Market).
This term describes the conditions of the whole market in regard to its layout. Among other descriptive parameters, we can mention:

* Where is the price coming from?
* Where does it seem to be going?
* Is the market trending or non-trending?
* What is the market's exact location within the whole context?
* How high/low is the morning, afternoon or day's apogee (highest high)?
* What is the trend's slope like, or how did the price reach the current location?
* Was there continuous movement, or did the price jump directly towards the high/low of the chart?
* How did the day finish – perhaps at an extreme point of the chart, or was there a last gasp in pre-close with the market closing with a huge counter price bar?

Contextual Market.
The entire market containing the local market.

Correction.
This term refers to a counter-move with regard to a prior trending move. One can also use the word *retracement*. The trader uses the Fibonacci ratio tools to quantify the degree of correction.

Criss-Cross Pattern Technique.
It is a sort of market mapping used through the *dispersion* mechanism of two different Action & Reaction Lines set-ups, sharing the same Center Line, A double overlapped Center Line is created, which is represented on the chart as a single trend line.

The particularity of this technique is that the Action Line of one set-up is mixed with the other set-up's Reaction Line, on the same side of the double Center Line. The widths of these dual A&R Lines set-ups are not identical. Each of them has its own equally spaced size.

This charting structure will allow a better understanding of the contextual market and is done in order to study its influence on the outcome of the profitability of the whole trade.

Demand.
This term designates the number of buyers participating in the market. If demand exceeds supply then the market will be rising. See also **Supply.**

'Despair' Return Points.
Many traders consider the 50% or the 61.8% Fibonacci ratio level as an exit or an entry level in a trade opposite to this retracement. We employ the *'Despair'* **Return Points** term to psychologically illustrate the possible *despair* of a trader when he/she is in a trade and the market price retraces more than half of the previous swing, which we repeat, is considered by many traders as a reversal level – *a return limit*. In our experience, a better threshold for this *return limit* would be the 78.6% or 88.6% Fibonacci ratios levels. We have noted, more often than not, that once these two levels are exceeded it is highly probable that the ongoing correction will continue towards the 100% or even overpass it.

Dominant Trend.
Every time frame has a specific trend. In spite of this, the trader ought to establish, which trend is dominant. The concept *'a trend within a trend'* takes here all its importance. The trader should look at a minimum of three time frames: the operational time frame, the one above and the one below. *Does this mean that the trader should be able to identify the trend in its own operational time frame or rather on the upper time frame?* Well, the answer is not easy because of the complexity of the interrelationships between the multiple time frames.

One thing is sure, though! We should identify the most dominant trend, in other words, find out who is in control: the bulls or the bears. Knowing that the operational time frame is only a portion of the upper time frame, it is only common sense to go and look for the dominant trend in the upper time frame.

Dow Ratios.
This pertains to the specific ratios used in retracements, projections or expansions market techniques. The most frequently used are: 0.33, 0.66, 1.33, 1.66, 2.33 and 2.66.

Eighty/Twenty Rule.
It proclaims that if the market closes in its daily bar's upper 80–100 percent, the next day will have an up-trending morning if not an up-sloping day. On the contrary, if the market closes in its daily bar's lower 0–20 percent, the next day will be a downtrend morning, if not a down day. In short:

- the nearer the close is to the top of the daily bar, the more probable an up-sloping day will follow;
- the nearer the close is to the bottom of the daily bar, the more probable a down-sloping day will follow.

Elliott Wave Theory.
Firstly described by Ralph Nelson Elliott in the early 1930s, the *Elliott Wave theory* takes up the hard task of defining a structured market based on *pattern, ratio* and *time*. The theory

describes the market flow as a series of variable length price movements forming the impulsive and corrective chart patterns. The former are cruising in the direction of dominant trend and the latter, are counter-trending it. The impulsive pattern contains five waves and the corrective pattern only three waves. More details on this topic can be found in Volume 2 (in preparation).

Energy-Building Rectangles.
The energy-building patterns are the hallmarks of a trend's development, from inception to development through to its termination. It is difficult to identify the energy-building rectangle as it begins to develop. It is defined as a rectangular pattern, which has a minimum of two touches on each boundary line that forms its upper and lower limits (see Fig. 17.1). In the event of a breakout energy pattern, a rectangle can also be identified by having three touching points, with the fourth counted as the breakout point. Its characteristics can be interdependent and widely diversified: location, height, width, bar volume and bars' internal structure including an inner trend line.

Exacerbation (of Market Energy).
This event occurs in a virtual jailbreak manner, expressed by a few big bars, each with a height of 2-4 times the Average True Range. The slope of the trend is over 60°. The huge liberated energy will be tremendous but of short duration, and a reversal or an associated consolidation will be imminent.

Exhaustion (of Market Energy).
It is a state of market's energy, which represents the lowest energy level, which will be restored in an ergonomic rhythm so that the market flow will be partially or totally revitalized, ready to continue the trend's development. The trader should be aware that this mechanism cannot be forced nor readily influenced. It occurs *as* and *when* the market judges that it is necessary.

Exhaustion Gap.
As the name indicates, this type of gap will illustrate the degree of the price exhaustion, which will be reached during the terminal part of the ongoing trend. The saying is '*for every trend, one exhaustion gap*'. At the end of the up-sloping trend the enthusiasm is no longer there. There are only a few buyers left, the demand diminishes and, by default, prices drop. The volume is less than that of the runaway gap, but still substantial.

Exogenous Factors.
Exogenous factors of the market are any factors outside the chart. It can be the news of a sudden unexpected happening, like a terrorist act or an election result that nobody expected... We mention also the fluctuations of the crude oil, euro against the US dollar, gold, interest rates, etc.

'*Expect the Unexpected*'.
This term refers to the psychological side of trading. The trader should always be prepared to react to the market's moves and think in probabilities.

External Retracement.
When applied this type of retracement is greater than 100%, which illustrates the percentage retracement of the prior swing, in the process of building a counter-trend (123.6, 127.2, 161.8, 200.0, 261.8 and 423.6%).

Failures.

This signals a progressive decrease of the market directional momentum followed by a final cut off. An imminent reversal will follow but in the opposite direction. *The counter move will be more powerful than the initial approaching ML movement.* The space between the ML and the newly created failure pivot can and should be measured in order to evaluate the degree of momentum weakness. A price failure will convert a trigger line into a Hagopian line, which has the merit to confirm the failure set-up.

Another confirming market failure factor is the sliding parallel line (PH), but this has a different degree of reliability than that of the Hagopian line. The main difference between these two confirming factors is in timing of the failure phenomena. The sliding parallel line is created right at the extremity's reversal bar (the inception site of the failure process). When the counter-trend is well developed the Hagopian line is created. Then the trigger line is converted into a Hagopian line.

Fan Lines.

Multiple slope trend lines having the same original point are called *fan lines*. The construction of the accelerating trend lines is done by linking the same departure pivot, usually the highest high in a downtrend, with the following three accelerating pivots (next lower highs). In the case of the decelerating trend lines of an up-trend, the linkage is done from the same lowest low with the following three decelerating pivots (next higher lows). The fan lines can be drawn on a bar/candle chart or on a line chart. The latter type of chart seems to be more visible.

Most of the traders expect a reversal, more often than not, after three fan lines or at least a small correction or testing. In the absence of the expected reversal, be ready for a zooming-through phenomenon, which will enhance the strength of the ongoing trend. And don't forget the old adage... *An old resistance may become a new support and vice versa.*

Fibonacci Numbers.

The dictionary defines the Fibonacci numbers as follows: '*An integer* (number) *in the infinite sequence 1, 1, 2, 3, 5, 8, 13, 21, 34, 55, 89, 144 ... of which the first two terms are 1 and 1 and each succeeding term is the sum of the two immediately preceding*'. (Merriam-Webster's Collegiate Dictionary 10th edition, 2002).

Fibonacci Percentages.

They are obtained from the Fibonacci ratios by multiplying a specific ratio with the number 100. (For instance: 0.146 becomes 14.6%, 0.236 is 23.6%, 1.382 becomes 138.6%, and so on.)

Fibonacci Percentage Trend Lines.

This term designates a trend line, which is parallel to the pitchfork's median line and is guided by the Fibonacci percentages. The median line is considered as the origin, being located at 0% level, and the upper/lower median line locations at the upper 100% level and lower 100% level, respectively. The first warning lines are located at 200% level, relative to the median line origin. Thus, the Fibonacci percentage lines are calibrated with regard to the origin level of the median line and also in comparison with the upper or lower part of the median line. We can take as examples: *the upper 50% Fibonacci line* situated at the midpoint of the median line and the upper median line; *the lower 250% Fibonacci line* located at the midpoint of the first lower warning line and the second.

Fibonacci Ratios.
They are obtained by dividing the Fibonacci numbers among them in a certain order. Over the years, traders have noticed that certain Fibonacci ratios predominate and have more applicability than others: 0.146, 0.236, 0.382, 0.500, 0.618, 0.786, 0.886 and also 1.00, 1.146, 1.236, 1.272, 1.382, 1.500, 1.618, 2.000, 2.618, 4.236 and 6.85.

Fibonacci Ratios Tools.
If there is a trading secret, it is to learn how to anticipate market movements, by using the Fibonacci tools (see Fig. 14.25). They are frequently used by the astute trader: internal and external retracements, alternate price projections and price expansions. The latter is only used to confirm the others. The main purpose of these tools is to obtain the clusters and/or the confluences, these precious level zones, which will increase the profit probability.

Final Indicator.
Throughout the experience the traders reached the conclusion that 'the final indicator is a tried and tested trend line'.

Finding the Optimal Trade Set-Up.
The best trade set-up is usually found by employing various patterns that the trader has already learnt. One of these examples is the presence of narrow range consolidation, which is forming an energy building rectangle. The trader will wait patiently for the breakout. Then, just before the entry, he/she will have to establish the aggressive or conservative type of trade.

Other sourcing patterns for profitable trades would be: the *mirror bars* – the bigger the better, the presence of a *pullback* unveiling the commencement of an up-trend, the *events around the median line* – zooming through, testing or retesting, the *failure* near the U-MLH, L-MLH or trigger lines, the weight of evidence of a *trend line breakout,* which is pleading an immediate reversal, the *market approaching a numerous multi-layers confluence* or a *numerous multi-levels cluster* – especially if they coincide, etc.

Fractals.
The fractals are entities that remain constant through magnification and this constancy explains why in the financial markets, whatever the time frame used, we always get the same pattern formations in charts of various time frames. A set of Russian dolls perfectly describes this phenomenon: a bigger doll holds a smaller one, which contains an even smaller one, and so on.

Gann Ratios.
This pertains to the specific ratios used in retracements, projections or expansions market techniques. The most frequently used are 0.25, 0.50, 0.75 and 1.00 with their halves.

Gap.
The definition of a *gap* on a daily chart is the *interval between yesterday's close and today's open*. We should take into consideration: the height, the midpoint of the gap, the time frame and how many gap points are already filled (if any at all).

Recall in a few words the identification footprint of each type of gap: common (*change signal*), breaking away (*strong trend signal*), continuation (*ensures momentum's inertia*) and exhaustion (*termination and reversal possible signal*). Be aware that a gap can always introduce one or more other gaps.

The measuring technique of a gap should be a trading routine when a gap has occurred. The drawing of the gap's measure extensions should be systematically done.

Gap Median Line.
A gap is seen as an interrupting factor that perturbs the well-being of a trend's development flow. A closely related pitchfork to the gap's charting characteristics will optimally describe the market flow. The only – and the most important – criterion in selecting the three pivots with the corresponding swing midpoint, is to match the gap median line with the trend's direction. Optimally the gap median line should serve as a symmetry axis in order to do its best in describing the market flow.

The anchor (P0) of a gap median line is usually situated within the gap's immediate environment:

- on the high, the low or the midpoint of the gap location;
- on the close level (*yesterday's last bar*) or the open level (*today's opening bar*).

The P1-P2 swing is usually located right at the beginning of the ongoing trend, when the first swing is terminated. Sometimes, the trader uses the second or even the third post-gap swing. The gap median line is obtained by linking the P0 pivot and the midpoint of the P1-P2 swing.

Be prepared for the transformation of a traditional median line into a gap median line as soon as the day's gap is unlatched.

Hagopian Rule and Line.
This rule applies when an up-sloping market is approaching a significant trend line (slant, horizontal or curvilinear) but the market momentum is not strong enough to reach and test it (for example, the ML of an up-sloping pitchfork). The same is valid for a down-sloping market.

The rule states that after nearing this significant trend line (for instance an up-sloping ML), the price will reverse vigorously in a big counter-move. It will drop rapidly towards an opposite strong trend line (L-MLH and the L-TL), called the *Hagopian line,* which also has the role of confirming and completing the failure set-up. Its reverse momentum is usually stronger than the initial momentum, which was previously approaching. In its strong counter-move, the price will meet the same trend line that it was drifting along before reversing.

Another confirming market failure factor is the sliding parallel line (PH), which has a different degree of reliability than that of the Hagopian line. The main difference between them is in timing of the failure phenomena. The sliding parallel line is created right at the extremity's reversal bar (the inception site of the failure process). The Hagopian line is created only when the counter-trend is well developed, when the trigger line is converted into a Hagopian line.

Homeostasis.
This term is defined as '*a relatively stable state of equilibrium or a tendency toward such a state between the different but interdependent elements of a group*' (*Merriam-Webster's Collegiate Dictionary* 10th edition, 2002). By analogy, this term has been used to describe the market return to equilibrium, after a huge gap movement. The market's recovery (*a correction move*) to the initial market level will cause a remediation process, which will ensure the *before the event* market flow homeostasis.

Hybrid Pitchfork.
This pattern is also called a 'suspended' anchor pitchfork because it is constructed by using a 'suspended' P0 anchor pivot and a P1-P2 swing issued out of an A&R Line set-up.

Image Mirroring Technique.
This technique is of the utmost importance in the construction of the three lines of the A&R Lines set-up. We can calculate the exact pivotal Cartesian coordinate locations with the assistance of Fibonacci tools, in such a way that the symmetry of the set-up's lines is preserved (refer to Figs. 11.10, 11.11 and 11.12).

Impulsive.
This term refers to a strong momentum move starting a new trending pattern, which encloses, multiple smaller degree impulsive and corrective swings.

Inter-Distance.
It is the distance between the current market and the nearest stop loss, whatever it is: *initial, break-even* or *trailing stop loss*.

Intermediate Pivot (I).
It is a kind of *go-between* major (J) and minor (M) pivots.

Internal Retracement.
When applied this type of retracement is less than 100%, which illustrates the percentage retracement of the prior swing, in the process of building a correction (23.6, 38.2, 50.0, 61.8, 78.6 and 88.6%).

'Ladder-Like' Rectangles.
This term designates a *pile of rectangles* with their power and also their role in detecting the up/down-sloping failure. A whole chapter is dedicated to the relationship of pitchforks and rectangles, in Volume 2 (in preparation).

Local Market.
It means the current market, the most recent within the contextual market.

Logical Profit Objective.
This term designates the first target of the trade. See also **Three Pawn Technique.**

Lower Median Line (LML or L-MLH).
It is the lower parallel line to the median line.

L-TL.
Acronym of the lower trigger line.

Major Accumulation Patterns.
They were described by Richard W. Schabacker and he used the term *seven cardinal formations*: Head and Shoulder Bottom; Common Upward Turn; Triangular Bottom; Ascending Bottom; Double Bottom; Complex Bottom; Broadening Bottom.

Major Distribution Patterns.
They were described by Richard W. Schabacker and he used the term *seven cardinal formations*: Head and Shoulder Top; Common Downward Turn; Triangular Top; Descending Top; Double Top; Complex Top; Broadening Top.

Major Pitchfork.
It is a large pitchfork that encapsulates the context of the market or at least a big portion of it. Its pivots are usually marked P0 (anchor), P1 and P2.

Major Pivot (J).
It is frequently seen immediately before the trend is completed.

Manual Trading Mode.
When *all three* progressive trading orders, labelled the *three-pawn technique,* are *not prearranged,* at the moment of the trade decision then the trade is performed in *manual mode.*

Market Description.
It means the way that the pitchfork encompasses the market. The best-constructed pitchfork will fully encompass the market within its main body, delineated by the upper and the lower median lines. We call this the most optimal market description.

Measuring Technique.
It measures the height of the pattern, which is price dependent, and projects it vertically from the lower/upper boundary in order to obtain the measuring upwards/downwards projection (see Fig. 17.9). We can also measure the width of the pattern as a horizontal distance (segment), and project it vertically from the lower/upper boundary in order to obtain the most probable measuring upwards/downwards projection.

Median Line (ML or MLH).
Dr Alan Hall Andrews' concept of median line first appears in the work of Roger W. Babson (1875–1967) under the *Normal Line* name in the first decades of the twentieth century.

The essence of a pitchfork resides in its median line with its acolytes: U-MLH, L-MLH, U-MLH, WL, TL, etc. The median line is the main component of a pitchfork's framework, not only for linking the anchor to the midpoint of the P1–P2 swing but also for constituting a foundation guideline for drawing its acolyte subordinates.

The median line's main role is to attract the market price. Alan Andrews taught his students that the price returns to the median line most of the time. Thus, the median line becomes the minimum price objective. The median line can also play the role of a symmetry axis meaning that the market flow will be equally spaced above or below the median line. One of the most important components of the pitchfork, the median line is a powerful tool in optimally encompassing the market flow. When the price approaches the median line, it creates one of the following movements: a reversal (a top pivot is made); a violent piercing, a zooming through – well exceeding the ML; or a narrow range, which will prepare the market flow for the next price outburst.

Mini-Median Line (mml).
It is the median line of a small pitchfork within the minor pitchfork frequently used to identify a reversal. Moreover, the following factors need to be considered:

- the number of pullbacks;
- the length of the already-developed trend (use bar count and momentum bars);
- the number of any eventual gaps within the current trend;
- the type of pattern at the beginning of the trend's movement; knowing this greatly enhances our knowledge of its strength and our understanding of its behaviour.

Mini-Median Line (Border).
This type of mini-median line is located at the border of the encompassing minor pitchfork usually parallel to the market direction.

Mini-Median Line (Inside).
This type of mini-median line is located inside the minor pitchfork usually parallel to the market direction.

Mini-Median Line (Reverse).
This type of mini-median line is located inside the minor pitchfork. It projects the price opposite to market direction.

Mini-Median Line (Twin Pivot).
The twin pivot mini-median line is frequently used at market turning points. They are called *twin* because they both have the same price/time Cartesian coordinates, with the difference that one belongs to a major pitchfork and the other to a minor pitchfork.

Minor Pitchfork.
It encompasses a small portion of the market flow, usually within the territory of a major pitchfork. Its pivots are usually marked p0 (anchor), p1 and p2.

Minor Pivot (M).
It is also called pullback pivot. These pivots are often present at the beginning and at the end of the pullbacks chart formation.

Mirror Bars.
The mirror bar pattern is classically formed of two bars of almost identical size, with the second bar catalogued as a reversal bar. Its characteristics are very appropriate for trading because it will reveal the exhaustion of the entire preceding trend. There may be three or even four bars in a row of almost identical size. In that case the middle bar(s) can play the role of an inside bar, and their presence greatly enhances the reversing power of the entire pattern (Fig. 16.4).

The momentum that initializes huge mirror bars is often so strong that it induces a runaway gap, especially after the sharp retracement occurs, which will greatly contribute to the enhancement of the countertrend's kinetic energy storage. The reliability of the mirror bar as a trading tool is greatly enhanced by a synergetic association with the pitchfork tool.

Mirror Sliding Parallel Lines.
This term depicts the mirroring of two PHs with regard to a symmetry line, which can be a pitchfork's median line or one of its acolytes. See also **Twin Sliding Parallel Lines.**

ML or MLH.
Acronym of the median line, usually pertaining to a major pitchfork. The letter H in this annotation is inherited from our 20th century teachers of the period and mimics the parallelism of the two vertical lines of the letter H and those of MLHs.

ml or mlh.
Acronym of the median line of a minor pitchfork, encompassed by the major pitchfork.

mml or mmlh.
Acronym of the mini-median line.

Momentum Bars.
The higher bars are only counted in an up-trend and vice versa, in view of determining the end of the trend. More on this bar counting technique in Volumes 2 and 3 (in preparation).

Momentum Indicators.
The word *momentum* is a characteristic of a moving entity that quantifies the strength of its movement. The price momentum is the strength of a market move that propels the trend. It is measured through the momentum indicators. More details on this topic in Volumes 2 and 3 (in preparation).

MTF.
Acronym of multiple time frames.

Multiple Pitchforks.
This set-up is constituted, at a minimum, of two pitchforks: the major pitchfork encompassing the minor pitchfork. A third pitchfork can be added to enhance the efficiency of the overall structure: a small pitchfork having a mini-median line or a bigger-size upper time frame pitchfork. One of the main purposes of having various median lines intersect is to reveal the eventual *confluences,* which are decisive trading landmarks.

Follow closely the nuts-and-bolts techniques: double channelling, the magnet-like power of the ML, confluence zones with their energy-building clusters, classic components of an entry (*piercing, testing, retesting and zooming*) and multiple time-frame pitchforks. Be aware that the market is mostly attracted by the recent market, more often than not.

Multiple Time Frames Concept.
A *cross-referencing* among three or more time frames, closely inter-related within the market analysis process.

Robert Krausz, a well-known trader and prolific writer, has dedicated a great deal of his work to the study of multiple time frames. Whatever trading programs he has conceived, his six rules are constant:

1. Every time frame has its own structure.
2. Higher time frames overrule lower time frames.
3. Prices in the lower time frame structure tend to respect the energy points of the higher time frame structure.
4. The energy points of support/resistance created by the higher time frame's vibration (prices) can be validated by the action of the lower time periods.
5. The trend created by the next time period enables the definition of the tradable trend.
6. What appears to be chaos in one time period can be orderly in another time period.

NR4 and NR7.
Acronyms of 4-bar and 7-bar trading ranges, respectively. It is well known that a small trading range will prepare the market flow for an explosion. Its direction is not obvious, except when the market is at the top or the bottom of the trend. Toby Crabel – a great trader and

teacher – has done extensive research about the NR4 and NR7 (see his 1990 book *Day Trading with Short Term Price Patterns and Opening Breakout*).

Orthodox Trend Line.
The term designates the traditional trend line. See **Trend Line.**

PH.
Acronym of the sliding parallel line. See also **SH.**

Piercing.
Piercing a trend line is defined as a temporary penetration of a trend line, which is mostly done through a long tail bar. Its relative importance is situated between zooming and testing (retesting). No trade should be set up if only this element is present.

Pitchfork (PF).
The geometrical structure of the pitchfork closely resembles a channel made out of three equidistant parallel trend lines, where the median is anchored farther away from the channel's main body. The cardinal orientation is usually slanted; otherwise it would have been named a rectangle. Most of the time the pitchfork is optimally drawn by suitable software and the trader only has to choose the best landmarks, which could be a single type of pivot or a mixture of different types: primary, major, intermediate and minor pivots.

Pitchfork Construction.
The constructing procedure is fully respected when there is only one criterion in trader's mind: *an ideal market description*. The choice of P0, P1 and P2 consecutive pivots, as well as their compatibility – how well they work together – must ideally embed the tortuous market flow, converting a seemingly random market into a railroad-like structured market, less random than it first appeared.

There are programs that display the Andrews' pitchfork with a few simple mouse clicks.

If manually constructed then carefully select the P0 anchor with regard to the probable direction of the market's up or down trend. The P1 and P2 pivots correspond to the extreme levels of the swing opposite to the anchor. After you found the midpoint of the P1/P2 swing, draw a straight line from the P0 anchor through this midpoint and then draw additional parallel lines through the P1 and P2 pivots. If the market exceeds the pitchfork's main body then draw equally spaced additional parallel lines to these!

What is the best-constructed pitchfork? The one that fully encompasses the market within its main body, delineated by the upper and the lower median lines!

How do we know, which are the best-chosen pivots? There is no way to know it before hand! A well-trained eye will easily find a good way to determine the most adequate pivots! This doesn't come easily, but with experience it will be possible!

Pitchfork Guidelines.
They are defined as the parameters that make possible the construction of a pitchfork that would encompass close to 100% of the market flow. They become obvious after the trader has practised and acquired the necessary experience in pitchfork analysis: the quality of the chosen pivots and the way the market relates to the pitchfork's lines.

Multiple tests of the median line or of its acolytes will definitively confirm the best pitchfork choice. The anchor will influence the pitchfork's outcome, so its best location must be carefully verified.

The exact count of the pivots is of great assistance for the trader. Most often than not, a reversal of the *P0-P1-P2-P3-P4-P5 trend* is probable when the market flow reaches the P5 pivot. If not, then watch for the incoming P7, P9 or P11 pivots.

Pitchfork (Holy Grail of).

The '*holy grail of the pitchfork*' principle occurs when '*the choice of pivots engenders the efficiency of pitchfork trading, which in turn is expressed by how well the market is encompassed*'.

Pitchfork Rules.

There are two decisive parameters in pitchfork trading: the quality of the chosen pivots and the degree of encompassing the market. They are intimately related! One will never work without the other.

The supreme rule, in our opinion, is to construct the directional pitchfork showing the market direction, in such a way that the market encompassing is reaching the 100% threshold. This will be possible only by trying several pitchfork versions, and then select the best choice!

Dr Alan H. Andrews course's rules specify that the median line and the slopes of alternate median lines of similar length indicate the price direction. He mentioned that the first target of the *just constructed pitchfork* is mostly the median line.

Pivots.

They constitute the basement of pitchfork construction. The pivot is defined as: '*a critical point having a major or central role, function or effect...a shaft or pin on which something turns*' (*Merriam-Webster's Collegiate Dictionary* 10th edition, 2002). The trader can mark the pivots on the chart and this requires some experience in evaluating the degree of importance of each type of pivot. The trader can also utilize ergonomic charting software. Among the most important pivot quality criteria we can mention are the location, the body configuration including bar's size, the types of bars that precede or follow them and the kind of swing that they belong to. A longer swing terminating with a big tail reversal bar gives, more often than not, an optimal pivot.

P&L Statement.

Acronym of the **Profit & Loss Statement.**

Plains Plateau.

This term is a cliché relating to the *land of green grass grazing profit*.

Pre-Close Breaking-Up/Down Trend Lines.

This covers the opening period of trading through the trend lines' breaking-out process. It is a kind of opening framework, prepared in advance and in detail, right after the close of the day's market. The configuration of these trend lines is various:

*   The *slant trend line* detects the probable breaking-out of the opening movements.
*   The *horizontal trend line* forms a pre-close rectangle, composed of upper and lower horizontal limits.

- The *border line guarantor* sanctions the location of the border of the day's market, in regard to projecting tomorrow's up/down market's bias. Its market level can be the close of the day, or the symmetrical level of a chart pattern formation.
- Many other choices are possible.

The purpose of this opening framework is to prepare the first trade of the day (*morning's trade*). We noticed that a profitable morning trade will really contribute to a better morale of the day!

Pre-Open Breaking-Up/Down Trend Lines.
See **Pre-close Breaking-Up/Down Trend Lines.**

Price Expansion.
This illustrates the price expansion of the same swing(s), in the direction of the current trend, especially applied to the inceptive swing. The degree of expansion is measured in percentages. As the name indicates this tool mostly expands the momentum of the initial A-B swing, thus finding its possible exhaustion location. These price expansions complement the other two Fibonacci ratios techniques and are used only to confirm them. The most commonly used percentage values are: 61.8, 100.0, 161.8, 200.0, 261.8, 423.6 and 685%. See also **Fibonacci Ratios Tools.**

Primary Pivot (P).
This term is mainly associated with the high/low of a trend.

Probability Degree (of a Trend).
This term designates the degree of obtaining the best profitability at an established risk. See also **Aggressive Trade** and **Conservative Trade**.

Profit & Loss Statement.
This term designates the financial outcome of the trade performance.

Pullback.
It is a small corrective chart formation that signals an eventual trend continuation. It is formed of one to several bars and it takes the form of a flag or a pennant. We affectionately call it the *'propagating pullback'* because of its synergetic function in continuing the propagation of the restored kinetic energy. It contributes greatly to the inception of the new trend.

Reaction Line.
The *reaction phase* of the market flow is graphically expressed by the Reaction Line (RL). This is a component of the newly-created market flow embedding process, having the Center Line encapsulated by the Reaction and Action Lines, each mirroring the other. This *reaction phase* usually borders and may or may not contain the impulse of the vectorial forces implemented by the Center Line's measurement. The origin of these impulses comes mostly from the Action Line Zone.

Resistance Line.
This term indicates that the market has reached a level line where the number of sellers exceeds the number of buyers; thus the supply is becoming dominant. As a consequence, a down-sloping move will occur.

Retesting.
Retesting is the rich parent of testing. Easy to understand, it happens when multiple tests occur. More often than not, the number of tests determines the strength of the S/R trend line. The more numerous the tests, the stronger the trend line becomes. We can give the example of a support trend line, which has been tested four times compared with a resistance trend line, which has been tested only two times. The market will selectively choose to break, more often than not, the resistance (only two touches), since it is not as strong as the support (four touches).

'Retrograde' Pitchfork.
The pitchfork shown in Fig. 2.33 is a 'retrograde' variation of the traditional pitchfork. Its median line is drawn through the middle of the P1–P2 swing and the P5 pivot, with the purpose of projecting the market price of the ongoing reversal movement (p0-p1-p2). Comparing the pitchforks of Figs 2.32 and 2.33, the latter optimally describes the market flow and shows the p0 to p3 correction more efficiently. Its disadvantage is that it can be drawn only after the P5 pivot has already formed, but right on time for trading the up-sloping correction, with the assistance of the p0 to p3 pitchfork.

Return to Mean.
This term describes the return of the market, after a hyper-extended move, to an average position, expressed by a moving average. See also *'Rubber Band' Effect.*

Reversal Island.
The exhaustion zone of a trend line can naturally be converted into an *island reversal zone*, which is formed by an exhaustion gap on its upward slope and by a breakaway gap on the other side (Fig. 13.12). The occurrence of the second gap will definitely signal the labelling of the exhaustion gap, especially when the ongoing market price drops all the way down under the low of the bar that opened the exhaustion gap. Once the reversal is confirmed, a new median line is required.

Reverse Pitchfork.
We begin to consider constructing a reverse pitchfork right after the weight of evidence has confirmed the trend reversal (P2 pivot). We have set up the P0-P1-P2 backward-looking pitchfork sequence (Fig. 10.29), which is ready to project into the future the inherent market vibration ratios of the immediate past. We should draw the first level of the warning line, in order to prepare the trading scene for the next movements.

Reward/Risk Ratio.
This is one of the most important tools of money management. This ratio ought to be, most of the time, bigger than 2.5 value. We take 2 to 2.5 *R/R ratio* trades seldom and only if they have a high probability. Do not forget that our main purpose is *capital preservation*. There is always another day and another opportunity, but only if you are still in possession of your capital. Our purpose is not to make any *home runs*. We are only looking for low-risk high-probability trades.

RL.
Acronym for Reaction Line.

R/R Ratio.
Acronym of the Reward/Risk ratio.

'Rubber Band'-Like Phenomenon.
This term describes the market's *return to mean*, expressed by a moving average, after a hyper-extended move.

Runaway Gap.
This type of gap projects the termination of the ongoing trend. It is also called the *continuation* or *measuring* gap. Its inception nest is usually in the middle of the trend, and it is thus much appreciated by the astute trader for its forecasting ability. The intensity of the volume is of a lesser degree compared to the volume of the breakaway gap.

Scale In.
This is a money management technique, which consists of progressively adding trading units, as long as the trade is running in trade's direction.

Scale Out.
This is a money management technique, which consists in progressive trading units exiting.

Schiff Pitchfork.
Jerome Schiff, a student of Dr Alan Andrews, invented this type of pitchfork. The necessity for it became obvious when the three pivots necessary to draw a more traditional pitchfork could not be found. The set-up choice of three pivots was replaced with a substitute: two pivots and the midpoint of a preceding swing. The purpose of this innovative pitchfork structure remains the same: to find the optimal encompassing of the market flow.

Schiff Pitchfork Construction.
We will take as example the end of a down-sloping trend. The midpoint of the trend's last swing (A–B) will create the anchor (P0) for the Schiff pitchfork. The market begins an up-sloping correction pattern from the B reversal pivot, the lowest low. The P1 reversal pivot terminates the first impulsive swing of the new trend. The first correction (P1–P2 swing) is complete. The P2 reversal pivot is ready to continue the third swing of the correction pattern, which is also its second impulsive swing. The P0-P1-P2 Schiff pitchfork is now ready to describe the market.

Semi-Automatic Trading Mode.
When *only two* of the three progressive trading orders, labelled the *three-pawn technique*, are *pre-arranged*, at the moment of trade decision, then the trade is performed in *semi-automatic pilot mode*.

SH.
Acronym of the sliding parallel line. See also **PH** & **Sliding Parallel Lines**.

Single Bar Pitchfork.
A very little-known ML is a single bar pitchfork. The four components of a bar (*open, close, high and low*) are selected to get the three optimal pivots necessary to construct the minuscule pitchfork. However, the natural question is. . . *What is the sense for such a tiny pitchfork*? The

answer is not obvious – the only possible use at this small fractal scale level of the trend is in money management with setting up or verifying the stop loss strategy.

Sliding Parallel Lines (PH or SH).
Part of the pitchfork line family, the sliding parallel line (PH or SH) is a line, which passes through a high, a low or (even better) through multiple highs/lows. It is drawn parallel to another pitchfork's trend line, which can be a ML or its associated lines, a multi-pivot trend line (also called an unorthodox trend line) or a traditional trend line.

The uniqueness of these sliding parallel lines resides in the fact that their construction is not based on pivots, like all the other median lines, and we do not use a pitchfork's pivots to draw them. It is not a fixed pivot-related line, but rather an unanchored trend line.

When testing, piercing and zooming, SH behaves in the same way as any median or non-pitchfork related trend line, even if the SH is constructed without any ML pivots.

Slope (of a Trend Line).
The slope of a trend line represents the degree of inclination (angle) with regard to the horizontal (time) axis. The *degree of the slope* is one of the most important features when using a trend line. It is known that a steep slope reveals either a sharp reversal or an imminent consolidation of the market, and a shallower slope informs about an incoming trading range. Generally, the steeper the slope of the trend, the stronger the momentum becomes, but the move tends to be of a shorter duration.

The 45° angle trend line has a primordial role in the trending process, being the only angle capable of giving the direction and the strength of a trend. If this line is broken with huge bars, we can be sure that the market momentum is very strong. Alternatively, if the breakout or the price approach occurs with small trading range bars, we know that the current trend is starting to lose its power and that its termination could well be imminent.

Snugging.
This word describes the process of securing a safe place. By analogy, we snug a stop loss.

Speed Lines.
Edson Gould, a prolific contributor to the science of technical analysis, first used them. They can be drawn only after the completion of the attributed swing by linking its highest high with the progressive ratios levels marked on its measured vertical line. The first ratios used were Dow's 33%, 50% and 66% with a later Fibonacci addition of 38.2% and 61.8% ratios.

Spotting the Trade Opportunity.
This process of finding a '*would be*' profitable trade must follow a strict systematized procedure. The trader should visually scan the various choices of the operational time frame charts: 60-min, 30-min, 15-min and seldom the 5-min chart. Our goal is to detect trade candidates representing low-risk high-probability trades. Once these opportunities are revealed, we will employ different techniques with all the recommended disciplined rigour and patience.

Staircase Concept.
This is defined as the trending process where the market flow takes the form of a wooden staircase that terminates on the upper floors. Every floor is a virtual energy consolidation structure that will greatly assist the trend to continue.

Straight Pivot Alignment Pitchfork.

This term is employed when an A&R Lines set-up is overlapping a P0-P1-P2 straight alignment of a pitchfork-like structure (refer to Fig. 11.36).

The particularity of this pitchfork is that:

- the P0-P1–P2 pivots are all aligned within the swing's trend line, just before the reversal;
- the anchor (P0) is located within the P1-P0-P2 swing, rather than on the preceding P1–P2 swing, as is the case with the traditional pitchfork;
- the median line links the P0 pivot and the P3 pivot, rather than joining the P0 pivot and the midpoint of the P1–P2 swing, as is the case with the traditional pitchfork.

Supply.

This term designates the number of sellers participating in the market. If supply exceeds demand then the market will be dropping. See also **Demand.**

Support Line.

This term indicates that the market has reached a level line where the number of buyers exceeds the number of sellers; thus the demand is becoming dominant. As a consequence, an up-sloping move will occur.

'Suspended' Anchor Pitchfork.
See **Hybrid Pitchfork.**

Swing Distribution Technique.

This tool consists of revealing the swings of the market through the use of a swing trend line, which is drawn from its lowest low to its highest high (or vice versa). Thus, the market zigzagging is unveiled and the trader can much better visualize the market context with its trend.

Symmetrical Pattern Technique.

It is another method of *dispersing* the Action and Reaction Lines around the Center Line. Like the A&R Criss-Cross Pattern Technique, the *A&R Symmetrical Pattern Technique* has a double set of A&R Lines, but differs in that both the Action Lines are on one side of the Center Line, and both Reaction Lines are on the other. We have purposely modified the previous technique in our search for the low-risk high-probability trades.

Symmetry Axis.

This is defined as an axis around which the market flow fluctuates, in equally spaced moves, on both parts. The dynamics of the market price around this axis (*trend line*) will temporarily create oscillatory movements illustrated by a sinusoidal curve, travelling from one side of the axis to another whilst at the same time piercing, zooming, testing or retesting it.

Synergy.

This is defined as *'a mutually advantageous conjunction or compatibility of distinct elements'* (*Merriam-Webster's Collegiate Dictionary* 10th edition, 2002). By analogy, we employ this term to illustrate that the elements of charting structures (*here A&R Lines set-up and pitchfork*) can be closely interwoven so that they can build up highly inter-dependent phenomena.

Systematized Visualization.
This simple tool of *systematized visualization* will immediately reveal (Fig. 13.2) that the whole chart consists of several types of modules, creating portions of the chart that optimally describe the market.

Territorial Distribution Technique.
The purpose of this tool is the same as that of the *swing distribution technique*. The trader will better understand the contextual concept. This technique immediately reveals the whole market concept composed of multiple territories, from left to right (see Fig. 13.3). See also **Swing Distribution Technique.**

Testing.
This process implies a pinpoint touch of the price on the support/resistance (S/R) level. No piercing or slight zooming is allowed. The price must rest exactly on the testing line. The degree of importance of the halt is greatly enhanced in studying the touching bar's close.

TF.
Acronym of time frame.

Three Pawn Technique.
This is a triple orders preparation and trade execution formed of:

* *Step 1* – Find the most *optimal entry* and place the *first order*.
* *Step 2* – Look for the best *initial stop loss location* – and then immediately enter a *stop order*, right after the *entry order* was executed. This will be the *second order*.
* *Step 3* – Find the most appropriate *logical profit objective* and then calculate the optimal *reward/risk ratio (R/R ratio)* which should not be under 2.5 value; if that is the case, place the *third order*, right after the stop loss order is working on broker's waiting list.

The *three pawns technique* must be understood, learned and practised everyday, with no exceptions. This requires discipline and patience.

Throwback.
This pattern occurs when the returned price of the failed breakout goes farther through the breaking line, until it is quickly halted by a stronger support level.

Time Frame.
This is the amount of time corresponding to the duration of the chart's bar. We mostly use for intra-day trades the 15- or 60-minute operational time frame. The upper time frame considered by the intra-day traders can be the daily TF (*mostly used for the market context*) and the lower time frames is 5-min TF (*mostly used to pinpoint the entries and exits*).

Time Frame Alignment.
Before taking any trading decisions we have to ensure that the operational time frame has the same direction as the upper time frame. We never buck the trend. This will greatly improve the probability of the trade.

Time-Price Virtual Space.

This term designates a hypothetical space of the time/price chart. We use it to emphasize the inter-relations between these dual parameters. The best reversals are where the time meets the price. *How do we know it?* By using the bar count technique and the time and price Fibonacci ratios, in order to unveil the cluster levels, where the reversals are most fitted to occur. More details on this topic are provided in Volumes 2 and 3 (in preparation).

TL.

Acronym of a trigger line or a common trend line.

T-Pitchfork.

A pitchfork constructed using an anchor (P0) at the midpoint of an A–B virtual swing is called a *T-pitchfork* (Fig. 10.18). The purpose of this pattern is to optimally encompass the market flow, when the other type of pitchfork is not able to do it. It will greatly assist the trader to have an edge.

Trader's Journal.

This step is one of the most important in becoming a consistent trader. It is the consistency barometer, which will tell you the '*Whys*' and the '*Hows*'.

We should *write* the trader's journal. . . Yes, *write it*, especially the main points, just after you have exited it, otherwise you risk forgetting the details. Whatever the outcome of the trade is, good or bad, just do it!

Trading Approach Steps.

We will list below, in chronological order, the different decision making steps of our trading approach:

* Spotting the Trade Opportunity;
* Finding the Optimal Set-Up;
* Time Frame Alignment;
* Three Pawn Technique – Triple Order Preparation and Trade Execution;
* Profit & Loss – P/L Statement;
* Trader's Journal - Keep Your Written Records

Trailing Stop Loss.

This designates the *follow-up stop loss* of an ongoing profitable trade. The *first trailing stop loss* is established after the *break-even stop loss* when the market advanced in the trade's direction and is at 1.5 to 2.5 ATRs inter-distance. The same procedure should be implemented for the next trailing stops with a remark. . . *Quantify the market position within the ongoing trend in such a way that you can progressively decrease the ATR value of the inter-distance to one ATR.* When you reached the conclusion that the trend termination is imminent, just snug behind the nearest low (in an up trend). See also **Break-Even Stop Loss.**

Translation across the Market Slots.

From the mechanical point of view the *translation* is a linear movement. By analogy, we use it in the markets as the price movement in almost linear form (except volatile markets or reversals) from the left to the right side of the chart. In our case these movements will occur across the various slots delineated by the median line and its acolytes. The transition from an upper-left space slot to the lower-right space slot (and vice versa) usually confirms a change of market tendency.

Trend.
An up-trend is defined by higher highs and higher lows, and lower highs and lower lows for a down-trend. A trend continues until the weight of evidence negates it and its corresponding trend line is definitely broken. In order to be at ease with trend determination, the trader should assimilate the four indispensable tools to detect the trend: *the pitchfork analysis, zigzagging technique, trough analysis* and *momentum related indicators*. Try all of them, and select the one(s) that you are comfortable with.

Trend Line.
The orthodox (*traditional*) trend line, which joins at least two points: a series of higher highs (*in an up-trend*) or lower lows (*in a down-trend*). Its characteristic is that it does not traverse the market (the price bars).

Not all trend lines are linear. Where neither of the two (*traditional or unorthodox*) TLs is of any value, we can use a moving average (21 or 50-MA) to detect the slope and where the trend is in its development. In this case we are talking about a *curvilinear trend line*.

The *degree of trend's strength* depends on the number of trend *touches* (pivots or not) produced when the price reaches (*and just touches*) the trend line. If there are many touches, there is a *stronger legitimacy*: the more touches mean a more significant event will occur when the price tries to break the trend line. The strength of the legitimacy builds the authority of the trend line. Longer trends, which are more tested, give stronger signals than shorter trends. A trend line touched 6 times is harder to break than a trend line touched only 3 times. A higher time frame trend line is much more difficult to break than a lower time frame trend line.

Trend Line (Orthodox or Traditional).
This trend line joins at least two points: a series of higher highs (in an up-trend) or lower lows (in a down-trend). Its characteristic is that *it does not traverse* the market (the price bars).

Trend Line (Un-Orthodox).
See **Un-Orthodox trend line**.

Trigger Line.
This line joints the pivotal anchor (P0) with one of the P1 or P2 pivots. It is also called a *multi-pivot trend line*. The upper trigger line (U-TL) is drawn above the pitchfork's main body and the lower trigger line (L-TL) is below it.

The trigger line is mainly used as a signal line for routine trade confirmations and for a conservative trade entry. It can be successfully used in case of a trend's failure.

This trigger line can also serve as a borderline for the whole market when it belongs to a contextual (major) pitchfork: the upper side of the market is found above the trigger line, and the lower side below it. The transition of the market flow from one side to another must inevitably pass through the strong support/resistance wall of the trigger line. The same thing happens if we draw a trigger line belonging to a higher time frame on the operational time frame.

When testing, piercing and zooming, the trigger lines behave in the same way as any other median or non-pitchfork related trend lines.

'Trigger-Shy' Syndrome.
This covers the psychological aspect of a trader whose triggering mechanism of performing a trade is impaired. There are several causes but the prominent ones are the precarious level of the learning curve and the analysis paralysis syndrome.

Trough Analysis.
The trough is the lowest level of a shallow valley or depression. By analogy, the chart's troughs are the lowest levels of the pullbacks. The strength of an up-sloping trend is directly proportional to the degree of the separating distance between the troughs. The larger this distance, the stronger the trend becomes, and vice versa. If the trend makes a lower high, it means that it is still developing. If the trend makes a lower high and a lower low, only then can we pronounce the trend terminated.

Twin Sliding Parallel Lines.
An SH can be an individual line alongside a trend line or be accompanied by other SHs, on the same side or opposite the symmetry axis which can be represented by MLs, U/L-MLHs, WLs, Fibonacci lines or trigger lines (TLs). The two SHs having a symmetry axis (see Fig. 7.4) constitute a drifting channel inside or outside the pitchfork's main body, which has the potential to guide the price farther away. Where these two SHs are valid only for a portion of the drifting away channel, we call them a *twin SH set-up* or a *mirror sliding parallel line set-up*.

UML or U-MLH.
Acronym of the upper median line.

Uncertainty Bar.
This is a bar whose open coincides with its close. If located in the middle of a swing within a consolidation it means strictly nothing, but located at the top/bottom of a long trend may be a sign of weakness or even a reversal. In candlesticks terms this uncertainty bar is called *a doji*.

Un-Orthodox Trend Line.
The unorthodox or *multi-pivoted* trend line links a series of higher highs or lower highs belonging to the same trend and/or other trends. It differs from the traditional trend lines because *it traverses* the market, camouflaged between the numerous valleys and peaks.

Upper Median Line (UML or U-MLH).
This is the upper parallel line to the median line.

U-TL.
Acronym of the upper trigger line.

Volume.
This represents the fuelling of a trade. Whenever the price rises with an enhanced volume, the trend is in a good shape. A weak volume might signal the waning of a trend. On the contrary, on a down trend, the price's drop may be associated with a weak volume.

Warning Line Territory.
It is located outside the pitchfork's main body delineated by the upper and the lower median line, where the slope of the pitchfork tells a great deal about its ability to describe the market:

- the steeper the slope, the stronger the trend will be. However, it is also probable that the trend will not last and the market will enter into a consolidation.
- in the case of a trading range, the zigzagging of the mmls of the multiple trend and counter-trend oriented pitchforks will give away the market's accumulation process.

Warning Lines (WL).
These lines are defined as the trend lines which are parallel to the upper or lower median lines, at the same distance as that of the separating space between the ML and the MLH. Drawn at equally spaced multiple distances, they are numbered from one to whatever level the market flow will attain. No warning lines should be drawn as long as the price is within the main body area of the pitchfork, in order to avoid clouding of the chart. On the other hand don't be shy about going to seven levels of WL if the market progresses and demands it! *Always be ahead of the market by at least one level of warning line!* See also **Warning Line Territory.**

Wedge.
This is a chart formation having the shape of converging straight lines either slope up or slope down. When it is trend-oriented, the wedge might signal the end of the trend. On the contrary, if it's counter-trend-oriented, it has a high probability to signal a continuation of the ongoing trend.

'What If' Concept.
The *'What If'* concept protects the trader from the unexpected events. This goes *hand in hand* with *'expect the unexpected'* concept. The trader must be always aware of the overall picture and react rather than act, at the market's fluctuations. See also **Expect the Unexpected.**

WL.
Acronym of the warning line.

Zigzagging.
This is a visual method, revealing the orientation of each swing participating in the trend's development or in its post-termination correction. By linking the lowest low and the highest high of each swing, we create the swing's trend line. Put all together, they will unveil not only the trend line but also the market context. It will also efficiently and prolifically allow an easier application of the Fibonacci tools. Moreover, it will help the trader anticipate the slope of the developing swing (see Figs 18.1, 18.2 and 18.3).

Zooming.
This is mostly used when a volatile bar hastily penetrates a trend line and closes above it. Zooming through the median line is the signature of a highly charged momentum movement. It can be used to consider a potential low-risk high-probability trade. As soon as a level is broken, either the market will move on to the next level or the ML needs to be retested.

Index

1-minute time frame charts, multiple time frames 332–3
15-minute time frame charts
   multiple time frames 332–3, 338–9, 349–53, 355–6,
      366, 374–8, 382–9
   pitchforks 349–53, 355–6, 366, 374–8, 382–9
30-minute time frame charts
   multiple time frames 332–53, 374–8, 382–9
   pitchforks 347–53, 374–8, 382–9
60-minute time frame charts
   multiple time frames 332–3, 334–5, 338–53, 355–6,
      366, 374–8, 382–9
   pitchforks 347–8, 355–6, 366, 374–8, 382–9
80/20 rule 338, 401
A&R lines see action and reaction lines
'act locally think globally' 20, 29, 37–9, 297–9, 398
action lines (AL) 10–15, 32, 38–41, 54–8, 63, 185–216,
      234–6, 241, 344–7, 397–400
   concepts 176–84, 234–6, 241, 344–7, 397–400
   definition 176–8
   gap median lines 234–6, 241
action and reaction lines (A&R lines)
   see also center lines; hybrid/suspended pitchforks
   border guarantor 208–15
   characteristics 186–7
   comprehension issues 186
   concepts 13–15, 32, 38–41, 54–8, 59, 63, 176–84,
      185–216, 231–6, 241, 243–4, 257–9, 344–7, 375–7,
      397–400
   construction processes 185–216
   criss-cross pattern techniques 197–205, 215,
      292–9
   definition 176–8, 185–6
   double action and reaction lines 197–207, 215
   foundation 187–8
   functions 185–216, 231–6, 241, 344–7
   gap median lines 231–6, 241, 257–9
   historical background 185–6, 397–400
   horizontal trend lines 208–15

hybrid/suspended pitchforks 189–92, 194–5
image mirroring technique 192–5, 215
key learning points 215–16
median lines 63, 176–7
Newton's principles 185
obscurity 185
pitchfork distinctions 214–15, 344–7
pre-close breaking-up/down trend lines 207–16
price translation across the market stops 194–7,
   215
slant trend lines 208–15
straight pivot alignment pitchfork 214–15
symmetrical pattern technique 204–7, 215
traditional action and reaction lines 188–93
add-on technique 253–4, 374–82
adjusted trend lines, concepts 135
Advanced GET Charting 2, 20, 34–5
AL see action lines
alternative price projections, Fibonacci tools 264–83,
   287–98
analysis paralysis syndrome 102
anchors
   see also pivots
   concepts 23–9, 32–3, 38–40, 45–7, 55–8, 59–60, 67,
      103–19, 150–9, 161–84, 189–216, 217–41, 251
   definition 23, 32, 58
Ancient Egypt (4000BC), pitchfork concepts 395–9
Andrews, Alan H. 3, 22, 59, 103, 104, 185, 400
Andrew's pitchfork trading technique 1, 22–3, 59
antepenultimate pivot of an ending correction 54–8, 148,
   367–72
appendices 395–405
ascending bottom formations 250
ATR see average true range
automatic trade mode, concepts 357–9, 372–3
average true range (ATR), concepts 187, 201–2, 230–3,
      237–40, 288–300, 302–3, 315–16, 336–7, 355–9,
      369, 373–4

Babson, Roger W. 22, 59, 185, 243, 399–400
bar counts
    see also Fibonacci bars; momentum...
    breakouts 135–6
Baron, Jonathan 2
bars 60, 75–95, 99–102, 115, 135–6, 187, 208–16, 255–6,
        301–13, 338–53, 393
    see also mirror bars
bibliography and references 402
Bonacci, filius 261
    see also Fibonacci...
border guarantor, action and reaction lines 208–15
border mini-median lines
    see also mini-median lines
    concepts 76–80, 95
borderline concepts of median lines 63, 105, 114–15,
        275–83
breakaway gaps
    see also gaps
    concepts 246, 247, 248–59
    critical elements 252–3
    definition 248
    end run 252–3
    gap median lines 251–3
    key learning points 259
    seven cardinal formations 250, 335
    trading potential 249–53, 259
breakouts 98–102, 103–19, 134–45, 189–90, 208–16,
        226–41, 294–300, 315–28, 355–6, 364–5,
        387–93
    bar counts 135–6
    closing prices 135–6
    concepts 135–45, 229–33, 294–300, 315–28, 387–93
    confirmations 135–6
    culmination of a trend 136, 229–33
    energy-building rectangles 315–28
    false breakouts 136, 229–33, 251–2
    trend lines 136, 139–45, 208–16, 229–33
'breathing areas' 334–5
broadening bottom formations 250
broadening top formations 250
Brownian motion 330–1
bull traps 136, 229–33, 253
buy stop 10–15, 366

cascades, energy-building rectangles 321–8
CBOT *see* Chicago Board of Trade
center lines (CL) 10–15, 63, 176–84, 186–216, 233–6,
        241, 344–7, 375–7, 397–400
    see also action and reaction lines; median lines
    concepts 176–84, 186–216, 233–6, 241, 344–7, 375–7,
        397–400
    definition 176–8, 186
charts
    homework 7–15
    seven cardinal formations 250, 335, 383–93

Chicago Board of Trade (CBOT) 3
Chicago Mercantile Exchange (CME) 3
choice of pivots
    case studies 33–58
    concepts 22–3, 24–5, 29, 31–58, 75–6, 148, 217–18
    gap median lines 217–18
    key learning points 55–8
    penultimate pivots of an ending correction 54–8,
        148
classic pivots 48–52
close level of yesterday's closing bar anchor-location
        version, gap median lines 220–4
closing prices, breakouts 135–6
clouded charts, warning lines 102
clusters
    characteristics 297, 300
    confluences 287, 292–300
    Fibonacci lines 281–3, 287, 292–300, 340–1
    functions 297–300
    global view 297–300
CME *see* Chicago Mercantile Exchange
commensalism 236
common downward turn formations 250
common gaps
    see also gaps
    concepts 246–8, 250, 259
common upward turn formations 250
commonality principle 241
complex bottom formations 250
complex top formations 250
Computer Analysis on the Futures Market (LeBeau and
        Lucas) 374
confirmations, concepts 103–19, 135–6
confluences
    case studies 286–99, 369–72
    clusters 287, 292–300
    concepts 11–15, 97–102, 145, 148–60, 163–8, 187,
        209–15, 257–9, 285–300, 310–13, 341–2, 369–72
    definition 285–6, 292
    double line intersection confluences 286–9
    dynamic-related criteria 149
    functions 285–300
    implementation procedure triad 285–6
    key learning points 298–300
    levels 295–300
    multi-level line intersection confluences 289–300,
        369–72
    multi-zone confluences with multi-level intersections
        291–300
    multiple pitchforks 148–60
    timing trajectory 286–300
consecutive pivots 32, 55
conservative trade entries, trigger lines 103–19
consistency needs 3–4, 149–50, 361
consolidations 246–59, 294–300, 355–6, 364–72,
        388–93

contextual market
    see also market context
    concept 18–19, 37–42, 58, 133–4, 137–41, 147–8,
        244–6, 327–8, 341–4
continuation gaps *see* runaway gaps
coordination issues, multiple time frames 338–53
corrections 33–4, 37–41, 51, 54–8, 63, 137, 148–60,
    162–84, 238–41, 375–7
count technique characteristic of energy-building
    rectangles 316
Crabel, Toby 303
Crime and Punishment (Dostoyevsky) 149
criss-cross pattern techniques, action and reaction lines
    197–205, 215, 292–9
cross-referencing aspects, time frames 329–53
culmination of a trend, breakouts 136, 229–33
currencies 201, 288, 338–9

daily time frame charts
    multiple time frames 331, 334–53
    pitchforks 344–7
    procedures 337–8
decision-making processes 2–5, 97–8, 355–93
degrees of importance, pivots 31–2, 55
descending top formations 250
despair return points 270, 274–6, 283
differential gap diagnosis 249
disclaimer 5
diversified efficiency 5
dominant trends
    identification tools 335
    multiple time frames 334–53
Dostoyevsky, Fyodor 149
double action and reaction lines
    see also action and reaction lines; criss-cross...;
        symmetrical pattern...
    concepts 197–207, 215
double bottom formations 250
double channelling, concepts 138–9, 148–60
double line intersection confluences
    see also confluences
    concepts 286–9
double mirror bars 99–102, 303–13
    see also mirror bars
double six parameter rules, median lines 62–3, 72
double top formations 250, 383, 386
Dow Jones Indexes 2, 33–58, 112–18, 189, 191,
    339–52
Dow ratios 4, 216, 217
down-sloping trend lines 9–15, 19, 31, 33–6, 37–9, 43–7,
    62–3, 65–72, 76–80, 99–102, 103–19, 123–45,
    152–60, 162–84, 192–216, 221–41, 256–9, 271–82,
    355–6, 364–72, 393
    see also peaks
    double six parameter rules 62–3, 72
    gap median lines 221–41

dual pitchforks
    see also multiple...
    concepts 149–60
duration of trend lines, concepts 136, 229–33
Dynamic Trading (Miner) 263

efficient first time breakouts 136
Einstein, Albert 329–30
embedding the global market flow role, pitchforks 33,
    148, 149–60, 161–84
emergency medicine analogies 17
empty charts 37–41
end run, breakaway gaps 252–3
energy-building rectangles 13–15, 60, 68–70, 92–4, 101,
    112–13, 131, 140–5, 148–60, 187–216, 286–300,
    301, 315–28, 334–5, 355–93
    cascades 321–8
    case studies 317–28, 355–74
    characteristics 316
    concepts 315–28, 355–74
    definition 315–16
    double trending characteristics 326–8
    exacerbation concepts 315–28
    exhaustion concepts 246, 247, 249, 250, 255–9, 315–28
    functions 315–28
    key learning points 328
    ladder-like trend structures 321–8, 392–3
    measuring techniques 316, 324–8
    micro/macro aspects 317–24
    multiple energy-building rectangles 323–4
    synergy 327–8
    trading approach steps 355–74
entry 7–15, 355–93
epilogue 404–5
epistemology 4
ergonomics 4, 5, 20, 136, 176, 270, 315–16
eSignal 20, 34–5
Euro/US dollar 201, 288
exacerbation concepts 315–28
excursion analysis, concepts 374
exhaustion concepts 246, 247, 249, 250, 255–9, 315–28
exhaustion gaps
    see also gaps
    concepts 246, 247, 249, 250, 255–9
    island reversal zones 256–9
    trading potential 255–9
exit decisions 7–15, 355–93
expansions, Fibonacci tools 265–83, 287–98
'expect the unexpected' awareness 201–7, 215, 239, 241
external price retracements, Fibonacci tools 263–83,
    287–98

failures
    see also reversals; sliding parallel lines; trigger lines
    concepts 2, 61–2, 64–5, 72, 99–102, 103–19, 121–32,
        157–60, 164–84, 257–9, 386–7

false breakouts 136, 229–33, 251–2
false reversals 149–60
fan lines, concepts 134, 142, 145
Federal Trade Commission (FTC) 5
Fibonacci bars, breakouts 135–6
Fibonacci lines/tools (FL) 9–15, 23, 29, 38–40, 43–5,
    51–3, 55–8, 59, 64–72, 77–94, 97–101, 106–18,
    122–36, 150–9, 161–84, 192–216, 219–40, 255–9,
    261–83, 287–98, 303–12, 335, 337, 390
  alternative price projections 264–83, 287–98
  case studies 266–83
  clusters 281–3, 287, 292–300, 340–1
  concepts 135–6, 261–83, 303–12, 335
  definition 261–2, 276–8
  dynamics of pitchfork integration 269–83
  external price retracements 263–83, 287–98
  functions 262–83, 287–98
  historical background 261–2
  internal price retracements 263–83, 287–98
  key learning points 283
  mirror bars 303–12
  price expansions 265–83, 287–98
  projections 262–83, 287–98
  retracements 262–83, 287–98, 341–52
  synergy 283
Fibonacci numbers, definition 261–2
Fibonacci ratios, concepts 4, 9–15, 23, 61, 216, 217,
    238–40, 261–83
fifth day gap period, gap median lines 240
filling of the gap phenomenon 68, 204
'the final indicator is a tried and tested trend line' factors,
    median lines 60, 73
finding the optimal set-up, trading approach steps 13,
    355–6, 362, 364–5, 375–7, 382–4, 388–93
first day gap period, gap median lines 237–8
first orders, three-pawn technique 356–9, 366, 372–3,
    376–82, 383–5, 389–93
FL see Fibonacci lines
flexibility qualities, pitchforks 23, 26
fourth day gap period, gap median lines 239
fractals (fractional dimensions), multiple time frames
    330, 353
FTC see Federal Trade Commission
FTSE 100 charts 54–8, 137–44, 291–4, 317–28
fundamental analysis 22–3
future results, past performance 5
futures 23–7, 64–72, 77–94, 98–101, 104–7, 123–31,
    137–44, 150–9, 162–83, 188–240, 244–58, 266–82,
    302–13, 317–28, 338–9, 374

Gann ratios 4, 213–16, 217, 273, 276
gap action and reaction lines 192–5
  see also action and reaction lines
gap measure technique 226–33
gap median lines
  see also mini-median lines
  action and reaction lines 231–6, 241, 257–9

anchor-location versions 218–41
breakaway gaps 251–3
choice of pivots 217–18
close level of yesterday's closing bar anchor-location
    version 220–4
concepts 63, 76–80, 217–41, 251–3, 257–9
construction processes 217–41
definition 217–18
down-sloping markets 221–41
fifth day gap period 240
first day gap period 237–8
fourth day gap period 239
gap measure technique 226–8
gap-filling charts 236–41
key learning points 240–1
midpoint of the gap anchor-location version 220–5
multiple gap median lines 236–41
multiple price translations 221, 224
open level of today's opening bar anchor-location
    version 218–22
outside the gap, P1–P2 swing gap's measure,
    anchor-location version 221–41, 251
pitchforks 218–41
pre-gap period 237
second day gap period 238
sideways markets 226–33
sixth day gap period 240
specificities 221–3, 225
synergy 236
textbook example 231–2
third day gap period 239
versions 218–35
gap-filling charts 236–41
gaps 23, 63, 76–80, 81–5, 139–45, 163, 192–5, 217–41,
    243–59
  see also breakaway...; common...; exhaustion...;
      runaway...
  concepts 243–59
  context charts 244–6
  definition 243–4, 246–9
  historical background 243–4
  key learning points 240–1, 259
  mechanisms 246–50, 259
  rectangles 248–59
  swing distribution technique 244–9, 259
  systematized visualization tool 244–7, 259
  territorial distribution technique 245–9, 259
  trading potential 249–59
  types 246–9, 259
'gasping rectangles' 334–5
geometry 185, 330–53
German bund 201
German Dax Indexes 2, 23–7, 64–72, 77–94, 98–101,
    104–7, 123–31, 137–44, 150–9, 162–83, 188–240,
    244–58, 266–82, 302–13, 317–28, 355–93
German elections 201–5, 237–40
gliding bed 48, 51, 87, 91, 112–13, 148

global behaviour, multiple time frames 333–5
0.618 Golden Ratio 261–2
greed 392
Greenspan, Alan 320

H letter, U-MLH/L-MLH usage 59
Hagopian rule and line, concepts 104–5, 106–8, 114–19, 121–32, 157–9, 176–80, 197–9
handles 105–19, 150–9
head and shoulder bottom formations 250
head and shoulder top formations 250
height/width characteristic of energy-building rectangles 316, 355–6
higher time frames, concepts 336
hindsight 374
'Holy Grail of the pitchfork' 23, 29, 31, 35, 75–6, 207
homeostasis 212–13
homework 7–15
horizontal trend lines
    action and reaction lines 208–15
    Fibonacci lines 266–83
horizontal zigzagging 325–6
horizontally-oriented bisector 209
human nature 1
hybrid/suspended pitchforks
    see also action and reaction lines
    action and reaction lines 189–92
    concepts 32, 38–41, 54–8, 63, 176–80, 184, 189–92, 194–5, 234–6
    construction processes 176–80, 184
    definition 176–8
    functions 176–80, 184
    key learning points 184

ideal market descriptions 29
'if it ain't broke, don't fix it!' 353
image mirroring technique, action and reaction lines 192–5, 215
impulse patterns 10–15, 162–84, 288–300
inceptive chart formations 248–59
    see also gaps
initial stops, sliding parallel lines 122–32
inner sliding parallel lines 122–32
inside bars, mirror bars 302–13, 357–9
inside median lines, concepts 63, 84–5
inside mini-median lines
    see also mini-median lines
    concepts 78–86, 95, 292–3
integrated pitchfork analysis 1–5, 149–60
    see also pitchforks
    principles 4–5
interdependent pitchforks 23, 26
interest rates 320–1
intermediate pivots (I), concepts 19–22, 32, 34
internal price retracements, Fibonacci tools 263–83, 287–98

internal structure characteristic of energy-building rectangles 316
introduction 1–5
intuition 17
island reversal zones
    see also exhaustion gaps
    concepts 256–9

Joseph, Tom 20

Kase, Cynthia A. 329
KESA 292–9
key learning points
    action and reaction lines 215–16
    birth of pivots and pitchforks 27–9
    breakaway gaps 259
    choice of pivots 55–8
    confluences 298–300
    energy-building rectangles 328
    Fibonacci lines 283
    gap median lines 240–1
    gaps 240–1, 259
    hybrid/suspended pitchforks 184
    median lines 72–3
    mini-median lines 95
    mirror bars 313
    multiple pitchforks 159–60
    multiple time frames 353
    pitchforks 27–9, 159–60
    pivots 27–9, 55–8
    reverse pitchforks 184
    runaway gaps 259
    Schiff pitchforks 184
    sliding parallel lines 132
    T-pitchforks 184
    trigger lines 119
    unorthodox trend lines 145
    warning lines 101–2
kinematics, pivots 32–3, 58
knowledge 4, 17
Krausz, Robert 333–4

L-MLH see lower median lines
L-TL see lower trigger lines
'ladder climbing' 79–84, 97–102, 321–8, 392–3
learning curves 1–2, 13–15, 17, 236–41, 360–2, 370, 373, 382, 386–7, 391–3
LeBeau, Charles 374
LML see lower median lines
local action of the market, market context 20–3, 37–42, 58, 148–9, 297–9, 327–8, 349–53, 398
location characteristic of energy-building rectangles 316
logical price objectives 334–53, 356–8
logical profit objectives 13, 356–9, 362, 366, 372–3, 376–8, 383–5, 389–93
long-range monthly activity 51–2

low-risk high-probability trades, concepts 7–15, 60–1, 97–102, 112–19, 160, 207–16, 283, 297–300, 355–93
lower median lines (LML/L-MLH)
    concepts 11–15, 23–9, 40–58, 59, 62, 64–72, 76–95, 97–102, 105–19, 123–31, 150–9, 163–83, 219–41, 252–3, 265–83, 286–300, 323–8, 345–52, 365, 376–8, 383–5
    warning lines 97–102
lower time frames
    see also time frames
    concepts 39, 42, 329–53, 375–7
    median lines 329–53
lower trigger lines (L-TL)
    see also trigger lines
    concepts 103–19
lowest low pivot of an ending correction 54–8
Lucas, David W. 374

magnetic powers, median lines 39, 42–3, 59–73, 92–4, 148–60, 220, 233–6, 271–2, 326–8
major pitchforks
    confluences 286–300
    mirror bars 310–13
    multiple pitchforks 147–60
major pivots (J), concepts 19–22, 23–7, 32, 34, 38–40, 60, 76–84, 95
Mandelbrot, Benoit B. 330
manual mode, concepts 357–9
market bias 20, 31–2, 65–6, 155–9, 208–15, 338
market context
    see also contextual market
    concepts 18–19, 37–42, 58, 133–4, 137–41, 147–8, 244–6, 327–8, 341–4
    definition 18–19
    limits 18–19
    local action of the market 20–3, 37–42, 58, 148–9, 297–9, 327–8, 349–53, 398
market flows
    see also gap...
    concepts 18–19, 33, 45–7, 72, 149–60, 161–84, 187–216, 217–41, 243–59, 285–300, 315–28, 355–93
    confluences 285–300
    energy-building rectangles 13–15, 60, 68–70, 92–4, 101, 112–13, 131, 140–5, 148–60, 187–216, 286–300, 301, 315–28, 355–93
market future direction of energy-building rectangles 316
market modules, multiple time frames 215–16
measuring gaps see runaway gaps
measuring techniques, energy-building rectangles 316, 324–8
mechanisms, gaps 246–50, 259
median lines (ML)
    see also center lines; gap...
    A&R lines link 63, 176–7

borderline concepts 63, 105, 114–15, 275–83
case studies 64–73, 382–93
characteristics 59–73, 114
concepts 11–15, 23–9, 32, 35–6, 38–54, 59–73, 97–8, 114–15, 121–32, 163–82, 186, 217–41, 285–300, 382–93, 395–400
confluences 11–15, 97–102, 145, 148–60, 163–8, 187, 209–15, 257–9, 285–300
definition 59, 72–3
different versions 63
double six parameter rules 62–3, 72
failures 2, 61–2, 64–5, 72, 99–102, 114–15
'the final indicator is a tried and tested trend line' factors 60, 73
functions 59–73
Hagopian rule and line 104–5, 106–8, 114–19, 121–32, 157–9, 176–80, 197–9
historical background 59, 395–400
key learning points 72–3
lower time frames 329–53
magnetic powers 39, 42–3, 59–73, 92–4, 148–60, 220, 233–6, 271–2, 326–8
minimum price objectives 60, 72, 76–95
multiple median lines 64
multiple pitchforks 150–60
newest lines 63
seven parameter rules 63–4, 72
single bar pitchforks 63
strength/weakness of market evaluations (double six parameter rules) 62–3, 72
symmetry axis power 60, 70–2, 76–7, 114–19, 122–31, 138–45, 152–9, 163, 171–6, 192–4, 218, 233–6
territories 59
triple action potential 60
upper time frames 329–53
wide median line 63
micro/macro aspects, energy-building rectangles 317–24
midpoint of the gap anchor-location version, gap median lines 220–5
midpoint lines 209
Miner, Robert C. 263
mini channels, sliding parallel lines 125–8
mini-median lines (MML)
    see also median lines
    border mini-median lines 76–80, 95
    case studies 76–95
    characteristics 75–95
    concepts 63, 75–95, 102, 122–3
    construction processes 75–6
    definition 75–6, 95
    functions 75–95
    inside mini-median lines 78–86, 95, 292–3
    key learning points 95
    reverse mini-median lines 85–9, 95
    steep downsloping mini-median lines 86–91, 95
    trigger lines 105–6

twin pivots' mini-median lines 87, 92–5
warning lines 76, 102
minimum price objectives, median lines 60, 72, 76–95
minor pitchforks
  confluences 286–300
  mirror bars 310–13
  multiple pitchforks 147–60
minor pivots (M), concepts 20–3, 27–9, 32, 34, 38–40,
  60, 66, 81–95, 128–32
mirror bars
  see also double...; triple...
  case studies 302–13, 318–28
  characteristics 301–8
  concepts 92, 94, 99–102, 115, 255–6, 301–13, 318–28,
    375–7
  definition 301–2
  Fibonacci tools 303–12
  functions 301–13
  inside bars 302–13, 357–9
  key learning points 313
  money management 313
  NR4/NR7 303–13
  open/close duo 301–13, 367–8
  pattern origination and development 304–7
  pitchfork applicability 308–13
  reverberant pullback 304–13
  synergy 310–13
  time frames 302–13
mirror sliding parallel lines 128–32
mixed market situations, concepts 338
ML *see* median lines
MML *see* mini-median lines
modified median lines *see* Schiff pitchforks
module learning 215–16, 236–41
momentum bar counts 135
momentum indicators 179–83, 209–15, 255–9, 335
money management 3–4, 13, 105–19, 122–4, 136, 313,
  355–93
monthly time frame charts
  multiple time frames 331, 334–53
  pitchforks 341–3, 347
  procedures 336–7
Morge, Timothy 3
moving averages 31, 207, 231–3, 337
multi-level line intersection confluences
  see also confluences
  concepts 289–300, 369–72
multi-pivoted trend lines *see* unorthodox trend lines
multi-zone confluences with multi-level intersections
  see also confluences
  concepts 291–300
multiple aspects of trigger line characteristics 115, 118
multiple gap median lines
  see also gap median lines
  concepts 236–41
multiple median lines, concepts 64

multiple pitchforks
  case studies 150–9
  complexity problems 147, 159–60
  concepts 147–60
  construction methods 148–9, 150–1
  definition 147–8
  dynamic-related criteria 149
  functions 147–60
  key learning points 159–60
  kinematics 149–50
  reversals 149–60
  structure-related criteria 148–9
  'The workplace must be always clean' 148
multiple price translations, gap median lines 221, 224
multiple tests 45, 60, 73, 81–4, 99–102, 115–19, 139–45,
  155–60, 163–84
multiple time frames
  see also time frames
  1-minute time frame charts 332–3
  15-minute time frame charts 332–3, 338–9, 349–53,
    355–6, 366, 374–8, 382–9
  30-minute time frame charts 332–53, 374–8, 382–9
  60-minute time frame charts 332–3, 334–5, 338–53,
    355–6, 366, 374–8, 382–9
  concepts 215–16, 329–53, 356
  coordination issues 338–53
  daily time frame charts 331, 334–53
  definition 329–30
  dominant trends 334–53
  fractals 330, 353
  functions 329–53
  global behaviour 333–5
  guidelines 339
  key learning points 353
  logical price objectives 334–53
  monthly time frame charts 331, 334–53
  photographs from space analogy 330–3
  pitchforks 329–30, 339–53
  practical aspects 339–53
  Russian dolls 330, 352
  six rules 333–4
  trend analysis uses 334–53
  turning points 334–53
  weekly time frame charts 331, 334–53
  zigzagging techniques 334–53

narrow inside bars, mirror bars 302–13, 357–9
narrow range bars 303–13, 324–5, 355–6, 387–93
  see also NR...
New York City 331–3
newest median lines, concepts 63
Newtonian principles 135, 185, 399–400
Nikkei 225 201, 288
normal line
  see also median lines
  concepts 59, 399–400

novice traders 1–3, 17, 207, 261, 357
NR4/7 303–13, 324–5
NYSE 240

omission phenomenon 2
open/close duo, mirror bars 301–13, 367–8
operational time frames
  see also time frames
  15-minute time frame charts 332–3, 338–9, 349–53,
    355–6, 366, 374–8, 382–9
  30-minute time frame charts 332–53, 374–8, 382–9
  60-minute time frame charts 332–3, 334–5, 338–53,
    355–6, 366, 374–8, 382–9
  concepts 329–53
  pitchforks 347–53
  types 338–9
optimal pitchforks 13, 48, 51, 355–6, 362, 364–5, 375–7,
  382–4, 388–93
optimal pivots 13, 31–2, 38, 40, 45–51, 54–8, 75–95,
  148, 188–216, 355–6, 362, 364–5, 375–7, 382–4,
  388–93
outer sliding parallel lines 122–32
outside the gap, P1–P2 swing gap's measure
  anchor-location version, gap median lines 221–41,
  251
overview 1–5, 403–5

P1–P2 swing, concepts 23–9, 32, 51, 54, 58, 59–60, 72,
  105–19, 150–9, 161–84, 214–16, 217–41, 251
pain, pleasure 1
parallelism criteria, sliding parallel lines 122
past performance, future results 5
pattern gaps *see* common gaps
peaks 19, 31–2, 149–50
  see also down-sloping trend lines
penultimate pivots of an ending correction 54–8, 148
PH/SH *see* sliding parallel lines
photographs from space analogy, multiple time frames
  330–3
piercings
  concepts 45, 60–1, 63, 72, 95, 97–102, 119, 122–32,
    149–60, 163–84, 307–13, 371–2
  trigger lines 119
  warning lines 97–102, 371–2
pitchforks
  see also integrated...; multiple...; Schiff...
  15-minute time frame charts 349–53, 355–6, 366,
    374–8, 382–9
  30-minute time frame charts 347–53, 374–8, 382–9
  60-minute time frame charts 347–8, 355–6, 366,
    374–8, 382–9
  action and reaction line distinctions 214–15, 344–7
  Ancient Egypt (4000BC) 395–9
  concepts 1–4, 22–9, 32, 33, 59, 122, 147–60, 269–83,
    308–13, 392–3, 395–400
  confluences 285–300

construction methods 22–4, 27–9, 32, 148–9, 150–1,
  269–83
daily time frame charts 344–7
definition 22–3, 32, 59
efficiency determinants 22–3, 29, 148
embedding the global market flow role 33, 148,
  149–60, 161–84
Fibonacci lines integration dynamics 269–83
flexibility qualities 23, 26
gap median lines 218–41
handles 105–19, 150–9
historical background 22, 59, 395–400
'Holy Grail of the pitchfork' 23, 29, 31, 35, 75–6, 207
interdependent pitchforks 23, 26
key learning points 27–9, 159–60
kinematics 33
'ladder climbing' pitchforks 79–84
mirror bar applicability 308–13
monthly time frame charts 341–3, 347
multiple time frames 329–30, 339–53
operational time frames 347–53
optimal pitchforks 13, 48, 51, 355–6, 362, 364–5,
  375–7, 382–4, 388–93
origins 22–9
pivots choices 22–3, 24–5, 29, 31–58, 75–6, 148
practice benefits 2–4
qualities 23, 29
rectangles 157–8, 392–3
retrograde pitchforks 32, 51, 54, 58
upper time frames 329–53
versatility qualities 23, 26
weekly time frame charts 341–5, 347
pivots
  see also anchors
  case studies 23–7, 33–58, 137–45
  characteristics 19–21, 31–2, 55
  choice issues 22–3, 24–5, 29, 31–58, 75–6, 148,
    217–18
  classic pivots 48–52
  concepts 17–29, 31–58, 137–45, 148, 188–216, 251–2
  consecutive pivots 32, 55
  creation case studies 23–7
  definition 19–21
  degrees of importance 31–2, 55
  gap median lines 63, 76–80, 217–41
  key learning points 27–9, 55–8
  kinematics 32–3, 58
  optimal pivots 13, 31–2, 38, 40, 45–51, 54–8, 75–95,
    148, 188–216, 355–6, 362, 364–5, 375–7, 382–4,
    388–93
  origins 17–29
  penultimate pivots of an ending correction 54–8, 148
  pitchfork efficiency determinants 22–3, 29, 148
  swings 31–2, 55, 161–84
  twin pivots 35–7, 87, 92–5
  types 19–20, 32, 43–4, 55

pleasure and pain 1
powerful tools, simple concepts 19, 27
practice benefits 2–4
pre-close breaking-up/down trend lines, action and reaction lines 207–16
pre-close phase 203–4
pre gap period, gap median lines 237
prelude 7–15
price behaviour, sliding parallel lines 121–2
price expansions, Fibonacci tools 265–83, 287–98
price translation across the market stops, action and reaction lines 194–7, 215
price-related market features 18–19
primary pivots (P), concepts 19–22, 23–7, 32, 34
Principia (Newton) 185
prior swings 45–7, 262–83
probability thresholds 361–2
profit & loss statements 13, 359–60, 362, 372–3, 380–2, 385–6, 390–3
projections, Fibonacci tools 262–83, 287–98
propagating sharp retracements 302
pullbacks, concepts 31–2, 75–6, 92–4, 102, 122, 125–9, 149, 207, 213–15, 302, 304–13, 355–6, 378–80, 388–93

R/R ratio *see* reward/risk ratio
range
    see also average...; narrow...; triple action potential
    concepts 60, 67–8, 72, 76, 101, 187, 201–2, 230–3, 237–40, 288–300, 302–13, 315–16, 324–5, 336–7, 355–9, 369, 373–4, 387–93
reaction lines (RL) 10–15, 32, 63, 176–84, 185–216, 231–6, 241, 321–8, 344–7, 397–400
    see also action...
    concepts 185–216, 231–6, 241, 344–7, 397–400
    definition 186, 189–90
    functions 186, 189–90, 231–6, 241, 344–7
    gap median lines 231–6, 241
    image mirroring technique 192–5, 215
rectangles 2, 13–15, 22, 60, 68–70, 92–4, 101, 112–13, 122, 131, 140–5, 148–60, 187–216, 248–59, 321–8, 392–3
    gaps 248–59
    ladder-like trend structures 321–8, 392–3
    pitchforks 157–8, 392–3
references 402
resistance lines 10–15, 35–7, 45–51, 60–1, 66–7, 81–4, 101, 103–19, 226–41, 273–82, 287–9, 295–300
resting areas 31–2
retesting 10, 45–6, 60–1, 72, 86–91, 112–19, 149–60, 163–84, 230–3, 355–87
retracements
    concepts 262–83, 341–52
    despair return points 270, 274–6, 283
    Fibonacci tools 262–83, 287–98, 341–52

levels 13, 204, 211–15
    reversals 270–1
    types 263–5
retrograde pitchforks, concepts 32, 51, 54, 58
'return to mean' phenomenon 234
reverberant pullback 304–13
reversals 29, 31–43, 51, 54, 60, 64–95, 99–102, 104–19, 121–32, 138–45, 149–60, 161–84, 192–216, 219–41, 252–3, 268–83, 301–13, 372, 375–7, 382–4, 393
    see also failures; mirror bars
    despair return points 270, 274–6, 283
    false reversals 149–60
    Hagopian rule and line 104–5, 106–8, 114–19, 121–32, 157–9, 176–80, 197–9
    multiple pitchforks 149–60
    retracements 270–1
    sliding parallel lines 121–32
reverse mini-median lines
    see also mini-median lines
    concepts 85–9, 95
reverse pitchforks
    concepts 179–84
    construction processes 179–83
    definition 179
    functions 179–84
    key learning points 184
reward/risk ratio (R/R ratio) 13, 109–19, 121–2, 125, 357–9, 361–2, 366, 373, 378, 381–2, 384–5, 390
    accuracy assessments 361–2
    trigger lines 109–19, 373
risk controls 3–5
risk management 3–5, 13, 105–19, 121–2, 125, 357–9, 361–2, 366, 373, 378, 381–2, 384–5, 390
    see also trade risk
    R/R ratio 13, 109–19, 121–2, 125, 357–9, 361–2, 366, 373, 378, 381–2, 384–5, 390
    sliding parallel lines 122–4
    trigger lines 105–19
RL *see* reaction lines
'rubber band' effects 68, 204
runaway gaps
    see also gaps
    concepts 246, 247, 248–59, 378–80
    definition 248–9
    key learning points 259
    trading potential 253–4
Russian dolls, multiple time frames 330, 352

S&P 500 crude oil 201, 288–90
S&P 500 e-minis 33–57, 98–101, 112–16, 137–44, 269–82, 288–90, 302–13, 317–28, 339–52, 362–74
satellite photographs 330–3
scale-in technique, concepts 253–4, 374–82
Schabacker, Richard W. 243–4, 248, 249–50, 254, 259
Schiff, Jerome 161
Schiff median line 11–15

Schiff pitchforks 32, 55–7, 58, 155–6, 161–84, 219–22,
        288–300
    concepts 161–84, 219–22
    construction processes 161–84, 219–22
    definition 161–2
    functions 161–84
    key learning points 184
    up-gap exploitation example 163–5
    version 1 efficiency 163–72, 184
    version 2 efficiency 165–72, 184
second day gap period, gap median lines 238
semi-automatic trade mode, concepts 357–9, 372–3
seven cardinal formations 250, 335, 383–93
seven parameter rules, median lines 63–4, 72
SH see sliding parallel lines
shooting stars 29, 58
short-term trading, overview 2–5
sideways markets 4–5, 31, 37–40, 87–93, 163–4, 226–33,
        272–82
signal line function, trigger lines 103–19
simple concepts, powerful tools 19, 27
single bar pitchforks
    see also median lines
    concepts 63
sixth day gap period, gap median lines 240
slant trend lines, action and reaction lines 208–15
sliding parallel lines (PH/SH)
    case studies 123–31, 310–11
    classic location 125–6
    concepts 59, 121–32, 164, 169–70, 179–83, 196–7,
        209–11, 310–11, 376–8
    definition 121
    double pitchfork criss-cross 125–6
    double testing 128–32
    failures 121–32, 164, 169–70, 179–83
    functions 121–32
    key learning points 132
    mini channels 125–8
    mirror sliding parallel lines 128–32
    money management 122–4
    parallelism criteria 122
    price behaviour 121–2
    up-sloping failures 123–4, 164, 169–70
    zooms 125–32
slope factors, unorthodox trend lines 134–45
smart money 3–4
snugging concept, trend lines 145
specificities, gap median lines 221–3, 225
spotting the trade opportunity, trading approach steps 13,
        355–6, 362–4, 374–7, 382, 387
staircase concepts, dominant trends 335
steep downsloping mini-median lines
    see also mini-median lines
    concepts 86–91, 95
stock market crash of 1929 59

stop loss 10–15, 122–32, 136, 302–13, 316–28, 356–9,
        366, 374, 376–8, 383–5, 389–93
stops, sliding parallel lines 122–32
straight pivot alignment pitchfork 214–15
strength factors, trend lines 135–45
strength/weakness of market evaluations (double six
        parameter rules), median lines 62–3, 72
support/resistance levels (S/R levels) 61, 103–19,
        122–32, 134, 144–5, 157–9, 226–41, 252–3,
        273–82, 287–9, 295–300
suspended pitchforks
    see also hybrid...
    concepts 32, 38–41, 54–8, 63, 176–80, 184, 189–93,
        194–5, 234–6
Sweeney, John 374
swings
    distribution technique 244–9, 259
    pivots 31–2, 55, 161–84
    trigger lines 105–19
symmetrical pattern technique, action and reaction lines
        204–7, 215
symmetry axis, concepts 48, 51, 60, 70–2, 76–7, 98–9,
        114–19, 122–31, 138–45, 152–9, 163, 171–6,
        192–4, 218, 233–6
synergy 5, 123–5, 140–5, 209–16, 236, 283
    A&R lines and pre-close breaking-up/down trend lines
        209–16
    energy-building rectangles 327–8
    Fibonacci tools 283
    gap median lines 236
    mirror bars 310–13
    multiple time frames 329–53
systematized visualization tool, gaps 244–7, 259

T-pitchforks
    concepts 32, 43, 54–8, 172–7, 184
    construction processes 172–7
    definition 172–3
    functions 172–7
    key learning points 184
    traditional pitchfork comparison 173, 175
technical analysis 1–5, 22–3, 185, 243, 259, 374, 392–3,
        395–400
    historical background 22–3, 185, 243, 395–400
    'Who knows the past, preferably the immediate past,
        controls the future' 393
techniques, overview 1–5
terminating phase of trends 34–5, 136, 145, 302–13,
        340–1
territorial distribution technique, gaps 245–9, 259
terrorist attacks 201
test-and-retest trades 10, 13–14, 60–1, 72, 99–102,
        112–19, 149–60, 163–84, 230–3, 355–87
    concepts 13–14, 60–1, 72, 112–19, 149, 355–87
    trigger lines 112–19

'think globally act locally' 20, 29, 37–9, 297–9, 398

third day gap period, gap median lines 239

third pitchforks 150

three-pawn technique, concepts 10, 13, 35, 356–9, 362, 366, 372–3, 376–82, 383–5, 389–93

throwbacks, concepts 136, 229–33, 253, 388–93

time frame alignment, concepts 13, 356, 362, 366, 375–7, 382–3, 389–93

time frames 13, 38–42, 45–6, 215–16, 302–13, 329–53, 356

   see also multiple time frames

   concepts 13, 215–16, 302–13, 329–53, 356

   cross-referencing aspects 329–53

   definition 329–30

   functions 329–53

   mirror bars 302–13

   types 334–53

time–price virtual spaces, concepts 3–4, 18–19, 27, 33, 59, 187–216

timing trajectory of the confluence 286–300

TL *see* trend lines; trigger lines

trade progression, case studies 366–72, 378–9

trade risk

   see also risk...

   trigger lines function 105–19

trader's journals, concepts 13–15, 360–2, 370, 373, 382, 386–7, 391–3

trading 1–5, 7–15, 355–93

   homework 7–15

   learning curves 1–2, 236–41

   overview 1–5

trading approach steps

   case studies 355–93

   energy-building rectangles 355–74

   finding the optimal set-up 13, 355–6, 362, 364–5, 375–7, 382–4, 388–93

   profit & loss statements 13, 359–60, 362, 372–3, 380–2, 385–6, 390–3

   spotting the trade opportunity 13, 355–6, 362–4, 374–7, 382, 387

   three-pawn technique 10, 13, 35, 356–9, 362, 366, 372–3, 376–82, 383–5, 389–93

   time frame alignment 13, 356, 362, 366, 375–7, 382–3, 389–93

   trade progression 366–72, 378–9

   trader's journals 13–15, 360–2, 370, 373, 382, 386–7, 391–3

   zoom and retest techniques 355–87

Trading and Deciding (Baron) 2

Trading with the Odds (Kase) 329

trading words, vocabulary warning 4

traditional pitchforks 32, 51, 58, 105–7, 161–84, 215, 269–82, 308–13

trailing stops 12–15, 122–32, 136, 302–13, 366–74

trend continuations, concepts 76–7

trend lines (TL)

   breakouts 136, 139–45, 208–16, 229–33

   case studies 137–45

   concepts 133–45, 208–16, 248–59, 334–53

   confirmations 135

   confluences 11–15, 97–102, 145, 148–60, 163–8, 187, 209–15, 257–9, 285–300, 310–13, 341–2

   dual aspects 137–8

   duration 136, 229–33

   key learning points 145

   money management 136

   multiple time frames 334–53

   snugging concept 145

   types 133–4, 137–45, 208–16

trending markets

   concepts 4–5, 31, 37–40, 335

   identification tools 335

'trends within a trend' 334–53

triangular bottom formations 250

triangular top formations 250

trigger lines (TL)

   borderline function 105

   case studies 112–19, 150–9, 251–9, 362–74

   concepts 29, 59, 85, 88, 99–100, 103–19, 128–32, 150–9, 251–9, 289–300, 327–8, 362–74

   construction processes 103–4

   definition 103–5

   functions 103–19

   Hagopian rule and line 104–5, 106–8, 114–19, 157–9, 176–80, 197–9

   key learning points 119

   mini-median lines 105–6

   multiple aspects of the characteristics 115, 118

   P1–P2 swing 105–19

   reward/risk ratio 109–19

   signal line function 103–19

   trade risk quantifying function 105–19

triple action potential

   see also piercings; range; reversals

   median lines 60

triple fan lines 139–45

triple mirror bars 92, 94, 99–102, 115, 255–6, 302–13, 375–7

   see also mirror bars

troughs 19, 335

   see also up-sloping trend lines

twin pivots 35–7, 87, 92–5

U-MLH *see* upper median lines

U-TL *see* upper trigger lines

UML *see* upper median lines

uncertainty bars 112–19, 125–31, 312–13

unorthodox trend lines

   case studies 137–45

   concepts 61, 121–32, 133–45, 187, 301–13, 327–8

unorthodox trend lines (*Continued*)
    definition 133–4
    fan lines 134
    functions 133–45
    key learning points 145
    money management 136
    opening breakout trend lines 139–45
    orthodox trend lines 133–42
    slope factors 134–45
    strength factors 135–45
    synergy 140–5
    systematized trend lines approach 144–5
unpredictable events 201–7, 215, 239, 241
up-sloping trend lines 15, 19, 29, 31, 35–7, 43–7, 51–3,
    62–87, 103–19, 123–45, 150–9, 162–84, 194–216,
    227–41, 265–83, 317–28, 334–53, 357–9, 395–400
    see also troughs
    double six parameter rules 62–3, 72
upper median lines (UML/U-MLH)
    concepts 11–15, 23–9, 35–62, 64–72, 76–102, 105–19,
    123–31, 150–9, 163–83, 219–41, 252–3, 265–83,
    286–300, 323–8, 345–52, 357–9, 365, 376–8, 383–5
    warning lines 97–102
upper time frames
    see also time frames
    concepts 39, 42, 329–53, 356, 362, 366, 375–7, 382–4,
    388–93
    median lines 329–53
upper trigger lines (U-TL)
    see also trigger lines
    concepts 103–19
upper warning lines 98–102, 230–3
    see also warning lines

vectors, concepts 186–7, 395–400
versatility qualities, pitchforks 23, 26
version 1 efficiency, Schiff pitchforks 163–72, 184
vocabulary warning 4

Vodaphone 291–4
volatility 101
volume indicators 66, 248–59, 315–28, 364–72
Volumes II and III 1, 403–4

warning lines (WL)
    case studies 98–101, 150–9, 230–3, 254–7, 365–72
    characteristics 97–102
    clouded charts 102
    concepts 23, 25–9, 41, 48, 51, 55–8, 59, 67, 76, 80, 87,
    91, 92–4, 97–102, 114, 116–18, 123–31, 150–60,
    164–83, 221–4, 230–3, 254–7, 263–83, 289–300,
    344–5, 365–72
    definition 97–8, 102
    functions 97–102, 150–60
    key learning points 101–2
    levels 97–8, 102
    mini-median lines 76, 102
    reverse pitchforks 179–93
web references 2–3
weekly time frame charts
    multiple time frames 331, 334–53
    pitchforks 341–5, 347
    procedures 337
whipsaw bars 123
'Who knows the past, preferably the immediate past,
    controls the future' 393
wide median line, concepts 63
WL *see* warning lines
words, vocabulary warning 4
'The workplace must be always clean', multiple
    pitchforks 148

zigzagging 325–6, 334–53
zooms
    concepts 45, 60, 68–70, 72, 76–80, 92–5, 97–102,
    112–19, 122–32, 149–60, 355–87
    trading approach steps 355–87

Index compiled by Terry Halliday